Group Work

Group Work

A Practical Guide to Developing Groups
in Agency Settings

Lupe Alle-Corliss
Randall Alle-Corliss

WILEY

JOHN WILEY & SONS, INC.

Copyright © 2009 by John Wiley & Sons, Inc. All rights reserved.

Published by John Wiley & Sons, Inc., Hoboken, New Jersey.
Published simultaneously in Canada.

Library of Congress Cataloging-in-Publication Data

Alle-Corliss, Lupe, 1956-
  Group work : a practical guide to developing groups in agency settings / by Lupe
Alle-Corliss and Randall Alle-Corliss.
      p. cm.
  Includes bibliographical references and index.
  ISBN 978-0-470-28896-2 (pbk.)
  1. Social group work. 2. Social groups. 3. Social service. I. Alle-Corliss, Randy,
1953- II. Title.
  HV45.A45 2009
  361.4--dc22

                                                                    2008044680

Printed in the United States of America

10 9 8 7 6 5 4 3 2 1

To Jessica and Justin—our wonderful children.

We are so proud of the young adults you have come to be.
May you continue to grow spiritually, intellectually, and emotionally.
We appreciate your accepting attitudes as they have allowed us to
persevere in our professional endeavors.

Lupe Alle-Corliss is a bilingual/bicultural licensed clinical social worker with a wealth of experience working in a variety of human service agencies and the coauthor (with Randall Alle-Corliss) of two texts: *Human Service Agencies: An Orientation to Fieldwork,* Second edition (2006) and *Advanced Practice in Human Service Agencies: Issues, Trends, and Treatment Perspectives* (1999), both published by Brooks/Cole. She attended the University of Southern California, obtaining a bachelor's in social gerontology (1978) and a master's in social work (1980). Professional positions that Lupe has held include medical social worker, minority outreach coordinator, lead clinician, graduate fieldwork supervisor, private practitioner Employee Assistance Provider, managed care provider, outreach/crisis intervention counselor, group leader, and university lecturer. Agencies where Lupe has worked range from a rehabilitation hospital, a family service agency, a county-contracted mental health clinic, a county department of behavioral health, a psychiatry department at Kaiser Permanente, and private practice. For the past 23 years, Lupe has also served as an instructor in the Human Services Program at California State University, Fullerton. She has been a faculty liaison and professor in the Graduate School of Social Work at California State University, San Bernardino, and was involved in developing curriculum for the new MSW program at California State University, Fullerton. She has also taught at the University of Southern California. Currently Lupe is the department administrator of a mental health clinic in the Department of Psychiatry for Kaiser Permanente in Ontario, California. In addition, Lupe continues to teach as a part-time lecturer and remains active in clinical work in psychiatry and private practice. She frequently provides in-services on a variety of topics to diverse audiences and agencies.

Randall Alle-Corliss, formerly Randall Mark Corliss, is a licensed clinical social worker with a broad range of professional experience. He has worked in a variety of community agencies and with many different client populations. At California State University, Fullerton, he earned a bachelor's degree in psychology. After he graduated, he began taking courses in the Human Services at California State University, Fullerton, where he received considerable training and experience in facilitating groups. After working several years as a community worker in a county- and state-funded mental health center, Randy entered the Graduate School of Social

Work at the University of Southern California, concentrating in mental health. The professional positions Randy has held include community worker, clinical therapist/psychiatric social worker, community outreach coordinator, outreach/crisis intervention counselor, group counselor, licensed clinical social worker, graduate fieldwork supervisor, university lecturer, and fieldwork instructor. For several years, Randy also served the human services department and the community as the fieldwork coordinator. He has worked for the last 18 years in the Department of Psychiatry at Kaiser Permanente, both as a licensed clinical social worker seeing adult clients and more recently as the department administrator in the Department of Psychiatry at Kaiser Permanente in Fontana, California. At the 1995 National Organization of Human Service Educators annual conference, he was a featured speaker on men's issues and men's groups. In addition to helping clients therapeutically, Randy is committed to human service education. For the last 24 years, he has taught undergraduate courses at California State University, Fullerton. For two of those years he taught full time. More recently, he has divided his time among managing the Department of Psychiatry for Kaiser Permanente, part-time teaching, and direct clinical practice.

Group work has become a preferred treatment modality in many human service agencies. This emerging trend reflects the current emphasis on providing needed therapeutic services to clients in the most cost-effective and efficient manner possible. In an era when funding is shrinking and there exists the ever-present threat of budget cuts, many organizations are faced with the dilemma of offering quality and timely treatment while simultaneously limiting the high cost of care. The challenges resulting from these pressures are great for both agency administrators and human service professionals alike, although each is affected in different ways. Human service practitioners, specifically, must develop sound clinical and specialized group skills as well as learn how to navigate their way successfully within a variety of agency settings if they hope to be effective.

This text is a practical guide to developing groups in agency settings. The idea for this text resulted from several class presentations on group work to undergraduate- and graduate-level human service and social work programs. The emphasis of our presentations was on the agency perspective of group work. Both students and professors welcomed our ideas and indicated a desire for more information on this specific facet of group practice. This interest, coupled with our own direct experience in agencies where the demands for group work have also increased, led us to explore the need for a specific text in this area. Certainly, excellent textbooks on group work are plentiful. However, a gap in the area of agency group work does seem to exist. This gap influenced us to explore ways in which we might add to the existing literature on group work.

Successful group practice cannot be realized without an understanding of the agency systems in which they exist. Knowledge of group skills alone is often insufficient; the many facets of agency life also must be taken into consideration. Understanding certain agency dimensions—such as the agency structure, policies and history, the current staff makeup and possible political issues at hand, the formal and informal lines of command, client demographics, and the existing needs of both the clients and the agency itself—are all equally as important and vital for a helper to examine.

This text attempts to address these various dimensions by providing the beginning human service professional with a practical guide from which to gain the knowledge, skills, and awareness of the many intricacies of working in groups within diverse agency systems.

Recognizing the value of strategic planning is a requisite for a helper to succeed in developing and maintaining a quality group practice. The goal of providing effective group treatment is enhanced when helpers learn how to strategically and positively maximize the use of available resources within themselves, their agencies, and the surrounding community. A dual emphasis on clinical group skills and the understanding of agency systems is therefore deemed the most conducive to meeting the objectives of rapid access and low-cost care. Furthermore, in a time when the struggle for economic survival is a priority for most agencies, it becomes imperative that the ethical mandate of providing quality care also remain a high priority.

This text is organized in a manner that facilitates learning and allows for direct translation into practice. The book is divided into four parts: (1) Introduction, (2) Developing Group Skills, (3) Developing Agency Skills, and (4) Applying Group and Agency Skills. As noted, the first two parts focus on introducing group work and in the development of group work skills. Part III focuses on enhancing overall knowledge of agency systems and learning how to engage in group practice within an agency setting. Part IV integrates both knowledge and skills by focusing on skill application. The last chapter takes a developmental lifespan approach by discussing group work in each major stage of life. In separate sections, we discuss working with children, adolescents, adults, and older adults. We also briefly address the medically ill. In each of these sections, we research a variety of age-related topics and present relevant issues and statistics. Common treatment considerations are examined with emphasis on the benefits of group work. A group proposal, overall objectives, and outline of sessions are offered, detailing session-by-session goals and activities. It is hoped that by providing this broad view of age-related topics, the reader will recognize the value of group work. A CD-ROM has been included that will provide additional information on many other issues relevant to working with individuals throughout the lifespan. An array of topics and corresponding "Group Profiles" are addressed in depth in this accompanying CD-ROM.

Perhaps the most beneficial aspect of this text is its practicality. Because the material is presented in a clear, concise, and relevant manner, the reader can easily apply various concepts, ideas, and skills into practice. Furthermore, application can be immediate, and thus it is more likely to benefit both clients and helpers alike.

Given the broad range of agencies that employ a group modality, we advocate use of this text by any helping professional working in some type of human service agency. We believe that learning about group work within agency systems will be an asset for anyone who hopes to work in the helping professions. Students, beginning human service practitioners, and advanced professionals (such as case managers, chemical dependency counselors, family therapists, human service workers, marriage, family, and child counselors, mental health specialists, psychiatrists, psychiatric nurses, psychologists, school counselors, and social workers) will benefit from the additional training in this book.

Acknowledgments

Special thanks and gratitude goes to our very dear friend and editor, Lisa Gebo. We have previously described her as a "kind and gentle soul," yet she is much more than that. Lisa is a courageous and caring person who strives to persevere despite life's obstacles. We admire her strength, resolve, and zest for life and are indebted to her for believing in our ideas and encouraging our writing endeavors.

We thank the many other staff at John Wiley & Sons for their various roles in the production of this text, including Rachel Livsey, Senior Editor, Susan Moran, Senior Production Editor, Sweta Gupta, Editorial Program Coordinator, Stevie Belchak, Editorial Assistant, Rose Sullivan, Senior Production Manager, Debra Manette, Copy Editor, and all the others who worked behind the scenes in helping make this text a reality.

Our gratitude must also go to our friends and colleagues who have encouraged us through the years and have been supportive of this project. Although there are many more, we would like to thank Margie Atkisson, Irene Bacus, Victoria Delgadillo, Debbie Sirignano, Susan Stewart, Christine Williams, and Jeannette Wilson here.

Special mention must be given to the many group members we have had the pleasure of working with in the capacity of group leaders. These clients have taught us the most about group practice and it is because of them that we have gained the knowledge and skills we impart in the many pages that follow. In a similar fashion, our students over the past 25 years have taught us about the many facets of learning, and we owe them for their special contributions. We thank Dr. Susan Larsen for her special contributions to various chapters within the text and Dr. Gerald Corey and Marianne Schneider Corey for their positive reinforcement, enduring support, and enthusiasm.

We also thank the many staff at the various agencies where we have had the privilege of working for providing us with such rich learning environments. Our experience in counseling, mental health, and group work could not have been possible without the support and encouragement of certain supervisors and managers who believed in our abilities and fostered our growth; they include Bruce Hume, Leo Juarez, Glen Roberts, David Rodriquez, and most recently, Larry Oliver.

Our daughter, Jessica, and son, Justin, also deserve recognition for their unconditional love, patience, and sense of humor. We thank them for their ability to endure our intensity at times as we researched and prepared the manuscript and engaged in rigorous revisions. Their love and support of higher education is a special gift they have given us. We hope to continue to positively influence them in their pursuit of their future career and life goals. Last, thanks to our adorable puppy, Sunny, who came into our lives just as we were finishing this text and helped us realize how special man's best friend can be.

Introduction

1

Introduction to Group Practice

As helping professionals working in different types of agencies, it is essential to be well versed in both direct and indirect practice. Developing skills in individual, family, group, and community work is essential. Becoming skillful in group work practice is especially important in today's competitive marketplace. Practitioners who are knowledgeable and experienced in group treatment are better able to meet the challenges of providing services to a variety of clients in a timely and cost-efficient manner. Group counseling is an increasingly popular and accepted form of treatment available in a variety of agency settings. Although group work practice has long been used with specific populations, such as individuals with mental health issues, even in these settings professionals are being challenged to develop new approaches in the prevention and treatment of psychological problems. In fact, the days of providing individual therapy alone are slowly dissipating. Notable authors in the fields of group counseling and group psychotherapy speak to this issue. For example, G. Corey (2004) states: "Group counseling offers real promise in meeting today's challenges. Group counseling enable practitioners to work with more clients—a decided advantage in these tight financial times—in addition, the group process also has a unique learning advantages" (p. 3).

Group psychotherapy is becoming as effective a treatment for a wide range of psychological problems as individual therapy. The benefits of therapeutic groups are being recognized increasingly in mental health settings, and group treatments are more widely used today than they were in the past. Yalom (2005) agrees, asserting that "a persuasive body of outcome research has demonstrated unequivocally that group therapy is a highly effective form of psychotherapy and that it is at least equal to individual psychotherapy in its power to provide meaningful benefit" (p. 1).

Group therapy is a powerful venue for growth and change. Not only do members receive tremendous understanding, support, and encouragement from others facing similar issues, but they also gain different perspectives, ideas, and viewpoints on those issues. Most group members, although somewhat apprehensive at first, report that the group experience was helpful far beyond their expectations.

Even when group counseling or psychotherapy is the preferred treatment modality, practitioners need to have specialized knowledge of group theory and practice in order to be effective. In addition, practitioners must be creative and spontaneous in applying group theory to real-life practice. In this chapter we begin by examining the various ways in which group work itself is defined. We explore the many different types of classifications, followed by a brief history of group work. Benefits and drawbacks of group work are to be delineated and current trends in the field are to be addressed.

Group Work

Group Work Defined

Definitions of the term *group work* vary. Often such terms as *group practice, group treatment, group counseling,* and *group therapy* are used interchangeably. In 1959, Olmstead authored a text titled *The Small Group* in which he defines a group as a

> plurality of individuals who are in contact with one another, who take one another into account, and who are aware of some significant commonality. An essential feature of a group is that its members have something in common and that they believe what they have in common makes a difference. (pp. 21–22)

Interestingly, despite the evolution of groups in these last 50-odd years, this definition still seems to hold true today. A more current definition proposed by the Association of Specialists in Group Work (ASGW), is similar:

> A broad professional practice that refers to the giving of help of the accomplishment of tasks in a group setting. It involves the application of

group theory and process by a capable professional practitioner to assist an interdependent collection of people to reach their mutual goals, which may be personal, interpersonal, or task related in nature. (1991, p. 9)

According to Toseland and Rivas (2001), group work is defined as "goal-directed activity with small groups of people aimed at meeting socio-emotional needs and accomplishing tasks. This task is directed to individual members or a group and as a whole within a system of delivery" (p. 12).

Groups can be categorized into two major types, *task groups* and *treatment groups*, which can then be further subdivided into more specific categories. We delineate the distinctions between these groups in further detail later in the chapter.

Task groups are developed to achieve a specific set of objectives or tasks; they are "focused on completion of a project or development of a product" (Hepworth, Rooney, & Larsen, 2002, p. 299). According to Hull and Kirst-Ashman (2004), in such groups, "concerted attention is paid to the tasks, and attainment of the desired ends assumes great importance. The objectives help determine how the group operates as well as the roles played by the members" (p. 361).

Treatment groups are more clinical and therapeutic in nature and are "aimed at enhancing the socio-emotional well-being of members through provision of social skills, education, and therapy using the vehicle of group process" (Hepworth et al., 2002, p. 299). Treatment groups are considered therapeutic groups in that they encourage behavior change in their members, serve to increase self-awareness and knowledge of others, help members clarify the changes they wish to make in their lives, and provide them with the necessary tools to make these changes. Through the group process, a trusting and accepting environment is created that allows members to experiment with new behaviors, take healthy risks, and receive constructive feedback that allows them to become aware of how they appear to others.

Treatment groups are composed of group counseling and group therapy or group psychotherapy. The major difference between group therapy and group counseling lies in goals. Whereas counseling groups focus on growth, development, enhancement, prevention, and self-awareness, therapy groups typically focus on remediation, treatment, and personality reconstruction (Brabender, Fallon, & Smolar, 2004; G. Corey, 2004; M.S. Corey & G. Corey, 2006; Jacobs, Masson, & Harvill, 2006).

Differences between group counseling and group therapy are examined further when we discuss the many different types of groups.

In general, however, group counseling typically focuses on a specific problem, whether personal, educational, social, or vocational; treatment is generally oriented toward the resolution of specific and short-term issues. Group therapy is also a form of psychosocial treatment where a small group of individuals meets regularly to talk, interact, and discuss problems with each other and the group leader. A major purpose of group therapy is to provide members with a safe and comfortable place where they can work on more severe psychological and behavioral problems. Members gain insight into their own thoughts and behaviors, and offer suggestions and support to others. Additionally, members who may have difficulties in interpersonal relations can benefit from the social interactions that are a basic part of the group therapy experience. In group psychotherapy focus is on both conscious and unconscious awareness, present and past issues are explored, and reeducation occurs. Depending on the orientation of the group leader and his or her personality, some groups may be primarily aimed at problem solving and skill building, while others focus on more in-depth behavior and personality change.

Since therapeutic goals may be more complex, group therapy tends to be longer term in nature than group counseling as it deals with more severe emotional problems that are deeply rooted in past history. Brabender et al. (2004) add that group therapy "is designed to promote psychological growth and ameliorate psychological problems through the cognitive and affective exploration of the interactions among members and the therapist" (pp. 14–15).

Group Classifications

Literature on the different types of group treatment prevalent today is vast. Various authors have classified groups differently. The ASGW, a national division of the American Counseling Association, provides training for four kinds of groups: (1) task/work groups; (2) guidance/psychoeducational groups; (3) counseling/interpersonal problem solving; (4) psychotherapy/psychoeducational. (M. S. Corey & G. Corey, 2006; Jacobs et al., 2006) In addition to these, support groups, brief groups, and self-help groups are well known in the field of group practice.

Task/Work Groups
Task groups, also known as facilitation groups, are common in many organizations and agencies. These groups are designed to achieve a

specific task, such as consulting regarding a patient on a psychiatric ward, resolving conflicts among house residents in a group home, or deciding policies in a school setting (Jacobs et al., 2006). Different types of task groups include committees, planning groups, staff development groups, treatment conferences, community organizations, social action groups, task forces, discussion groups, and learning groups.

Task groups use the principles and processes of group dynamics to improve practices within organizations and to achieve specified goals. Basically, task groups are intended to meet clients' needs, organizational needs, and community needs (Corey & Corey, 2006; Toseland & Rivas, 2009). Task groups are considered most effective when these nine characteristics are in place:

1. The group purpose is clear.
2. A balance of process (dynamics) and content (information) exists.
3. Culture building is encouraged and differences are both recognized and appreciated.
4. Cooperation, collaboration, and mutual respect exist.
5. Conflict is addressed.
6. Clear and immediate feedback is exchanged.
7. "Here-and-now" group issues are addressed.
8. Group members are encouraged to be active participants.
9. Time is given to both leaders and members to reflect on their work (M. S. Corey & G. Corey, 2006; Gladding 2004; Hulse-Killacky, Killacky, & Donigan 2001).

Task groups are useful in a variety of settings, such as athletic departments, employment settings, businesses, and counseling agencies. Task groups are used whenever professionals work in teams to resolve internal and/or external situations and to plan and implement ideas. Community workers, especially, will find the use of task groups essential in their daily functioning. According to G. Corey (2004):

> *Working in the community usually means working with a specific group or in a situation in which competing or collaborating groups are dealing with an issue or set of issues in a community. Most of the work in community change will be done in a small group context, and skills in organizing task groups are essential. (p. 12)*

Group workers need to be aware of and understand how socio-political influences impact various racial and ethic minority groups. Arredondo et al. (1996) address such concerns as immigration issues, racism, stereotyping, poverty, and powerlessness further in their discussion of multicultural counseling.

Guidance/Psychoeducational Groups

"Psychoeducational groups, also known as guidance or educational groups, are a large force in group practice today. These types of groups are structured by a central theme, are usually short term in nature, and are often preventive and instructional; focus is on teaching and learning. Neukrug (2008) specifies that "psychoeducational groups attempt to increase self-understanding, promote personal and interpersonal growth, and prevent future problems through the dissemination of mental health education in group settings" (p. 169). Through involvement in psychoeducational groups, members can gain knowledge about specific issues, share common concerns, receive and provide needed support within the group, learn necessary problem-solving skills, and are encouraged to develop healthy support systems outside of the group setting. Since there is both an instructional and self-development component, these groups are both educational and therapeutic in nature. Psychoeducational groups often are found in educational settings as well as in hospitals, mental health centers, social service agencies, and universities (Jones & Robinson, 2000).

The purpose of psychoeducational groups may vary, from helping participants learn skills to reduce depression or to deal with a potential threat such as AIDS or a terminal illness; to deal with a developmental life event, such as entering adolescence or growing older; or to cope with an immediate life crisis, such as the death of a loved one or a pending divorce. Generally, psychoeducational groups involve training individuals in psychological skills or knowledge that is either preventive or remedial in nature. Specifically, these types of groups have been helpful in providing general coping skills and guidance during transitional times; reducing anxiety, anger, aggression, and other emotional stressors; improving interpersonal skills; and strengthening study skills. In general, the ultimate goal is to enhance self-awareness of group members and teach them a repertoire of healthy coping skills that they can use when needed.

Many psychoeducational groups are based on a learning theory model and incorporate behavioral and cognitive techniques, such as social skills training and assertiveness training, stress management, cognitive therapy, and multimodal therapy (Gladding, 2004). Page and Jencius (2009) emphasize that a psychoeducational group must "highlight the fact that the group's primary focus is on teaching and learning" (p. 28). They encourage using words 'teaching' and 'learning' in the purpose statement, along with other relevant information. Several examples of group purpose statements are as follows:

- *Children's learning disabilities support group.* This is an 8-week support and psychoeducational group focused on helping children with disabilities share their struggles with feeling different, learn appropriate social skills, recognize maladaptive behaviors, and learn proper coping skills.
- *Teen anger management.* This is a 12-week psychoeducational group for teens ages 13 to 17 who have experienced mild problems with anger and want to learn skills to be able to manage their anger in more positive ways.
- *Adult substance abuse group.* This pyschoeducational group is designed to help individuals suffering from substance abuse learn about addiction, stress management, problem solving, and relapse prevention.
- *Alzheimer's caregiving support group.* This group is aimed at providing a safe environment for caregivers to vent their frustrations and possible ambivalent feelings and to educate them on a variety of matters including the disease process of Alzheimer's, caregiving techniques, community resources, and self-care.
- *Breast cancer support group.* This is a 12-week psychoeducational support group designed for women who have been recently diagnosed with similar forms of breast cancer. Group goals include helping women to: learn how to cope with the physical, emotional, and lifestyle changes associated with cancer; deal with medical treatments that can be painful and traumatic; assist with choosing the right hospital and medical treatment; learn how to control stress, anxiety, or depression; learn problem-solving strategies in a supportive environment; and assist women to cope with such issues as fears about reoccurrence.

An important aspect of the process in such groups revolves around group discussions of how members will personalize the information presented in the group context. Often in the beginning of such groups, a questionnaire is given to members to determine how well they are coping with the particular area of concern. Structured exercises, readings, homework assignments, and contracts are typically used to help group members learn and practice specific skills. Watching certain films or movies can be especially useful in bringing to life a specific issue or concept discussed in groups (e.g., *Ordinary People* to deal with loss; *Kramer versus Kramer* to illustrate the impact of divorce on children; *The Notebook,* which demonstrates how Alzheimer's disease affects family, etc.). Some therapists may also invite guest speakers to a group session in an effort to solidify or enhance group learning. For instance, someone from public health may be invited to speak to a teen group regarding high-risk behavior, such as sexually transmitted diseases or the dangers of drug use; in a support group for parents of children with Attention Deficit Hyperactivity Disorder(ADHD), a guest might be a parent who has been successful in using behavior modification techniques at home; and in a group for chronic pain, a physical therapist might be invited to help teach body-mechanics and the use of specific exercises to alleviate pain.

Examples of psychoeducational groups prevalent today include:

- Anxiety, depression, and bipolar groups
- Bereavement groups for children and spouses
- Groups for children of divorce, alcoholics, and domestic violence
- Incest survivors and post traumatic stress groups
- Social skills and relationships groups for children, teens, men, and women
- Support groups for HIV/AIDS, Alzheimer's caregivers, breast cancer
- Teen pregnancy and parenting groups

Clearly, psychoeducational groups vary in theme and content and can be structured in a multitude of ways. Perhaps most noteworthy is the flexibility that these types of groups offer. Not only can they be designed for use with many different client populations, but they can be tailored to meet the specific needs of group members. Furthermore, because psychoeducational groups offer treatment in an efficient and cost-effective manner, they are becoming a most popular type of group treatment used by practitioners today.

Counseling/Interpersonal Problem-Solving Groups
Counseling groups, also known as interpersonal problem-solving groups, strive to help group members "to resolve, the usual, yet often difficult, problems of living through interpersonal support and problem

solving" (ASGW, 1992, p. 143). Counseling groups are similar to psychoeducational groups, and sometimes distinguishing between the two can be difficult. Normally, group counseling is more direct than a psychoeducational group in its attempt to modify attitudes and behaviors. For example, the affective involvement of group members is stressed in group counseling; members' cognitive understanding is emphasized in a psychoeducational group. Group counseling is generally conducted in a small, intimate setting; a psychoeducational group can be conducted in a larger, room-size environment (Gazda, Ginter, & Horne, 2001). Additionally, in counseling groups, interaction among group members is greater than in psychoeducational groups (Gladding, 2004).

Counseling groups also vary in their purpose and populations they serve. Personal, education, career, social, and developmental concerns are commonly addressed. Unlike psychotherapy groups, which are discussed in the next section, counseling groups focus on "interpersonal process and problem-solving strategies that stress conscious thoughts, feelings, and behaviors" and are "geared toward resolution of specific short-term issues," not the treatment of more severe psychological and behavioral disorders (M. S. Corey & G. Corey, 2006, p. 12).

Members attend counseling groups because of certain problems in their lives. Interactive feedback is used among members, and here-and-now support methods are central to helping participants deal with developmental concerns or to resolve problems relating to daily life. Group members may be dealing with situational crises and short-lived conflicts or may be working on changing self-defeating behaviors. Group members often determine the focus of the group and with the group leader's guidance are encouraged to help one another. Members are generally well-functioning individuals who are encouraged to discover internal resources and strengths. The premise is that by helping other group members discover their inner resources and learn to deal constructively with barriers preventing their optimal functioning, they will learn interpersonal skills that can help them better cope with both existing difficulties and future problems. Self-exploration is fostered by a supportive group atmosphere that challenges members to engage in honest self-exploration.

Counseling groups may vary in terms of how they are structured; some are open, while others have a more specific focus. There is no consensus on how these groups should be conducted. Opinions vary regarding the role of the members and of the leader, the appropriate tone, and the theoretical orientation to be used. However, three goals are common to all counseling groups:

1. Helping individuals develop more positive attitudes and improved interpersonal skills
2. Using the group process to facilitate behavior change
3. Helping members transfer newly acquired skills and behaviors learned in group to everyday life (M. S. Corey & G. Corey, 2006, p. 13)

In essence, then, the group leader is assigned the task of developing a favorable climate for productive work to take place. Engendering an open and trusting group environment allows members to feel safe in giving and receiving feedback and in exploring different ways of relating and problem solving. Ideally, the group leader guides members into translating general goals into more concrete behavioral changes and encourages active participation. As the group becomes more of a microcosm of society, group process provides a sample of reality. Essentially, when the struggles that people experience in group mirror those conflicts faced in their daily lives, group members can learn to respect differences and to recognize that they are often more alike than different. As we discuss later, this sense of universality offers support and hope. When these conditions are met, group members feel most empowered to accept their situations and/or to make changes for the better.

Psychotherapy/Personality Reconstruction Groups

Psychotherapy groups differ from task, psychoeducational, and counseling groups in that they are often more long term in nature and group members typically are dealing with more severe problems. Psychotherapy groups are sometimes called personality reconstruction groups, given their emphasis on helping individual group members to remediate in-depth psychological problems (Gladding, 2004, p. 252). G. Corey (2004) contends that the difference between group therapy and group counseling is rooted in their goals:

> Whereas counseling groups focus on growth, development, enhancement, prevention, self-awareness, and releasing blocks to growth, therapy groups typically focus on remediation, treatment, and personality reconstruction. Group psychotherapy is a process of reeducation that includes both conscious and unconscious awareness and both the present and the past. (pp. 8–9)

According to the ASGW (1992), "because the depth and the extent of the psychological disturbance is significant, the goal [of personality reconstruction groups] is to aid each individual to reconstruct major personality dimensions" (p. 13).

Because the focus is on helping individual group members resolve deeply rooted psychological problems, treatment can take a long time. Group members may present with acute or chronic emotional conditions. They are likely to feel extreme emotional distress and impairment in their daily functioning level. Since a major goal of this group is to help individual members to reconstruct major personality dimensions, emphasis is often on connecting past history to current-day issues. Group leaders use interpersonal and intrapersonal assessment, diagnosis, and interpretation to assist them; they are usually clinicians of some type (e.g., psychologists, licensed mental health counselors, and licensed clinical social workers) and are well versed in psychotherapeutic interventions.

Group therapists often encourage regression to earlier experiences that require exploring the unconscious and the reexperiencing of traumatic events. Theoretically, as catharsis occurs, these past experiences are relived in the group, helping individual members to gain awareness and insight into the past and its impact on current functioning. A primary characteristic of group psychotherapy is this working through unfinished business from the past in an effort to reconstruct one's personality. Past exploration, delving into unconscious territory, and promoting new behavior patterns requires both insight and patience on behalf of both group members and therapists, and can be a long-term endeavor.

Techniques used in group psychotherapy are numerous; the most common involve exploration of dreams, interpretation of resistance, management of transference issues, and assisting individual group members to consider alternate viewpoints on unfinished business with significant others. Involvement in group psychotherapy requires specialized training beyond what is necessary for task, psychoeducational, and counseling groups. In-depth knowledge regarding abnormal psychology, psychopathology, and diagnostic assessment is a prerequisite.

Other Groups

Brief Groups

Brief groups differ from group psychotherapy in terms of duration and focus. The term *brief group therapy* (BGT) refers to groups that are structured and time limited. In the literature, there is no consensus regarding the specific time span for a brief group. In our experience, such groups can last from 2 to 4 months and consist of 8 to 16 weekly sessions. Mackenzie (1995) distinguishes between brief groups and short-term, time-limited groups in this way: Brief groups meet for up to 8 sessions and are tailored to help individuals successfully negotiate a crisis, while time-limited groups have a lifespan from 6 weeks to 6 months and are designed to treat persons with more severe or complicated problems or move them to a higher level of psychological functioning.

Despite the different opinions regarding the exact number of sessions required for a brief therapy group, there is agreement that in today's era of managed care, brief interventions and short-term groups have become essential. Due to economic pressures and a shortage of resources, the mental health delivery system has seen major changes. With the advent of managed care, the trend in mental health is for briefer forms of treatment, including group treatment. Piper and Ogrodniczuk (2004) advocate brief therapy. Besides being cost effective, brief group therapy is more effective and applicable to a wide range of client problems than long-term group approaches. Likewise, Rosenberg and Zimet (1995) found evidence that behavioral and cognitive behavioral approaches were particularly effective when used in a brief group therapy format. Certain populations for which brief group therapy has been successful in treating include: cancer patients; those with medical illnesses, personality disorders, trauma reactions, or adjustment problems; and those dealing with grief and bereavement (Piper & Ogrodniczuk, 2004). Despite these positive findings, caution should be taken in considering brief group therapy for all types of clients; some individuals are best suited for longer-term group psychotherapy. Furthermore, it is imperative that group leaders engaging in brief group therapy be well trained in both group process and brief therapy. As a fast-paced, specific form of treatment, brief therapy requires leaders to possess specialized skills in goal setting and treatment planning.

Support Groups

A support group consists of members who share something in common and meet on a regular basis for support. Group members share similar thoughts and feelings and help one another examine issues and concerns (Jacobs et al., 2006). Support groups enable members to learn that other people struggle with the same problems, feel similar emotions, and think similar thoughts. Brabender et al. (2004) highlight the use of support groups for the medically ill:

> Support group psychotherapy can be effective for patients through the experience of universality in reducing the feelings of stigma and isolation often associated with medical illness. Across many medical diagnoses,

outcome studies have demonstrated the reduction in psychological morbidity and, in some, a change in the primary disease process. (p. 267)

Additional support groups that have proven to be effective through the years include groups for staff members, for chronically ill psychiatric patients, and groups for families of psychiatric and medically ill patients. Actually, a support group can occur any time clients who share a similar condition gather together for support. As with the other groups described, support groups benefit from professional group leadership. Brabender et al. (2004), Rutan and Stone (2001), and Yalom (1995) all emphasize the importance of group leadership. Group leaders with knowledge of the etiology of the illness or condition and who understand the many intricacies of group dynamics are often better equipped than those with limited knowledge of the specific population they are treating, or of group dynamics, to lead effectively. Yalom (1995) highlights such existential concerns as personal struggles with death, isolation, meaning of life, and freedom that often become the focus of certain support groups as an environment of trust is built.

Spira (1997) has identified three fundamental approaches to support groups with the medically ill:

1. The deductive approach, whereby the group leader acts as a health educator whom group members pose questions to.
2. The interactive approach, whereby the group leader introduces a theme that group members are encouraged to discuss.
3. The inductive approach, whereby the floor is open for group members to raise their own themes.

Today many support groups combine these different approaches in a way that is most conducive to the specific issue for which the support group is developed for (Abbey & Farrow, 1998; Allan & Scheidt, 1998).

Self-Help Groups

The self-help group has become increasingly popular in the last 25 years. Self-help groups enable individuals with a specific problem or life issue to create a support system that provides them with encouragement to begin working on positive life changes. Basically a self-help group is made up of laypeople with similar concerns who meet on a regular basis to help and support one another. Perhaps the most popular of self-help groups is Alcoholics Anonymous (AA), which follows a 12-step program. Many other types of self-help groups follow the AA model, including Narcotics Anonymous, Gamblers Anonymous, and Overeaters Anonymous. Additionally, with the Internet, individuals can develop a supportive network online that provides them with needed support and validation.

Common to both self-help groups and therapy groups is the notion that individuals suffer from unexpressed feelings and thoughts and can benefit from expression of these feelings/thoughts or catharsis. Both these types of groups bring together people with similar issues, encourage support, emphasize group connections, and strive for behavioral change.

Despite these commonalities, differences between self-help groups and therapy groups also exist. According to G. Corey (2004) and Riordan and Beggs (1987), self-help groups focus on a single topic, such as addiction or illness, whereas therapy groups consider more global goals, such as improving general mental health, increasing self-awareness, or enhancing self-esteem and interpersonal functioning. A further difference is in their leadership. Self-help groups are typically led by a group member who suffers from the same condition as the others. In group therapy, the leader is a professional who is trained in group practice and promotes a therapeutic atmosphere in which change results through group process.

Self-help groups and therapy groups both provide a vital function. It is important to understand the role of both in working with clients.

Historical Roots of Group Work

Group work has a long and interesting history that highlights the enduring quality of group practice. A brief look at the historical roots of group work is valuable in understanding how today's group practice came to be.

Brief History

In the late 19th century, group work followed early casework within charity organizations. Toseland and Rivas (2009) note that group work emerged in England and the United States in settlement houses as an outcome of casework in charity organizations. Early writers such as Brackett (1895) and Boyd (1935) chronicle group work as evolving primarily from the leaders of socialization groups, adult education groups, and recreation groups in settlement houses and youth service agencies.

In the early part of the 20th century, various other workers—adult educators, recreation leaders, and community workers, among others— began to recognize the potential of group work to help individuals participate in their communities, enrich their lives, obtain support, and learn needed social skills and problem-solving strategies. The first therapy group was conducted by a Boston internist, Joseph Pratt, with patients who suffered from tuberculosis. Pratt became "impressed with the power of the interactional components of group" (Brabender et al., 2004, p. 2). Pratt is considered a "trailblazer" in the area of group work and prepared the pathway for future group treatment with the medically ill (Gladding, 2004).

Around that time, group work was beginning to be used for therapeutic purposes in state mental institutions. L. Cody Marsh is credited in developing a group treatment format for those suffering from psychiatric disorders. As the founder of milieu therapy, Marsh "recognized that members could act altruistically toward one another, find common ground in their thoughts and feelings, experience accep- tance, and enjoy an esprit de corps, all of which would ameliorate suffering" (Brabender et al., 2004, p. 2). Marsh too can be credited for setting the stage for today's use of psychoeducational techniques in group therapy. During this time, psychiatrist Edward Lazell used a group approach in the treatment of schizophrenic and manic-depressive pop- ulations. Lazell, March, and Pratt were pioneers of group therapy and believed in tracking members' progress, again foreshadowing today's emphasis on empirical evidence of treatment success.

In the 1920s a French scholar used the term *contagion* to describe the readiness of members to take on the psychological elements manifested by those around them. The term *group psychotherapy* was introduced into the counseling literature during this time by Jacob L. Moreno (Gladding, 2004). In 1921, Sigmund Freud published *Group Psychology and the Analysis of the Ego*, which primarily focused on the role of the leader as an important determinant of group development. As early as 1921, Alfred Adler and his coworkers used a group approach in their child guidance centers in Vienna (Dreikurs, 1967). Many practitioners of this era introduced group therapy to save time but quickly recognized that it was an effective means of encouraging change in clients. For instance, it was found that feelings of inferiority can be effectively challenged in groups. The group itself becomes influential in changing concepts and values that are believed to be at the root of social and emotional problems. This emphasis on group leadership skills remains prevalent today. The role of identification, empathy, and aggression were also beginning to be explored in relationship to groups.

During the 1930s and 1940s, Kurt Lewin's field theory concepts led to Tavistock small study groups in Great Britain and the Training (T)-group movement in the United States (Gladding, 2004). Kurt Lewin was instrumental in developing a metatheory of group life. His position was that "the group possesses properties that transcend those of any individual" (Agazarian & Janoff, 1993; Brabender et al., 2004, p. 10). In the 1930s, the first psychoanalytic group was conducted by Louis Wender, who emphasized the importance of cognition and foresaw the concept of interpersonal learning and strategies used by modern-day cognitive therapists. Samuel Slavson was the first to use group therapy in the treatment of children and adolescents. He valued each member's individualism within the group progress and believed that treatment needed to be tailored to the individual's specific needs. This focus on developing specialized groups based on age or theme remains prevalent today (Anthony, 1972; Brabender et al., 2004; Yalom, 1995, 2005).

The American Group Psychotherapy Association (AGPA) was founded by Slavson in 1943 and remains an important organization. Also, in the early 1940s, Jacob Moreno founded the American Society for Group Psychotherapy and Psychodrama. Both psychoanalytic and action-oriented approaches to group treatment were developed (Brabender et al., 2004).

The 1940s and 1950s were considered an age of expansion in regard to group treatment. During this era, group work was credited with positive therapeutic results in the area of juvenile delinquency and rehabilitation for those who suffered from a mental illness. The trend of using groups in a curative capacity in mental health settings continued. The emphasis of groups during this era changed from a recreational and educational focus used earlier in settlement houses to a more insight-oriented focus on diagnosis and treatment of members' problems (Alle-Corliss & Alle-Corliss, 1999; Reid, 1981).

The increase in curative groups in the mental health arena likely resulted from the influence of Freudian psychoanalysis and ego psychology, which was burgeoning during this time, and the shortage during World War II of personnel trained to provide individual therapy to disabled war veterans. Brabender et al. (2004, p. 9) note that "whereas World War I created an interest in group psychology, World War II precipitated the establishment of group therapy as a major treatment modality."

At the same time that the use of group work grew within child guidance, mental health, and psychiatric settings, group work was increasingly used in recreational, educational, and community arenas, as for example in Jewish community centers, in youth organizations such as Girl Scouts and the YMCA, and in the area of community development and social action. As this interest in the use of group work spread, so did the examination of small groups as a social phenomenon. This era during the 1950s was aptly coined the golden age of the study of groups (Alle-Corliss & Alle-Corliss, 1999; Hare, 1976). During this time, many theoretical approaches to group work were expanded and the existence of group dynamics received added attention.

The 1960s continued to see growth in the community mental health movement that led to widespread group practice. Since group therapy was considered a cost-efficient treatment modality, much as it is today, many human service professionals without specific training began to conduct groups. More generic and less specialized types of practice began to dominate, resulting in fewer professionally trained group practitioners (Toseland & Rivas, 2009). It was during this time that the need for group therapy training became increasingly apparent.

During this period of growth in the group movement, many new techniques and methods were introduced. Some of the more non-traditional groups of this time include: T-groups (*T* for training), sensitivity groups, encounter groups, and marathon training groups. William Schultz and Jack Gibb are other pioneers in the group movement who are known for emphasizing a humanistic approach to T-groups that focused on personal growth as a legitimate goal (Gladding, 2004). Carl Rogers, well known for his humanistic approach to counseling and psychotherapy, is noted for devising the basic encounter groups in the 1960s that became the model for growth-oriented group approaches that followed (Corey, 2004; Day, 2004; Gladding, 2004). All of these groups tended to focus more than previous groups on the here-and-now and used a variety of experimental techniques, some which are still used in today's group practice.

Gestalt therapy, which originated in the 1940s, was used extensively during the 1960s in the form of group therapy at the famous Esalen Institute in Big Sur, California. Fritz Perls and his wife, Laura, developed this "existential-phenomenological approach" that emphasized helping clients understand their interactions with their environment (Corey, 2005; Day, 2004). Grounded in field theory, Gestalt therapy assumes that individuals have the capacity to regulate themselves when they are aware of the interaction between their internal states and their environment. Groups were often short term in nature with one member at a time sitting in what was called the "hot seat" to work with the therapist while others observed and participated when called on by the therapist. Even silent members were believed to benefit by "spectator learning," as they had the opportunity to identify with the interaction and became aware of their own inner responses to the session (Day, 2004). Gestalt therapy also encouraged use of body awareness, experimentation, role playing, empty-chair techniques, dream work, and psychodrama, which allowed for a lively experience that promoted direct experiencing versus a more abstract style of merely talking about situations.

In 1970 the famous text *The Theory and Practice of Group Psychotherapy* written by Irvin Yalom (2005) introduced interpersonal theory, which emphasized enabling the individual group member to improve his or her capacity to have positive relationships with others. Additionally, Yalom coined the term *therapeutic factors*, referring to factors intrinsic to groups. We elaborate on these later within the chapter. Outcome research during the 1970s became more rigorous in nature and suggested that group therapy was at least as effective as other modalities (Brabender et al., 2004).

From 1985 to the present time, the helping field has seen continued growth in the use of group work as a major form of treatment. With the emergence of managed care systems that control reimbursements for health care services, including mental health, short-term group therapy has flourished. Basically, since group treatment tends to be more cost effective and short term in nature, it has become increasingly popular during today's push for fiscal restraints. Accordingly, MacKenzie (1994) asserts that the managed care industry has positive regard for group therapy, as it enables the provision of cost-effective treatment.

Besides the trend toward using cost-reduction modalities, practitioners are also being held more accountable for the usefulness of their intentions. "Vaguely defined goals pursued through unspecified processes and measures" are no longer an option for group therapists. "Third-party payers require clear treatment plans. Goals must be operationalized, methods clearly detailed, and outcomes explicitly identified. Group therapists are expected to use validated approaches" (Brabender et al., 2004, p. 13).

Another notable change seen in the provision of group therapy today is the support for a multiplicity of approaches. The use of a more integrative style is encouraged; practitioners draw from a variety of therapeutic approaches in an effort to provide more comprehensive and effective services. This emphasis on integration has led to a more collegial atmosphere among practitioners, yet specialized training for group leaders remains a must. Training and credentialing opportunities for group leaders are greater. The American Group Psychotherapy Association (2001), for instance, has taken greater responsibility in this capacity. Legal and ethical issues tied to group work are being scrutinized more closely. Additionally, today's emphasis on diversity-sensitive practice requires that practitioners consider such issues as race, culture, gender, religion, and geography in their preparation and treatment.

Group therapy, which developed as a response to diverse needs for educational, recreational, mental health, and social services, has an eclectic base that continues to foster diversity within group practice. In short, "group therapy continues to be widely used across different psychological populations and settings" (Brabender et al., p. 16).

Benefits and Drawbacks of Group Work

Benefits

The benefits of group work are numerous. Jacobs et al. (2006) ask the basic question, "Which is better, group counseling or individual counseling?" Their honest and succinct response sums up our views as well.

This is difficult to answer because people and situations are so different. Sometimes one or the other is best, and sometimes the combination of individual and group counseling produces the most benefit. For most people, groups can be quite valuable. For some people, group counseling is better because members need the input from others, plus they learn more from listening than talking. (p. 19)

Simply put, why does group therapy work? Consider that all of us have been raised in group environments, either through our families, schools, organized activities, or work. These are the environments in which we grow and develop as human beings. Group therapy is no different; it also provides a place where individuals can come together with others to share problems or concerns, to better understand one's situation and to learn from and with each other. Group therapy helps individuals learn about themselves and enrich their interpersonal relationships. Group therapy can address feelings of isolation, depression, and anxiety and can help members make significant changes so they can feel better about the quality of their lives.

When individuals enter a group and are able to interact freely with other group members, they often re-create those difficulties that brought them to group therapy in the first place. Under the skilled direction of a group leader, the group is able to give support, offer alternatives, or gently confront the person. In this way the difficulty becomes resolved, alternative behaviors are learned, and the individual develops new ways of socializing. During group therapy, members often recognize that they are not alone. Since many individuals feel they are unique because of their problems, it is encouraging to hear that others experience similar difficulties. In the climate of trust provided by the group, group members often feel free to care about and help each other.

The benefits are obvious to anyone who has conducted group therapy and witnessed the positive outcome of group process at work. These benefits are also well outlined in the literature. Jacobs et al. (2006), for example, identify nine reasons for leading groups: efficiency, experience of commonality, greater variety of resources and viewpoints, sense of belonging, skills practice, feedback, vicarious learning, real-life approximation, and commitment.

Efficiency

"Having several clients meet as a group for a common purpose can save considerable time and effort" (Jacobs et al., 2006). There are many situations where clients can be well served using a group format. The psychoeducational group discussed is a great example, as are developmental-type groups, such as those conducted with children, teens, and the elderly.

Experience of Commonality

Typically clients believe that their problems are unique and believe they are helpless to make any changes. Group therapy helps members recognize that they are not alone with their problems; others also struggle with similar issues. Many group members are comforted knowing that others have the same anxieties and emotional issues they have; this realization tends to reduce the sense of isolation and shame that is common. "Groups provide a natural laboratory that demonstrates to people that they are not alone and that there is hope for creating a different life" (M. S. Corey & G. Corey, 2006, p. 5).

Greater Variety of Resources and Viewpoints

Groups, by their very nature, provide a greater variety of viewpoints and resources. "Whether they are sharing information, solving a problem, exploring personal values, or discovering they have common feelings, a group of people can offer more viewpoint and, hence, more resources" (Jacobs, et al., 2006, p. 3). Shulman (1984) calls this cooperative element of sharing multiple resources in group "sharing data"; it has proven very useful, because many individuals on their own have very limited resources at their disposal.

Sense of Belonging

Many in the field have pointed out the powerful human need to belong (Adler, 1927; Berne, 1964; Kottler, 1994; Maslow, 1962; Trotzer, 1999; Yalom, 2005), and group provides this sense of belonging. This need is especially valuable with certain populations, such as veterans; those who suffer from substance abuse, eating disorders, or mental illness; or incest survivors. "Members will often identify with each other and then feel part of a whole" (Jacobs et al., 2006, p. 3). G. Corey (2005) adds: "The group provides the social context in which members can develop a sense of belonging and a sense of community" (p. 113). Sonstegard (1998b) writes that group participants come to see that many of their problems are interpersonal in nature, that their behavior has social meaning, and that their goals can best be understood in the framework of social purposes."

Skills Practice

Group therapy members benefit by working through personal issues in a supportive and confidential atmosphere and by helping others to work through their issues. When the group environment is safe and nurturing, members can practice new skills and behaviors in a supportive environment before trying them in real-world situations. Essentially, the group provides a safe forum in which to practice new behaviors.

Learning to reflect on the "process" in relationships and handle conflict successfully are very important process skills that group members acquire. Many group members have avoided conflict and have not known how to resolve conflict in relationships. As a result, they have missed out on intimacy, closeness, and commitment.

Reiter (2008) highlights the opportunity for skills practice that groups afford. Through group process, members can "gain a sense of how other people perceive them and can, in the moment, work at developing better relating skills. They are then able to take this interpersonal learning and apply it to their life outside of the therapy room" (p. 304).

Feedback

Group therapy offers an opportunity to give and receive immediate feedback about concerns, issues, and problems affecting one's life. It has been well documented that by providing help to others, clients are also helped to feel good about themselves (Yalom, 2005). By helping others in the group work through their problems, group therapy members often gain more self-esteem.

Group feedback is often more powerful than individual feedback. It is easier to dismiss one person's feedback than when six or seven individuals are saying the same thing. Also, some individuals behave and react more like themselves in a group setting than they would one to one with a therapist. Group therapy clients gain a certain sense of identity and social acceptance from their membership in the group. Members learn how to relate on an emotional level to peers, not just to a therapist who is a trained listener. The transfer of skills to outside relationships is potentially greater in group therapy than in individual psychotherapy.

Vicarious Learning

Group therapy provides the opportunity to benefit both through active participation and through observation. The opportunity for vicarious learning exists when group members actually learn from observing how others resolve their personal conflicts. Seeing how others deal with these issues may give group members new solutions to their problems and provide new options.

Group therapy is an interpersonal learning environment; clients learn in vivo about healthy relationships. Peers model effective communication styles and healthy behavior. As members learn these more effective patterns, they receive increasingly positive feedback from their peers, and this feedback increases self-esteem. Effective group therapy is a team approach and a truly cooperative effort. Individuals learn about problem solving, trusting their peers, and community spirit.

Real-Life Approximation

Group therapy allows the exploration of issues in an interpersonal context that more accurately reflects real life. It has been said by Yalom (1975), for one, that group therapy is a microcosm of the client's interpersonal world. Interpersonal difficulties (i.e., projections and distortions) may emerge in the relationships with others. Often a member's habitual ways of relating are reproduced in the group setting. This gives the group the opportunity to examine and understand the difficulties that arise, which in turn allows the member to develop and establish new, more productive patterns of relating. Group therapy may also simulate members' family experiences and allow family dynamic issues to emerge. Clients may experience an increased need to resolve the underlying relationship issues as they come to understand how these interpersonal difficulties create barriers. Group therapy provides the opportunity to observe and reflect on one's own and others' inter- personal skills; it also provides an opportunity for a group of people to develop an intimate, social, interactive environment without having to commit emotionally to members outside of the group. A skilled group leader can assist members in learning how to interact with others based on how they interact in the group. The assumption is that individuals respond in the therapy group in much the same manner as they respond in other groups (family, friends, and work).

Commitment

Group members are often more committed toward goal attainment than they would likely be if in individual therapy. "The combination of support, subtle expectations, and the desire not to let down the group is often a powerful motivation for behavior change" (Jacobs, Masson, & Harvill, 2006, p. 5). The group process fosters empowerment.

In addition to the benefits just outlined, groups can be most effective with certain age groups, such as children, adolescents, and elderly persons. Group members can learn appropriate social skills and to develop identity, self-esteem, and character formation through interac- tion with their peer groups. Developmental tasks can be addressed best in a group format.

Group therapy can be a corrective emotional experience, especially if many past relationships have been painful and difficult. Individuals often replicated childhood patterns in their adult relationships. In group therapy, members often become part of a community that is more like a healthy family and have the opportunity to experience positive and healing relationships.

Despite these well-identified values of group work, many miscon- ceptions about group work exist. Some of these misconceptions include:

- *Group therapy will take longer than individual therapy as members have to share time with others.* Group therapy can be more efficient than individual therapy for two reasons. First, even during sessions when members say little, they gain from group work by listening carefully to others. Members may find that they have much in common with other group members, and as they work on a concern, they can learn more about themselves. Second, group members often bring up issues that will strike a chord with others, although the others might not have been aware of the issue or brought it up themselves.

- *Individual members will be forced to tell all their deepest thoughts, feelings, and secrets in the group.* Ideally, no one will be forced to do anything in group counseling. Each member can control what, how much, and when to share with the group. Members do not have to share when they are not ready to disclose. Members can be helped by listening to others and thinking about how what they are saying might apply to them. When a member feels safe enough to share, then the group will likely be helpful and affirming. If there is pressure to disclose, the group leader should deal appropriately with this issue.

- *If individual members struggle with talking to others in general, they will never be able to share in a group.* Most people are anxious about talking in group. Almost without exception, within a few sessions individuals find that they do begin to talk in the group. Group members remember what it is like to be new to the group, so they will likely give newcomers a lot of support for beginning to talk openly.

Prior to joining a group, prospective members often are given a handout identifying the benefits of group. Such a handout might say:

Group therapy can help you
- Form goals.
- Increase self-awareness and self-esteem.
- Gain insight into the ways others perceive you.
- Discover effective patterns of relating to others.
- Develop more satisfying relationships.
- Receive support for sharing common problems.
- Learn how to apply new behaviors to situations outside the group.

Drawbacks to Group Therapy

As we have seen, engaging in group work can be very advantageous for those participating. Nonetheless, group therapy or counseling is not a cure-all. According to Gladding (2004), "Groups are not a panacea for all people and problems. They have definite limitations and disadvantages" (p. 250). Clear counterindications for group therapy include:

- Certain client concerns and personalities are not well suited for group.
- The problems of some individuals may not be dealt with in enough depth in groups
- Group pressure may force a client to take action, such as in self-disclosure, before being ready.
- Groups may also lapse into a *groupthink* mentality, in which stereotypical, defensive, and stale thought processes become the norm and creativity and problem solving are squelched.
- Individuals may try to use groups for escape or for selfish purposes and disrupt the group process.
- Groups may not reflect the social milieu in which individual members normally operate. Therefore, what is learned from the group experience may not be relevant.
- If groups do not work through their conflicts or developmental stages successfully, they may become more regressive and engage in nonproductive and even destructive behaviors, such as scapegoating, group narcissism, and projection (McClure, 1994).
- Agency mandates may require clients to enter group treatment despite their lack of readiness or desire to do so. "Individuals who do not want to be or are not ready to be in a group can disrupt it or be harmed because group pressure may cause them to take some action or self-disclose before they are ready" (Jacobs et al., 2006, p. 19).
- At times, a specific group member's concerns are not dealt with adequately in a group setting due to constraints of time.

Current Trends

Today, group work is being used by a wide variety of helping professionals and is becoming the treatment modality most effective with certain populations.

> *This emerging trend reflects the current emphasis in the human services field of providing needed therapeutic services to clients in the most cost-effective*

and efficient manner possible. In an era when available funding is shrinking and the threat of budget cuts is ever present, many organizations are faced with the dilemma or providing quality and timely treatment while simultaneously limiting the high cost of case. (Alle-Corliss & Alle-Corliss, 1999, p. 194)

Funding reductions that most human service agencies faced during the last few decades has resulted in efforts by administrators and human service professionals to explore more cost-effective treatment methods. Group work has a rich history. It has proven pivotal in providing sound therapeutic services to individuals in an array of settings, including educational, medical, community mental health, rehabilitative, and psychiatric settings. Cosby and Sabin (1995), who practice in a large health maintenance organization (HMO), write about the challenge of providing quality professional treatment to an ever-increasing number of clients with shrinking resources. Their HMO faced a problem familiar to virtually all organizations with limited budgets that serve large populations—increased demand for mental health services and unacceptably long waiting lists. One of the strategies pursued for "increasing efficacy and effectiveness of outpatient programs was to make increased use of therapy groups, especially time-limited groups" (Cosby & Sabin, 1995, p. 7). This plan provided needed services to more clients and was economical as well. Treatment outcomes from their work, as well as from other researchers, reflects that group therapy is becoming the treatment of choice.

Piper and Ogrodniczuk (2004) identify efficacy, applicability, and cost efficiency as the main benefits of group therapy: "Given that group therapy is as efficacious as individual therapy and requires less therapist time, it appears to be the more cost-effective treatment" (p. 642).

Groups are being designed for use in many different types of settings and for various client groups. Brief and short-term groups for specialized populations seem prevalent. Since the trend seems to be toward time-limited groups that are more cost effective, they may have narrower goals. Focus is likely to be on "symptomatic relief, teaching participants problem-solving strategies and interpersonal skills that can accelerate personal changes" (M. S. Corey & G. Corey, 2006, p. 5).

A number of researchers underscore the many possibilities of group work in the future (see Gladding, 2004; DeLucia-Waack, 1996; LaFountain, Garner, & Eliason, 1996; Shapiro, Peltz, & Bernadett-Shapiro, 1998). Increased emphasis is on developing new ways of working with groups that are grounded in a specific theory. For instance, there has been an increase in solution-focused counseling and brief therapy groups, which differ from problem-solving groups in their "focus on beliefs about change, beliefs about complaints, and creating solutions" (LaFountain et al., 1996, p. 256). Similarly, there is a trend toward creating more preventive-type groups.

Brabender et al. (2004) gathered abundant empirical evidence that suggests that "in most cases group therapy is as effective as individual interventions, and in some cases it is more effective. Insofar as group therapy is more cost efficient, it would seem to be the preferred modality when treatment must be limited" (p. 181).

Jacobs et al. (2006) specify specific problem areas of diagnostic criteria that have been found most conducive to group therapy. These include: depression and anxiety, grief therapy, substance abuse, eating disorders, childhood sexual abuse, and psychotic disorders. Groups are likely effective for developmental-type issues such as working with children, adolescents, or geriatric clients and for patients suffering from such medical conditions as heart disease, cancer, and gastrointestinal illness (pp. 165–174). As suggested, group may be the best treatment modality for certain clients and certain problems/issues.

Unlike individual therapy, group therapy offers "input from peers, multiple feedback, efficient use of therapist's time, and observational learning" (Sharf, 2008, p. 605) and is therefore likely to continue to remain an attractive alternative for today's practitioner.

Using an Integrative Approach in Group Work

Given our present-day managed care system, where treatment services are often limited to crisis and brief treatment, developing an integrative approach to helping is indispensable. According to G. Corey (2009, p. 448):

> Since the early 1980s psychotherapy integration has developed into a clearly delineated field. It is now an established and respected movement that is based on combining the best of differing orientations so that more complete theoretical models can be articulated and more efficient treatment developed.

Many authors advocate an integrated approach that embodies features from a number of theoretical models. "An integrative focus involves selecting concepts and methods from a variety of systems to create a model that is most suitable for working with specific clients in a way that meets agency demands for brief treatment" (Alle-Corliss & Alle-Corliss, 1999, p. 106).

Eight motives have been cited as being responsible for promoting this trend toward psychotherapy integration:

1. The greater number of therapies that are available
2. The fact that no one theoretical model is adequate to address the needs of all clients and all problems
3. The restrictions by insurance companies and healthcare companies that mandate short-term treatment
4. The increased popularity of short-term, perspective- and problem-focused therapies
5. The opportunity this climate affords clinicians to experiment with a variety of therapies
6. The deficiency of differential effectiveness among existing therapies
7. Increased awareness that therapeutic commonalities play a major role in determining therapy outcomes
8. The development of professional groups that foster this integrative movement (Dattilio & Norcross, 2006; Lazarus, 1986; Norcross, Beutler, & Levant, 2006; Norcross, Karpiak, & Lister, 2005).

Overall, one major reason summarizes this trend toward psychotherapy integration: "the recognition that no single theory is comprehensive enough to account for the complexities of human behavior, especially when the range of client types and their specific problems are taken into consideration" (Corey, 2009, p. 450).

In our own practice, we have found that an integrated approach is preferable in accommodating practitioners with different styles and practice preferences. An integrative approach allows practitioners to adopt the facets of various theories and treatment modalities they have found most effective with their particular clientele, allows them more opportunities to tailor treatment to meet specific client needs, and allows them to use the modalities with which they are most comfortable and confident. Chapter 4 presents a complete review of the most common therapies used by group therapists today.

In Closing

This chapter introduced readers to group practice. We presented definitions of group work along with specific group classifications, including task, counseling, psychotherapy, brief, support, and self-help groups. We outlined the history of group, discussed the benefits and drawbacks of group, and presented the merits of an integrative approach. Chapter 2 begins Part II, "Developing Group Skills."

Developing Group Skills

Part

Fundamentals of Group Work

U nderstanding the fundamentals of group work is a pre-requisite to becoming an effective group leader. This chapter addresses various important issues regarding group work. Group dynamics and process are reviewed and the therapeutic aspects of group work are detailed. Group leadership skills are considered along with the value of co-leadership and the necessity for consultation and supervision. We end by encouraging practitioners to develop their own group leadership style.

2

Chapter

Understanding Group Dynamics and Process

Group Process and Dynamics

Group process and *group dynamics* are terms used to refer to the attitudes and interaction of group members and leaders. Some authors define these terms separately; others agree that these terms can be used interchangeably (Posthuma, 2002, p. 7)

Group process refers to the interactions individuals within a group have with one another. *Group dynamics* refers to the unique forces that influence both group members and the group as a whole. Yalom (2005) defines process as "the nature of the relationship between interacting individuals—members and therapists" and goes on to elaborate on the importance of each member's internal psychological world, interpersonal interactions, group-as-a-whole forces, and the clinical environment of the group as important to understanding group process (p. 143). M. S. Corey and G. Corey (2006) present similar views:

> *Group process consists of all the elements basic to the unfolding of a group from the time it begins to its termination. Group process pertains to dynamics such as the norms that govern a group, the*

level of cohesion in the group, how trust is generated, how resistance is manifested, how conflict emerges and is dealt with, the forces that bring about healing, inter member reactions, and the various stages of group's development. (p. 5)

Understanding group process is essential when engaging in group work; being aware of the interaction and energy exchanged between members and leaders is said to be key in being an effective group leader (Jacobs, Masson, & Harvill, 2006; Reiter, 2008). Gladding (2004) concurs: "Before the group begins, group members and leaders need to be informed as much as possible about group process" (p. 258). He differentiates between homogenous groups (in which members are more alike) and heterogeneous groups (when members are more unalike) in terms of conflict. Generally, in homogenous groups, conflict and risk taking is less likely as there is usually more cohesion, support, and better attendance. In heterogeneous groups, conflict and risk taking is generally greater at the onset with support and cohesion lagging behind. Donigian and Malnati (1997), Gladding (2004), Kraus and Hulse-Killacky (1996), Merta (1995), and Nelligan (1994) all highlight the importance of the group process: "It is the process of the group, not the content, focus, or purpose, that will eventually determine whether a group succeeds" (Gladding, 2004, p. 258). In fact, authorities in the field maintain that in successful groups, "the process and content is balanced. It is this group process itself that is often more helpful than the therapist's efforts in getting people to change" (Schaefer, Johnson, & Wherry, 1982, p. 4).

Group process is important in determining the outcome of group. The presence of specific therapeutic factors are also critical to the successful group practice. In his classic text, *The Theory and Practice of Group Psycho-therapy*, Yalom (1975) first proposed 11 primary "therapeutic factors" that represent "different parts of the change process" (pp. 3–4); these include: instillation of hope, universality, imparting information, altruism, the corrective recapitulation of the primary family group, development of socializing techniques, imitative behavior, interpersonal learning, group cohesiveness, catharsis, and existential factors (Yalom, 1975, 2005). As we will see, these factors are interdependent. Although they exist in every group, their interplay and importance will differ from group to group.

Therapeutic Aspects of Group Work

The literature regarding the therapeutic aspects of group work is plentiful. In this chapter we examine Yalom's curative factors; MacKenzie's therapeutic categories; Corey's therapeutic factors; and Jacobs, Masson, and Harvill's therapeutic forces.

Yalom's Curative Factors

Yalom considers 11 therapeutic factors to be curative forces that typically occur in groups, and which are essential for positive change.

1. Instillation of Hope
   - According to Yalom (1975, 1985, 2005), a crucial ingredient in helping clients is the leader's belief in the value of their work and the power of the group. "The instillation and maintenance of hope is crucial in any psychotherapy. Not only is hope required to keep the client in therapy so that other therapeutic factors may take effect, but faith in a treatment mode can in itself be therapeutically effective (Yalom, 2005, p. 4). Group leaders who encourage positive change from the beginning set a hopeful tone that grows as members witness growth in themselves and others. Seen as a foundation, instillation of hope is at the core of any therapeutic attempt (Donigan & Malnati, 2006).
   - *Example:* Assurance that treatment will work can be evident in how the group leader interacts with others, sets ground rules, and reinforces the process.

2. Universality
   - We have already touched on the importance of not feeling alone with one's problems. "The notion of universality—that a person is not a solitary being disconnected from the rest of humanity—can be a very powerful realization for clients" (Reiter, 2008, p. 305). Usually as a group progresses, members become more aware of the universality of their life issues; it is this awareness that encourages cohesion, catharsis, and ultimately, therapeutic gains.
   - *Example:* The realization that one is not alone, unique, or abnormal. Young-adult groups for college students have been shown to help members recognize that others are struggling with similar issues of intimacy and loneliness.

3. Imparting Information
   - Imparting information to group members can be very curative. Whether directly or indirectly, group leaders often share information with members that is therapeutic in nature. Knowledge is power and can lead to awareness and be the impetus for change, individually and collectively.

- *Example:* Instruction about mental health and problem solving. For instance, in an anxiety group, clients can be taught how anxiety affects them physically and emotionally. This information, in and of itself, is a motivating force in helping members learn to manage their anxiety more effectively.

4. Altruism
   - Yalom (2005) believes that "members gain through giving, not only in receiving help as part of the reciprocal giving-receiving sequence, but also in profiting from something intrinsic to the act of giving" (p. 13). This act of giving and receiving can be very satisfying to individual group members. "By being an active member in the group, members realize that they are not only working toward their own positive change, but also that they are helping multiple members of the group" (Reiter, 2008, p. 306).
   - *Example:* Sharing experiences and thoughts with others, helping them by giving of one's self, working for the common good. In a men's group, members really enjoyed helping each other and were helped by the process of supporting others.

5. The Corrective Recapitulation of the Primary Family Group
   - The therapy group often resembles a family in various aspects. For instance, there are authority/parental figures, peer/sibling figures, deep personal revelations, strong emotions, deep intimacy, and sometimes hostile and competitive feelings (Yalom, 2005). Since many individuals entering therapy have experienced problems in their family of origin, the therapy group can be seen as the corrective recapitulation of the primary family group.
   - By reliving earlier family patterns with the guidance of the group leader, individual members are able to "experience a more positive way of relating, that did not occur in the client's family" (Reiter, 2008, p. 306). Ideally, a sound group therapist can recognize various families' reenactments at play within the group and can help group members work through any old emotional impasses and unfinished family business (Donigan & Malnati, 2006).
   - *Example:* Reliving early family conflicts and resolving them. In a weeklong group therapy experience, group members were able to work on issues with parents through interactions with a male and female coleader who were instrumental in identifying unresolved issues tied to childhood.

6. Development of Socializing Techniques
   - Individuals learn from their interactions through the process of socializing. This social learning "is a therapeutic factor that operates in all therapy groups, although the nature of the skills taught and the explicitness of the process vary greatly, depending on the type of group therapy"(Yalom, 2005, p. 16). By learning and practicing social skills within the group, group members eventually can begin to practice them outside of the group in their everyday life.
   - *Example:* Interacting with others and learning social skills as well as more about oneself in social situations. In a teen support group, members were able to learn skills in socialization through direct involvement with one another. Group work with children with attention deficit hyperactivity disorder also allows group leaders to directly witness social skills problems they can specifically target.

7. Imitative Behavior
   - A common phenomenon among members in a group is the imitative behavior that can occur. One way in which individuals learn social skills is by imitating those behaviors they observe in the group environment. Group therapists and members alike model certain behaviors that may influence other group members. When the behavior learned is positive, both individual and group growth is possible.
   - *Example:* Modeling positive actions of other group members. In a women's support group, a more aggressive member can benefit by observing how more assertive members interact within the group.

8. Interpersonal Learning
   - Earlier we talked about the value of group being a social microcosm for members. One of the most important therapeutic factors of group therapy is the transfer of the interpersonal learning that occurs in group to interpersonal relationships outside of group. Essentially, when group members exhibit the problematic behaviors they have shown throughout their lives within the group, group leaders and members can provide constructive feedback that encourages members to work toward changing their maladaptive ways in real-life situations.
   - *Example:* Gaining insight and correctively working through past experiences. In an adult support group, a member with a very abusive history is able to deal with early experiences and realize that not all relationships are abusive in nature.

9. Group Cohesiveness
   • By being in a group, members join together along with the group leader to develop a sense of "we-ness" in which they feel a sense of connection to one another. By virtue of being part of the group, individual members feel more connected to others outside of the group as well. Group cohesion results when members feel enough trust to be willing to let others know them in meaningful ways. Because cohesion usually takes time to build, often cohesion is not evident until the working stage of groups. Typically, the more cohesive the group, the more positive the therapeutic outcome.
   • Various authors have noted that group attraction is integrally related to cohesion (Cartwright, 1968; Henry, 1992; Zastrow, 1985). Cohesion develops, in part, due to the attraction of members to each other, to the activities the group members do together, or to the goals the group is working on (Henry, 1992). Cohesion may also develop as a result of external pressures to remain together. Zastrow (1985) discusses payoffs and costs of membership that he considers instrumental in determining group attraction. Companionship, attaining personal goals, prestige, enjoyment, and emotional support are examples of possible payoffs. Costs may include being with people one dislikes, expending time and effort, criticism, distasteful tasks, and dull meetings. Actual monetary costs may also be a hindrance, especially during troubling economic times. Clearly, when costs are too great, there is a greater likelihood for cohesion to be limited or to never truly develop, which could result in group dispersion.
   • *Example:* Bonding with other members of the group. In women's incest survivors' groups, bonds among members can be extremely strong and conducive to improved feelings of self-worth.

10. Catharsis
    • Catharsis is a therapeutic ability for individuals to be able to express their emotions freely and outwardly, to be able to emote. Yalom (2005) summarizes that

    > *the open expression of affect is vital to the group therapeutic process; in its absence, a group would degenerate into a sterile academic exercise. . . . The intensity of emotional expression is highly relative and must be appreciated not from the leader's perspective but from that of each member's experiential world. (p. 91)*

    • Simply emoting is not sufficient for change unless a connected type of cognitive learning goes along with this expression.

Logically, catharsis and cohesion seem to be related; when group members are able to express themselves openly, this reflects a trusting atmosphere, which, in turn, enhances the development of cohesiveness.
- *Example:* Experiencing and expressing feelings. In a men's group, the ability to express hurt and disappointment is important to men and is instrumental in building cohesion.

11. Existential Factors
- Existential factors are related to issues of mortality and individual responsibility. Basically, every person is responsible for his or her own actions, and in group every member is encouraged to take ownership of his or her feelings and behaviors. Although individual members may ask for feedback and support from others in the group, it will be up to each person to pave a path toward confronting pain in their lives and making changes in their lives for the better.
- *Example:* Accepting responsibility for one's life in basic isolation from others, recognizing one's own mortality and the capriciousness of existence. Empowerment groups emphasize the importance of choice and responsibility. Members learn that ultimately they are the only ones who have the power to change their lives.

MacKenzie's Therapeutic Categories

Brabendar, Fallon, and Smolar (2004), in their text *Essentials of Group Therapy*, also discuss therapeutic factors inherent in group practice. Many of the factors described are those initially presented by Yalom. These, along with additional factors are further cataloged by MacKenzie (1990); these are outlined in Table 2.1.

Corey's Therapeutic Factors

G. Corey (2004) has identified various factors that he believes are essential in ensuring that a group will become cohesive and productive. These factors are especially important during the working stage of a group (which we address in detail in Chapter 3). Some of these factors have been previously identified and/or alluded to in our discussion regarding group process. These therapeutic factors include: trust and acceptance, empathy and caring, intimacy, hope, freedom to experiment, catharsis, cognitive restructuring, commitment to change, self-disclosure, confrontation, and benefiting from feedback.

Table 2.1 **MacKenzie's Therapeutic Categories**

Category	Elements	Purpose
Supportive Factors	Instillation of Hope Acceptance Altrusim Universality Cohesion	Helps members gain access to the psychological skills they possess.
Self-Revelation Factors	Self-disclosure Catharsis	Involves sharing of emotional information.
Factors in Learning from Others	Modeling Vicarious Learning Guidance Education	Provides an educational focus.
Psychological Work Forces	Interpersonal Learning Self-understanding	Captures the unique features of group life.

Source: Adapted from Brabender et al. (2004), p. 104; MacKenzie (1990).

Jacobs, Masson, and Harvill's Therapeutic Forces

Jacobs et al. (2006) outline 15 forces that are important to consider as a group leader. These forces can be positive or therapeutic, neutral, or negative or antitherapeutic. Jacobs et al. believe that in a successful group, most of the forces are positive or neutral; an unsuccessful group has at least one or more negative forces at play.

1. *Clarity of purpose.* Both the leader and the members must clearly understand the purpose of the group.
2. *Relevance of purpose.* The purpose of the group must be relevant to the needs and desires of the group members.
3. *Group size.* Group size must fit with the purpose, length of time of each session, the setting available, and the experience of the leader.
4. *Length of each session.* Sufficient time must exist for members to have sufficient time to express themselves, but not so long that boredom sets in.
5. *Frequency of meetings.* Purpose and group composition will determine how often the group needs to meet.

6. *Adequacy of the setting.* Convenience, privacy, comfort, and appropriate physical arrangements are all important to consider.

7. *Time of day.* Choosing a time that meets the needs of the majority is important.

8. *Leader's attitude.* A positive attitude that reflects a willingness and strong belief in group process is essential in setting an encouraging tone.

9. *Closed or open groups.* It is important to determine the purpose of the group and the population being serviced in order to decide whether an open or closed group is appropriate.

10. *Voluntary or nonvoluntary membership.* Adapting the group to whether group members choose to be in the group or are mandated to attend is essential.

11. *Members' level of commitment.* Group leaders must take into account the level of commitment in developing group structure and activities.

12. *Level of trust.* In most groups, trust levels increase or decrease as the group cohesion develops. Group leaders must remain alert to changes in the trust level and be prepared to explore possible underlying reasons.

13. *Members' attitude toward the leader.* A group leader who is viewed positively, is trusted and respected, will have a greater impact on group process and success. When negative feelings exist toward the group leader, it is important to understand the leader's possible role in this dynamic.

14. *Leader's experience in leading groups.* Certainly, a more seasoned group leader will be more confident. Experience in both individual and group counseling is important, as is having knowledge about different counseling theories.

15. *Coleadership harmony.* When coleaders are in sync with each other, the group is apt to run more smoothly. Group leaders who clash are more likely to create a negative tone.

Facilitating Interpersonal Relationships

Interpersonal learning is a therapeutic factor central to group work and is most useful in our practice. Groups provide clients with a great opportunity to learn about relationships in a safe and supportive environment that may not otherwise exist outside the group environment. This is especially true if group cohesion is strong.

Defeating isolation is a clear benefit of encouraging healthy interpersonal relationships in and outside of group. For many clients who are alone or find themselves isolated, a group can provide the necessary link to the real world that provides them with hope and courage to overcome their fears and take appropriate risks in reaching out to others.

Group work also enables members to develop effective communication skills, which are a necessary element of strong and healthy interpersonal relationships. Communication, whether verbal or nonverbal, is an essential component of any group and greatly impacts treatment outcomes. Clear communication patterns develop within a group. The way in which groups make decisions is also closely connected to communication within the group. Generally, members must communicate their ideas, beliefs, and points of view in order to reach a consensus on common goals. More specifically, communication among members will determine what issues are entertained during the group session and what ones are not. How individual members communicate within a particular group setting affects future group sessions. What is and is not communicated within a group may influence members to decide whom they can and cannot trust as well as what is safe to disclose and what is not.

Group leaders must possess sound communication skills in order to be effective.

Group Leadership

Our discussion on group process and dynamics underscores the notion that strong group leadership skills are an essential component to successful group practice. Strong cohesion and effective communication skills within a group are closely related to how proficient the leader is in conducting the group.

A professional group leader is skilled in guiding the development of the group and its members. The leader acts like a pilot in order to ensure that the group as a whole and each of its members achieve their specified goals. Although mastering basic leadership skills is essential to becoming an effective leader, it is the personhood of the group leader that is most important.

Personhood of Group Leader
In any realm of practice within human services, the personality and self of the helper is integral to the overall success and outcome of any treatment

provided. As professional helpers, we are often the greatest tool in helping our clients. Our ability to establish solid relationships with group members is tied directly to who we are as people. M. S. Corey and G. Corey (2006) agree that "the professional practice of leading groups is bound up with who the counselor is as a person. Indeed, the leader's ability to establish solid relationships with others in the group is probably the most important tool he or she has in facilitating group process" (p. 27).

Group leaders are persons first and, as such, bring their personal qualities, values, and life experiences to each group meeting. More-over, when group leaders demonstrate a commitment to ongoing self-awareness, they model this to their group members. This modeling is perhaps the most powerful aspect of the helping process. Recognizing and taking responsibility for our personhood is therefore key to remaining therapeutic and ethical in our work.

Self-Awareness Although self-awareness is important for any practi-tioner, when working in a group setting, the group leader's self-aware-ness is even greater necessary due to the simple fact that there are more individuals to trigger countertransference issues. Similarly, competency issues may be more at question for group leaders merely because of the dynamic nature of groups that makes it more difficult to hide or ignore one's feelings and self-perceptions. Becoming overwhelmed or not knowing which direction to go while conducting a group is common and can take its toll on both the leader and the group process if it is not acknowledged. Remaining aware of our own feelings, thoughts, and actions and their impact on the groups we conduct is critical to better understanding ourselves and our clients. Emotionally, professionally, and ethically, self-awareness plays a key role in our ongoing growth and success. Those professionals who remain committed to looking at themselves and taking responsibility for the role they play in the group process typically are more effective and energized by their leadership role.

Values Introspection occurs often results in the recognition of values that helping professionals may not have been aware of. There can be no question that our own individual value systems influence our group work; values impact our intervention styles, the skills we use and the reactions clients have to them, and even the goals we set and the methods we use to attain them. Even in cases where leaders are completely permissive and nondirective, their nonaction reflects their values and reveals much about who they are.

According to Morales and Sheafor (1995), a group leader's actions in the group are affected by contextual values, client value systems, and the worker's personal value system. Contextual sources of values are the values of society, of the agency sponsoring the group, and of the helping professions. Also, since each group member brings with him or her an individual value system, every group is a unique constellation of its members' values. Last, the group leader's personal value system, whether conscious or unconscious, cannot help but enter the therapeutic environment. Examples of how personal values can be tapped include when practitioners are uncomfortable discussing certain value-laden topics that they may masterfully evade, when they unknowingly impose their own values on the group, or when they engage in a debate with those whose values are dissimilar from theirs. Because of the potentially harmful nature of any one of these situations, practitioners must be self-aware and always receptive to considering how their own values affect the group they are leading. When group leaders struggle with some facet of their practice that is value laden, we advocate seeking supervision and/or consultation.

Personal Characteristics of Effective Group Leaders Along with understanding oneself, being aware of our own issues, and recognizing the impact of our values on our work, the literature has identified additional personal characteristics that are instrumental to group leadership; these are summarized in the next sections. It is critical to note that these personal characteristics exist on a continuum. No one possesses 100% of these characteristics. In reviewing the list, be mindful of both those strengths that you can build on and those limitations that you can strive to work on.

Courage Courageous leaders demonstrate their courage in their daily interactions with group members: They are honest, caring, take risks, gently and respectfully confront members as needed, share their own feelings and intuitions with the group, and are willing to acknowledge their imperfections.

Presence Being present emotionally refers to "being there" for group members, both physically and emotionally. Leaders who are affected by the pain, struggles, and joys of others are more able to be empathetic and caring in their responses. Being present also requires keeping feelings and thoughts about other issues outside of the therapy hour.

Willingness to Model Group leaders serve as models for their group members. The leader's behaviors and attitudes can help set a positive tone for working together. The group leader who hopes to lead by example can model such group norms as "openness, seriousness or purpose, acceptance of others, respect for diversity of values, and for the desirability of taking risks. Engaging in honest, appropriate, and timely self-disclosure can be a way to fulfill the leadership function of modeling" (M. S. Corey & G. Corey, 2006, p. 29).

Personal Power A group leader's personal power is directly linked to empowering group members by promoting a sense of power toward positive growth and change. Group leaders who are confident and able to encourage change in others are most effective in their role. The personal power suggested here does not refer to domination or exploitation; rather, this power is portrayed through honest and enthusiastic behaviors and attitudes that reflect energy and a feeling of being alive.

Goodwill, Genuineness, and Caring The basic human qualities of genuineness and caring set the foundation for any type of helping. An effective group leader is one who shows warmth, concern, and support and knows when it is appropriate to gently confront members. Trust and cohesion within the group are more likely when a positive and affirming mood is set.

Belief in Group Process: The successful group leader believes in group process and the beneficial role one plays as a group leader is a prerequisite. Group members can tell when leaders are confident in both the modality being used and in themselves. Likewise, when leaders do not believe in the process, this feeling is conveyed to the group and creates a sense of doubt that hinders progress.

Enthusiasm Enthusiasm radiated by the leader is contagious and sets a positive climate that encourages group members to have faith in the group process. When those in the leadership position are apathetic or even angry, this directly influences how members themselves view the group.

Inventiveness and Creativity Opposite to becoming encapsulated and stagnant in one's work, a leader who remains inventive and creative is more apt to succeed in encouraging creativity within the group. When the same preplanned activities are followed, both the leader and the group do not benefit from new, fresh, and innovative ideas and approaches to working on life issues.

Openness Group leaders who are appropriately open in attitude, to others' opinions, to new ideas, and to themselves foster an atmosphere of openness within the group. Once again, the tone set by the group leader impacts the overall functioning of the group.

Nondefensiveness in Coping with Criticism Group leaders often are viewed as authority figures. As such, they may engender frustration in certain group members, who act out as a result. For instance, it is not uncommon for many clients to work through unfinished business with authority figures in group. As a result, they may project angry feelings onto the group leader. In these situations, it is helpful for the leader to remain objective and not react to these projections. There may also be times when the leader legitimately deserves some critical or negative feedback. In either case, a nondefensive response is the most appropriate. A savvy leader can take this opportunity to model an assertive response that is honest and fair.

Becoming Aware of Your Own Culture A provision to being diversity sensitive involves being aware of how one's own culture affects interactions with others who are different from us. A group leader who embraces diversity will likely be more accepting and open with the group, which, in turn, creates a more trusting group atmosphere. Diversity in group membership can be challenging as well.

Willingness to Seek New Experiences Group leaders who are open to experiencing different emotions are better able to empathize with their clients. Group leaders who are closed to their own feelings will have greater difficulties in understanding and allowing clients to share their feelings.

Sense of Humor Often a healthy and appropriate sense of humor is what is needed to lighten a heavy atmosphere within a group. Laughter often is the best medicine for stress. Humor helps us relax and enjoy our work more fully, and it also takes the edge off intense emotional situations.

Some consider laughter a form of internal jogging, saying that it serves a psychological purpose as well. Vergeer (1995) has studied the psychological changes caused by laughter; these include the release of endorphins, lowered heart rate and blood pressure, stimulation of respiratory activity and oxygen exchange, and enhanced immune and endocrine function.

Humor also allows us to perceive the paradoxes of life from an emotional distance. We can separate ourselves from worrisome incidents and perhaps gain a more realistic perspective.

"Genuine humor can heal. Laughter is good for the soul" (M. S. Corey & G. Corey, 2006, p. 33). Group leaders who are able to laugh at themselves and foster a lighter mood are more well rounded. Humor helps in seeing life from a new perspective.

Personal Dedication and Commitment Dedication and commitment are necessary ingredients for any effective helping practitioner. Committed professionals possess humility, remain current with changes in the field, attend professional seminars, and read professional journals and books.

Stamina Group leaders must possess physical and psychological stamina in order to maintain a functioning group. Group leaders who cannot keep a heightened energy level are more likely to succumb to group pressures. Perseverance is needed as performance demands are often high.

Willingness to Confront Oneself (Self-Awareness) A last characteristic is a willingness to confront oneself, which we have discussed earlier as self-awareness. Simply said, self-awareness is central to becoming a leader who manifests the many characteristics we have just identified (G. Corey, 2004; M. S. Corey & G. Corey, 2006; Gladding, 2004).

Others in the field (Gladding, 2004; Kottler, 1994; Osborne, 1982; Yalom, 1995, 2005) have identified additional qualities of effective group leaders, including a caring attitude and "intentionality." Intentionality on part of the leader has been found to very important; a group leader who can anticipate the group's direction is better able to prepare for its needs. Other characteristics basic to helping are flexibility, warmth, objectivity, trustworthiness, honesty, strength, patience, and sensitivity (Cormier & Nurius, 2003; DeLucia-Waack, 1999; Egan, 2002).

Additional leadership characteristics and traits that are important consist of: being comfortable with oneself, others, and in a position of authority; confidence in one's ability to lead; capacity to tune into others' feelings, reactions, moods, and words; possessing sound psychological health; strong planning and organizational skills; a good understanding of basic human conflicts and dilemmas, such as issues of guilt, fear of failure, self-worth, parents, anger, love relationships, and death; and a commitment to learn from experience so as to avoid repeating the same mistakes.

Group Leadership Skills

As we have seen, group leaders with many of the personality characteristics discussed are well on their way of becoming effective leaders. Additional group leadership skills, however, are also necessary. In general, skill attainment is a process that develops gradually with ongoing practice and evaluation. This is especially true in regard to developing group leadership skills. Table 2.2 outlines group leadership skills most often identified in the literature.

Table 2.2 **Group Leadership Skills**

Specific Skill	Definition and Purpose
Active Listening	Attending to verbal and nonverbal aspects of communication. Determining if communication is congruent, and sensing underlying messages.
	Purpose: Encourages trust which when in place increases client self-disclosure and exploration. Allows members to feel heard and misunderstood.
Restating	Restating involves paraphrasing what has been said by using slightly different words in order to clarify meaning.
	Purpose: Helps determine if communication has been understood correctly and provides support and clarification.
Clarifying	Involves simplifying client statements by focusing on the core of the message; Capturing the essence of the message sent at both emotional and cognitive levels.
	Purpose: Assists both leader and members in sorting out conflicting and confusing feelings and thoughts and leads to a more meaningful understanding of what has been communicated.
Summarizing	Recapping, condensing, and crystallizing the essence of what was communicated.
	Purpose: Provides direction, continuity, and meaning to a session. Helps prevent fragmentation as a concise summary tightens focus, is helpful in making a transition, and highlights key points.
Assessing	Ability to evaluate certain behavioral problems and choose appropriate interventions and referrals.
	Purpose: Allows for proper intervention and referrals.
Questioning	Open-ended questions that help explore issues or feelings more extensively.

Purpose: Elicits further discussion, gathers added information, stimulates thinking, increases clarity, promotes further exploration, and reduces experiencing of intense feelings when unwarranted.

Interpreting

Offers certain hypothesis and a new frame of reference for certain behaviors, feelings, and thoughts.

Purpose: Encourages deeper exploration; offers new perspectives and alternatives from which to view issues and better understand them.

Confronting

A powerful way of challenging members to take an honest look at themselves; an effective way of pointing out discrepancies among thoughts, feelings, and behaviors.

Purpose: Encourages honest self-exploration, which can heighten client's self awareness and the ability to explore new avenues for problem resolution.

Reflecting Feelings

Conveying understanding of the content of feelings.

Purpose: Provides validation that clients have been heard and understood. Fosters further contact and involvement, and promotes increased self awareness.

Supporting

By listening attentively and being psychologically present, leaders provide encouragement and reinforcement.

Purpose: Promotes an atmosphere that encourages trust, allows for positive reinforcement for desired behaviors, and the opportunity to learn new behaviors.

Empathizing

In a caring and open way being able to sensitively grasp the clients' subjective world; identifying with client by assuming their frames of references.

Purpose: Fosters trust in the therapeutic relationship, communicates understanding, and encourages deeper levels of self-exploration.

Facilitating

Through active listening and a sense of caring, the leader opens up clear and direct communication within the group that encourages members to assume increasing responsibility for their involvement.

Purpose: Promotes effective communication among members, encourages more active participation within the group, and supports successful goal attainment.

Initiating

Actively encourages group participation by providing direction, offering structure, and suggesting group activities.

Purpose: Prevents group mismanagement; increases pace of group; and helps members identify and resolve conflict, be able to work through issues, and to focus on their goals.

Goal Setting

Use of intervention skills necessary to challenge members to formulate clear, meaningful, and realistic goals; Plans specific goals for group process.

Purpose: Offers direction for group's activities; assists members in setting individual goals.

Evaluating

Leader's ongoing assessment of individual and group dynamics.

Purpose: Promotes deeper self-awareness and better understanding of group process, dynamics, and movement. An honest assessment of the group's functioning allows considering if change in direction is necessary.

(Continued)

Table 2.2 (Continued)

Specific Skill	Definition and Purpose
Giving Feedback	Communicating honest reactions based on direct behavioral observation. **Purpose:** Gives individual group members insight into how others view them; serves to increase self.
Suggesting	Offers advice and information to group members; Encourages direction and ideas for new behavior. **Purpose:** By giving information and providing appropriate suggestions, members are challenged to develop alternative courses of thinking and action.
Protecting	Safeguarding members from unnecessary psychological or physical risks by discouraging unwarranted and/or inappropriate attacks or confrontation. **Purpose:** Minimizes possible risks that are possible when participation in group treatment.
Disclosing Oneself	Skillful revelation of personal reactions to group process/here-and-now events in the group. **Purpose:** When group leaders appropriately self-disclose this serves to create trust within the group, models openness, and facilitates deeper levels of interaction within the group.
Modeling	Demonstrating desired behaviors (honesty, respect, openness, risk-taking, and assertiveness through action in group. **Purpose:** Provides group with live examples of these desirable behaviors; encourages developing positive skills of interpersonal relating.
Dealing with Silence	Suspending from verbal and nonverbal communication when therapeutically advised. **Purpose:** Appropriate use of silence can be beneficial to group by allowing for reflection and assimilation, helping to sharpen focus, integrating emotionally intense material, and encouraging group interaction and work.
Linking	Connect themes in group to specific group or member issues as is appropriate. **Purpose:** Promotes interaction among members; encourages working together.
Blocking	In a direct, sensitive, and therapeutic manner, the leader intervenes by stopping counterproductive behaviors in group. **Purpose:** Protects unfair and inappropriate attacking of members; models appropriate assertion and communication; enhances the flow of group process.
Terminating	Connect themes in group to specific group or member issues as is appropriate. **Purpose:** Provides members with opportunity to deal with feelings of loss about ending, offers them suggestions of how to apply skills they have learned in group to their daily lives, prepares them for possible problems outside of group, allows for evaluation and review of group, and encourages anticipatory planning.

Source: Adapted from Alle-Corliss & Alle-Corliss (1999); Brabender et al. (2004); G. Corey (2004); M. S. Corey & G. Corey (2006); Gladding (2004); Jacobs et al. (2006); Kottler (1994); Reiter (2008); Spitz & Spitz (1999).

Determining which group leadership skills one has and which one lacks can help group leaders explore additional learning opportunities in which they can cultivate additional skills.

Brabender et al. (2004) present their views on group leadership by identifying five general categories, which are summarized here:

1. *Attitudes and styles of relating of successful therapists*. These attitudes include believing in group therapy as a legitimate and effective treatment, being optimistic in one's approach, being empathic and caring, and remaining self-aware. Ability to deal with narcissism and shame, having the capacity to be aware of multiple levels of interaction, and the ability to manage fear and anxiety are additional areas that are important for group leaders to be well versed in.

2. *Creating a therapeutic frame*. A therapeutic frame provides adequate structure in which group work can take place, enables leaders to be aware of external (membership, time, unhealthy alliances both inside and outside group, and informational) and internal (boundary between therapist and group) boundaries, and creates a safe environment.

3. *Cognitive framing*. Cognitive framing encourages members to "regularly and consistently reframe their experiences into a coherent world view" that helps them find meaning in their experiences and behaviors, especially their problem behaviors (Brabender et al., 2004, p. 117). The specific methods and techniques found most useful include education, reflection, clarification, confrontation, and interpretation.

4. *Putting the leadership structure to good use*. Determining if group will be co-led or solo led is important for leader(s) to address when initially developing a group.

5. *Therapist self-monitoring (self-awareness)*. This self-awareness is important to better understand subjective and objective types of countertransference and identification with group members.

In 2000, the Association for Specialists in Group Work developed *Core Competencies of Group Work*. These professional standards for training of group workers specify certain competencies that are divided into two categories: (1) knowledge objectives and (2) skill objectives .

When considering attainment of group leadership skills, humility is important. How do we acknowledge strengths, remain open and struggle with growth and change, and remain human? Group leadership is a very human endeavor.

Different Group Leadership Styles and Approaches

Effective group leadership facilitates the attainment of group and individual goals and ensures the maintenance of the group. Every group is unique as each leader brings their own style and personality into the group, and the leadership style used will undoubtedly impact the overall functioning of the group. Group leaders bring their personality, value systems, biases, unique skills, and theoretical preferences to the group they lead. Traits that have been found specifically to enhance group cohesion and encourage member commitment include acceptance, responsiveness, and confidence. In contrast, leaders who are more neutral, professional, and distant will be less successful in achieving such cohesion within the group. Ultimately, creating a trusting, open, and fair group environment seems to be the most conducive to positive treatment outcomes. Leaders who are either too dominant or too passive tend to be more ineffective.

The style and role of the group in large part depends on its purpose. A current debate exists over how active, directive, and structured the leader should be. Jacobs et al. (2006) believe that "an active style of leadership works bests for most groups" as "most members of most groups need some structure, organization, and direction" (p. 22). Reiter (2008) concurs:

> It is usually safer to be a bit more active with a group than passive, as a passive leadership style might allow the group to lose focus and become chaotic. The active leader can begin the group by employing more structure at the start, and then loosening the structure and how active and directive they are throughout the process of therapy. It is more difficult to move from more passive to more active. (p. 315)

It is important for leaders who conduct short-term groups to be active, directive, and conscious of time limitations and to show versatility.

Another issue tied to leadership style is the approach to be used, leader directed versus group directed. In the first approach, the leader understands group members' needs and structures the group to meet those needs; in the latter approach, the leader turns over the group to the members and has them determine the direction and content. Either approach can be beneficial; much depends on the overall qualities of the group leader and the composition of the group itself.

Leadership styles exist on a continuum of being interpersonally or intrapersonally oriented. An interpersonally oriented leader tends to focus on the group as a whole, the here-and-now, interactions among individual group members, ongoing group dynamics, and obstacles to effective group leadership. In contrast, intrapersonally oriented leaders are interested primarily in focusing on individual members' needs and concerns (G. Corey, 2004; Jacobs et al., 2004; Reiter, 2008). Both styles are useful, yet the ideal is a balance.

Diversity Sensitivity and Competent Group Leadership

Group practice, by its very nature, brings together many individuals who may be different from each other and from the group leader. Understanding diversity is a prerequisite within the helping profession, as Brill and Levine (2000) highlight:

> *Human diversity is a significant factor in working with people. It is not only a determinant of individual and social functioning; it also affects every aspect of practice in human service. Only as workers are sensitive to differences among people, knowledgeable about their causes and effects, and skillful in recognizing and working with them will practice be effective. (p. 67)*

Alle-Corliss and Alle-Corliss (2006) note that "successfully helping diverse clients necessitates not only the desire and willingness to help but also sensitivity to diversity itself" (p. 132).

Awareness of beliefs and attitudes, knowledge, and skills have been identified within the literature (Lum, 2004; Sue, Arredondo, & McDavis 1992; Sue & Sue, 2003) as keys to becoming competent in working with those who are different from ourselves. According to Pack-Brown, Whittington-Clark, and Parker (1998), culturally competent group counselors will be: (1) aware of their own personal biases, stereotypes, and prejudices; (2) knowledgeable about the members of their groups; and (3) able to practice skills that are appropriate for the life experiences of their clients. We address these three areas briefly next.

Need for Self-Awareness
Developing self-awareness is a vital element in learning to work effectively with those from different backgrounds. Self-knowledge requires becoming aware of "one's own perceptions of difference on basis of race, ethnicity, gender, and other factors" (Lum, 2004, p. 5).

M.S. Corey and G. Corey (2006) add that "effective group counselors must have some level of understanding of their own cultural conditioning, the cultural conditioning of their clients, and an awareness of the sociopolitical system of which they are a part" (p. 41). As we learn to appreciate our own diversity and understand how it relates to our view of others, then we can better learn to accept and appreciate this diversity in others (Alle-Corliss & Alle-Corliss, 2006). In essence, then, it is imperative that helpers understand their own culture in order to be sensitive to those from other cultures and recognize their own biases and ethnocentric beliefs.

DeLucia-Waack and Donigan (2004) propose eight basic steps group leaders can take to become multiculturally competent. Group leaders should:

1. Clarify their personal values, beliefs, and how they view people interacting in productive ways.

2. Be aware of the values inherent in their theoretical approach to group work.

3. Learn which group interventions have been found most effective in working with specific cultural groups.

4. Identify specific instances where their personal or theoretical values, views, and beliefs may be contrary to the values of individuals from diverse backgrounds.

5. Abstain from imposing their worldview on group members.

6. Recognize situations in which there may be a need to refer clients due to a conflict of personal or cultural values.

7. Recognize the need to seek supervision or consultation in working through biases or views.

8. Develop a resource list with information about different cultures and potential conflicts related to group work. (p. 29)

According to M.S. Corey and G. Corey (2006, p. 42), beliefs and attitudes of diversity-competent group workers are also important. Effective group leaders are able "to recognize and understand their own stereotypes and preconceived notions about other racial and ethnic groups" and strive to accept and respect those who are different. An open and accepting tone is encouraged in working with clients of diverse value orientations. Likewise, ongoing consultation, supervision, and continuing education is suggested to maintain self-awareness.

Developing a Solid Knowledge Base

Along with self-awareness and knowledge about their own culture and values and their impact in working with others who are different, it is important for group leaders to learn as much as possible about the clients they will be working with. This entails understanding the dynamics of oppression, racism, discrimination, and stereotyping and becoming aware of the institutional barriers that often prevent certain minorities from accessing necessary services.

Additionally, competent practitioners strive to understand their clients' worldviews and to learn about their historical backgrounds, traditions, and values. Learning about minority family structures, hierarchies, values, beliefs, and communication style differences is equally important. Developing a solid knowledge base about clients is a dynamic process; helpers who are honest and open to continually learning are more likely to be successful. "The greater their depth and breadth of knowledge of culturally diverse groups, the more likely they are to be effective group workers" (G. Corey, 2004, p. 43.).

Skill Application

The term *skill application* refers to developing intervention strategies and techniques that are appropriate to the client group being served. Skill application entails incorporating awareness and knowledge into the services provided. The effectiveness of working with diverse client groups is enhanced when helping modalities and defined goals are consistent with the life experiences and the cultural values of these clients. "Because groups and individuals differ from one another, the blind application of techniques to all situations is ludicrous. Differential approaches are necessary" (Sue & Sue, 2003, p. 45). For instance, it may not be appropriate to encourage certain clients to journal, log, or chart their behavior, to read self-help books, or to use cognitive restructuring techniques. Similarly, certain clients may not be receptive to self-disclosure or to an active or directive approach. Leaders must take care to understand different communication styles and be willing to explore alternative approaches to helping that are congruent with the client group being served. In groups, it is especially important to be sensitive to differences among group members and to respect these differences.

Cormier and Hackney (2005) and Sue (2001) all address cultural competence and emphasize its importance. They also recommend that leaders learn about their own cultural background and affiliations and how these might impact their work with clients. They also recommend that therapists:

- Be willing to learn about others different from themselves by becoming immersed in other cultures and pursing opportunities to interact with others who are from different cultures.

- Remain honest and open about their own range of experiences and possible limitations.

- Recognize issues tied to power, privilege, and poverty and how these might affect different ethnic groups.

- Take responsibility for becoming educated about the various dimensions of culture and differences among clients.

M.S. Corey and G. Corey (2006, p. 44) believe that "diversity-competent group counselors possess a wide range of skills, which they are able to use with diverse client populations." They encourage leaders to invite group members to openly discuss issues about diversity, such as race and ethnicity. Cardemil and Battle (2003) concur that providing members with this opportunity to discuss differences openly enhances the therapeutic relationship and promotes better treatment outcomes.

Value of Coleadership

Although many group practitioners continue to debate the value of coleadership, the consensus is that this model offers many more advantages than disadvantages. Those who favor working with a coleader cite these benefits:

- Coleadership provides the leader with a source of support, feedback, and the opportunity for professional development.

- Coleader peer supervision is possible without breaking confidentiality. Coleaders are better able to understand each other, as they were both present during the group session. Issues of countertransference can be readily discussed and worked through.

- Coleadership increases the leader's objectivity by providing alternative frames of reference.

- Coleaders may complement one another; one leader may be able to supplement skills that the other may not excel in.

- The process may help train an inexperienced coleader by matching a novice with a more seasoned helper. Doing so helps reduce anxiety for the new group leader who is appropriately nervous about group leadership.

- Coleadership models appropriate communication, interaction, and conflict resolutions to group members. Some leaders may even plan a conflictual situation for members to witness; knowledge is gained when the leaders resolve the situation successfully.
- Leaders can more easily engage in role plays, simulations, and program activities with the assistance of a coleader.
- Coleadership affords members the opportunity to receive feedback from two leaders rather than just one. Members can benefit from the life experience and insights of two therapists. Even when leaders are different in their views, they can complement each other.
- Coleadership assists with limit setting and structuring the group experience. The addition of another leader helps in situations where a particular group member is out of control or requires additional support and guidance.
- Coleadership helps reduce burnout rates; coleaders can help leaders with difficult and draining members and can validate a leader's experience. Leaders can work together to prepare and plan for future sessions.
- Coleadership allows the group to continue meeting even if one leader is absent.
- Coleadership allows coleaders to learn from other, just as group members can learn from one another.

Clearly, "many possibilities exist for linking members, for facilitating interaction between members, and for orchestrating the flow of a group when co-leaders are sensitively and harmoniously working as a team" (M. S. Corey & G. Corey, 2006, p. 48). Despite the benefits of coleadership, however, it is important to acknowledge that limitations can also exist:

- Coleadership is more expensive and time consuming.
- Communication between sessions may be a problem for coleaders. Problems are more likely when coleaders rarely meet and are not synchronized.
- Leaders may not work well together, even if they generally agree on how to conduct the group.
- Coleaders may view group process and engage in group practice in very different ways, and these differences may adversely impact the group.

- The interactions of group leaders who do not trust or respect one another often set a negative tone in the group.
- Group members may favor one leader over another, thereby creating conflict and division. Competition and rivalry can occur, which can create added stress within the group. One leader siding with members against the other leader can lead to serious problems in group dynamics.
- Group members may attempt to pit one leader against the other, placing additional pressure on the group leaders to function properly.
- Coleaders who are intimately involved may unwittingly attempt to work through some of their own relationship issues in group or become distant and uninvolved in group due to problems in their relationship.

These disadvantages are more likely when coleaders do not respect or value each other. Ideally, leaders with complementary styles and personalities work best together. Whether coleaders are similar or different, an effort to create and maintain an effective relationship is crucial. Meeting regularly before a group for planning purposes is helpful, as is meeting after the group to process.

Roller and Nelson (1991) encourage examining coleadership dilemmas through what they call the *Five Cs*: competition, countertransference, confusion, lack of communication, lack of congruence between coleaders, and codependency between coleaders. Taking time to consider these possible difficulties before the group begins or as they arise is certainly indicated.

Need for Consultation and Supervision

Ongoing self-awareness is essential for all helping professionals. The complexity and ever-changing nature of group practice magnifies the need for self-awareness. Ongoing supervision is necessary when beginning to engage in group work. Issues related to group dynamics and process will need to be discussed, as will concerns of a more personal nature that may surface when leading a group. Supervision may not be essential for more seasoned practitioners, yet remaining open to consultation is highly recommended. Sometimes even the most experienced providers can become stale and narrow-minded and may need someone to share their struggles with and to bounce new ideas off. This is especially true for leaders who conduct groups alone and do not have the opportunity to process and receive feedback from coleaders.

Developing Your Own Group Leadership Style

Every practitioner and group leader must develop his or her own personal style. Doing this requires that each leader integrate personhood, experience, knowledge, and skills into a style that is uniquely his or hers. G. Corey (2004) says: "Know yourself and develop a style that fits your personality" (p. 51). Alle-Corliss and Alle-Corliss (1999) recommend that practitioners

> *become familiar with some of the basic theories in an attempt to find the one—or more likely, the synthesis of several—that is most suitable to you. Of equal importance is paying careful attention to what theoretical approaches and treatment methods work best with different types of clients or with specific types of issues. (p. 132)*

Learning about the various theoretical perspectives that guide group practice and determining which treatment modalities are best to use with certain populations is critical in developing a personal style.

Leadership style also depends on whether a group leader is planning on leading a short- or long-term group. Short-term groups are fast-paced and require leaders to be active, directive, and conscious of time and limitations. A structured format is necessary, and leaders must help members identify individual problem areas and set specific goals.

Equally important in cultivating a leadership style is to work from a theoretical base that is congruent with one's own personal values and that fits one's special talents and temperament. G. Corey (2004) agrees here as well: "The theoretical stand that you are challenged to develop must be closely related to your values, beliefs, and personal characteristics" (p. 51). Alle-Corliss and Alle-Corliss (1999) identify three main areas that will have a bearing on the style and approach group leaders develop:

> *(1) self-awareness, as your style and approach will be partially based on your own personality and interests; (2) your work setting, as your approach may depend in part on what kind of agency you work for; and (3) your experience level, which can also dictate, to some extent, what helping approach you apply. (p. 132)*

Additional training, supervision, or assistance may be intermittently necessary for any practitioner or group leader; this is especially true for beginning helpers. It is necessary to accept that becoming a sound group leader is an ongoing, evolutionary process. Table 2.3 provides a guide for practitioners in developing their own style of helping.

Table 2.3 **Steps to Developing Your Own Style of Helping**

Step 1. Consider your personal values and views about people.

Step 2. Review the major theories of group counseling and psychotherapy and decide on the one (s) that most closely resembles your own personal values and beliefs.

Step 3. Study this chosen theory in depth and partake in available workshops that will allow you opportunities to practice using associated techniques in a supervised environment.

Step 4. As you work with clients, begin to apply what you have learned, being careful to keep your clients' interests as the focal point.

Step 5. As you become comfortable with your chosen theory, be open to consider use of other theories that may also fit your theoretical base.

Step 6. Remain open to learning new ways of understanding and working with individuals and groups. In time you will become more aware of your own personal style.

Source: Adapted from Alle-Corliss & Alle-Corliss, 1999 (p. 133) and J. Harrow, M. Nelson-Brambir, & G. Harrow (1996).

In Closing

This chapter discussed group process and group dynamics, identified therapeutic aspects of group work, explored aspects of group leadership, and provided suggestions for developing one's own style of helping. Chapter 3 focuses on understanding group development.

Understanding Group Development

U nderstanding group dynamics and developing the skills necessary to be an effective leader are fundamental to becoming a successful leader. Likewise, understanding group development is essential to group planning and actual group practice. In this chapter we detail the stages of group work starting with group planning during the pregroup stage. We explore beginning, middle, working, and ending stages and address common issues and concerns.

Stages of Group

Information on the various stages of group is well documented in the literature (Brabender, Fallon, & Smolar, 2004; G. Corey, 2004; M.S. Corey & G. Corey, 2006; Gladding, 2004; Jacobs, Masson, & Harvill, 2006; Yalom, 2005). There are various perspectives on the number or stages and the specifics of what exactly happens during each stage, yet the overall consensus is that groups have a pregroup period and a beginning, middle, and ending. Table 3.1 illustrates how various authors have identified these stages.

In general, our view mirrors the various stage models shown in the table. We believe that our version of group development is both comprehensive and sensible. It contains a pregroup stage followed by a beginning, middle/working, and final stage. Pregroup issues that involve group planning and group formation are summarized here and addressed in further detail in Chapter 7, which addresses how to successfully engage in group practice within an agency. Our primary focus in this chapter is on the stages of group work that follow the pregroup stage.

Table 3.1 **Various Views on Stages of Group**

Researchers	Stages
Jacobs, Masson, & Harvill	Beginning
	Working
	Closing
Tuckman	Forming
	Storming
	Norming
	Performing
Donigan & Malnati	Orientation
	Conflict and Confrontation
	Cohesiveness
	Work
	Termination
Brabender, Fallon, & Smolar	Forming a Group
	Authority and Power Issues
	Intimacy
	Dealing with Differences
	Termination
G. Corey; M. S. Corey & G. Corey	Forming the Group
	Initial Stage of Group
	Transition Stage
	Working Stage
	Final Stage

Pregroup Issues

Group Planning and Group Formation

Sound group planning is the foundation for an effective group. The seven-step "Planning Model for Group Work" proposed by Toseland and Rivas (2009) provides a framework from which to begin to explore group development:

1. Establishing a group purpose
2. Determining potential group sponsorship and membership
3. Recruiting members/attracting members
4. Group composition: Forming the group

5. Orienting members to the group
6. Contracting
7. Preparing the group's environment

Beginning Stages of Group

The first session marks the beginning of the group. During this "orientation and exploration" stage, members are "determining the structure of the group, getting acquainted, and exploring the member expectations" (G. Corey, 2004, p. 90). One of the primary tasks of this first phase is that of "inclusion and identity" whereby group members strive to find an identity in the group and decide how much they will allow themselves to be involved. According to Tuckman (1965), it is in the first stage of "forming" where emphasis is on helping members feel they are part of the group and when trust and inclusiveness is developed. Yalom (2005) considers the "initial stage" as one of orientation. Box 3.1 outlines factors that leaders should consider in the first session.

Factors to Consider in First Session

- Beginning the group
- Helping members get acquainted
- Setting a positive tone
- Clarifying purpose
- Explaining leader's role
- Explaining how the group will be conducted
- Helping members verbalize expectations
- Drawing out members during the first session
- Use of exercises during the first session
- Checking out the comfort level
- Explaining group rules
- Explaining terms
- Assessing members' interaction styles
- Being sensitive to multicultural/diversity issues and any dynamics that may be present

(Continued)

- Cutting Off members during the first session
- Focusing on the content
- Addressing questions
- Getting members to look at other members
- Other first-session considerations
- Closing the first session

Initial Session(s)

The initial meeting is often filled with both excitement and apprehension, regardless of how well the leader(s) planned for the group or how prospective members were prepared. Members are often anxiously observing other members and assessing their own level of comfort about sharing in the group. G. Corey, Schneider-Corey, Callanan, and Russell (2004) note that "members are typically anxious about not fitting in, about revealing themselves, about meeting new people, and about being in a new situation" (p. 70). Reid (1997) offers his view of this first session:

> *The beginning of the first session is marked by hesitant statements, awkward pauses, and reoccurrence of previously answered questions. In the initial stages of the group, clients are preoccupied with themselves rather than with group concerns, and they experience only a limited sense of connection with other group members. (p. 191)*

M.S. Corey and G. Corey (2006) made similar observations. They note that at the onset, members are getting acquainted and discovering how the group functions. This is a time when spoken and unspoken norms that will govern group behavior are developed; ideally it can be a time for the promotion of healthy norms. Members are consciously or unconsciously exploring their fears and hopes concerning their participation in the group. Their expectations are clarified, personal goals are identified, and ultimately members are determining if the group is safe and appropriate for them to continue in.

We concur with Reiter (2008) who feels that "getting off to a good start" is extremely important. "The beginning of the group interview sets the tone for how that session and subsequent sessions will go. Clients feel out the therapist, along with other members, and judge how safe it is for them to open up in this multiple-person format" (pp. 315–316). We, like many others have (G. Corey, 2004; M.S. Corey & G. Corey, 2006; Jacobs et al., 2006; Yalom, 2005), advocate allowing members to express their expectations, concerns, and anxieties openly during this initial phase. During this time, the leader should clear up any misconceptions about the group process in general. G. Corey (1996) sees this initial phase "as akin to the first few days one spends in a foreign land, having to learn the rudiments of a new language and different ways of expressing oneself" (p. 95).

Earlier literature has emphasized the importance of leadership preparation in conducting this first session. We agree that it is critical for group leader(s) to permit members to stay involved with the group's beginning by allowing them to experience the inevitable awkwardness and tentativeness rather than to push for a perfect climate where everyone feels positive, which is impossible anyway. The primary goal during this initial phase of a group is to facilitate the discovery of a common base that will set the foundation for future work together. Doing this requires skillful work by the group leader, who must not only be sensitive to the normal anxiety typical at the onset of any new group but also be cognizant of each individual member's dynamics and needs, all the while attempting to integrate material presented into a common theme from which to start.

Logically, the first session is often the most difficult. Jacobs et al. (2006) note that the leader has "many different dynamics and logistics to manage: starting the group, introducing the content to the members, and monitoring the members' reactions both to being in the group and to the content" (p. 85). Numerous factors must be considered in the first session: how to begin the group, help members get acquainted, set a positive tone, clarify the purpose of the group, explain the leader's role, explain how the group will be conducted, check out members' comfort levels, assess members' interaction styles, and be sensitive to multicultural/diversity issues. Using exercises, focusing on content, cutting off members who are inappropriate, addressing questions from group members, getting members to acknowledge others in the group, and closing the first session are additional topics that should be considered.

Group Structure
Early on in most groups, members look to the leader for direction and understanding. Reid (1997) maintains that one way group leaders can help lessen the anxiety in a group and enhance commitment by members is by reiterating information previously presented in pregroup interviews and reviewing the overall purpose, objectives, and expectations of the group. Providing the group with structure is especially important during this initial stage, when members are apt to be anxious and confused about what is expected of them in the group.

"Groups function best when members feel a sense of confidentiality" (Gladding, 2004, p. 260). The subject of confidentiality, initially discussed during the prescreening interview, is important to raise at this juncture as well. Corey et al. (2004) concur that confidentiality needs to be stressed during the first meeting of the group and on a regular basis thereafter; doing this entails defining confidentiality, discussing why it is difficult to enforce, and addressing issues regarding betrayal of confidentiality. Group leaders can guarantee only their own adherence to the principles of confidentiality, yet they are ethically and legally bound to strive to ensure the rights of all group members (Gladding, 2004; Olsen, 1971). Group members will likely want to talk about their group experience. What they say about *what* they have learned about themselves does not violate confidentiality, yet when "they talk about *how* others made changes by describing what others did or what techniques were used," then confidentiality is likely to be breached (Corey et al., 2004, p. 13).

Careful attention is needed in structuring every session, especially the very first one. Shulman (1999) believes that the first few meetings should be structured to meet these objectives:

- Introduce group members to one another.
- Present a brief but simple opening statement to clarify the agency's reasons for sponsoring the group. Members raise issues and concerns they feel most important.
- Encourage feedback from group members about their feelings of the match between their needs and the agency's view of the treatment it can provide them.
- Clarify the role and method of conducting group.
- Deal directly with any obstacles that present themselves.
- Encourage intermember interaction versus discussions held between individual members and group leaders.
- Develop a supportive environment that engenders a sense of safety and trust among members.
- Support members to develop a tentative agenda that addresses both individual and group needs.
- Identify the mutual expectations of the agency and group members.
- Gain some consensus about how to proceed within group.
- Advocate honest feedback from members about the group's effectiveness.

Some of these objectives are simple and easily met during the first session. Others, however, may require more time for members to feel enough trust to verbalize their views. Groups vary as to what marks the beginning and end of this initial stage. For instance, some groups engage in open and honest dialogue almost from the onset, creating a trusting and comfortable environment that allows the group to quickly move to the working stage. Typically groups take a couple of sessions, at the very least, to coalesce and develop a working environment. Some groups many never reach the working stage. Leaders must be careful to not allow the group to remain too long in the beginning stage; this could lead to boredom, frustration, and early dropouts. Leaders who move the group too quickly into the working stage, however, may also create a situation where members feel frustrated, confused, and perhaps even angry.

Group structuring allows for positive *group norms* to emerge. Group norms are those "shared beliefs about expected behaviors aimed at making groups function more effectively" (M.S. Corey & G. Corey, 2006, p. 149). Typically, norms develop early on during a group's life and have a huge impact on its overall success. When standards that govern group behavior are unclear, there is likely to be more tension within the group. When norms are explicitly stated, members may understand more clearly what is expected of them. Implicit norms may develop as well. They are more likely when members make false assumptions, when leaders modeled by leaders themselves, and as a result of condoned group interactions.

Group Composition and Characteristics
Group characteristics of the initial stage of group work are additional key areas that must be addressed during this early stage. First, various types of reactions by members are likely; some may be tentative and vague about the group, appear impatient and ready to work, appear hesitant and uninvolved, or seem eager to find quick solutions to their problems. The group leader must know how to deal with each type of reaction and work toward developing cohesion in the group.

Most group members typically experience some form of initial resistance during the first session(s). Members may be hesitant, suspicious, or struggle with cultural dictates that reinforce keeping family matters private. Often members complain about the place or time of meetings or what appears to be inconsequential matters, yet these complaints may serve to hide underlying fear and anxiety. "Although members may have very particular fears about the group, a shared concern is the loss of autonomy, individuality, and privacy that accompanies connection with others" (Brabender et al., 2004, p. 145). A more qualified group leader will be sensitive to these reactions and help members identify and discuss these fears early on. Sometimes the very act of sharing fears helps members begin to bond with one another and to recognize that their fears are very similar.

Hidden agendas often plague the initial stages of a group. Often certain issues that affect the way a group progresses are not openly discussed.

> *If encouragement to face these issues is lacking, the group process gets bogged down because the norm of being closed, cautious, and defensive replaces the norm of being open . . . trust is low, interpersonal tensions emerge, people are guarded and unwilling to take risks, the leader seems to be working harder than the members, and there is a vague feeling that something just does not make sense. (M.S. Corey & G. Corey, 2006, p. 135)*

Clearly, the group suffers when hidden agendas are not challenged; in extreme cases, the group may even disband. To avoid this, leaders must remain persistent in assessing and exploring underlying issues.

In beginning groups, it is common for group members to talk about others and focus on people and situations outside the group instead of focusing on themselves. "The content of initial sessions frequently focuses on those member concerns that lie outside the group, and a high level of externalization will be evident" (Brabender et al., 2004, p. 145).

Since this is a normal reaction, group leaders must be careful to respect members' anxiety yet still work toward encouraging them to focus on themselves and explore their own reactions to others. If leaders wait too long to challenge members on this, not discussing personal issues may become a group norm.

The "here-and-now" and "there-and-then" focuses are both encouraged during the initial phases of group work. It has been said that "members studiously avoid focusing on the here and now" (Brabender et al., 2004, p. 145). Since members may wish to focus on problems outside the group, they are encouraged to connect these to their experiences in the group. Ideally, members can benefit most when they are able to see how their behavior in the group may be similar to that in their personal lives. Since the manner in which group members behave within the group is indicative of how they interact with others outside the group, this allows for valuable interpersonal learning through group. When interventions are used to encourage members to gain awareness of what they are experiencing in the here-and-now by paying attention to what they are thinking, feeling, and doing in the moment, they are challenged to recognize how they may similarly interact with others in their daily lives. "The more members are able to immerse themselves in the here and now, the greater chance they have to enhance the quality of their interpersonal relationships in everyday life" (M.S. Corey & G. Corey, 2006, p. 139).

Group Cohesion
Effective group practice is difficult without cohesion. Cohesion is considered the glue that holds a group together (Coyle, 1930; Henry, 1992). Deemed universally as an essential ingredient for effective group practice, cohesion is thought of as a "bond that permits members to feel close enough to each other to allow their individuality to be expressed" (Henry, 1992, p.13).

> *The greater a member's feelings of attraction to or belongingness to the group, the more likely the member will be to feel his or her presence is vital to the group and the more likely the member will be to ''risk'' participating in and contributing to the group. (Donigan & Malnati, 2006, p. 44)*

Cohesion has also been connected to "a sense of belonging or attraction to a group" (Donigan & Malnati, 2006, p. 44). Aspects of a cohesive group include members who are invested in remaining in the group and feel they belong and can relate to other group members. Zastrow (1985) asserts that cohesion is "the sum of all the variable influencing members to stay in a group. . . . It occurs when the positive attraction of a group outweighs any negative implications a member might encounter" (p. 21). This notion tends to parallel lasting relationships in real life where positives outweigh the negatives. For instance, many people have been able to surmount difficult times in order to maintain long-term relationships because of the overall good between them.

Cohesion has been described by Yalom (2005) as analogous to the relationship in individual therapy; that is, group cohesion is "regarded as the group counterpart to the therapeutic alliance in individual therapy" (Brabender et al., 2004, p. 93).

Cartwright (1968) wrote about cohesion early on. He discusses "group attraction," which is essential for cohesion to develop. In his work

Cartwright identifies four interacting sets of variables that are believed to determine a member's attraction to a group. Alle-Corliss and Alle-Corliss (1999) outline these variables in this way:

1. Needs and affiliation, recognition, and security
2. Incentives and resources of the group, such as the prestige of its members, the group's goals, its program activities, and its style of operation
3. The subjective expectations of members about the beneficial or detrimental consequences of the group
4. A comparison of the group to other experiences

Others cite similar reasons as to why cohesion tends to develop within a group: attraction of members to each other, to the activities group members do together, or to the goals the group is working on (Henry, 1992). Zastrow (2009) writes about the payoffs and cost of group membership that affect group attraction. Payoffs may include: companionship, attaining personal goals, prestige, enjoyment, and emotional support. Costs may include: being with people one dislikes, expending time and effort, criticism, distasteful tasks, and uneventful sessions. When costs are too high, cohesion is limited and group viability is threatened.

Cohesion that develops internally within the group forms gradually and may be affected by events that occur inside and outside the group; cohesion is ever changing. Groups are likely to be more productive and longer lasting when cohesion exists and when group and individual goals are met. Because cohesion is so vital to the success of the group, it is essential for leaders to assess the level of cohesion present in their groups regularly and make necessary adjustments to increase communication. Donigan and Malnati (2006) believe that "member behavior" must be elicited for cohesion to occur; that is, members must actively participate in sharing their concerns and expressing their feelings. Group leaders are therefore encouraged to use interventions that stimulate members to talk openly and interact freely with one another.

Creating Trust among Members, and with Leader(s)
Trust is said to be at the core of any successful group. "Trust is an important factor throughout the group's development, but even more so in the early stages" (Reid, 1997, p. 64). Developing trust early on

sets a strong foundation for the future of any group; without it, "group interaction will be superficial, little self-exploration will take place, constructive challenging of one another will not occur, and the group will operate under the handicap of hidden feelings" (G. Corey, 2004, p. 91).

Two levels of trust exist: (1) membership trust in the group leader, and (2) member trust with one another. Long (1996) writes that trust and rapport are related:

> *Trust is an effective experience and a desired outcome within the helping relationship. It grows from rapport and is built on acknowledged cognitive beliefs, particularly the belief that individuals have the right to be themselves and to have their own feelings, thoughts, and actions. (p. 81)*

Many factors contribute to the level of trust that develops within a group. The leader's preparation and planning demonstrates interest and commitment to the group process. Structuring the group reduces the amount of anxiety and ambiguity that is common at the beginning session. Introducing confidentiality and informing the group of guidelines, responsibilities, and expectations early creates a climate of trust. Encouraging diverse members to be respectful of one another also inspires trust. A leader with a positive attitude who demonstrates a genuine interest in the welfare of individual members engenders trust as well. Encouraging members to share their fears and concerns early on also fosters trust; members begin to feel they are not alone when others are able to share similar feelings and concerns.

Once trust is developed group leaders must continue to explore ways of maintaining this trust. When group members are allowed to jump in and give advice instead of allowing problem solving to occur, a sense of distrust and uneasiness may emerge. Also, when negative feelings about other members or the group leader arise and they are not handled properly, trust can break down. Brabender et al. (2004), G. Corey (2004), and Donigan and Malnati (2006) all consider the way in which conflict is dealt with as instrumental in ensuring that trust is maintained; if issues are brought out into the open and negative feelings are listened to in a nondefensive way, resolution is more likely.

It is important to keep in mind that levels of trust are dynamic within a group; levels of trust will likely change as the group progresses and members begin to form more intimate bonds. However, a trusting climate created during the initial stages of the group sets the tone for a more trusting environment during the group's more difficult transition and working stages.

Group Goals and Individual Member Goals

Once trust and rapport is established, group leaders must turn their focus on helping members, as well as the group as a whole, to identify and clarify goals. According to Reid (1997), establishing manageable goals:

1. *Focuses the member's attention and action and provides a vision toward which the member can direct his or her energy,*
2. *Mobilizes the member's energy and effort,*
3. *Increases the member's persistence, that is, ability to work harder and longer, and*
4. *Motivates the member toward action and away from the inclination to engage in aimless behavior. (p. 198)*

For some members, developing realistic goals is a fairly simple matter. These persons are usually clear about their problem, are able to articulate their expectations, and can identify strategies to achieve these goals. Also, members who have been in counseling previously may be more familiar with the goal-setting process. In turn, goals are much more difficult to develop for involuntary clients, for those who are vague about the reasons for entering therapy, or for those who have sought treatment to placate others (i.e., significant others, school, work, etc.). Often initial goals as defined by clients are too broad, unrealistic, and difficult to measure. When this is the case, the group leader will need to be more active in helping shape these goals into more specific and concrete ones. When leaders are unwilling or unable to use intervention skills necessary to challenge group members to identify concrete goals, groups are likely to be unproductive and directionless.

Workable goals must contain four elements:

1. Goals must be defined in explicit terms and stated as specific outcomes.
2. They must be both realistic and attainable during the length of the group.
3. Goals must be measurable and verifiable, allowing members (and the leader) to be able to measure their own progress.
4. The goals must truly be owned by the client, not imposed by others, including the group leader.

When clients are fully invested in the therapeutic process, the likelihood for success is much greater. Similarly, group leaders must be careful to not create a group that is solely goal governed, so tense and rigid that the beauty and freedom of the group experience is lost. DeShazer (1991) identifies seven characteristics of workable goals, some of which echo views just cited: Goals should be small rather than large; salient to clients; described in specific, concrete behavioral terms; and achievable within the practical contexts of clients' lives. In addition, goals should "be perceived by the clients as involving their hard work; be described as the 'start of something' and not as 'the end of something'; and treated as involving new behavior(s) rather than the absence or cessation of existing behaviors" (p. 112).

Along with developing workable goals, being able to prioritize them is often necessary. Group members often present with more than one issue on which to work and become confused when they attempt to work on too many goals at once. Reiter (2008) explains that "client goals are usually based on intensity levels, with some goals being more important and significant for the client" (p. 155). He believes that it is the group leaders' responsibility to help members determine which are the primary, secondary, and tertiary goals. When goals are clear and prioritized, members will be more likely to see them through completion.

Once members identify their individual goals, the group leader may need to cement these goals by establishing a contract that allows clients to be more precise in their goals, encourages them to be responsible for assuming an active role in their treatment, and holds them accountable. Group exercises and homework assignments can also be used to encourage clients to work on their goals, both inside the group and outside.

Group goals are also important to consider and have been separated into two general categories: general group goals and general process goals (M.S. Corey & G. Corey, 2006). General group goals differ from group to group and are based largely on the purpose of the group. For instance, goals for an incest survivors' group may be to assist clients to resolve past issues that will allow them to lead more fulfilling lives.

Group process goals are those that apply to most groups. For example, in a men's group, members are encouraged to express feelings and thoughts directly. In a pain management group, members learn skills to decrease pain. Generally, group process goals consist of:

- Staying in the here-and-now
- Challenging one another
- Taking healthy risks

- Giving and receiving feedback
- Using active listening
- Honest and specific responses
- Willingness to deal with conflict
- Openness to dealing with feelings as they arise in the group
- Mutually agreeing on what the group focus will be
- Acting on new insights
- Practicing new behavior in and out of the group

Inherent in these process goals is the creation of trust and acceptance, the promotion of an appropriate level of self-disclosure, and the encouragement to take healthy risks. Since these goals are for the group as a whole, they must be clearly stated, and the leader must make every attempt to ensure that each member understands and accepts these goals.

Middle Stages of Group

When members are ready to focus on the purpose of the group, they have entered the "middle" stage of group work. Stages of group development have been compared to developmental life stages: initial stage (childhood), middle stage (young adulthood), working stage (mid-life), and final stage (later life). Reid (1997) states:

> *The middle, or adulthood, stage of group evolves as a result of each group member's growing sense of trust in the other members, in the worker, and in the group process. There is a definite move from the tentative involvement typical of the childhood stage to a greater feeling of commitment. (p. 230)*

Movement from one stage to another is a process. Although movement usually means that one stage leads to another, this progression does not always flow smoothly. In most groups, a great deal of work occurs during the middle stage. For this reason, this stage is often broken down into two phases: the "transition phase" and the "working phase."

Transition Phase
It is commonplace for members to begin to truly work on various issues at a deeper level as they transition into the middle stage. Characteristics of this stage include anxiety, establishing trust, defensiveness, resistance,

struggle for control, member conflicts, confrontation, challenges to the group leaders, and the emergence of problem behaviors among difficult group members (G. Corey, 2004; M.S. Corey & G. Corey, 2006; Corey, Schneider-Corey, Callanan, & Russell, 2004).

In order for the group to successfully progress to the working stage that follows, these issues must be recognized and dealt with appropriately. If insufficient time is spent acknowledging and dealing with members' feelings or concerns, the ability to be genuinely open and trusting in the group process will be minimal and ultimately may serve to stifle more intense, realistic therapeutic work by members to be genuinely open and trusting in the group process.

Anxiety and Defensiveness

Anxiety and defensiveness at this stage are to be expected when you consider that members are now ready to let their guard down and allow others to see their true colors. Most of us can attest to feeling anxious when embarking in any new venture we are not completely sure of; this is what many group members experience as they embark into new territory. Sources of anxiety at this stage can be many. For instance, some clients feel anxious by the mere notion of letting others see them in a different light from how they present publicly. Others may feel anxious simply due to the lack of structure within the group or the lack of clarity regarding purpose, goals, or expectations. For still others, there is the fear of appearing foolish or different, of being misunderstood or feeling alone, and of being rejected. In most cases, a normal human reaction to feeling anxious is to respond defensively and with resistance. Anxiety is normal in new situations. G. Corey (2004) contends that anxiety can result "from the fear of being judged and misunderstood, from the need for more structure, and from a lack of clarity about goals, norms, and expected behavior in the group situation" (p. 98). Group leaders must be sensitive and accepting, and certainly be careful not to push clients too hard to open up. Depending on the clients' diagnosis and their level of crisis, encouraging them to open up may not be therapeutic. Respecting clients' emotional states while gently encouraging them to move forward is a delicate matter that requires continual examination by group leaders.

Resistance

Since anxiety is often high as group members enter the middle stage, true resistance often manifests itself at this time. Reacting defensively is often an outcome of anxiety and can be considered a form of resistance. Corey et al. (2004) consider resistance "as behavior that keeps us from exploring personal conflicts or painful feelings" (p. 181). As a defense to protect us from anxiety, resistance is a normal process that is inevitable in groups. Because resistance is often misunderstood, we explore it in further depth here.

According to Brammer (1998), resistance that is experienced in any beginning therapeutic work represents a client's "conscious or unconscious reluctance to begin a helping relationship as well as their covert thwarting of the goals of the interview once the process is under way" (p. 52). Egan (2002) believes that clients are often reluctant and ambivalent about making changes that will require some discomfort. Resistance then is any behavior that deters clients from exploring personal issues or painful feelings in any depth, and as such, serves as an "obstacle presented by the client that blocks treatment" (Meier & Davis, 1993, p. 15). Resistance is not always clearly stated as "I don't want to go on any further"; it can take many forms, from open hostility to passive-resistive behaviors. When resistance is not recognized or explored, it can serve to block the group's progress. In fact, resistance is often the very material that leads to further productive exploration within the group. Also, an individual member's defensiveness may be a clue to how the person relates interpersonally outside of the group. Ormont (1988) believes that often resistance is tied to a fear of intimacy, which may take on various forms, such as conflict, detachment, distrust, or diverting. Underlying these behaviors is the basic fear "of getting close and the vulnerability this implies" (Corey et al. 2006, p. 181).

The group leader must attempt to understand the many underlying reasons for resistance. Alle-Corliss and Alle-Corliss (2006) cite these causes for resistance: as a defense mechanism, fear of change, cultural factors, authority issues, manipulation, depression, and being involuntary clients.

Additional fears experienced by group members that must be explored during this transition phase include fear of: appearing foolish, rejection, emptiness, losing control, and self-disclosure. Savvy group leaders will be able to assess for these conditions by recognizing certain behaviors that group members manifest. Such leaders will know to expect and respect resistance. Expecting resistance helps them not to become defensive. Leaders who respect resistance can work more creatively in understanding and confronting it. Following we provide some considerations in therapeutically working with resistance.

Considerations for Dealing with Resistance

- Emphasize the importance of developing a trusting relationship that sets a positive tone from which to better deal with resistance.
- Display acceptance and strive to develop a respect for resistance, as it may serve a valuable purpose.
- Be open to examine your own issues with regard to resistance.
- Express a desire to explore the significance of the resistance and its inherent dynamics.
- Be open to addressing the resistance directly and empathetically.
- As appropriate, use constructive confrontation; that is, confront in a caring and concerned way that is descriptive, specific, and well timed.
- Recognize that dealing with resistance may lead to an opportunity for positive change and growth.
- Refrain from pushing your own agenda and accept that change is not universally accepted or rigidly defined. Thus, what appears as resistance may not necessarily be.
- Consider that resistance may be a result of poor communication or underlying depression.
- Be flexible, creative, and willing to work with the resistance, not against it.
- Be willing to relax and listen to the client; this might allow you to gain new insights and awareness.

(Adapted from Alle-Corliss & Alle-Corliss, 1999, p. 64)

Conflict, Control, and Confrontation

Like resistance, conflict has been said to be ever present during the transition phase, where the struggle for power and control seems to be the greatest. Group members may be openly negative, critical, judgmental, or quietly observing the group dynamics to determine who will gain the power. According to Yalom (2005), this stage is a time when there is a struggle for power among the members and with the leader. "Each member attempts to establish his or her preferred amount of initiative and power. Gradually, a control hierarchy, as social pecking order emerges" (Yalom, 2005, p. 314). Although likely to be manifested differently, this struggle for power is evident in every group. Yalom

(2005) notes that "this struggle for control is part of the infrastructure of every group" and "is always present, sometimes quiescent, sometimes smoldering, sometimes in full conflagration" (p. 314). Group members may become competitive, jealous, and judgmental of others in group, and may challenge the group leader over the division of responsibility and decision-making procedures (G. Corey, 2004; M.S. Corey & G. Corey, 2006).

Recognizing and openly discussing issues tied to control as they arise is best; ignoring these behaviors can further problems and thwart group cohesion. Also, as with resistance, control issues that surface may be clues that members struggle with similar issues outside the group and may warrant further exploration. Conflict is unavoidable in any group setting; leaders who demonstrate an openness and willingness to deal with conflict as it arises show members that conflict is an important aspect of group development that they will not shy away from.

Conflict is an inevitable outcome of challenging or confronting group members. Too often, however, conflict is feared, ignored, or avoided, due to its negative connotation. Nonetheless, for group work to be productive, group leaders first must acknowledge that conflict exists and then make an effort to explore the underlying dynamics that are present.

Toseland and Rivas (2009) distinguish between *task conflict* and *relationship conflict*. Task conflict, also called instrumental and substantive, is

> based on members' differing opinions about ideas, information and facts presented during the task group's work. Relationship conflict [also known as affective, social, or process conflict] is based on the emotional and interpersonal relationships among members within and outside of the group. (p. 323)

Task conflict is said to be helpful to development and maintenance of group cohesion; relationship conflict is more detrimental to group process since it is generally resistant to persuasive reasoning.

Besides understanding the different types of conflicts, leaders must be aware that certain personality characteristics have also been associated with productive and nonproductive conflict. A win-win orientation and flexibility are connected to productive conflict whereas "zero-sum" orientation and rigidity is associated with conflict escalation (Jehn & Chartman, 2000; Wall & Nolan, 1987).

The manner is which conflict is handled by both the group leader and group members will undoubtedly set the tone for how the group views and handles conflict. Fisher, Ury, and Patton (1997) suggest that group leaders educate group members on four steps of conflict resolution:

1. Separate the person from the issue or conflict being addressed.
2. Focus on interests or attributes of the conflict rather than on the group member's positions on the issue.
3. Generate a variety of possible options before deciding how to proceed.
4. Insist that the decision about how to proceed be based on an objective standard rather than on subjective feelings.

Practitioners must learn to instill in the group an acceptance of conflict as a natural part of relationships and help members learn to deal with conflict constructively. When this occurs, members not only gain a deeper respect for the leader but may also realize that working through conflict is actually more therapeutic and psychologically healthier than avoiding it. G. Corey (2004) sums up the importance of dealing with conflict:

> *The way conflict is recognized, accepted, and worked with has a critical effect on the progress of the group. If it is poorly handled, the group may retreat and never reach a productive stage of development. If it is dealt with openly and with concern, the members discover that their relationships are strong enough to withstand an honest level of challenge. (p. 98)*

During this transition stage, conflict with the group leader is also possible as members are feeling more trusting, safe, and courageous enough to challenge him or her. A leader must be able to distinguish between a challenge and an attack and to respond nondefensively and in an assertive manner. The ability to challenge the group leader positively is an important step for group members and can serve to empower them with a sense of autonomy. When members are able to speak up and be heard successfully this signifies that the group has reached a level where there is trust. This of course depends largely on how effective group leaders are able to deal with challenges to their authority and in managing their own anger. Leaders with many unresolved anger issues themselves will find it difficult to respond therapeutically. Also, leaders must consider the tendency to avoid conflict by caretaking and rescuing; such actions will not only stifle the group process but also get in the way of modeling healthy conflict resolution.

Confrontation is also common during the transition phase of group process. When skillfully used, confrontation can help members overcome resistance and motivate them to continue working. In the literature, confrontation is viewed as the ability to clarify, examine, and challenge behaviors to help group members overcome distortions and discrepancies among behaviors, thoughts, and feelings (Egan, 2002; Toseland & Spielberg, 1982).

Toseland and Rivas (2009) caution that since confrontations are often "potent and emotionally charged," group leaders must be prepared for strong reactions and be willing to explore underlying feelings before making "direct, full-scale confrontation" (p. 116). They further maintain that "although confrontations are often associated with pointing out member's flaws and weaknesses, they can be used to help members recognize strengths and assets." There is a difference between "caring confrontation" and "inappropriate confrontation." It is the leader's responsibility to teach clients about confrontation and appropriate ways of challenging comembers and leaders in constructive manners.

Confrontation should not be "tearing others down carelessly; hitting others with negative feedback and then retreating; being hostile with the aim at hurting others; telling others what is basically wrong with them; and, assaulting others' integrity." (M.S. Corey & G. Corey, 2006, p. 188). Rather, caring confrontation can be viewed "as a form of constructive feedback an invitation for participants to look at some aspect of their interpersonal style or their lives to determine if they want to make changes" (M.S. Corey & G. Corey, 2006, p. 188). Through caring confrontation, helpers are able to point out discrepancies in members' thoughts, feelings, and actions. Such confrontations must be well timed, presented in a genuinely caring manner, and be clear and specific (Alle-Corliss & Alle-Corliss, 1999, 2006).

Group leaders must continually assess confrontational styles within the group, strive to understand their underlying meaning, and attempt to ensure that only caring confrontation is used. When used appropriately, confrontation helps foster growth and promote change.

Problem Behaviors and Difficult Group Members

It is often during the transition phase that leaders and members become aware of the deeper problems of certain members. Certain problem behaviors are more apt to emerge at this time as well. According to the literature and from our own group leading experience, leaders are often challenged to deal with member silence and lack of participation, sexual feelings, monopolistic behavior, storytelling, questioning, advice giving, band-aiding, hostile behavior, dependency, acting superior, prejudice and narrow-mindedness, socializing, intellectualizing, and emotionalizing. Jacobs et al. (2006) have identified various types of group members;

these include the chronic talker, talkative member, dominator, distracter, rescuing member, negative member, resistant member, and member who tries to get to the leader. In Table 3.2 we provide suggestions for intervening with different types of problematic behaviors or clients.

Table 3.2 **Problematic Behaviors/Clients**

Type of Client	Suggested Intervention
Talkative clients	Be aware that clients may feel intimidated, angry, or anxious. Point out body language. Discuss your own reaction in a nonjudgmental way.
Overwhelmed clients	Resist becoming overwhelmed yourself. Explore with the client ways in which he or she becomes overwhelmed.
Involuntary clients	Be careful to not become apologetic or defensive.
	Place the responsibility on the client.
Silent or withdrawn clients	Be aware of the possible purposes of the silence: protection, lack of knowledge regarding the helping interaction, cultural issues, or intimidation.
"Yes-but" clients	Such clients are seldom satisfied, so you may find yourself working too hard. If so, place the responsibility back on the client. Point out the behavior. Clients who deny needing help—refrain from trying to convince such clients that they have problems.
Blaming clients	Place the responsibility and focus for change back on the client.
Overly dependent clients	Explore how you might possibly be fostering dependence. Encourage individuation and separation in a supportive way.
Moralistic clients	Help them recognize how their judgments of others affect their relationships and may distance them from others.
	Ask them to indulge their tendency to lecture. Have them make up very stern diatribe. This may reveal how they possibly have incorporated a critical parent.
Intellectualizing clients	Recognize that intellectualization is often a defense mechanism, developed out of a need to insulate people from their deeper feelings. Refrain from insisting that these clients dig deeply into their feelings. Rather, gradually encourage their expression of feelings.
Emotionalizing clients	These clients are similar to intellectualizing clients in that they may also be defending against deeper emotions and have become stuck in their pain.
Passive-aggressive clients	Explore the underlying dynamics. Be aware of how the client's behavior affects you. Share your reactions while avoiding making judgments about the behavior.

Source: Adapted from Alle-Corliss & Alle-Corliss, 2006; G. Corey, 2004; M. S. Corey & G. Corey, 2006; Corey, Schneider. Adapted from Corey, Callanan, & Russell, 2004; Donigan & Malnati, 2006; Jacobs et al., 2006; and Yalom (2005).

Transference and Countertransference

Transference and countertransference issues are likely to surface during the transition phase. Transference is considered an unconscious process "whereby clients project onto their therapist past feelings or attitudes they had toward significant people in their life" (M. Corey & G. Corey, 2003, p. 143). Common feelings evoked by transference range from love, lust, high praise, and regard to anger, ambivalence, hate, and dependence.

Transference *Transference* is common to some degree in every relationship, yet it is more likely when emotional intensity is so great that objectivity is lost and the client begins to relate to the therapist or group leader as a significant person in his or her life (Cormier & Cormier, 1998, p. 49). Transference can be positive, negative, or neutral. Furthermore, it may be easily recognizable or very subtle and difficult to pinpoint. In groups, recognizing transference becomes even more complex since there is an opportunity for multiple transferences to exist. "Members may project not only onto the leaders but also onto other members in the group" (M.S. Corey & G. Corey, 2006, p. 211). When transference is not handled properly, it can seriously interfere with the helping process. Group leaders must be astute in recognizing signs of transference and in deciding what and how much needs to be discussed directly with the client. Group leaders must continually assess if and what kind of transference exists and weigh the advantages and disadvantages of exploring it further. The decision to explore transference further will depend in large part on the type of group being conducted and its purpose. In less clinical, more psychoeducational groups, for instance, it may be enough for the leader to be aware of the transference. In more therapeutic types of groups, the transference issues may require in-depth discussion and working through. Either way, "paying attention to your client's feelings can give you key insights into how they interact with others in their social sphere" (Alle-Corliss & Alle-Corliss, 1999, p. 59).

Countertransference *Countertransference* is defined as feelings helpers have toward their clients. Viewed as any projection that could conceivably interfere with the helping process, countertransference must be recognized and addressed by the group leader. The possibility of experiencing countertransference is greater for group leaders, simply because a greater number of clients are present who are apt to trigger feelings in the leaders. When group leaders acknowledge the feelings evoked by the group members and make an effort to understand them, the risk of harm is greatly reduced. However, when group leaders ignore or do not recognize countertransference, more serious problems can ensue.

"Hurtful countertransference" as described by Cormier and Cormier (1998) can be dangerous to the therapeutic process if not dealt with early on. Such countertransference is more likely when group leaders are (1) blinded to an important area of exploration, (2) focus on issues that are more their own than their clients, (3) use clients for "vicarious or real gratification," (4) use "subtle cues" that lead the client, (5) make interventions not in the clients' best interest, and most important, (6) "adopt the roles the client wants [them] to play in his or her old script" (Alle-Corliss & Alle-Corliss, 1999, p. 60).

The group leader's unresolved conflicts and/or repressed needs can seriously interfere with the group process and create a situation where power may be abused (G. Corey, 2004). Because group members are sure to set off feelings in group leaders, especially where there are old or current wounds, it is crucial to be vigilant to triggers that may affect the client-worker relationship. Themes of separation, loss, dealing with anger or assertiveness, or denial of sexuality are common ones that tend to surface through work with our clients. According to Chiaferi and Griffin (1997): "Common reactions include a need for approval, identification with the client, sexual and/or romantic feelings toward a client, a tendency to refrain from confrontation, or a compelling need to rescue the client" (p. 50).

When these reactions "are intense, persistent, and compelling," they can become detrimental to members and group leaders alike. Group leaders must learn to recognize these themes and risk introspection; they need continual self-awareness. Many times, such awareness will be sufficient. Other times, group leaders may need to work through deeper issues and would benefit from seeking added supervision or even counseling themselves. An example might be when a leader is directly confronted within the group, as this situation can set off difficult emotions and reactions. Knowing how to react nondefensively is very important, as is the ability to engage in appropriate self-reflection.

Table 3.3 summarizes general guidelines for working with countertransference as described in the literature.

Since so much is apt to occur during the transition phase, new group leaders can feel overwhelmed and fearful. New leaders may be at a loss of how to handle problem behaviors, when to encourage members to take risks, how to set limits, or deal with their own

Table 3.3 **Guidelines for Working with Countertransference**

- Strive to accept your feelings as they may contain significant information about your clients or about yourself.
- Try not to judge or to disregard your own feelings.
- Be prepared to use your feelings and reactions appropriately to enhance the helping process. Be open to gaining insight by examining your countertransference feelings.
- Be willing to consult with professional colleagues or supervisors if your feelings are interfering in your work with your clients. A more objective viewpoint is often helpful and sometimes necessary to guide you in the right direction. At times the most appropriate action to take is to secure a referral.
- Be ready to engage in your own counseling or therapy if extreme countertransference reactions persist. Also seek therapy when a theme continues to surface with certain clients or issues.

Source: Adapted from Alle-Corliss & Alle-Corliss, (1999, p. 62).

countertransference. Being open to consultation at any time during group leading is necessary.

The transition phase is a challenging one that sets the stage for the working phase that follows. When all the different facets of this stage are recognized and properly handled, the group can proceed smoothly. When not, the group process may be affected, and in most severe cases, permanently stifled.

Working Phase

The title *working phase* reflects how pivotal this stage is in the overall scheme of group development. Considered "the core of the group process, "it is the period when members benefit most from being in group" (Jacobs et al., 2006, p. 30). Tentative feelings about being in a group have pretty much dissipated. The discomfort and anxiety characteristic of the transition phase have been expressed along with conflicts and resistance. At this point, members are ready to work through many of their issues, cohesion is usually stronger, and productivity within the group generally increases. Reid (1997) suggests that members are more willing to identify their goals and concerns and more open to assuming responsibility for making changes. Members tend to engage in more risk-taking and action-oriented behaviors and are more honest as they self-disclose. Members may express stronger emotions more freely as they feel more comfortable with the group process. "The members are also more likely than before to talk directly to one another rather than to the worker. And they appear more secure and therefore less concerned about the other members' and the worker's expectations" (Reid, 1997, p. 230). During this stage, more in-depth exploration of important issues is the norm because members are more ready to work.

Cohesion A sense of belonging, inclusion, and solidarity necessary for cohesion are typically present at this stage. The initial testing period is over, and group members seem to trust each other and the leader more. By this point, members have developed common history. Through the disclosure of their feelings, thoughts, and experiences, they have developed a better understanding and appreciation for one another that leads to greater cohesion.

Members may not always agree, conflict may still arise, and trust may be tested from time to time, yet there is no longer a threat to the group's very existence, as is typical in the beginning stages, when group cohesion was weak. A sense of family and working together to help one another indicates that the group has reached a place where deeper issues can be dealt with. "Cohesion provides the group with the impetus to move forward and is a prerequisite for the group's success. Without a sense of 'groupness,' the group remains fragmented, members become frozen behind their defenses, and their work is of necessity superficial" (G. Corey, 2004, p. 107). Yalom (2005) contends that cohesion allows for other therapeutic factors to exist and serves to foster action-oriented behaviors, which include immediacy, mutuality, confrontation, risk taking, and translating insight into action.

Common themes among members evolve during this phase, which lead to a sense of belonging within the group. For instance, members feel more understood, more lovable, more positive about having the capacity to change, more hopeful, and more willing to share and be close to others. Painful experiences of childhood and adolescence can be revealed, and members become more aware of the need for, and fear of, love. Repressed feelings are expressed, and members seem more focused on struggling to find meaning in life. Similarities and differences among members are noted and generally more accepted during this stage. Members often feel guilt over past mistakes and for inaction. Many during this stage are open about their longing for meaningful connections with others and their search for their own identity.

Cohesion alone is not sufficient, however, for the group to prosper. Sometimes groups may feel so comfortable and secure in their cohesive state that they resist challenging themselves further. When members are no longer challenged to move forward either by fellow group members or by the group leader, the group can reach a plateau. It is the leader's responsibility to continue to encourage members to note their commonalities and focus on a common bond that links them. To prevent cohesion from resulting in passivity or inertia, at this juncture leaders must encourage members to actually work on goals and challenges.

Movement toward Goal Attainment The existence of trust and acceptance, empathy and caring, hope, freedom to experiment, a commitment to change, and intimacy are common therapeutic factors that are critical during this stage. Catharsis, or the expression of pent-up feelings, and self-disclosure are more prevalent, and clients seem to benefit most from feedback since they feel more accepted and committed to the therapeutic process. Given the presence of these factors, clients are more ready to move toward goal attainment than in earlier stages.

Characteristics of an Effective Working Phase An effective working group is focused on goal identification and attainment (Corey et al., 2004). A here-and-now focus typically exists. Members themselves can readily identify goals and concerns. Members have learned to take responsibility for setting and reaching their goals and are clearer about expectations. They are more willing to practice outside the group to bring about behavioral changes that will lead to goal fulfillment. They complete homework assignments and are more willing to share with the group the difficulties they experience outside group. Most members have a feeling of inclusion, even if they are not as active as others in the group. During this stage, the group is encouraged by the leader to challenge members who appear distant to deal with issues that may be contributing to their withdrawal. Members recognize that they are responsible for their own growth; they must be active in assessing their level of satisfaction and making the necessary changes if they feel unsatisfied.

Leadership Responsibilities
A major responsibility for group leaders is to continually encourage active participation among group members. At times this is easy enough, as the group is a dynamic one that has taken charge. At other times, however, group participation may be limited. In such cases, the group leader must assess possible underlying reasons and challenge the group to become more involved in the group process.

The group leader has to be continually in tune with the group process and forever assessing both individual members and overall group dynamics. The leader often has to choose to which direction to move in. According to M. S. Corey and G. Corey, (2006), some of the choices that must be made during the working stage that help to shape the future of the group itself include: disclosure versus anonymity, honesty versus superficiality, spontaneity versus control, acceptance versus rejection, cohesion versus fragmentation, and responsibility versus blaming. We concur with their belief that "a group's identity is shaped by the way its members resolve these critical issues" (p. 237). Group leaders must be knowledgeable and open to exploring the best way of dealing with each of these issues.

Especially difficult is the emergence or reemergence of conflict or anger, which can plague a group if it is not handled properly. Leaders must openly acknowledge any conflict or anger that exists and make every effort to work it through. To do so, leaders must be open and willing to accept that working through conflict and anger can be productive.

Role Models Leaders, by the very nature of their role, are models to the clients they work with. They often set the tone for what will be discussed in the group and how feelings and conflicts will be handled. Through verbal and nonverbal channels, leaders communicate their values, their preferences, and what is acceptable and unacceptable to discuss.

Self-Disclosure The leader's type and extent of self-disclosure will also influence group dynamics. The term *self-disclosure,* in this context, refers to the personal revelations made by a leader to group members. Such revelations may be verbal or nonverbal in nature and may not be intentional. Cormier and Hackney (2005) identify four forms of self-disclosure: (1) disclosing the helper's own problems, (2) disclosing facts about the helper's role, (3) disclosing the helper's reactions to the client, and (4) disclosing the helper's reactions to the client-helper relationship. Danish, D'Aguielli, and Hauer (1980) have categorized self-disclosures into two major types: self-involving and personal self-disclosure.

Alle-Corliss and Alle-Corliss (1999) define self-disclosure as

> *self-involving statements that include messages that express the helper's personal reaction to the client during the helping process. . . . Personal self-disclosing messages are related to struggles or problems the helper is currently experiencing or has dealt with in the past that are similar to the clients' problems. (p. 45)*

"Self-involving statements" are lower risk whereas "personal self-disclosing messages" can be more problematic. Group leaders must be judicious in disclosures of a personal nature. Not only can excess disclosures serve to undermine the group's confidence in the leader, but they may also divert attention from the group process.

Guidelines for the leader to consider regarding the appropriate use of self-disclosure are:

1. Determine the purpose of the disclosure.
2. Consider if the disclosure is beneficial to the group.
3. Decide how much of the leader's private life will be shared in a group setting.
4. Accept responsibility to seek counseling if it becomes clear that there are issues that require further exploration.

Simply put, self-disclosure is appropriate when it is used to help the group. In situations when the leader's needs take precedence, self-disclosure may be more harmful than helpful.

Additional Leadership Functions Ultimately, the leader must be aware of and ready to explore common themes within the group that foster a sense of universality and allow members to work together in the pursuit of shared goals. The leader must remain attentive to the intensification and further development of group norms that impact the group and be continually open and willing to help members translate insight into action.

When goals are attained and the group has accomplished its goals, it may be ready for the final stage of group, the termination process.

Ending (Final) Stages of Group

The final, closing, or ending stage of group is devoted to bring definitive closure to the group. During this stage, members are encouraged to share what they have learned, note how they have changed, and consider how they plan to use what they have learned. Additionally, members prepare to say good-bye and deal with the group's end. Toseland and Rivas (2009) identify a variety of tasks that are associated with ending a group as a whole:

- Learning from members
- Maintaining and generalizing change efforts

- Reducing group attraction and promoting independent functioning of individual members
- Helping members deal with their feelings about ending
- Planning for the future
- Making referrals
- Evaluating the work of the group

There is no specific time when discussion about ending should take place; however, "as a general rule, the greater number of sessions and the more personal and sharing, the longer the closing stage will be" (Jacobs et al., 2006, p. 362). Far too often, group leaders who themselves are ambivalent regarding ending may avoid the topic until the final few sessions; not only is this professionally inappropriate, but it can create animosity toward the group leader and impede proper closure.

Review and Consolidation

Review Reviewing the group process is an essential part of the final phase. Members are invited to review the entire history of the group experience. They are encouraged to explore what they have learned during their time in the group, cite turning points, share likes and dislikes, and consider ways in which the group could have been more helpful. This review helps members begin the process of ending and also serves as a meaningful evaluative tool. Members are asked to be concrete and specific in their sharing and to feel free to express whatever comes to mind. The manner in which this review takes place varies from group to group and is determined in part by how the leader presents it.

> *This technique of recalling special moments may bring back to life incidents of conflict in the group, of closeness and warmth, or humor and lightness, of pain, or of tension and anxiety. The more members can verbalize their experiences the more they can recall what actually happened, the greater their chances of integrating and using the lessons they have learned. (Corey et al, 2004, p. 171)*

Brabender et al. (2004) contend that by reviewing their accomplishments, group members are able to prepare for the future: "Sometimes members may be helped by recalling a critical incident, an event in the group that was significant because it entailed successfully handling a stressor" (p. 155).

In our groups, we have found this review process to be most important in helping members to acknowledge their strengths, to develop a positive view of the therapeutic process, and to put cognitive meanings to their experience that they can take with them after the group has ended. Giving and receiving summary feedback during this stage is especially valuable if done so in a concise and concrete way. We developed a "personal poster" to encourage the provision of individual support and constructive feedback. Specifically, as a memento of the group, each member personalizes a card with his or her name. The card is then passed around the group during the last session. Each member and the group leader sign the card and offer positive feelings and hopes. The rationale for this exercise is that all group members are able to take with them some useful feedback or supportive comments. When the group ends then, each member has a written account of positive affirmation and wishes. This personal poster can serve as a reminder of the group process and reinforce individual strengths and potential.

Unfinished business is common in most groups. The ending phase can be an excellent opportunity to discuss the many unfinished issues that may exist. Sometimes this working through is the most memorable part of group for the member and perhaps even for the group. Because there is a natural tendency to disengage as the group approaches closure, the leader may have to challenge members to carefully explore any unfinished business that may exist.

Care should be taken to not wait until the very last session, however, as doing so could trigger a crisis for certain members who will need additional support. Corey et al. (2004) concur "that leaders must be cognizant of the timing of discussing new material and be ever so careful to not encourage discussion of deeper issues toward the end of a group."

Consolidation of Gains   In reviewing the group experience, members are challenged to consolidate their learning. This process is often a very important one for both group leader and members, since this is when members transfer what they have learned in the group to their outside world. To ensure that group members complete this task of consolidation of their learning, the group leader must prepare them for this work early on. From the onset, leaders must inform members that ending is an eventuality and provide as many specifics about the length of the group as are feasible. Also, members may need periodic reminders, especially as the termination phase approaches. Despite the difficulties inherent in ending, we believe members respond much better when well prepared.

During this ending phase, it is important for group members to examine the effects of the group on themselves. When group members have an opportunity to put into words what they learned from the entire group experience, they are able to begin the process of letting go. Leaders should encourage members to be as specific and open as possible in describing what they have learned; this will increase their ability to retain and use what has been gleaned. In order for permanent learning to take place, the leader must provide members with the structure to help them review and assimilate what they have learned.

Assisting clients to identify their growth and acknowledge the attainment of their goals is an exciting endeavor when the group has been a successful one. Group leaders often feel invigorated and professionally satisfied with this process and welcome the opportunity to help group members recognize their progress. However, when members have not accomplished much or when the group as a whole has not been effective, the task of consolidating gains becomes much more difficult. Since not every group will be a success, it is important to be prepared to deal with such instances. In such cases, we recommend encouraging members to explore what did not go well and why. Sometimes this process is a positive one that results in members feeling that something was gained. In reality, most groups have mixed success and difficulties.

Group leaders are not immune to reactions about ending. Fortune, Pearlingi, and Rochelle (1992) and Toseland and Rivas (2009) list some of the strong reactions group leaders often experience upon termination:

- Pride and accomplishment in the client's success
- Pride in their own therapeutic skill
- A renewed sense of therapeutic process
- Sadness, sense of loss, or ambivalence about no longer working with the client
- Doubt or disappointment about the client's progress or ability to function independently
- A reexperiencing of their own losses
- Relief, doubt, or guilt about their therapeutic effectiveness

Anticipatory Planning As we have seen, often during the termination phase, members are helped to consider ways in which they can incorporate their gains into their daily lives. It is important to be specific, clear, and realistic when helping clients with this process. Similarly, we advocate use of anticipatory planning with clients at this juncture. Anticipatory planning involves presenting members with realistic situations they may encounter in the future and encouraging them to apply what they have learned in their therapy. Because this process helps solidify their growth and learning, it is an excellent technique to use during closure. In essence, in this final stage of termination, "leaders help members make the transition from the group to their other social environments" (Donigan & Malanti, 2006, p. 43).

Termination Issues

Review and consolidation of learning is often overwhelming as members are aware that termination is eminent and may be reluctant to end. Some members will avoid bringing up new issues or tying up any loose ends as they feel discouraged that the group is ending. When members realize that the group is coming to an end, it is not uncommon for them to begin distancing themselves from the group experience. There is a tendency to avoid examining what they learned and how it can affect their out-of-group behavior. Members should be encouraged to deal directly with their feelings of loss, if possible, as this can be both an enriching and a learning experience for individual group members and the group as a whole. Some members may already be mourning the loss of the group and are therefore not invested in the group process during this time. To prevent premature separation, leaders must alert members to this possibility and encourage them to share their feelings of loss openly. Since grief and sadness are common, a supportive climate is essential to allow members to experience these emotions freely.

As the final phase nears, some members disengage in order to avoid deeper feelings. It is important to learn to deal with loss and ending relationships, as this is an important life task.

The leader is challenged to deal gently with underlying feelings of loss. There may be times when the group's ending will spur feelings related to other losses that must be acknowledged and dealt with. When issues tied to loss and abandonment are triggered, the leader can take the opportunity to help members work through those feelings in a therapeutic manner.

Some members will have no difficulty ending. They feel little or no attachment to the group and simply consider termination as an indication that the group has accomplished its goals. In groups where there has been conflict that has not been managed properly, members may feel relieved that the group is coming to an end. Conversely, members in groups where a strong level of cohesion and conflict resolution has existed may find ending very difficult. In either of these instances, the emphasis must remain on the feelings evoked by the pending end of the group. The exploration of feelings engendered, no matter how painful, will help bring proper closure to the group.

This final stage in the life of the group is often an awkward one that is met with apprehension by both group members and the leader alike. "This apprehension will elicit all types of personal ways of dealing with endings, loss, separation, and aloneness. The overall climate of the group will range from sadness to euphoria" (Donigan & Malnati, 2006, p. 77). Since feelings and reactions will vary, it is the group leader's responsibility to make sure closure is dealt with in a therapeutic manner. When group leaders have not adequately dealt with their own existential issues concerning endings, this stage may prove to be more difficult than expected. As a result, some leaders may end prematurely to avoid their feelings, while others may delay ending the group indefinitely. Ending is apt to be particularly painful for a group that has been very emotionally close, cohesive, and worked hard to achieve their individual goals.

Coleadership Issues and Ending Leaders need to be in agreement on termination and in tune as to how and when to approach the issue of ending. Coleaders must also be prepared to support one another in not allowing members to continue bringing up new issues for group discussion that may thwart movement toward termination. To ensure that group leaders are working together at this point, they must meet to discuss such issues as:

- Their own feelings about separation and ending
- Concerns about individual group members
- The need to share perceptions about the group prior to the last session
- Plans on how to help individual members and the group as whole review their growth and be able to translate this learning in their everyday lives
- Ideas for how to assist group members with the consolidation process

Overall Evaluation of Group Experience
Termination, no matter how difficult, affords both the members and the leader the opportunity to evaluate how successful the therapeutic process was. Although evaluation begins at the start of treatment,

and should be continuous throughout the process, often a complete examination of the process cannot take place until the end. Much like a review, this summative evaluation involves determining the outcomes of the therapeutic process, assesses client satisfaction, and checks for success. In order for a successful summative evaluation to occur, the original goals that were set must be examined and efforts made to explore goals that were met as well as those not attained. This process is a gratifying one when treatment has gone well; client strengths can be validated, their courage to participate in the group commended, and their ongoing commitment to change reinforced.

Further examination of unanticipated outcomes is also essential in determining what was effective and what was not. This process is especially important when outcomes were undesirable. Many clients who felt dissatisfied with the process likely discontinued treatment early on, felt insecure about their abilities, or questioned the value of helping. When this occurs, members are more likely to avoid seeking help in the future.

> *Disappointment and unsuccessful outcomes can be caused by incomplete assessment, unclear or unrealistic goals, unrealistic expectations about the helping process, and mismatch between helper and client. Also, the client may not have been completely ready or able to engage in the helping process. (Alle-Corliss & Alle-Corliss, 2006, p.120)*

Clearly, this evaluation process may not be pleasant or easy for either client or helper, yet it can lead to a renewed positive view of the therapeutic process. Also, the feedback gained through this evaluation can provide the helper with useful information as to which skills or interventions were most effective and which require closer scrutiny. A nondefensive attitude on behalf of the leader and a willingness to look objectively at him- or herself is critical during this evaluation process. Upon ending, it is recommended that leaders meet to discuss their own experiences with one another and with the group process.

Coleadership Evaluations Ending also provides leaders with a chance to receive feedback from one another and consolidate their own learning. Reviewing the similarities and differences in how they perceived the group is important during this stage. The "Best Practice Guidelines" (ASGW, 1998) supports leaders in processing the workings of the group with themselves, group members, supervisors, and other colleagues. Taking time to prepare a summary of the group's work is helpful for each group leader to identify feelings and perceptions and can also be useful in providing feedback to one another.

Follow-up Follow-up sessions after the completion of the formal group treatment program are not mandatory, although they are an excellent way to encourage that group members sustain treatment goals and apply them to individual life situations. Ideally, such

> *follow-up sessions reinforce members commitment to maintaining changes. They remind members of the changes in their lives since they began treatment. Members can share similar experiences about their difficulties in maintaining changes and trying to generalize changes to new situations and new life experiences. (Toseland & Rivas, 2009, p. 389)*

Gladding (2004) states that "follow-up is used in a group to keep in touch with members after the group has terminated to determine how well they are progressing on personal and group goals." (p. 262). Further, ASGW's "Best Practice Guidelines" (1998) stipulate that group workers provide for follow-up after the termination of a group as appropriate to assess outcomes or when requested by group member(s).

Follow-up can be helpful to both the group members and group leader(s) in assessing what they have gained from the group experience and in determining if additional referrals are necessary. In sum, follow-up sessions serve to maximize the effects of a group experience and encourage members to keep pursuing the original individual and group goals set while they were in group (Jacobs, Harvill, & Masson, 2002). Furthermore, it has been found that when members are aware during the termination stage of their group that a follow-up session is planned, they are more likely to continue pursing their goals (G. Corey, 2001; Gladding, 2004).

An example of how effective follow-up can be is noted in the success of a 12-week women's support group for incest survivors:

- Building follow-up procedures allowed a basis for understanding the long-term value of the group experience and the opportunity to improve the design for future groups.
- Several follow-up meetings were scheduled to help members make the transition from weekly group meetings to being on their own and relying on newly developed support networks.
- An additional purpose for this follow-up was to reinforce what was learned and to provide renewed support.

- Postevaluation questions were given along with a rating measure. Members were asked to rate themselves as "better," "worse," or "the same" in regard to these areas:
  - Work
  - Friendships
  - Relationships with family members
  - Intimate relationships
  - Feelings about sex
  - Feelings about oneself
  - The ability to protect and take care of themselves

- Based on the many follow-up groups conducted, it became clear that a well-developed group format with proper screening can result in a therapeutic group experience. Such a group was found to greatly enhance the treatment of incest survivors as it allowed clients to be seen on a regular basis and provided them with the continuity and support necessary for healing.

- As evidenced in the follow-up groups, many members developed a strong support network that provided them with the strength and courage to begin to resolve past incest, overcome old, negative patterns, and set healthy, challenging goals for the future. The greatest message members shared they received was that "they deserve to feel good about themselves and to lead more productive lives."

In Closing

This chapter focused on understanding group development. Pregroup, beginning, middle/working, and final stages of group were outlined. Important topics such as group structure, composition, cohesion, trust, individual and group goal setting, anxiety and defensiveness, conflict, control and confrontation, problem behaviors and difficult group members, transference and countertransference, and leadership responsibilities were presented as they relate to the different stages of group. Chapter 4 discusses the theory and practice of group work.

Theory and Practice of Group Work

4

This chapter begins by exploring the various theoretical perspectives that guide group practice and determine which treatment modalities are best to use with certain populations. Theories from analytic, experiential and relationship oriented, action, and systems perspectives are explored, including psychodynamic and Adlerian, person-centered and Gestalt, cognitive-behavioral and developmental/lifespan. Crisis theory also is discussed, given current emphasis on crisis intervention and brief treatment. After essential concepts and common strategies of each theory are presented, group applicability is discussed, followed by a brief group illustration. The chapter ends with a discussion of the integrative approach.

Theoretical Orientation and Perspectives

Successful treatment cannot exist without understanding the connection between theory and practice. Theory lies at the foundation of any treatment, whether working individually with clients; providing conjoint, marital, or family therapy; or engaging in group work. In fact, most theories underlying group work today were initially developed for individual counseling and have been adapted for use with groups. Developing a theoretical orientation affords the group leader a general framework from which to understand group dynamics and to develop specified treatment strategies. Jacobs, Masson, and Harvill (2006) highlight this premise:

> Those who do not have a good working knowledge of at least one theoretical perspective often lead a very shallow group; this is, the group never goes below surface interaction and sharing. If the

members do not become more involved, the leader who does not have a theoretical base is usually overwhelmed. (p. 20)

M.S. Corey and G. Corey (2006) use an analogy to emphasize the importance of theory in practice:

Leading groups without having an explicit theoretical rationale is like flying a plane without a flight plan—although you may eventually get there, you're equally likely to run out of gas. If you operate in a theoretical vacuum and are unable to draw on theory to support your interventions, your groups may not reach a productive stage. (p. 8)

A theoretical base is essential in determining which approach(s) will be used; "otherwise, everyone would be 'just doing their own thing' and there would be no rhyme or reason to client interventions" (Neukrug, 1994, p. 57). Although most group leaders have a preference for one or several theoretical perspectives, we believe a general understanding of the major contemporary theories is necessary to determine which concepts and techniques fit best with the leader's personality, values, and leadership style. Learning about the different theories can assist leaders in developing their own individual leadership style. Gladding (2004) agrees that being aware of "multiple theoretical models provides richness and diversity for conducting groups" (p. 333).

We encourage group leaders to remain open to exploring the many facets of helping that are rooted in theory. Whether it is through learning about new theories or refreshing our current knowledge base, we are better able to help clients in new, innovative ways.

Considerations for Group Practice: Building a Foundation

Before elaborating on any specific theory, it is important to understand concepts from general systems theory and the biopsychosocial approach that are central to our work with clients and to set a foundation from which to work.

Systems Theory

A main theoretical base in which most group practice is grounded is systems theory, which basically attempts to explain the group as a system of elements that are interacting. According to general systems theory, there are interrelationships between systems and their subsystems, and a change in one part of the system will affect the entire system. Basically, "the focus in general systems theory is on how the interaction of parts influences the operation of the system as a whole" (Gladding, 2004, p. 224). This systems approach is useful in understanding both family systems and small groups. Specific to group, systems theory provides a way for group leaders to conceptualize how the group functions as a system and how change in one part of the group will affect every other part.

The concept of circular causality explains how intervention with one member will impact every other member of the group as well as the group as a whole. Donigan and Malnati (2006) believe that

> group therapists who think systemically believe that is shortsighted to perceive member A's issue in isolation of other group members' issues, the leader, and the whole group. . . . Systemically thinking leaders do not observe events that occur within the group in isolation, but rather in terms of their interdependence and the subsequent patterned responses these events evoke in each of the subsystems over time. (p. 3)

Viewing groups with this general systems philosophy in mind is helpful in both treatment planning and actual group interventions. "System groupings facilitate relationship building, problem identification, assessment, intervention, and termination and provide a schematic framework to conceptualize interaction in the helping process" (Lum, 2004, p. 89). Furthermore, leaders who use systems theory place less emphasis on psychopathology and more emphasis on the influence of interaction between clients and the various other systems in the environment.

Biopsychosocial Approach

Those who advocate using the biopsychosocial approach highlight the importance of understanding clients through an ecological approach that considers all systems within the social environment. George Engel (1977), a psychiatrist, first proposed the biopsychosocial model. He criticized medicine's dominant biomedical model, writing that "it leaves no room within its framework for the social, psychological, and behavioral dimensions of illness. Alle-Corliss and Alle-Corliss (2006) write that the biopsychosocial approach

> emphasizes transactions between people and their physical and social environments. . . . An ecological model gives attention to both internal and external factors. . . . Three major areas (biological, psychological, and societal) are assessed; when they are viewed together, a complete picture emerges. (pp. 104–105)

Lum (2004) goes on to share that ecological theory "focuses on the reciprocal relationship of person and environment. The emphasis is on the consequences of exchanges between the two entities and the changes or modifications that are made as a result" (p. 90).

According to Brooks-Harris (2008, p. 233), "the biopsychosocial model has been pivotal in the development of Health Psychology, has been embraced by social workers who work in healthcare settings and has redefined the way psychiatrists think about diagnosis." The biopsychosocial model has also influenced preventive medicine by encouraging individuals to take better care of their physical and emotional health and reduce stress within their social environment.

Use of this model within group work is also important. By applying this approach, group leaders are challenged to assess each group member individually in these three spheres as well as consider their role within the group setting. The biopsychosocial approach "focuses on the study, diagnosis (assessment), and treatment of individuals in transaction with their social environments" (Goldstein, 1995, p. 1948). A perfect example is leading an incest survivors' group where past sexual abuse and molestation has impacted every client in the group; some members may be traumatized and depressed; others may be angry and acting out; still others may isolate themselves and are determined to never trust again. Each of these reactions to the past impact the present, both internally (biologically and psychologically) and externally (socially). These reactions are the very crux of what is to be dealt with in group therapy. A sound group leader will be in tune to each member's specific issues tied to members' past and to their involvement in the group process. Leaders who ignore the past might miss important clues to a client's current functioning. Likewise, clients' pasts are likely to affect how they interact within the group and with their social environment; thus they must be continually assessed.

Common Theoretical Perspectives

There is an abundance of theoretical perspectives from which to choose. We concentrate here on those theories that are most useful to group practice. For ease in presentation, we have categorized the theories in this way:

- Analytic: Psychodynamic and Adlerian therapies
- Experiential and relationship oriented: Person-centered and Gestalt therapies

- Action: Cognitive-behavioral therapies
- Systems: Developmental/lifespan therapy
- Others: Crisis theory and crisis intervention

Analytic Approaches

Psychodynamic Therapeutic Approach

The psychodynamic therapeutic approach is rooted in Freudian psycho-analytic theory, which can be dated to the 1800s, when Sigmund Freud discovered psychological origins for physical problems through his practice of hypnosis. Before this time, physical symptoms were thought to be principally organic in origin. Freud, the "originator of psycho-analysis" is credited with contributing his views as one of the most complete theories of human development to date. Besides introducing a uniquely different view of human nature, Freud's often-controversial methods have greatly influenced contemporary practice. Many theorists have borrowed Freud's concepts as a basis for their own theoretical views and approaches. In fact, many new theories and advances about human nature developed directly from psychoanalytic theory. Psychosocial theory is rooted primarily in a traditional psychoanalytic base, while the humanistic perspective is in direct opposition to psychoanalysis.

Essential Concepts
Freud emphasized the importance of understanding the dynamics of behavior, the functioning of the ego defenses, the workings of the unconscious, psychosexual stages of development, and the ways in which the past impacts the present (Brooks-Harris, 2008; G. Corey, 2004; Day, 2008; Sharf, 2008). Psychoanalysis practiced traditionally, although revered by many theorists and practitioners alike, is both costly and long term and therefore not as conducive to work with many clients in today's climate. However, the psychodynamic approach that devel-oped from psychoanalytic theory can be more readily incorporated into short-term treatment.

Three beliefs are central to the psychodynamic approach:

1. Drives motivate human behavior.
2. These drives are at least somewhat unconscious.
3. Most important, "our perceptions of our childhood and the actual events that occurred in our early years, together with our drives,

greatly affect our development and who we become as adults" (Alle-Corliss & Alle-Corliss, 1999, p. 92).

Sharf (2008) adds that the term *psychodynamic* "generally refers to the idea that feelings, unconscious motives, or drives unconsciously influence people's behavior and that defense mechanisms are used to reduce tension" (p. 61).

According to Neukrug (2002), the "purpose of psychodynamic therapy is to help the individual understand his or her early childhood experiences and how those experiences, in combination with the individual's drives, motivates the person today" (p. 38). Brooks-Harris (2008) concurs, saying:

> The way people perceive interpersonal relationships can be distorted by painful experiences in the past. The purpose of psychodynamic psychotherapy is to help clients work through past events in order to decrease interpersonal distortions more accurately so they can adapt to interpersonal relationships. (p. 279)

Examining relationship patterns that may be influencing how a person interacts with others is also inherent to a psychodynamic approach. In fact, when a client's primary concerns appear to be related to repetitive relationship patterns, a psychodynamic perspective can be used to direct treatment. Many contemporary psychodynamic treatments focus on identifying interpersonal patterns revealed in both past and present relationships as well as the client's relationship to the psychotherapist (Brook-Harris, 2008; Loborsky, 1984; Strupp & Binder, 1984).

Common Strategies

In our practice, we have found that clients, whether in individual or group therapy, benefit greatly when they are helped to connect current concerns to past issues. Further growth occurs when clients are able to understand how their current interactions with significant others are related to their past. Brooks-Harris (2008) encourages therapists to listen closely "to the way clients describe their interactions with significant others and to watch for common themes" (p. 279). Loborsky (1984) introduced a specific method called the core conflictual relationship theme (CCRT) to describe recurrent interpersonal patterns. In order to use this CCRT method, the therapist must pay close attention to the description of several different *relationship episodes* and identify three different components:

1. *A client's wish*. The goal or wish represents what clients are trying to achieve interpersonally. What do you want from another person in a particular interaction?

2. *A response from another person*. What is the actual or anticipated response from the other person in the context of the client's wish?

3. *A response to self*. Based on the response of the other, what is the subsequent response (affectively and behaviorally) of the self?

A psychodynamic view contends that individuals tend to act out old patterns in new relationships. Involvement in group therapy allows both group leaders and members to witness these repetitive relationship patterns as displayed and discussed within the group. When these patterns are closely examined, group leaders are able to identify interpersonal themes of each member that may merit further exploration and intervention. Further, by learning more about the client's past, group leaders can be more proactive in planning treatment interventions.

Brooks-Harris (2008) identifies 16 key psychodynamic strategies that were drawn from both psychodynamic (Loborsky, 1984; Strupp & Binder, 1984) and interpersonal (Teyber, 2000; Weissman, Markowitz, & Klerman, 2000) approaches to psychotherapy. Table 4.1 presents these strategies organized into four different categories: "Focus on Past," "Unconscious Thoughts and Feelings," "Current Relationships," and "Therapeutic Relationships between Helper and Client."

Erik Erikson (1963), who built on some of Freud's ideas, expanded his own theory by highlighting the fact that the psychosocial aspects of development beyond early childhood are important contributors to the psychodynamic perspective. Originally aligned with Freud, Erikson eventually developed his own model of human development. Because Erikson's psychosocial theory is also a developmental one, we discuss it in further detail in the section titled "Developmental/Lifespan Therapy."

Group Applications

Although presented for use in individual psychodynamic treatment, the strategies and considerations just outlined can be as effective when used in group therapy. This, of course, requires a group leader who is well versed in psychodynamic theory and comfortable with potentially intense work. Even though many psychodynamic techniques have limited usefulness for the group counselor, some analytic concepts are helpful in understanding the dynamics operating both in individual group members and in the group as a whole.

Table 4.1   **Psychodynamic-Interpersonal Strategies for Psychotherapy**

Focus on Past

- Honoring resistance
- Exploring childhood experiences
- Working through past conflicts
- Identifying attachment styles

Unconscious Thoughts and Feelings

- Listening to narratives
- Encourages free association
- Interpreting dreams

Current Relationships

- Identifying relationship themes
- Making interpersonal interpretations
- Modifying relational interactions
- Adapting to interpersonal losses or disputes
- Encouraging new relationships

Therapeutic Relationship between Helper and Client

- Observing the therapeutic relationship
- Attending to subjective responses
- Resolving conflicts in the therapeutic relationship
- Learning from termination

Source: Adapted from Brooks-Harris (2008, p. 284), Loborsky, 1984; Strupp & Binder, 1984; Teyber, 2000; Weissman, Markowitz, & Klerman, 2000.

As we have noted, the psychodynamic approach centers on exploring the past in order to fully understand present behavior. Groups can be an ideal place to engage in this exploration. Because many of the issues and unresolved conflicts brought to a group are rooted in early childhood experiences, overlooking the influence of the past can limit the group experience; groups may function at a superficial level. However, helping group members to understand the influence of their past offers them more control over their current behavior.

Psychodynamic group therapists may also attend to unconscious determinants of behavior that are based on past experiences. Rutan and Stone (2001), Sharf (2008), Wolf (1975), and Wolf and Kutash (1986) suggest that many psychodynamic conceptual approaches to group therapy have taken a drive-ego psychology approach whereby group therapists attend to "repressed sexual and aggressive drives as they affect the individual's psychological processes in group behavior" (Sharf, 2008, p. 67).

Group leaders need to recognize the use of ego defense mechanisms within the group that often surface as a means to cope with anxiety. Leaders should respect these defense mechanisms and recognize how they develop and are manifested in group interactions. G. Corey (2004) finds that "dealing with the defenses against anxiety provides a useful framework for intense group work. Members have the opportunity to challenge some of their defensive strategies, and in the process of learning how to communicate in non-defensive ways they can also learn new ways of responding" (p. 171).

Resistance is another important psychodynamic concept that is manifested in group therapy. Often the resistance exhibited suggests underlying fears about exploring the past or participating in the group itself. Wolf and Kutash (1986) have described various types of resistance that group leaders are apt to encounter: being "in love with" or attaching first to the therapist and then to another group member; taking on the role of the parent by attempting to dominate or lead the group; observing versus participating; and analyzing others to avoid introspection. Sharf (2008) notes that "all of these examples divert attention away from the patient's awareness of his own mental processes and the issues he struggles with" (p. 68). The group therapist needs to be aware of when and how resistance manifests itself and know about how to intervene within the group.

Since transference and countertransference are central to psycho-dynamic theory, it is important for the group leader to recognize and understand their presence within the group. A seasoned group leader can deal with projections effectively by exploring certain feelings within the group. More often than not, projections onto the leader or other members provide valuable clues about unresolved conflicts within a group member's own life that can be successfully worked through in the group.

Last, since the group can become a re-creation of an individual member's family of origin, it is important to understand early life situations and the feelings expressed during group that are connected to the past (G. Corey, 2004; Rutan, 2003; Rutan & Stone, 2001; Sharf, 2008). For instance, many members are apt to find symbolic mothers, fathers, siblings, and significant others in their group that provide perfect material to explore further.

Group Illustration: An 'adults molested as children' group is a prime example of a psychodynamic group, in that past childhood traumas are explored and connected to present-day functioning. Members are encouraged to work through their feelings about the past in an effort to move on and be able live more productive lives in the present. The goal is to move from being a victim to a survivor and even a thriver.

Adlerian Psychology

Adlerian psychology, also known as individual psychology, was founded by Alfred Adler around 1912. Adlerian counseling is a cognitive, goal-oriented, social psychology that is interested in an individual's beliefs and perceptions as well as the effect that an individual's behavior has on others (Milliren, Evans, & Newbauer, 2003). Adler was also aligned with the psychodynamic approach and is considered by some to be a neo-Freudian. Like Freud, Adler believed that an individual's perceptions of the past and interpretation of early events have an impact on their current functioning. "Their similarity is mainly in their belief that the personalities of individuals are formed in their early years, before the age of 6" (Sharf, 2008, p. 112). Adler, however, departed from Freudian view as he contended that "neurosis was the result of a person's retreat from the required tasks in life with the symptoms serving an ego-protective or safeguarding function to protect the individual from perceived failure in a life task" (G. Corey, 2004, p. 177). Adler thought it was the individual's interpretation of early events that mattered most, not what actually happened. He emphasized encouraging each individual to reach his or her highest potential by striving for perfection.

Essential Concepts
This concept of striving for perfection is a major one in Adlerian therapy. Adler's focus on the psychology of growth differed significantly from Freud's emphasis on abnormal personality and pathology. Adler believed that individuals are primarily motivated by social relatedness rather than by sexual urges. He considered behavior to be purposeful and goal-directed and strongly felt that individuals have choice and responsibility to strive for success, completion, and perfection.

According to Capuzzi and Gross (2003): "Individual Psychology promotes social equality, which means granting each other mutual respect and dignity regardless of our inherent differences. It is not a set of techniques, but rather a comprehensive philosophy of living" (p. 91). Adler stresses that people are better understood when viewed as individuals with their individual history that fashions their personality in a unique way.

Ferguson (1984) highlights the three most fundamental principles of Adlerian theory: (1) behavior is goal oriented; (2) humans are fundamentally social, with a desire to belong and have a place of value as an equal human being; and (3) the individual is indivisible and functions with unity of personality. Milliren et al. (2003) note that these aspects of individual psychology are unique from other approaches. "The principles of *'purposiveness, social interest, and holism'* describe the person as moving in unity toward self-chosen goals that reflect a human value for belonging and social contribution" (Capuzzi & Gross, 2003, p. 91). According to Gladding (2004), "Adlerian theory focuses on social interests as well as the purposefulness behavior and the importance of developing a healthy style of life" (p. 195).

Adler believed that humans naturally strive toward growth and expansion, live by goals and purpose, and anticipate the future. His view of human nature centered on his philosophy that individuals are primarily motivated by *social interest*. Simply stated, social interest is the ability to cooperate and contribute to the welfare of others (Milliren & Clemmer, 2006). Mosak (2000) explains this social interest view as having two components:

1. A feeling of being connected to society as a part of the social whole that requires an active interest and empathy with others.
2. Possessing a need and willingness to contribute to the general social good.

Gladding (2004) adds that "those with social interest take responsibility for themselves and others and are cooperative and positive in regard to their mental health" (p. 196). Adler used the concept of social interest as a means of measuring psychological health: "If a person has little social interest, then that person is self-centered, tends to put down others, and lacks constructive goals" (Sharf, 2008, p. 117). Adler was especially interested in helping the criminal and antisocial populations that demonstrated a problematic development of social interest (Ansbacher, 1977).

Holism is also central to the Adlerian philosophy in that Adler emphasized striving to understand the whole person. Day (2004) writes about Adler's holistic and existentialist core: "His theory is a holistic one, a theory that takes each person as unified rather than as a collection of symptoms or a battlefield where psychic structures struggle with each other" (p. 118). G. Corey (2009) adds that individuals are seen as an "integral part of a social system" and that the focus of treatment is more on "interpersonal factors than on intrapersonal ones" (p. 179).

Adler believed that both the future (technological) goals and the past influence an individual. He placed less emphasis on genetics than Freud did and instead proposed that the main influence on each individual's *style of life* was the social world as a child, with the family playing a significant role in personality development. *Family atmosphere* is defined as "the climate of relationships among family members" whereas *family constellation* is "the social configuration of the family group, the system of relationships in which self-awareness develops" (G. Corey, 2004, p. 183). Day (2004) adds that the "psychological make-up of the family as a whole affects the style of life established by each child" (p. 121). Adler maintained that this *style of life* or *lifestyle* is "created early in childhood within a social context . . . [and] serves as a blueprint for coping with tasks and challenges of life" (Frew & Speigler, 2008, p. 109). In essence, then, the role of family is very important to those who adhere to Adler's theory. Observing how individuals approach five major interrelated tasks—self-development, spiritual development, occupation, society, and love—also has a bearing on the lifestyle they will pursue (Ansbacher & Ansbacher, 1956; Mosak & Maniacci, 1999; Sharf, 2008). Sharf (2008) offers the example of the lifestyle of a child who is bullied and later becomes an insurance salesperson "persuading and convincing others, yet providing a service that helps others in a catastrophe".

Family Environment: Adler placed considerable emphasis on *birth order analysis*, "a typological system that assigns personality characteristics according to chronological place in the family" (Day, 2004, p. 121). Mosak (2005) notes that birth order often has a major impact on how a child relates to society and the development of his or her style of life. Basically, those who share ordinal birth positions, such as firstborns, are thought to have more in common with one another than siblings from the same family. Much has been written about birth order. Five ordinal or psychological positions that are typically described include: firstborns, secondborns, middle children, youngest children, and the only child (Adler, 1964; Capuzzi & Gross, 2003; G. Corey, 2004; Day, 2008; Dreikurs, 1967; Gladding, 2004; Sweeney, 1998). Although the specific birth order is important, it is the perceived role in the family that is the most critical. G. Corey (2009) stresses that "birth order is not a deterministic concept but does increase an individual's probability of having a certain set of experiences. Actual birth order is less important than the individual's interpretation of his or her place in the family" (p. 103).

Common Strategies

Central to successful treatment is the role of emotions, which Adlerians view as an element of motivation. "Without emotions, no strong acts are possible" (Dreikurs, 1967b, p. 213). Emotions are viewed as the fuel necessary to propel one to achieve their goals:

> *Emotions help one ''move out'' of a situation in a way that is consistent with the life style and one's immediate goals. . . . Emotions are not something that control the individual, rather, the individual learns to use emotions to pursue goals. (Capuzzi & Gross, 2003, pp. 109–111)*

Counselors are continually making assessments "by gathering information of the family constellation and client's earliest memories. . . . The client is encouraged to examine and change a family lifestyle by developing social interest" (Gladding, 2004, p. 197). The goals of Adlerian counseling center around assisting clients to develop healthy, holistic lifestyles. Counselor and client build interpretations together, and insight is viewed as crucial to behavioral change.

Robert Dreikurs is credited as being "the most significant figure in bringing Adlerian psychology to the United States" after Adler's death (G. Corey, 2009, p. 98). Dreikurs identified three phases of the therapeutic process: *understanding* the client, *explaining* the client's behavior to him or her in a way that makes sense, and *strengthening social interest*, the working-through part of counseling or therapy. *Building the relationship* was eventually added as the initial step in treatment, given the belief that developing mutual trust, respect, and rapport is essential to the therapeutic process (Ansbacher & Ansbacher, 1956; Capuzzi & Gross, 2003; Dreikurs, 1967; Milliren, Evans, & Newbauer 2003). Today, these four main phases of Adlerian therapy include:

1. Establish the proper therapeutic relationship.
2. Explore the psychological dynamics operating in the client (an assessment).
3. Encourage the development of self understanding (insight into purpose).
4. Help the client make new choices (reorientation and reeducation).

Day (2008) has divided customary techniques used by Adlerian therapists into three categories: reframing, behavior experiments, and resource development. Table 4.2 describes each of these techniques.

Table 4.2   Adlerian Techniques

Reframing: Involves altering habitual ways of thinking by substituting these new, more positive ways.

The Question: If you could magically eliminate your symptom immediately and completely, what would be different in your life?

The Push-Button: Imagine pushing a button and then picturing a pleasant experience from the past by remembering details while noting the positive feelings it elicited. The same technique is used to imagine unpleasant events and the negative feelings that are experienced. Repetition of this technique is used while having clients switch back and forth from pleasant to unpleasant memories in an effort to have them realize they have inner control over how they feel.

Role Playing: Acting out a distressing event by taking on the character of different persons so as to encourage clients to reframe the situation from a different perspective.

Brainstorming: Once basic mistakes in thinking are identified, clients are encouraged to brainstorm alternative thoughts that can be substituted. Implications of this change are then discussed.

Humor: Clients are encouraged to see the lighter side of life. Therapists model using laughter and a sense of humor where appropriate.

Behavior: Experiments Active experiments used outside the counseling session are encouraged.

Acting: "As If" Clients are encouraged to behave as if they are psychologically better.

Task Setting: Homework tasks are often given to clients to help them work on their issues and become more involved in social interest type activities.

Catching Oneself: Clients are encouraged to *catch* their use of habitual ways of thinking and acting by becoming aware of when habitual ways of thinking and acting tend to surface and short-circuiting them.

Countersuggestions: A form of paradoxical intention in which clients are asked to increase or intensify a pattern they wish to eliminate.

Compensation: Clients are asked to inventory their strengths and together with the therapist explore ways to make use of these.

Dreams: Clients are encouraged to use dreams to solve problems they are experiencing.

Confrontation: A means for therapists to challenge clients to consider their own private logic and realize they do have power to change their behavior.

Spitting in the client's soup: Spitting in the client's soup is when the therapist points out certain behaviors to clients and thus ruins the payoff of their behavior

Source: Adapted from Capuzzi & Gross (2003); G. Corey (2004, 2009); S. X. Day (2004); S. T. Gladding (2004); and J. Frew & M. D. Speigler (2008).

Group Applications

Group therapy is ideal for Adlerians, who consider problems individuals face to be mostly of a social nature. Groups provide a perfect social milieu that fosters a sense of belonging and sense of community in group members. By participating in a group, individual clients are able to see that many of their problems are interpersonal in nature and that their behavior has social meaning.

As with individual counseling, Adlerian group therapists "promote an egalitarian, person-to-person relationship which is basic to

Adlerian approach to groups" (G. Corey, 2004, p. 185). Also, group leaders serve as a role model; hence their actions in the group are critical. Important group leader characteristics as described by Sonstegard (1998b, p. 184) include: presence, acceptance, caring, attentive listening, confidence, healthy risk taking, role modeling, belief in group treatment, self-confidence, sense of humor, and collaboration. Ideally, group therapists need to have a clear sense of their own identity, beliefs, and feelings as well as awareness of the basic conditions essential for the growth.

According to Sonstegard and Bitter (2001), Adlerian group leaders must be adept at: promoting involvement and interaction among members, providing structure, assisting with goal identification, conducting assessments offering interpretations, and guiding group assessments. Sonstegard (1998b) has outlined four fundamental tasks Adlerian group leaders perform in order to build a sense of community within the group: (1) establishing and maintaining a group relationship; (2) examining the patterns and purposes of group members' actions and behaviors; (3) disclosing to individuals the goals pursued and the private logic that supports these goals; and (4) implementing a reeducation experience that enhances social interest. Table 4.3 lists stages of group that correspond to these tasks.

Dinkmeyer and Sperry (2000) note that Adlerian group leaders use educational and creative methods in their application of Adlerian principles. Common types of groups used by Adlerians include the lifestyle group and the teleoanalytic workshop. In the lifestyle group, members "develop a mini-lifestyle that includes family relationships, comparisons with siblings, and early recollections" (Sharf, 2008, p. 141). The leader is responsible for summarizing mistaken perceptions, assets, and goals of each member. Once this is accomplished, the group is able to examine each member's lifestyle and connect it to the person's beliefs and goals.

Table 4.3 **Stages of Adlerian Groups**

Stage 1. Establishing and maintaining cohesive relationships with members
Stage 2. Analysis and assessment (exploring the individual's dynamics that includes family constellation, early recollections, and integration and summary)
Stage 3. Awareness and insight
Stage 4. Reorientation

Source: Adapted from G. Corey (2004, 2009); M. A. Sonstegard (1998b); M. A. Sonstegard & J. R. Bitter (2001).

Members are encouraged to help each other develop strategies and goals for change. Similar to this is the teleoanalytic workshop, where group members are encouraged to activate their social interest in an attempt to engage in more effective interpersonal relationships. "This workshop combines lectures on topics such as social interest, life tasks and challenges, and encouragement and courage. For each topic, exercises help individuals improve their communication skills" (Sharf, 2008, p. 142). Exercises are initially practiced in groups of 2 to 3 and eventually involve the entire group.

Moreno's psychodrama technique, which is also used in Gestalt therapy, is used in a modified form by Adlerian therapists (Blatner, 2000, 2003). By having members and the leader act out problems within the group, individual group members are able to "see the problem acted out in front of them," which leads to "insights and new strategies for dealing with their issues" (Sharf, 2008, p. 142).

The collaborative effort and the importance of active listening that is fundamental in Adlerian theory is also the case for the person-centered approach we discuss next.

Group Illustration: Adler's philosophy is a great model for understanding children and adolescent behavior. His concepts of social interest, mistaken goals, and purposive behaviors have been found extremely useful in treating a wide range of adolescent problems and issues. Applying Adlerian concepts to a group for high-risk teens that deals with sexuality, school problems, classroom management, delinquency, and drug use has been found to be very productive.

Experiential and Relationship-Oriented Approaches

The importance of the therapeutic relationship is basic to experiential and relationship-oriented approaches of which person-centered is the most well known. This approach is a basic foundation to helping in our work.

Person-Centered Approach

The person-centered approach is grounded in the humanistic perspective that emerged in the 1940s as a reaction to both the psychoanalytic (psychodynamic) and behavioral approaches that required a trained expert utilizing well-defined therapeutic skills and techniques to bring about determined changes in the client. "Humanistic and existential approaches to psychotherapy gained prominence during the middle of the twentieth century and came to be known as the 'third force,' emerging after psychoanalysis and behaviorism" (Brooks-Harris, 2008, p. 195).

Essential Concepts

The humanistic view differs from both psychodynamic and behavioral approaches in that it highlights the value of a positive helping relationship, which is believed to be the most instrumental factor in promoting positive client change. Alle-Corliss and Alle-Corliss (1999) state:

> *the deterministic views inherent in the psychodynamic therapies, as well as the scientific reductionistic notions of the behavioral approach, were both challenged by the introduction of this more humanistic view whose origins lie in existential philosophy and phenomenology. (p. 94)*

Neukrug (2004) adds that the humanistic approach "highlights the strengths and the positive aspects of the individual and rejects the concept that people are determined by early childhood experiences or reinforcers in the environment" (p. 73).

Integral to the humanistic approach is the view that we all have a choice in creating our existence. This theory emphasizes the growth and potential existing within the human spirit. Further, it is believed that everyone has an actualizing tendency; each of us has the ability to transcend our current existence by moving toward a more fulfilling and harmonious one. Practitioners who adhere to the humanistic view strive to understand their clients' subjective reality in an effort to help them become self-actualized.

Well-known proponents of this nontraditional, humanistic perspective include Carl Rogers, Rollo May, and Abraham Maslow (Brooks-Harris, 2008; G. Corey, 2009; Day, 2008; Gladding, 2004; Sharf, 2008). Their divergent views during the 1940s about human nature and therapy created a revolution within the mental health field at the time. Today these theorists are highly respected, and many in the helping professions strongly advocate humanistic approaches. For instance, principles of the humanistic perspective can now be found in both educational and therapeutic environments that feature a nondirective and optimistic view to helping.

Person-centered therapy was first known as *nondirective therapy* and later as *client-centered therapy*. Essentially, "this therapeutic approach, developed by Carl Rogers, takes a positive view of individuals, believing that they tend to move toward becoming fully functioning" (Sharf, 2008, p. 87). It is believed that human beings are born with some type of "actualizing tendency," or growth force. Neukrug (2004, p. 74) describes this tendency to mean "that individuals have the ability to transcend their current existence and move toward a more fulfilling and harmonious existence."

Common Strategies

Person-centered practitioners have great confidence in their clients, given their belief that "all people have innate motivation to grow in positive ways and the ability to carry out such a growth process" (Capuzzi & Gross, 2003, p. 160). As a result of this positive view of human nature, clients are encouraged to be primarily responsible for the direction, style, and content of the helping relationship. This positive view of humanity is based on four key beliefs about people in general:

1. People are *trustworthy*.
2. People innately move toward *self-actualization* and health.
3. People have the *inner resources* to move themselves in positive directions.
4. People respond to their *uniquely perceived world* (phenomenological world). (Capuzzi & Gross, 2003, pp. 160–161)

According to Corey (2009, p. 169), a common theme of this approach is to "trust the client's ability to move forward in a constructive manner if the appropriate conditions fostering growth are present." The central hypothesis of this approach maintains that individuals have within themselves vast resources for self-understanding and for altering their self-concept, attitudes, and behavior. It is believed that these resources can be tapped most thoroughly when a positive atmosphere exists to facilitate this change process.

Rogers identified three specific conditions that constitute this growth-promoting climate:

1. *Genuineness, realness, or congruence.* When a helper is authentic, the client has a much greater likelihood of changing and growing in a constructive manner.

2. *The presence of acceptance, caring, and unconditional positive regard.* When a helper has a positive, nonjudgmental, accepting attitude toward clients, there is an increased potential for clients to change.

3. *The presence of empathic understanding.* The helper senses accurately the feelings and personal meanings that are being experienced by the clients and communicates this acceptance and understanding to clients (Brooks-Harris, 2008; G. Corey, 2009; Day, 2008; Gladding, 2003; Neukrug, 2004; Rogers, 1986; Sharf, 2008).

Unlike both the psychodynamic and Adlerian approaches, "advocates of the humanistic approach stress the personal qualities of the professional in the change process. Helpers using this non-directive approach believe that these qualities alone are the key to client growth" (Neukrug, 2004, p. 76).

The goals of person-centered therapy focus on helping the client become self-actualized, not to resolve his or her problems. Rogers believed that the main purpose of therapy was to assist clients in their growth process by teaching them more adaptive coping skills to cope with current and future problems. Furthermore, Rogers emphasized that "a fully functioning person develops a greater acceptance of self and others and becomes a better decision maker in the here and now" (Gladding, 2003, p. 201).

In sum, the ultimate goal of person-centered treatment is to help clients be able to identify, use, and integrate their own individual resources and potential (Boy & Pine, 1989; Gladding, 2003; Miller, 1996). Common methods that help foster a positive client-therapist relationship "include, but are not limited to, active and passive listening, accurate reflections of thoughts and feelings, clarification, summarization, confrontation, and general or open-ended leads" (Gladding, 2004, p. 201).

Group Applications

Rogers was a strong believer in the power of groups, "both those designed for personal growth and those designed to ease conflicts between people of different ethnic or national groups" (Sharf, 2008, p. 213). As noted in *Carl Rogers on Encounter Groups* (1970), Rogers believed that individual group members had the power to help each other through the group process and that the group leader's role was to be a facilitator and companion to each member. Ideally, group leaders used themselves as instruments of change within the group in hopes that this would lead to the establishment of a therapeutic climate that encouraged honest and meaningful interactions within the group. According to Rogers, the leader's role was to "facilitate core conditions so that individuals may become more genuine, accepting, and empathic with each other so that leadership, in the sense of direction, became less necessary" (Sharf, 2008, p. 214).

Rogers believed that promoting these core conditions of person-centered therapy is fundamental to the success of any group. For that reason, leaders had to possess these skills: active listening, acceptance, understanding, respect, reflection, clarification, summarization, sharing personal experiences, responding to and engaging others in the group, providing affirmations, and emphasizing every member's capacity for self-determination. Rogers believed in allowing the group to flow naturally; he discouraged directing the group process.

In person-centered therapy, trust is also considered paramount. Developing a trusting atmosphere is viewed as a process. At first, clients may feel confused, resistant to share their personal issues, and fearful of becoming vulnerable. As members begin to disclose past feelings, trust begins to emerge, which leads members to begin to share more personal feelings and experiences. As a result, group members become more open and personal in their disclosures, and their interactions are more interpersonal and meaningful. This positive climate fosters honesty, deeper communication, and increased genuineness, which leads to positive feelings and closeness among group members. Ultimately, when these conditions exist, behavior change is more likely to occur. Clients can develop new insights into their problems and become more aware of the incongruities within themselves, and are able to find more effective ways of dealing with others.

As Rogers believed more in encouraging self-exploration and self-development, he minimized the mastery of skills, techniques, and leadership methods (Bozarth & Brodley, 1986). Boy and Pine (1999) emphasize this point:

> *A person-centered approach to group counseling puts far greater emphasis on the facilitative quality of the counselor as a person rather than emphasizing the counselor's knowledge and use of specific and predesigned procedures. It views the counselor's presence as the basic catalyst that prompts group participants to make progress. (p. 150)*

Rogers was very clear about promoting a trusting and open therapeutic climate. He had misgivings about certain functions and procedures, which he felt were counterproductive. These counter-productive procedures include:

- Encouraging the client toward a goal that is unclearly stated
- Use of exercises to evoke certain emotions
- Encouraging and planning dramatic performances within the group
- Allowing attacks and open hostility among members
- Pressuring involvement in group exercises
- Frequent interpretation of members' motives and behaviors
- Making interpretive comments about the group process
- Giving advice
- Highlighting the importance of diagnosis and evaluation to group work
- Hiding behind role of expert leader by remaining emotionally distant and anonymous (G. Corey, 2004; Rogers, 1970).

Even though Rogers was confident about his approach and the power of group work, he acknowledged that there were risks and dangers. He was concerned that positive change would not be long lasting and that the group would not be able to move forward without a clear and shared structure. In addition, he recognized that some group members might feel more vulnerable and exposed upon sharing deeper feelings and thoughts and thus would not be able to proceed. He worried that the cultivation of positive and warm relationships within the group might threaten intimate relationships outside the group. Despite these concerns, however, Rogers believed that the benefits of person-centered group therapy far outweighed the potential risks and drawbacks (Rogers, 1970; Sharf, 2008).

Group Illustration: A Grief support group is a person-centered approach, suited perfectly for a group designed to provide support after the loss of a loved one. Members are allowed to share their feelings freely and benefit from support, acceptance, validation, and unconditional positive regard. Therapists primarily offer support and help with developing coping skills to deal with loss.

Gestalt Therapy

Gestalt therapy is considered an experiential therapy. Its focus is on the client's experiencing events in the present. "Rather than talk about the problem, the client . . . experiences the problem by feeling it internally, talking it out, or re-enacting it" (Sharf, 2008, p. 219).

Gestalt therapy originated in the 1940s as a reaction to psycho-analysis and behaviorism (G. Corey, 2004; Gladding, 2004; Sharf, 2008). Fritz Perls, who is credited with establishing Gestalt therapy, developed this "process-based approach on the premise that individuals must be understood in the context of their ongoing relationship with the environment" (G. Corey, 2009, p. 198). Gestalt therapy emphasizes how people function in their totality. Therapists are concerned with the whole individual, who is viewed as more than the sum of her behaviors (Perls, 1969). Gladding (2004) adds that "Gestaltists believe that human beings work for wholeness and completeness in life. Each person has a self-actualizing tendency that emerges through personal interaction with the environment and the beginning of self-awareness" (p. 204).

Essential Concepts

Gestalt therapy is phenomenologically based in that the methods used value the "human experience" and emphasize the client and therapist's experience of reality (G. Corey, 2009; Sharf, 2008). The Gestalt approach is also existential, since it is "grounded in the notion that people are always in the process of becoming, remaking, and rediscovering themselves. . . . it gives special attention to existence as individuals experience it and affirms the human capacity for growth and healing through interpersonal contact and insight (G. Corey, 2009, p. 198).

This approach stresses individual responsibility for self and encourages bringing issues related to either the past or the future into the present. As in the person-centered approach, Gestalt therapists have a strong belief in human nature and trust that clients strive to live healthy and productive lives. Sharf (2008, p. 219) notes that the general goal of Gestalt therapy is "awareness of self, others, and the environment that brings about growth and integration of the individual." More specific goals are well defined, emphasize the here-and-now, focus on both nonverbal and verbal expression, and stress the concept of making choices.

For Gestaltists, the word *NOW* is very significant; Perls (1969) himself developed a formula that accentuates its essence:

Now = experience = awareness = reality. The past is no more and the future is not yet. Only the now exists. (p. 14)

Gladdings's (2004) comments sum up the gist of Gestalt therapy:

The Gestalt approach concentrates on helping a client resolve the past to become integrated. This goal includes the completion of mentally growing up. It emphasizes the coalescence of the emotional, cognitive, and behavioral aspects of the persons. A primary focus is the acceptance of polarities within the person. (pp. 205–206)

Common Strategies

It is important to differentiate among techniques, exercises, and experiments in Gestalt therapy. Covin (1977) considers exercises to be ready-made techniques, such as the enactment of fantasies, role-playing, and psychodrama. Typically, these techniques are used to evoke a certain response from the client, such as anger or sadness (Gladding, 2004). G. Corey (2004) adds that "techniques are exercises or procedures that are often used to bring about action or interaction" and "generally they are not invented in the moment as an integral part of the client's process" (p. 312). In contrast, experiments occur as a result of the interaction between therapist and client. They are unplanned, spontaneous events that invite clients to try out a new behavior. Experiments are phenomenologically based in that "they evolve out of what is occurring within a member or members in the present moment, and they usually grow out of the struggles members are experiencing" (G. Corey, 2004, p. 312).

   Body awareness is very important to Gestaltists, who strongly believe that the "mind versus the body polarity is one of the most misleading. . . . [Perls] believed that every emotion has a psychological component" (Day, 2004, p. 209; Perls, Hefferline, & Goodman, 1951). Noticing body signals is key to understanding suppressed impulses and areas of repression. One way to work on body awareness is to give the body symptom its own voice, such as "If your clenched jaw, tearful eyes, tense shoulders, shaky hands, and so on, could speak, what would they say?"

   Because it is common to describe emotions in physical terms, Gestaltists encourage clients to become aware of how and why they do this. Furthermore, since emotions can also be located in the body, Gestalt therapists often question where clients feel: "Where do you feel your sadness, anger, fear, and so on? Exploration of the physical feelings associated with emotions can fine-tune awareness of what the emotions are more effectively than mere discussion about them. For example, you can imagine that anger experienced as one's head about to blow up is different from anger experience as an ache in the stomach" (Day, 2004, p. 210).

Exaggeration is an exercise tied to body awareness. Here clients are asked to exaggerate body symptoms until their meaning emerges into awareness: "I notice that you are wringing your hands. Exaggerate your wringing hands. Wringing them really hard. Where do you feel the wringing?" (Day, 2004, p. 210). According to Gladding (2004, p. 206), "Clients accentuate unwitting movement or gestures. In doing so, the inner meaning of these behaviors becomes more apparent."

Experimentation was encouraged by Perls, who had a background in drama. This strategy of experimentation is related to the paradoxical theory of change described by Beisser (1970): Day (2004, p. 210) adds that when individuals get stuck in the same patterns, it might be best to "try something new just to see how it feels. Heightened emotions or awareness may result."

Role playing is an experiment where clients act out different perspectives in the therapy session. "The goal is to resolve unfinished business and integrate polarities by arousing emotions, discovering needs, and shifting one's point of view" (Day, 2004, p. 212). Additionally, clients are encouraged to focus on using their imagination in acting out different aspects of themselves and perspectives of others that they typically divert or suppress.

Role playing is a key feature of Gestalt *dream work*. Words by Perls (1969) himself illustrate the value of dream work:

> *In Gestalt Therapy we don't interpret dreams. We do something much more interesting with them. Instead of analyzing and further cutting up the dream, we want to bring it back to life. . . . We find all we need in the dream, or in the perimeter of the dream, the environment of the dream. The existential difficulty, the missing part of the personality, they are all there. (pp. 68–70)*

Basically, clients present their dreams in detail and then are directed to experience each part of the dream; the technique is "a type of dramatized free association. In this way, a client can get more in touch with the multiple aspects of the self" (Gladding, 2004, p. 206).

Psychodrama is a powerful technique popularized by J. L. Moreno that occurs when role-playing is performed by several people in a Gestalt group (Day, 2004; Moreno, 1972).

Instead of single acting out various parts, members of a group are assigned parts representing significant individuals in a directed re-enactment of a past experience. The client whose experience is being dramatized acts as the director, along with the therapist, to inform and guide the other characters in their actions and responses. (Day, 2004, p. 214)

Also, there are times when clients jump in and experiment with alternative ways of behaving in the situation. This allows the past to be brought into the present (Korb, Gorrell, & Van de Reit, 1989).

The *rehearsal* experiment is when clients speak out loud what they are thinking silently. Rehearsals are used to enhance awareness and are most helpful when it is obvious that clients are blocking or censoring their communication. By talking out loud, clients

become more aware of the preparatory means they use in bolstering their social roles. They also become increasingly aware of how they try to meet the expectations of others, of the degree to which they want to be approved, accepted, and liked, and of the extent to which they go to attain acceptance. (G. Corey, 2009, p. 217)

Rehearsal can also be useful when a client is expecting a future confrontation.

Confrontation has been used by Gestalt therapists since the early days, when Perlsian style of "boom-boom-boom therapy" was common (Yontef, 1993). During this era, Gestalt therapy was exemplified by theatrics, abrasive confrontation, and intense catharsis. During the 1960s and 1970s, the anything-goes environment was common. Since that time, a more kind, compassionate, and supportive style of Gestalt therapy has evolved. Yontef (1999) notes that this approach "combines sustained empathic inquiry with crisp, clear, and relevant awareness focusing" (p. 10). G. Corey (2009) suggests:

Confrontation can be done in such a way that clients cooperate, especially when they are invited to examine their behaviors, attitudes, and thoughts. Therapists can encourage clients to look at certain incongruities, especially gaps between their verbal and nonverbal expression. Further, confrontation does not have to be aimed at weaknesses or negative traits; clients can be challenged to recognize how they are blocking their strengths. (p. 215)

Dramatizing is another experiment to bring to the forefront painful memories, imagine an anxiety-provoking encounter, role-play one's parent, create a dialogue between two parts of oneself, attend to an unnoticed gesture, or exaggerate a certain posture. Because some of these experiments can be overwhelming and potentially emotionally dangerous, sensitivity and care are required on the part of the therapist (Polster, 1990).

Exercises

The *empty-chair* technique is a very commonly used and effective technique. Perls was inspired by the empty-chair technique created by J. L. Moreno, who began staging expressionist experimental theater in the 1920s in Europe. Essentially, "two chairs are used with each one assigned a character, attitude, emotion, or quality. The client moves back and forth between the two chairs, alternately speaking from the perspective of each" (Day, 2004, p. 212). Through this procedure clients are able to talk to various parts of their personality (e.g., passive/aggressive, passive/dominant, top dog/underdog). "In this dialogue, both rational and irrational parts of the client come into focus; the client not only sees these sides but also becomes able to deal with the dichotomies within the self" (Gladding, 2004, p. 206).

The *reversal exercise* is an example of experimental homework that requires doing the opposite of what one usually does. The theory underlying the reversal technique is to have clients plunge into the very thing that they are anxious and fearful about, which they have previously repressed, suppressed, or denied. This technique can help clients begin to accept certain personal characteristics they have tried to disown.

Making the rounds is an exercise routinely used in groups when the therapist believes the entire group would benefit from discussing a particular theme or feeling that is being expressed by an individual client. Usually, in this exercise, group members are asked to each say something that they usually do not communicate verbally in an effort to increase awareness of their inner feelings. This exercise is flexible and can also include expression of positive feelings.

''I take responsibility'' is an exercise that encourages clients to make statements about their perceptions and close each statement with the phrase "and I take responsibility for it." By engaging in this exercise, clients work on integrating and own their perceptions and behaviors. An example might be: "I am angry at you and take responsibility for feeling this way."

Language exercises are important for Gestalt therapists, who view the relationship between language patterns and personality to be important. Passons (1975) suggested that since our speech patterns are sometimes expressions of our feelings, thoughts, and attitudes, focusing on a client's overt speaking habits leads to increased self-awareness. Examples of language exercises commonly used in Gestalt group work include:

IT: Encouraging clients to change "it" to "I" or "I'm" helps clients take more personal responsibility for what they say.

YOU: Encouraging clients to change "you" to "I" statements helps them to be more authentic and responsible.

Questions are discouraged. It is felt that they distract and can easily put others on the defensive.

Qualifiers and disclaimers such as "but" are important for clients to notice since they often serve to downplay what clients are feeling. "By paying attention to the qualifiers they attach to their statements, members can increase their awareness of how they diminish the power of their messages" (G. Corey, 2004, p. 316). In group, clients are encouraged to pay attention to the impact of the use of various qualifiers and disclaimers.

''Can't'' statements are substituted with "won't" statements that are more precise and honest. When members are able to own responsibility for their choices, they can move forward.

''Shoulds'' and *''oughts''* are recognized in an effort to make clients aware of how powerless they must feel. Clients are encouraged to change "I should" or "I have to" to "I choose to," again in an effort to help them recognize their ability to choose.

Group Applications

Historically, Gestaltists have been strong proponents of group work interventions. The group leader may encourage members to take responsibility for their actions yet believes it is important to be active in creating experiments and using exercises to help members reach their fullest potential. Active involvement, use of self-disclosure, promoting a sense of mutuality, and cultivating a nurturing environment are all important for Gestalt leaders who strive to enhance relationships and assist group members to become more self-aware and experience their conflictual emotions more fully. Gestalt therapists believe that developing new ways to help clients experience their emotions will help them gain new insights that can lead to positive change (Strumpfel & Goldman, 2002). A nurturing environment allows for this process of self-discovery to occur while an unsafe atmosphere is felt to hinder the process (Fender, 1994). As active participants in therapy, clients need a safe environment in which they can feel free enough to experiment with new ways of being and behaving (Yontef, 1993).

Since Gestalt therapists use many exercises and experiments to encourage change and growth, it is important for the group leader to be well versed in the use of common techniques. Gestaltists are generally creative, spontaneous, and comfortable with dramatization. Because Gestalt therapists are seen as, "nothing less than an artist involved in creating new life" (Polster & Polster, 1973), they must take care not to become so caught up in devising procedures that they lose sight of the therapeutic process.

Zinker (1978) contends that creative therapists live rich and full lives that allow them to model this to their clients. Additional skills Zinker (1978) believes are important for the functioning of creative therapists include:

- Being able to identify energy within the members and know how to introduce experiments in a timely and appropriate manner
- Being flexible and open to moving to new areas of exploration that appear more dynamic
- Willingness and courage to gently push and confront group members to participate in group as well as to know when to refrain from doing so
- Capacity to assist members to express their feelings and be able to consolidate their learning from experimentation
- The wisdom to allow members to experience confusion in order to find their own way

Kepner (1994) describes a three-stage model of Gestalt group in this way:

Stage 1 (Initial Stage): Identity and dependence. Members are initially dependent on how group members and the leader perceive them. The leader engages in activities to encourage members to become aware of their identity within the group. Leaders need to create a climate of trust that will encourage interaction and experimentation.

Stage 2 (Transition Stage): Influence and counterdependence. This is a time when the group wrestles with issue of influence, authority, and control. By assuming the role of facilitators, leaders attempt to encourage members to recognize their differences and role flexibility.

Stage 3 (Working Stage): Intimacy and interdependence. Having worked through various issues, members are now ready for real contact and deeper level of work. The leader becomes less active and more of "an experience resource or consultant. The leader helps the group to arrive at closure and also assists members in recognizing unfinished business not worked through in the group" (G. Corey, 2004, p. 312).

Gestalt therapists made popular three types of groups in the 1960s and 1970s:

1. *Hot seat groups* are where individual group members work one to one with the therapist while others in the group observe. Later the group is asked to comment on what they observed. It was felt that the entire group benefitted by learning from others.

2. *Process groups* are exactly what their name suggests: groups where attention is paid to current group process. Since group members are said to often work on themes central to their everyday lives, these types of groups can be very powerful.

3. *Process-thematic groups* are those that attend to process, and themes that involve the entire group may be acted out. This type of group can also be powerful and therefore requires a skilled, sensitive, and respectful group leader.

Language exercises (discussed earlier) and *psychodrama* are commonly used in Gestalt groups. It is important not to challenge a group member's language too quickly. Trust and a sense of safety should exist before language patterns are explored. Similarly, psychodrama requires special care on the part of the group leader.

Because Gestalt group work is often intense and recommended for more seasoned therapists, beginning therapists can best learn by accepting opportunities to participate in and later colead a Gestalt group.

Group Illustration: Gestalt techniques are useful in many different types of groups. We have used Gestalt exercises successfully in men's, women's, young adult, anxiety, and depression groups in an effort to point out body language and its connection to certain life events or deeper feelings. Members who are struggling with unfinished business may be asked to use the empty-chair technique to talk to an individual in their past. Someone who wants to practice assertion skills may be asked to engage in a role play or role rehearsal.

Action Approaches

Cognitive-Behavioral Approaches

Cognitive-behavioral therapy has its roots in both behaviorism and cognitive therapy. Most practitioners who use this approach today integrate principles from both these schools of thought. According to Alle-Corliss and Alle-Corliss (1999), the "cognitive-behavioral strategies create a balanced approach to understanding and treating common problems of life" (p. 98). Two basic premises underlie this approach: "(1) being able to examine the manner in which individuals view themselves and their environment (cognition) and (2) the way in which they act on that environment (behavior)." In short, the primary goal of a cognitive-behavioral therapy is to bring about positive and lasting change by helping clients to modify maladaptive thoughts and/or behaviors.

Behavior Therapy
Behavior techniques are fundamental to cognitive-behavioral therapy. Historically, the advent of behaviorism led to a change in the psychological world. Brooks-Harris (2008) writes: "The rise of behaviorism marked a shift in psychology's interest; moving from a focus on human consciousness based on introspection [as seen in psychodynamic and Adlerian theories] toward a focus on behavior that is directly observable" (p. 151).

Essential Concepts
The literature identifies three main approaches in contemporary behavior therapy:

1. Neobehavioristic meditational stimulus-response model
2. Applied behavior analysis
3. Social-cognitive theory

> *These three approaches differ in the extent to which they use cognitive concepts and procedures. At one end of the continuum is applied behavior analysis, which focuses exclusively on observable behavior and rejects all cognitive mediating processes. At the other end is social-cognitive theory, which relies heavily on cognitive theories. (Corsini & Wedling, 2008, p. 224)*

Neobehavioristic Meditational Stimulus-Response Model The main premises of behavior therapy were proposed by Pavlov and Skinner, who are well known for their work on classical and operant conditioning. At the turn of the 20th century, Ivan Pavlov, a Russian scientist, discovered what was later called *classical conditioning*. Through his experiments, Pavlov found that "a hungry dog that salivated when shown food would learn to salivate to a tone if that tone had been repeatedly paired or associated with food" (Neukrug, 2004, p. 70). This observation led to the important premise, still held today, that individuals often respond in predictable ways to certain stimuli or life events as a result of experience or associative learning.

In the 1920s John Watson, an experimental psychologist, studied the principles of *classical conditioning* when he demonstrated the way a human infant's emotional reactions could be conditioned and generalized. In 1958, Joseph Wolpe, a psychiatrist and pioneer in behavior therapy, also used the principles of classical conditioning to develop the still widely used clinical intervention of systematic desensitization (Brooks-Harris, 2008; G. Corey, 2009; Day, 2009, 2008; Gladding, 2003; Neukrug, 2004; Rogers, 1986; Sharf, 2008). These and other techniques using classical conditioning have come to be known collectively as *behavior therapy*. In fact, Wolpe (1990) was influential in challenging the predominant Freudian perspective due to his focus on developing strategies designed to extinguish conditioned responses of maladaptive anxiety. "Behavior Therapy promised the field of psychotherapy specific techniques based on scientific principles that could be empirically tested and supported" (Brooks-Harris, 2008, p. 151).

The "Stimulus-Response approach features the application of the principles of classical conditioning, and is derived from the learning theories of Pavlov [and others]. . . . S-R theorists have been particularly interested in the study of anxiety; the techniques of systematic desensitization and flooding" are used in an effort to reduce or eliminate anxiety (Corsini & Wedding, 2008, p. 224).

Applied Behavior Analysis Approach Corsini and Wedding (2008) note that the applied behavior analysis approach "is a direct extension of Skinner's (1953) radical behaviorism" (p. 224). In the 1920s, the psychologist B. F. Skinner added to Pavlov's research by demonstrating that animals would learn specific behaviors as the target behavior was reinforced. Based on this finding, the theory of *operant conditioning* was born, based on the idea that behavioral change often occurs as a result of positive and negative reinforcements. A positive reinforcement occurs when an individual is presented with a stimulus that produces an increase in a desirable behavior. Conversely, a negative reinforcement occurs when there is a removal of a stimulus that results in an increase in behavior. "Essentially, then, an individual's behavior is thought to be governed by contingencies. Behavior that is rewarded or reinforced will be repeated and the individual will learn from his or her experience" (Alle-Corliss & Alle-Corliss, 1999, p. 99). It is said that "Skinner's research on operant conditioning in animals also led to psychotherapy applications and strategies based on principles of reinforcement that came to be known collectively as *behavior modification*" (Brooks-Harris, 2008, p. 151).

In the applied behavior analysis approach, "treatment procedures are based on altering relationships between overt behaviors and their consequences" (Corsini & Wedding, 2008, p. 224). Procedures typically used include reinforcement, punishment, extinction, and stimulus control.

A most important outcome of Skinner's pioneering work in the behavioral branch of psychology was the premise that maladaptive behaviors are learned and therefore can be unlearned. Skinner stressed the cause-and-effect relationships between the environmental conditions present and an individual's behavior. Also important was Skinner's finding that physical and social environments are critically important in determining human behavior.

Social-Cognitive Theory In the 1970s, Albert Bandura, a clinical psychologist, introduced *social learning theory,* known today as *social cognitive theory,* that "emphasized the role of thoughts and images in psychological functioning" (Sharf, 2008, p. 259). Bandura combined classical and operant conditioning with observational learning. The influence of the environment on behavior is thought to be "largely determined by cognitive processes governing how environmental influences are perceived and how the individual interprets them" (Corsini & Wedding, 2008, p. 224).

Social learning theory was viewed as a "new learning paradigm based on principles of modeling, imitation, and self-control" that "provided a more cognitive explanation of learning" (Brooks-Harris, 2008, p. 152). In this approach, which holds that humans are capable of self-directed behavior change, the person is the agent for change (Corsini & Wedding, 2008, p. 24). Perhaps more important, Bandura's work opened the door for an integrated form of cognitive-behavioral therapy that we elaborate on later. Notably, it is this "blend of cognitive and behavioral approaches" that is "more representative of currently practice (Sharf, 2008, p. 259).

Recent Developments in Behavior Therapy
According to Haynes, Follette, and Linehan (2004), the development of behavior therapy can be divided into three waves.

> *The first wave of behavior therapy focused primarily on modifying overt behavior. The second wave was the emphasis on cognitive factors, resulting in what is known as cognitive behavior therapy (CBT). . . . The "third wave" comprises a group of therapeutic approaches with overlapping conceptual and technical foundation. (p. 226)*

This group of approaches includes dialectical behavior therapy (DBT) (Linehan, 1993) and acceptance and commitment therapy (ACT) (Haynes, Luoma, Bond, Masuda, & Lillis, 2006).

DBT emerged in the 1990s with the work of Linehan (Brooks-Harris, 2008; Corsini & Wedding, 2008). DBT was developed by Marsha Linehan, psychologist and professor of psychiatry and behavioral sciences, to help clients who express distress due to their rigid or extreme patterns of thought, think in a more balanced manner. DBT is an integrative treatment model developed specifically to treat individuals suffering from borderline personality disorder. A primary goal of this approach is "to help clients recognize and overcome polarized thinking that often results in unstable relationships and intense emotional reactions" (Brooks-Harris, 2008, p. 135). Linehan (1993) writes:

> *Dialectical reasoning requires the individual to assume an active role, to let go of logical reasoning and intellectual analysis as the only route to truth, and to embrace experiential knowledge . . . The dialectical therapist helps the patient achieve synthesis of oppositions, rather than focusing on verifying either side of an oppositional argument. The therapist helps the patient move from "either or" to "both-and." (p. 204)*

Corsini and Wedding (2008, p. 226) contend that "a defining feature of DBT is its focus on balancing traditional behavior change with the value of acceptance, and the importance of the relationship between the two, which Linehan sees as central dialectic of therapy." Wilson (2004) suggests that the message in the Serenity Prayer—"God, give me the serenity to accept the things I cannot change, the courage to change the things I can, and the wisdom to know the difference"— illustrates the importance of balancing acceptance with change that is central to DBT. Corsini and Wedding (2008, p. 226) stress that according to Linehan, "acceptance" should not be interpreted as "giving up" or resigning oneself to life's problems but as an "active process of self-affirmation."

In addition to using traditional behavior therapy techniques, DBT also emphasizes the use of the distinctive therapeutic strategy of *mindfulness*, which consists of five core skills:

1. Observe or attend to emotions without trying to terminate them when painful.
2. Describe a thought or emotion.
3. Be nonjudgmental.
4. Stay in the present.
5. Focus on one thing at a time (one mindfully) (Corsini & Wedding, 2008; Linehan, 1993).

Segal, Teasdale, and Williams (2004) describe *mindfulness* in this manner:

> *Mindfulness can be seen as . . . an alternative cognitive mode, in which the focus of processing is at a level of representation that is not conceptual, and in which specific discrepancies are not the prime topic of processing. Traditionally, this aspect of mindfulness is described as ''being'' rather than ''doing.'' (p. 53)*

Mindfulness training emphasizes the importance of helping clients recognize that their distorted and at times painful thoughts are "just thoughts," not reality (Kabat-Zinn, 1990). Linehan (1993) highlights the importance of "observing, describing, and participating" in mindfulness training.

> *Observing . . . is attending to events, emotions, and other behavioral responses, even if these are distressing ones. . . . Describing events and personal responses [involves] the ability to apply verbal labels to behavioral and environmental events. . . . Participating without self-consciousness [involves] entering completely into the activities of the current moment, without separating oneself from ongoing events and interactions. (pp. 145–146)*

Three benefits of mindfulness training include:

1. Clients tend to experience "less emotional reactivity."

2. There is a "reduction of judgmental thinking, which may be at the core of dysfunctional cognition" (Brooks-Harris, 2008, p. 138).

3. Clients "deliberately [turn] toward the unpleasant with an attitude of openness and acceptance" (Segal et al., 2004, p. 53).

Although originally used to treat borderline personality disorder, the DBT concepts of acceptance and mindfulness have been found to be useful in the treatment of many other clinical conditions, including anxiety, depression, and eating disorders (Corsini & Wedding, 2008; Hayes, Follette, & Linehan, 2004).

Along with DBT, ACT is a new form of behavior therapy. According to Hayes et al. (2006), ACT uses traditional behaviorism together with a more innovative, post-Skinnerian model of language and cognition and their connection to psychopathology. Experiential avoidance lies at the core of ACT. Experiential avoidance is "the process of trying to avoid negative or distressing private experience, such as thoughts, feelings, memories, and sensations," which ultimately does not work and may "make matters worse" (Corsini & Wedding, 2008, p. 227). The three basic techniques of ACT have been well defined by Corsini and Wedding (2008, p. 228):

1. Acceptance in encouraged. Clients are taught that since experiential avoidance does not work, they need to learn how to "accept the thoughts and feelings they have been trying to get rid of."

2. Cognitive defusion refers to "separating thoughts from their referents and differentiating the thinker from the thoughts" or "not taking thoughts as inherent aspect of self or as necessarily valid reflections of reality." This concept is based on "the assumption that learning how to defuse language promotes acceptance and being in the present, and thus clients overcome psychological problems."

3. Commitment "refers to making mindful decisions about what is important in your life and what you are going to do in order to live a valued life. Therapy involves helping patients choose the values they hold dear, setting specific goals, and taking concrete steps to achieve these goals."

Corsini and Wedding (2008) eloquently discuss why ACT has become a widely used and popular behavioral treatment of many clinical problems:

One of the reasons for its popularity among clinicians is its foundation in core therapeutic principles that are linked to psychological science and have broad applicability to different disorders. It emphasizes common processes across clinical disorders, making it easier to teach fundamental treatment skills. Clinicians are then free to implement these basic principles in diverse and creative ways. (p. 228)

Brooks-Harris (2008, p. 152) adds that ACT is one of the new behavioral approaches being developed that are "revitalizing the field and redefining what behavioral psychotherapy will look like in the future."

Common Strategies

As noted, many behavior techniques used today are rooted in the earlier works of Pavlov and Skinner. Some of the more common ones include:

- Training in assertiveness and relationships
- Systematic desensitization, typically used to treat anxiety, chronic pain, and phobias
- Behavior modification, used in treating behavior disorders in children and providing parent effectiveness training to their parents
- Reinforcement schedules and token economies, commonly used in schools and psychiatric hospitals

Central to all of these behavioral techniques is the premise that treatment and assessment are interrelated since they occur simultaneously. The focus is primarily on changing specific behaviors. Some of the more traditional intervention strategies used are profiled next.

Behavioral Assessments Behavioral assessments are very important for the behavioral therapist. Sharf (2008) writes: "Assessing specific behaviors rather than broader characteristics or traits is the hallmark of behavioral assessment. The emphasis is on determining the unique details of a client's problem and situation" (p. 265). Essentially, behavioral assessments involve using a set of procedures to gather certain relevant information "that will guide the development of a tailor-made treatment plan for each client and help measure the effectiveness of treatment" (G. Corey, 2004, p. 361). Day (2004) considers the assessment an opportune time to ask questions related to "when the behavior occurs, how frequently it occurs, what usually comes before and after the behavior, what the client thinks and feels during the behavior, and what the client has already tried in order to solve the problem" (p. 252). Speigler and Guevremont (2003) note that behavioral procedures typically share five important characteristics. They are as follow.

1. Aimed at gathering detailed information about the problem the client presents with
2. Focused on current functioning and life conditions
3. Used to sample client behaviors in order to learn about a client's normal functioning
4. Narrowly rather than broadly focused
5. An important part of therapy

Contingency Management In contingency management, "contingencies can operate at two times: before a behavior and after it. Many behavioral treatments consist of manipulating the situation that precedes a behavior and the situation that follows it" (Day, 2004, p. 262). *Reinforcement* is perhaps one of the most notable of these behavior strategies. "Reinforcement occurs whenever the consequences of a behavior increase the likelihood that a person will engage in the behavior again. The reinforcing consequence is known as a reinforcer and is usually pleasant or desirable" (Frew & Spiegler, 2008, p. 292). Capuzzi and Gross (2007) differentiate between *positive* and *negative reinforcement*: "Positive reinforcement is a procedure in which some behavior is increased by following it with something rewarding. . . . Negative reinforcement is the removal of something aversive to increase behavior" (p. 252).

Punishment Punishment involves "changing the consequences of a behavior so that the client is less likely to engage in the behavior again" (Frew & Speigler, 2008, p. 294). Corsini and Wedding (2008) add that "in punishment, an aversive event is contingent on a response; the result is a decrease in the frequency of that response" (p. 235). *Differential reinforcement* is the most desirable strategy for decelerating undesirable behavior; rewards are delivered when the client is *not* performing an undesirable behavior. In other words, *responses are withdrawn* when undesirable behaviors occur such as use of 'time out'" (Day, 2004, p. 263).

Extinction Extinction is a behavior intervention designed to decrease a problematic behavior . . . [as] a reinforcer that has followed the behavior in the past is removed, and the problem behavior decreases" (Capuzzi & Gross, 2007, p. 252). Simply, in extinction, there is a cessation or removal of a response.

Overcorrection Overcorrection involves "having the clients correct the effects of their actions (restitution) and then intensely practice an appropriate alternative behavior (positive practice)" as a way to administer undesirable consequences (Frew & Speigler, 2008, p. 296).

Aversion Therapy Since interventions using punishment can pose potential risks, they are used less than other behavior techniques in therapy. Aversion therapy is used primarily when clients wish to break habits they dislike in themselves, such as excessive smoking, drinking, drug use, or overeating. In these instances, an undesirable consequence results after clients engage in the negative behavior.

Stimulus Control In stimulus control, preceding contingencies are analyzed and manipulated. Basically, stimulus control is used to modify (control) antecedents (stimuli) by modifying prompts or by modifying setting events (Capuzzi & Gross, 2007; Day, 2004). *Prompts* are "cues that remind or instruct us to perform a behavior" and include environmental, verbal, and physical prompts. "*Setting events* are broad conditions in the immediate environment that influence the likelihood that a client will engage in particular behaviors" (Frew & Spiegler, 2008, p. 291).

Shaping Shaping is a gradual approach to behavior management that occurs when therapists reward behaviors that come closer and closer to the desired goal in a process of *successive approximations*. This behavior intervention is used to gradually increase the quality of a behavior and typically is introduced when teaching a new skill (Capuzzi & Gross, 2007; Day, 2004).

Token Economy According to Frew and Spiegler (2008, p. 298) "A *Token Economy* is a system for motivating clients to perform desirable behaviors and to refrain from performing undesirable behaviors. Clients can earn tokens-reinforcers such as poker chips or points, and they lose tokens for maladaptive behaviors." Watson and Tharp (1997) suggest that tokens or points are used primarily "to bridge the delay between the time you perform the desired behavior and the time you can receive the reinforcer" (p. 222).

Reactivity Encouraging clients to keep track of a certain behavior results in the phenomenon called reactivity of measurement; just keeping track of something makes individuals behave differently.

Psychoeducation In psychoeducation, therapists become educators about the principles of behavior management. Clients are made aware of how they respond to cues or to the reinforcers they give or receive. Clients are also provided with factual information that may help them better understand their own behavior and explore ways they can change it.

Exposure Therapies Exposure therapies are used primarily to treat clients who suffer from such negative emotions as anxiety, fear, and anger by "exposing them—under carefully controlled and safe conditions—to whatever it is that is making them anxious" (Frew & Speigler, 2008, p. 298). *Systematic desensitization* and *flooding and implosion* are the best-known behavioral interventions that fall under this category.

Systematic desensitization is a very popular and extensively researched behavioral procedure developed by Joseph Wolpe to treat phobias (Emmelkamp, 1994). According to the theory as proposed by Wolpe (1958):

> *when a response incompatible with anxiety (e.g., relaxation) is paired with an anxiety-evoking stimuli (whatever the client reports as anxiety producing), the association between the anxiety-producing stimulus and anxiety will be lessened. . . . Clients are desensitized to their fears. (Capuzzi & Gross, 2007, p. 245)*

Two basic steps are involved in systematic desensitization:

1. Clients are taught to use progressive relaxation in order to become completely relaxed.
2. Using a hierarchy arranged with the least anxiety-provoking stimuli first and the most anxiety-provoking stimuli last, the therapist encourages the client to imagine each stimuli while continuing to use relaxation techniques (Kalodner, 1998).

In essence then, this type of technique "involves careful sequencing of anxiety and relaxation to ensure that anxiety loses" (Day, 2004, p. 267).

Flooding uses the same premise of desensitization: "Avoidance of exposure to a feared situation has been reinforced by the relief of not facing it. . . . Flooding assumes that with prolonged or repeated exposure to the situation, with no actual aversive consequences, anxiety cannot be sustained. Fear and avoidance of the situation will be reduced or extinguished" (Day, 2004, p. 269).

Flooding techinques are used in "Implosive therapy," however, the choice of an aversive situations have a conventional psychoanalytic aspect. In fact, "Implosive therapists report that the emotional release caused by thoroughly frightening imaginal exposure, with no adverse consequences in reality, exhausts the affect of the situation and leaves the client relieved" (Day, 2008, p. 337).

Modeling Therapies   Examples of modeling therapies are *social skills training* and *assertion training*, two of the most common types of behavior group therapies used today.

Skills training involves using a variety of techniques, such as: modeling, direct instruction, prompting, shaping, reinforcement, corrective feedback, behavior rehearsal, and role playing. Skills training is designed to teach clients to cope with skills deficits. Social skills training involves teaching "social skills," which are defined as "the interpersonal competencies necessary to successfully interact with others [that] are essential for functioning on a daily basis" (Frew & Speigler, 2008, p. 309). Many types of social skills training programs are used with different populations; most notable are those used with children (Spence, 2003) and with psychiatric patients (Tsang & Cheung, 2005).

Assertion training is another behavioral technique used to help clients who have difficulty asking for their needs to be met (passive) or those who express themselves in inappropriate ways (aggressive). Young (2001, p. 248) notes that "the term 'assertiveness training' became popular in the 1970s and refers to a broad set of social skills used to enhance self-esteem and deal effectively with emotions." Assertiveness involves "standing up for personal rights and expressing thoughts, feelings, and beliefs indirect, honest, and appropriate ways that do not violate another person's rights. The basic message is: 'This is what I think,' 'This is what I feel,' 'This is how I see the situation'" (Lange & Jakubowski, 1976, p. 7). Alberti and Emmons (2001) encourage differentiating among passive, assertive, and aggressive behaviors. They believe assertive behavior is not only a self-affirmation but also an expression of respect for others. It is important to teach clients that they need to respect themselves and therefore have a right to be assertive; yet, at the same time, it is essential to respect the rights of others. In sum, "assertiveness is a respectful communication technique that encourages mutuality and compromise and preserves a person's basic integrity" (Alle-Corliss & Alle-Corliss, 2006, p. 76).

Self-Management Methods The term *self-management methods* refers to applying behavioral strategies to one's own life. Since behavioral interventions are easy to understand, many clients can learn them by reading self-help books, such as *Mastery of Your Anxiety and Worry* (Craske, Barlow, & O'Leary, 1992), and *Feeling Good: The New Mood Therapy* (Burns, 1999). These and similar books take clients through the steps of behavioral treatment. Some clients are able to learn self-management techniques on their own; for others, the guidance of a therapist is useful, in either individual or group psychotherapies.

Group Applications
Behavioral approaches to groups have become more popular, given the increased emphasis on teaching clients self-management skills. Since behavior therapy is a very directive and structured process, group leaders must be detailed, concrete, and problem oriented in their style and comfortable with assuming a teacher role. Because treatment is often short term in nature, goals are more appropriate if they are limited and realistic. G. Corey (2004, p. 363) finds that "the time limitation can [actually] be a catalyst for members to make the best use of group time to achieve their goals."

Leaders serve as role models for their clients and often engage in role-playing during the group. Group leaders use positive reinforcement to encourage newly developing behavior and skills. Every achievement, no matter how small, is recognized in an effort to encourage continued work toward goal attainment.

Since the behavioral approach emphasizes a plan for change, behaviorists encourage clients to remain actively involved in their work, both in the group and outside the therapy. *Awareness and insight* is the first step toward change; *action* is the second. "Leaders help members understand that verbalizations and insight are not enough to produce change. To broaden their repertoire of adaptive behaviors, members are urged to experiment in the group and practice homework assignments" (G. Corey, 2004, p. 364).

Behavior therapy groups follow a sequential process: initial stage, working stage, and final stage.

During the Initial stage, intake and pregroup interviews are conducted with prospective members. Preliminary assessments are made and individual members are oriented to the group and how to get the most from it. The purpose and member expectations are reviewed with member commitment confirmed. Once a group is composed and orientated, at the beginning of each session, all members report on homework and any progress made. They are also encouraged to identify any other topics or issues they want to work on. Cohesion is all-important and requires a climate of trust, which behavior therapists are partially responsible for establishing. During this early stage, the leader is more directive and strives to keep members attracted to the group process.

The next stage is the Working stage where a *"Treatment Plan and Application of Techniques"* takes place. By continually assessing and evaluating individual group members, the group leader is better able to develop an individualized treatment plan that identifies the most appropriate set of procedures likely to achieve behavioral change (G. Corey, 2004, p. 366). Since individuals and the group are dynamic in nature, change is constant. As a result, a behavior therapist consistently re-evaluates the appropriateness of the treatment plan and use of specific strategies. Reinforcement, contingency contracts, modeling, behavior rehearsal, coaching, homework, feedback, cognitive restructuring, problem solving, and use of the buddy system to effect change are some of the more commonly used techniques during this phase of treatment.

In social skills training, for instance, group members are oriented to social skills and taught through role playing. They are asked to identify the specifics of their problem situations and to role-play. Each member is asked to keep a diary about what happens when the situation occurs during the week. During the group sessions, members are helped to develop goals for dealing with their specific situations and to explore ways to meet these goals. Modeling effective ways of dealing with difficult situations through role-plays is central to group process. Sometimes the group leader or fellow members use coaching to offer suggestions on how best to proceed in a challenging situation. Homework is often given to members to help them practice newly learned behavior in the real world. Sharf (2008) highlights the benefit of using group therapy:

> Because teaching, demonstrating, and modeling are behavioral strategies that can be applied as easily to group as to an individual, the use of group therapy with social skills and assertiveness issues is particularly appropriate. Groups provide members an opportunity to practice situations with different group members and to get feedback from several people rather than just one. Reinforcement from peers as well as from the leader can often be quite powerful. (p. 294)

As the group approaches the termination stage, group leaders are focused on helping members transfer changes they have exhibited in group to the outside world. Members are encouraged to practice and rehearse new behaviors in the group and with significant others in their lives. Reality testing, feedback by fellow group members, and anticipatory planning is important during this phase. "Sessions are systematically designed so that new behaviors are gradually carried into daily life" (G. Corey, 2004, p. 371; Rose, 1989; Rose & Edleson, 1987).

Group Illustration: Behavior therapy is very useful in working with children and teens. In a social skills training group for ADHD, specific measurable goals are set for latency-age children who struggle in completing homework, following rules at home and school, and relating to others. Positive reinforcement is used along with a token economy system whereby group members receive prizes for their positive behavior. They are taught how to complete their homework and manage their classroom behavior. The group leader is very active and directive.

Cognitive Approach

The cognitive approach, which emerged much later than behavior therapy, is now being effectively used with the behavioral approaches. This approach stresses "how the individual thinks, particularly how cognitions affect our behaviors, and how we feel" (Neukrug, 2004, p. 76). The cognitive approach was initially viewed as revolutionary, given the shift in clinical practice from a strong behavioral perspective to a cognitive one (Baars, 1986). Over time, however, pairing techniques from both these schools has resulted in the development of the cognitive-behavioral approaches that are widely used today.

Essential Concepts
Cognitive theory emerged in the 1960s and 1970s as a result of the pioneering work of Albert Ellis and Aaron T. Beck.

Cognitive Restructuring Therapies
In cognitive restructuring therapies, clients are encouraged to identify dysfunctional schemata and thinking patterns that are considered "ill formed and interfering with the pursuit and attainment of goals" (Gravold, 1994, p. 20). They are then helped to modify these patterns. Cognitive restructuring is most effective when used with other cognitive methods (i.e., thought stopping, covert sensitization, guided imagery) and behavioral methods (i.e., behavior rehearsal, skill training, deep muscle relaxation).

Self-talk is exactly what it sounds like: what people say to themselves while they are thinking. An important step in cognitive restructuring therapy involves becoming aware of one's self-talk, learning to monitor self-talk, identifying maladaptive self-talk, and substituting "adaptive self-talk for maladaptive self-talk" (Frew & Speigler, 2008, p. 320).

Thought stopping is a type of cognitive restructuring therapy that is used to "decrease the frequency, duration, and intensity of persistent, disturbing thoughts" and is performed in two stages: " (1) interrupting the disturbing thoughts, and then (2) replacing the disturbing thoughts with nondisturbing competing thoughts" (Frew & Speigler, 2008, p. 322).

Rational emotive therapy is perhaps one of the best-known types of cognitive restructuring therapies that is used to help clients change irrational thoughts that lead to psychological problems. Albery Ellis, from the field of clinical psychology, is well known for developing the rational-emotive behavior therapy (REBT), which

> *assumes individuals are born with the potential for rational thinking but tend to fall victim to the uncritical acceptance or irrational beliefs. The assumption is that thinking, evaluating, analyzing, questioning, doing, practicing, and redeciding are at the base of behavior change. (Alle-Corliss & Alle-Corliss, 1999, p. 100)*

According to Ellis, common irrational beliefs result from faulty reasoning or logical errors about the world and oneself (Bernard & Di Giuseppe, 1989; Ellis & Bernard, 1985). Absolute (dichotomous) thinking (black-or-white thinking), overgeneralizing, and catastrophizing are three ways in which irrational beliefs are maintained.

REBT is a didactic and directive model in which therapy is a process of reeducation based on the belief that a reorganization of one's self-statements will result in a corresponding reorganization of one's behavior. Basically, "the aim of REBT is to modify irrational beliefs, first by identifying thoughts based on the irrational beliefs, then by challenging the irrational beliefs, and finally by replacing thoughts based on irrational beliefs with thoughts based on rational beliefs" (Frew & Speigler, 2008, p. 324).

Cognitive therapy is a well-known cognitive restructuring therapy that was conceived by Aaron Beck (Beck, 1963, 1976). Beck's cognitive approach, from the field of psychiatry, emerged in the 1970s. Beck is renowned for his research and treatment applications in the cognitive approach and is known as the founder of cognitive therapy. Beck concurs with Ellis in his belief that our cognitions are the major determinants of how we feel and act. He contends that clients' internal dialogue plays a major role in their behavior (Brooks-Harris, 2008; G. Corey, 2009; Day, 2004; Gladding, 2003; Neukrug, 2004; Rogers, 1986; Sharf, 2008).

The central premise underlying cognitive therapy is the belief that people often have maladaptive patterns of thinking that must be understood and altered for positive changes to result. Essentially, the overriding focus of this therapy is changing dysfunctional cognitions (thoughts), emotions, and behaviors. Since certain individuals have maladaptive thinking patterns, a primary goal of cognitive therapy is the identification of negative and distorted automatic thoughts. These thoughts are relatively autonomous and tend to occur rapidly while a person is in the midst of a particular situation or is recalling significant events from his or her past.

Neukrug (2004) adds that professionals who use cognitive-oriented techniques tend to believe that a person's thinking is conditioned, starting in early childhood. Furthermore, they believe that these ways of thinking are reinforced throughout a person's life and are directly related to how a person acts and feels.

Goals of cognitive therapy include "(1) to correct client's faulty information processing, (2) to modify the irrational beliefs that maintain clients' maladaptive actions and emotions, and (3) to provide clients with skills and experiences that foster adaptive thinking" (Frew & Speigler, 2008, p. 329). A close client-therapist collaboration is essential in helping clients accomplish these goals (Beck & Weishaar, 1989; Burns & Nolen-Hoeksema, 1992).

Given its emphasis on changing negative thinking, cognitive therapy has been shown to be an excellent treatment of choice for those who suffer from depression and anxiety. Since these individuals experience more negative and fearful automatic thoughts that influence them and provoke painful emotional reactions, they seem to respond best to a technique that challenges their pessimistic outlook. Specifically, in cognitive therapy, clients are helped to uncover the irrational and problematic thinking styles that often accompany emotional distress.

Cognitive theorists believe that our feelings are a direct extension of our thoughts and that these feelings are influenced to a large extent by the way we view life events. Therefore, if clients can change their thoughts or thinking processes, they can change their feelings as well. In an effort to help clients become more productive and satisfied in their lives, therapeutic strategies concentrate on helping them to detect their cognitive errors and to develop more rational ways of thinking

(Brooks-Harris, 2008; G. Corey, 2009; Day, 2004; Gladding, 2003; Neukrug, 2004; Rogers, 1986; Sharf, 2008). Typical cognitive distortions of many clients include all-or-nothing thinking, personalization, ignoring the evidence, and overgeneralizing.

Cognitive-Behavioral Coping Skills Therapies

Problem-Solving Therapy Problem-solving therapy is "a cognitive-affective behavioral process through which an individual (group) attempts to identify, discover, or invent effective or adaptive means of coping with problems encountered in everyday living" (D'Zurilla, 1988, p. 86). This process is often enhanced when it is used with such methods as cognitive restructuring, social skills and assertiveness training, self-control techniques, and coping skills training.

Self-Instructional Training Self-instructional training involves the use of self-verbalizations to guide the performance of a task, skill, or problem-solving process. Through step-by-step self-statements, clients help themselves become competent in performing specific tasks and targeted skills. The premise behind this method is that when adaptive self-statements are inserted between a stimulus and response to prevent maladaptive behavior, the stimulus/response chain is broken, thereby inhibiting the maladaptive response from occurring (Meichenbaum, 1975).

Stress Inoculation Training Stress inoculation training is another intervention developed by Meichenbaum (1977, 1985) to "help clients learn coping skills and then practice using them while being exposed to stress-evoking events" (Frew & Speigler, 2008, p. 341). Poser (1970), Poser and King (1975), and Speigler (1980) compare stress inoculation to biological immunizations in which the body's immune system is prepared to deal with disease-causing microorganisms.

Common Strategies

Below we review cognitive-behavioral strategies that are drawn from various different thought-oriented approaches to psychotherapy, including, but not limited to, cognitive, rational emotive, cognitive-behavior modification, and dialectical behavior therapy.

1. *Identifying thoughts.* Identifying automatic (usually negative) thoughts and self-talk that lead to an awareness of existing cognitive patterns.

- *Clarifying the impact of thoughts.* Helping clients understand how their negative, irrational, and faulty thinking has impacted their behaviors and possibly resulted in the development of many psychological disorders.
- *Challenging irrational thoughts.* Clients are encouraged to challenge or dispute their irrational thoughts or inaccurate beliefs.
- *Illuminating core beliefs.* Involves helping clients explore the meaning of their thoughts and patterns in order to clarify what their core beliefs are. Sometimes these core beliefs are described as *maladaptive assumptions* that appear as themes in automatic thoughts.
- *Evaluating evidence.* Clients are encouraged to work collaboratively with the therapist in examining their thoughts and beliefs and to test their validity in real life.
- *Testing hypothesis.* In addition to evaluating evidence, clients are encouraged to make predictions and to test their hypotheses based on their belief system.
- *Modifying beliefs.* Once it is determined that irrational, faulty beliefs are at play, efforts are made to encourage clients to modify their beliefs to more functional and adaptive ones.
- *Reinforcing adaptive cognitions.* Once adaptive ways of thinking are developed, they are reinforced, and efforts are made to extinguish dysfunctional ones.
- *Encouraging accurate perceptions.* Following Glasser's (1965) reality therapy, clients are encouraged to "honestly look at their life situations and make active choices based on an accurate perception of reality."
- *Supporting dialectical thinking.* Clients are helped to move toward a synthesis rather than focusing only on one method of thinking.
- *Fostering mindful awareness.* Using dialectical behavior therapy, therapists foster mindful observation and awareness in clients in an effort to help them live in the present rather than make judgments.
- *Working with imagery.* Through the use of imagery, metaphors, and stories to reduce negative images, clients are encouraged to visualize adaptive images and to embrace positive metaphors.
- *Brainstorming solutions.* As part of engaging in active problem solving, clients are encouraged to brainstorm alternative solutions to their negative views.
- *Providing psychoeducation.* Clients are educated about relevant issues and provided with information from theory and research to help with therapeutic change.

- *Supporting bibliography*. Relevant books and articles that support therapeutic learning are recommended.

2. *Decatstraphizing or ''what if'' technique*. This technique helps clients prepare for feared consequences.

3. *Reattribution*. Here techniques are used to test automatic thoughts and assumptions by considering alternative causes of events.

4. *Redefining*. By making a problem more concrete and specific, this technique is used to mobilize clients who may believe they have no control over their thinking.

5. *Homework*. Homework is used to give clients the opportunity to apply cognitive techniques and practice behavioral changes. "Typical homework assignments focus on self-observation and self-monitoring, structuring time effectively, and implementing procedures for dealing with concrete situations" (Corsini & Wedding, 2008, p. 286).

6. *Behavioral rehearsal and role playing*. These techniques are used to practice skills via modeling and role-playing that can be applied to real-life situations.

7. *Diversion techniques*. The use of physical activities, social contacts, work, play, and visual imagery helps clients reduce strong emotions and decrease negative thinking.

8. *Activity scheduling*. By helping clients rate the degree of mastery and pleasure experienced during each activity, they are encouraged to continue working on changing their thoughts and behaviors.

9. *Graduated task assignment*. In this technique, therapists encourage clients to begin an activity at a nonthreatening level. Therapists then gradually increase the difficulty of the assigned tasks.

(Beck, 1967; Beck, Rush, Shaw, & Emery, 1979; Beck, 1995; Brooks-Harris, 2008; Corey, 2009; Corsini & Wedding, 2008; Day, 2008; Frew & Speigler, 2008; Capuzzi & Gross, 2007; Gladding, 2004, and McMullin, 2000.)

These cognitive and behavioral techniques have proven useful with a wide variety of client populations, specifically children who are hyperactive-impulsive and aggressive, those who are socially isolated, college students struggling with test anxiety, elderly persons, and mentally ill persons. Other behavioral interventions also have been found to encourage a reversal of behavioral pathology and influence cognitive functioning; these include activity scheduling and graded task assignments.

Cognitive therapy has become widely used in recent years, most likely due to its broad applicability to brief and short-term therapies. Cognitive therapy has proven very effective in the treatment of depression and anxiety. As a result, it is one of the most commonly researched forms of psychotherapy today.

Group Applications

Group therapy is ideal for the application of cognitive and behavioral techniques. G. Corey (2004) notes that "REBT [rational emotive group therapy] aims at providing group members with tools for reducing or eliminating unhealthy emotions so that they can live richer and more satisfying lives" (p. 400). Sharf (2008) writes:

> *The goal of the REBT is to show clients how they are assessing, blaming, and damning themselves for their behaviors. The group also endeavors to help them stop devaluing other people and evaluate only their behaviors, not their self or personhood. (p. 329)*

Given the variety of techniques available, group leaders often can use various methods in the group setting to help members recognize their irrational thinking, understand underlying beliefs, and be able to think more rationally. Group therapy offers "practical ways to identify [clients'] underlying faulty beliefs, to critically evaluate such beliefs, and to exchange them for constructive beliefs" (G. Corey, 2004, p. 400).

Group therapists continually teach group members to take responsibility for their emotions while challenging them to pay attention to their own negative self-talk in order to substitute more rational and realistic alternatives. Through feedback from fellow members and the group leader, clients become increasingly aware of their core beliefs and how these beliefs have negatively impacted their lives. It is the leader's job to educate members how to challenge their assumptions and stop the vicious cycle of blaming others.

REBT group treatment is typically a very active therapy that employs many cognitive and emotive techniques (G. Corey, 2004; Ellis, 1996; Ellis & Dryden, 1997; Sharf, 2008). Group therapists must be open to continually questioning and challenging group members to recognize their irrational thinking. Both planned and spontaneously designed exercises are used to encourage such understanding and awareness.

Once members are in touch with their faulty thinking, the group leader must encourage them to actively experiment with new ways of thinking, feeling, and doing. The group leader must be knowledgeable regarding the many different types of techniques and exercises that are cognitive-behaviorally based and be willing to encourage their appropriate use. Ideally, group leaders take on the role of teachers, collaborators, and mentors; they are respectful of their clients and are generally both supportive and encouraging.

REBT group leaders are active in teaching the theoretical model, proposing methods of coping, and teaching members strategies to try out their new behaviors. They are also directive in encouraging members to actively participate during and outside the group. The structure group leaders provide enables the group to come alive; structure is also important in making sure that no member is neglected or monopolizes the group. Group leaders must be active in discussing the "progress or lack of progress of individual group members as well as the results of their previously assigned homework or their failure to complete their homework" (Sharf, 2008, p. 329). The techniques used are designed to help the group as a whole as well as to treat individual problems that are issues in the group. Basically, group members are provided with tools they can use in their daily lives that will increase their self-esteem and ability to learn more adaptive coping.

Group Illustration: Psychoeducational groups for anxiety and depression are ideal examples of cognitive-behavioral groups. Focus is on teaching group members about cognitive behavior therapy and cognitive restructuring. Since many anxious and depressed feelings are rooted in negative thinking, members are challenged to change their negative and irrational thoughts to more positive and rational ones. As time goes on, group members are increasingly able to think more positively and feel less anxious or depressed.

Systems Perspective

Earlier we discussed the importance of systems theory in working with clients. Practitioners who understanding the various systems clients interact with and are affected by provides them with a more comprehensive view of clients.

Developmental/Life-Span Therapy

Ivey (1991) suggests that "the purpose of counseling, therapy, and all helping interventions, is the facilitation of human development over the lifespan" (p. 18). Considering an individual's developmental stage allows for a more thorough understanding of the client; using developmental strategies can assist individuals to reach their fullest developmental potential (Alle-Corliss & Alle-Corliss, 1999; Ivey, 1991).

Essential Concepts

Developmental theory considers the attachments and separations that repeat throughout the lifespan. Emphasis is on understanding the views of developmentalist John Bowlby (1969), who believed that to understand and appreciate clients' attachment-separation issues, helpers must be able to identify their own developmental connections and separations. Additionally, "helpers must be able to understand their struggles and to encourage them to make the changes necessary to improve their lives. Without connecting with others, change is essentially impossible" (Alle-Corliss & Alle-Corliss, 1999, p. 102). Ivey (1991) addresses this issue of connection in this way:

> *Connection is as vital as separation. . . . We have twin tasks in our developmental progression. To survive, we must be simultaneously attached to others but also separate. Relationship, connection, and attachment provide a foundation for a sense of trust and intimacy. As we move through the developmental tasks of autonomy and identity, we must define our separate boundaries from our family and others. (p. 158)*

In order to gain a client's trust and rapport, helpers must serve as role models who are self-aware of their own developmental issues.

Group Applications

When conducting a group, group leaders must assess (1) at which specific stage of development individual group members are at and (2) how they are coping with the particular psychosocial crises or conflicts typical of that stage. Therapeutic interventions often center on helping group members achieve the tasks of their particular stage of development or determining what factors may have interfered with their ability to continue successfully to the next stage.

Employing a developmental framework may not be as simple as it appears. One must be able to conduct a thorough assessment to determine the client's developmental level and the best course of action. The developmental perspective is very versatile; it can be readily incorporated into most therapeutic approaches.

Group treatment can be effective in working with many types of developmental issues. For instance, children's groups are often determined by age and life-skills issues (consider the social skills groups common for latency-age children). Similarly, there are many types of groups for adolescents who struggle with identity and peer issues typical for this phase of life. Adults also join age-related groups, such as a young adults' group or one for individuals dealing with midlife issues. Reminiscing or support groups for older adults to deal with end-of-life issues also are common.

Group Illustration: A preteen developmental life skills group and young adults' group are examples of groups that focus primarily on developmental issues. In the preteen group, members are helped to prepare for adolescence and to deal with stage-related issues. Similarly, in young adults' groups, members are assisted in understanding the crisis of 'isolation and intimacy' that is common at their developmental stage.

Other Approaches

Erikson's Psychosocial Theory

Like Freud, Erikson was concerned with the inner dynamics of the personality. Erikson considered psychosocial forces to be major motivators in an individual's development over the lifespan and believed that individuals have the capacity to overcome many of their issues. He proposed that the personality evolves through systematic changes and focused on the individual through the lifespan. Erikson is credited with outlining an eight-stage developmental model, from infancy to old age, that each person passes through.

> *Erikson postulated that as we approach each stage, we are confronted with specific age-related developmental tasks or crisis to overcome and must establish an equilibrium between ourselves and our social world. When these tasks or developmental milestones are successfully mastered, a positive identity is created, and the individual is ready to move on to the next level. (Neukrug, 2004, p. 41)*

When a person is unable to conquer the developmental tasks at hand, a low self-image and bruised ego results, impairing the person's ability to master future developmental stages. In Erikson's view, all people face critical turning points in their lives and can either successfully resolve existing conflicts or crises and move on or fail to resolve these conflicts and regress. Whether individuals successfully resolve the conflicts or crises of each distinct stage or not, they still will be pushed forward by both biological maturation and social demands into the next stage.

In essence, Erikson's model encourages examination and resolution of unresolved issues so as to be able to move forward and develop fully. Group therapy is often an appropriate forum to work toward resolving issues that impede client movement to the next level of development. G. Corey (2009) believes that Erikson's framework for understanding developmental issues as they appear in therapy is a very helpful one: "The key needs and developmental tasks, along with the challenges inherent at each stage of life, provide a model for understanding some of the core conflicts clients explore in their therapy sessions" (p. 68).

Crisis Theory

Crisis intervention is a process whereby clients are assisted in finding adaptive solutions to crisis situations in their lives. Historically, like many of the theories we have discussed, crisis theory is rooted in psychoanalytic theory. Freud influenced current-day clinicians in his view of people as complex beings capable of self-discovery and change. His emphasis on listening to the client and encouraging catharsis (the expression of feelings about a traumatic event) continues to be important for helpers and is especially necessary for effective crisis intervention.

Eric Lindemann (1944) and Gerald Caplan (1964) are two of the most prominent pioneers in the field of crisis counseling (Gladding, 2004; James, 2008). Lindemann studied bereavement following the Coconut Grove fire in 1942 and was instrumental in defining the grieving process families went through after relatives' sudden death. His work led to the notion that grief work involves the process of mourning the loss, experiencing the pain of such loss, and eventually accepting the loss and adjusting to life without the loved person or object (Lindemann, 1944; Slaikeu, 1990). Lindemann found that people who "allow themselves to go through the normal process of grieving can prevent negative outcomes of crisis due to loss" (Hoff, 1989, p. 11). Lindeman's work on grief has contributed greatly to contemporary crisis theory.

In 1964, Caplan developed a conceptual framework for understanding crisis that emphasizes the need for clients to take charge and believe that they can overcome their loss and continue to grow. He was instrumental in suggesting that when a crisis can be resolved during the intense and vulnerable four to six weeks after the trauma, clients are less likely to develop psychiatric disorders (Slaikeu, 1990, p. 7). Caplan also contributed to the development of a communitywide approach to crisis intervention that emphasized prevention. He believed that providing brief training in crisis intervention to community volunteers and clergy could be helpful in assisting clients to return to their pre-crisis levels of functioning.

Crisis theory has evolved over the years. The advent of suicide prevention centers, and the grassroots movements involving Alcoholics Anonymous (AA), Vietnam veterans, and participants in the women's movement in the 1970s have helped "shape crisis intervention into an emerging specialty" (James, 2008, p. 7).

Since the 1980s, managed care has flourished throughout the mental health system. Managed care has led to a shift to brief and short-term therapies that emphasize a cognitive-behavioral stance that is tied to crisis theory, which characterizes a person's crisis as being sustained through his or her maladaptive behaviors, negative thoughts, and destructive defense mechanisms. Crisis (adapational) theory asserts that a person's crisis will subside when maladaptive coping behaviors are changed to more adaptive ones (Alle-Corliss & Alle-Corliss, 1999).

Essential Concepts

Crises are commonplace today in our fast-paced, stressful lives. Likewise, loss is inevitable. As a result, clients are often in need of guidance and support to get through a crisis and are more likely to seek brief crisis intervention therapy than longer-term treatment.

A crisis has been summarized as "a perception or experiencing of an event or situation as intolerable difficulty that exceeds the person's current resources and coping mechanisms" (James, 2008, p. 3). Caplan (1961, p. 18) defines a crisis similarly, as "an obstacle that is, for a time, insurmountable by the use of customary methods of problem-solving. A period of disorganization ensues, a period of upset, during which many abortive attempts at a solution are made."

When literally translated, the Chinese character for crisis means "opportunity in the midst of crisis." (Aguilera & Messick, 1982; James, 2008; Gilliland & James, 1993). Essentially, "a crisis can be seen as a turning point in a person's life: It is an opportunity for growth in that it may require decisions that can be life changing. A crisis is typically time-limited with the resolution either being positive (opportunity) or negative (danger). Often the chance for a positive outcome is heightened when professional services are sought and crisis intervention techniques are sought" (Alle-Corliss & Alle-Corliss, 1999, p. 108). Hoff (1989) notes that "successful crisis interventions involves helping people take advantage of the opportunity and avoid the danger inherent in crisis" (p. 8). Brammer (1985) adds that when individuals take advantage of the opportunity, "intervention can help plant the seeds of self-growth and self-realization" (p. 95).

Crises come in many different shapes and sizes. Four of the most common types are:

1. Developmental (tied to stages of life, such as birth of a child, marriage, retirement, etc.)
2. Situational (unexpected and unfortunate events, such as an accident, loss of a job, or sudden death of a loved one)
3. Existential (includes inner conflicts and anxieties related to issues of power, responsibility, independence, freedom, and commitment, such as reaching 50 and feeling despair)
4. Environmental (a natural or human disaster: a hurricane, earthquake, or act of terrorism, robbery, etc.) (Gladding, 2004; James & Gilliland, 2001).

As a summary, we outline the various characteristics of crises as identified by James (2008) and Gilliland and James (1993):

Presence of both danger and opportunity. A crisis can be a dangerous time when suicidal thinking is more prominent, yet it can also be an opportunity to deal with deeper emotions and develop more adaptive coping skills (Aguilera & Messick, 1982; Brammer, 1985; James, 2008).

Seeds of growth and change. Sometimes the discomfort and anxiety present during a crisis state are the impetus for change (Janosik, 1984).

Complicated symptomatology. Complicated symptomatology often exists during a crisis. Crises can be complex and difficult to understand for both clients and significant others. Also, crises can be more complicated to work through non-crisis situations as they may exist at individual, interpersonal, and social levels (Bass & Yep, 2002; Brammer, 1985).

No panaceas or quick fixes. The fact that there are no panaceas or quick fixes suggests that crisis interventions are ineffective in the long run.

Gilliland and James (1993) note that sometimes clients' conditions worsen because they did not seek appropriate help during their bout with a crisis. Interestingly, it is during a crisis, when defenses are lowered and clients are more motivated to look at themselves and experience deeper feelings, that change often occurs.

Necessity of choice. The necessity of choice exists at the very basic level in crisis situations. Clients have a choice: seek help and benefit from the opportunity to make changes in their lives or choose to not obtain assistance (Carkhuff & Berenson, 1977).

Universality and idiosyncrasy. Disequilibrium or disorganization accompany most crises: "universally because no one is immune to crisis, and idiosyncratic because each of us will experience and cope with a similar crisis in different ways" (Alle-Corliss & Alle-Corliss, 1999, p. 109; Janosik, 1984).

The central premise behind crisis intervention is to provide a client in need with prompt and skillful intervention. Theorists believe that immediate involvement can help restore the client's previous state of equilibrium, can help prevent the development of serious long-term problems, and, most optimistically, may allow new coping patterns to emerge that can help the individual function at a higher level of equilibrium than before the crisis.

Treatment begins at the first moment of contact with clients. Since clients feel disorganized, they require a clear, direct, and gentle approach with only several goals to work toward. The literature identifies six primary goals of crisis interventions that emphasize stabilizing and strengthening the client and his or her family system (Alle-Corliss & Alle-Corliss, 1999; Rapport, 1996; Roberts, 2000):

1. Relieve the acute stress sympotomatology.
2. Restore the client to optimal pre-crisis level of functioning.
3. Identify and understand the relevant precipitating event(s).
4. Identify remedial measures that the family can take or that the community resources can provide to remedy the crisis situation.
5. Establish a connection between the current stressful situation and past experiences.
6. Initiate client development of new ways of perceiving, thinking, and feeling and of adaptive coping resources for future use.

Common Strategies

A versatile and succinct ABC model was proposed by Kanel (1999). This three-step model involves:

A. Developing and maintaining contact.

B. Identifying the problem and therapeutic interaction.

C. Developing coping skills.

The next, more comprehensive nine-step approach to crisis intervention includes facets of the various crisis models identified in the literature (Alle-Corliss & Alle-Corliss, 1999; Belkin, 1984; Gilliland & James, 1993; James, 2008; James & Gilliland, 2003; Kanel, 1999; Roberts, 2000).

1. *Rapidly establish a constructive relationship.* Establish this relationship through active listening, developing rapport and trust, and being sensitive to client's feelings and circumstances.

2. *Elicit and encourage expression of painful feelings and emotions.* Anger, frustration, and feelings may be related to the current crisis.

3. *Discuss the precipitating event.* Examine details about how, when, and why the crisis occurred. Linkages to the past are made later.

4. *Assess strengths and needs.* Begin assessment at the onset of treatment with emphasis on client's strengths that when tapped can improve self-esteem and enhance motivation.

5. *Formulate a dynamic explanation.* Explore the meaning and perceptions of the crisis.

6. *Restore cognitive functioning.* Assist clients in identifying alternatives to resolving the crisis that focus on reasonable solutions they feel motivated to work toward.

7. *Plan and implement treatment.* Assist clients to formulate goals, objectives, and appropriate action steps that are prioritized. Active participation on behalf of the client is especially important.

8. *Terminate.* Ideally clients achieve their goals and the crisis is successfully resolved. The therapist reviews the precipitating events, the response(s), and the newly acquired coping skills that can be applied in the future.

9. *Follow-up.* Continued contact and/or further referrals may be necessary.

Group Applications

Group therapy to treat a variety of crisis-type situations is becoming the treatment of choice. Because clients who are in crisis often need support and the knowledge that they are not alone, groups are very appropriate after a crisis. According to Gray (1988), teens who have lost a loved one found support groups of their peers to be "most helpful" and did not want to be singled out or treated differently. James (2008, p. 449) adds that since teens lack experience with grief, and since "social influence is powerful and pervasive in a setting such as high school, the use of adolescent group grief work is an ideal strategy for controlling distortions and rumors and for helping young people release grief energy and begin to resolve their feelings of loss."

Groups have also been found to be helpful when working with loss. Bereavement among elderly persons is common; many types of losses are frequent. At any age, grief over loss of a loved one through death or separation and loss of status, as seen in retirement, can be dealt with successfully in a group where others struggle with similar feelings.

Groups have been found to be very effective in treating addictions. Lawson, Ellis, and Rivers (1984 UKATT Research Team, 2005) have found that because those suffering from chemical dependency benefit most from positive social interaction, that can replace the temptation of isolating themselves with their substance of choice. Dinkemeyer and Muro (1979) identify belonging, acceptance, affection, social interaction, equality, and development of a new self-concept as relationship needs that are best met by group treatment.

Group therapy also is often the treatment of choice in working with child sexual abuse. Groups are valuable for both children and adults molested as children. Realizing that one is not alone, receiving support, and feeling understood are some of the major benefits of group therapy.

In sum, group therapy for those suffering from a crisis can be very effective.

James (2008) shares his positive view of group:

The group format offers opportunities for peers to successfully confront clients in ways that the individual therapist can rarely, if ever, do. It allows them to learn more effective social skills, self-disclose threatening issues and try out new behaviors in a safe environment, increase focus on here-and-now activities rather than past events, emotionally invest in others as well as themselves, produce tension that promotes change, instill hope, and regain a sense of humor. (p. 339)

Group Illustration: Many agencies offer actual crisis groups that focus specifically on life crises, including trauma, loss, divorce, serious illness, family, and upheaval. Emphasis is on providing needed support and education on adaptive coping methods in hopes of helping members either return to their previous level of coping or move to a higher level of functioning.

Using an Integrative Approach

Given our present-day managed care system, where treatment services are often limited to crisis and brief treatment, an integrative approach to helping is indispensable. According to G. Corey (2009):

> *Since the early 1980s psychotherapy integration has developed into a clearly delineated field. It is now an established and respected movement that is based on combining the best of differing orientations so that more complete theoretical models can be articulated and more efficient treatment developed. (p. 448)*

This trend is well documented by many authors, who advocate incorporating the best of many orientations into an integrated approach that embodies the most applicable feature of a number of theoretical models. "An integrative focus involves selecting concepts and methods from a variety of systems to create a model that is most suitable for working with specific clients in a way that meets agency demands for brief treatment" (Alle-Corliss & Alle-Corliss, 1999, p. 106).

G. Corey (2009, p. 2) in *The Art of Integrative Counseling* defines an integrative approach as "rooted in a theory with techniques borrowed from other approaches and tailored to a client's unique needs." Arkowitz (1997) notes that since the late 1970s, practitioners have examined "various ways to cross school boundaries, integrate theories and techniques from two or more approaches, or suggest factors that the different therapies have in common" (p. 262).

Trends

Many reasons have been cited as being responsible for promoting this trend toward psychotherapy integration (Alle-Corliss & Alle-Corliss, 1999; Dattilio & Norcross, 2006; Norcross & Beutler, 2008; Norcross,

Karpiak, & Lister, 2005). Norcross and Newman (1992) cite eight specific motives that include:

1. Mere expansion of therapies
2. The fact that no one theoretical model is adequate to address the needs of all clients and all problems
3. The restrictions by insurance companies and healthcare companies that mandate short-term and brief treatment
4. The increased popularity of brief, short-term, and problem-focused therapies
5. The opportunity this climate provides clinicians to experiment with a variety of therapies
6. The disparity in effectiveness among existing therapies
7. Increased awareness that commonalities among therapies play a major role in determining therapy outcomes
8. The development of professional groups that encourage this integrative movement

Overall, the one major reason that accounts for this trend toward psychotherapy integration "is the recognition that no single theory is comprehensive enough to account for the complexities of human behavior, especially when the range of client types and their specific problems are taken into consideration" (G. Corey, 2009, p. 450). According to Okun (1990), the current emphasis on connecting theories is based on the basic premise that "no one theoretical viewpoint can provide all answers for the clients we see today" (p. xvi). Moreover, it is estimated that approximately 60% to 70% of professionals identify themselves as eclectic in their use of theory and techniques (Gladding, 2004; Lazarus & Beutler, 1993). According to Cheston (2000), clinicians tend to use various theories and techniques to meet their clients' needs, with an "average of 4.4 theories making up their therapeutic work with clients" (p. 254).

In our own practice, we have found an integrated approach preferable in accommodating the diversity of practitioners' styles and practice preferences. An integrative approach not only allows practitioners to adopt the facets of various theories and treatment modalities they have found most effective with their particular clientele but also provides helpers with more opportunities to tailor their treatment to meet specific client needs and to use the modalities they are most comfortable with and confident in (Alle-Corliss & Alle-Corliss, 1999, p. 107).

Despite the inherent benefits of using an integrative approach, there are some drawbacks; the main one is the element of choice offered to clinicians (Alle-Corliss & Alle-Corliss, 1999, p. 107). Neukrug (1994) writes that clinicians should "carefully reflect on their views of human nature and draw techniques that fit their ways of viewing the world. . . . [Unfortunately, he] has seen many individuals who call themselves eclectic use a hodgepodge of techniques, which may end up confusing the client" (p. 71). Others (G. Corey, 2009; Lambert, 1992) assert that since this process is an intricate one, much care is needed in selecting appropriate theories. Practitioners should be "committed to learning about various techniques and be open to deciding which key concepts of each approach best fit their personality. . . . The helper must always put the needs of the clients first in selecting treatment techniques" (Alle-Corliss & Alle-Corliss, 1999, p. 107).

In Closing

This chapter focused on the various theoretical orientations and perspectives that are important for practitioners to understand if they are going to be effective in providing individual and group counseling. Concepts of systems theory and the biopsychosocial approach were outlined along with a detailed presentation of psychodynamic Adlerian, person-centered, cognitive-behavioral, developmental, and crisis theories. Group applications for each of these theories were discussed and group examples provided. Chapter 5 marks the beginning of Part III, "Developing Agency Skills."

Developing Agency Skills

Part

Understanding Agency Systems and Diverse Client Populations

5

Understanding the agency system in which one works and the specific client populations most commonly served is instrumental in successful group development and practice. Alle-Corliss and Alle-Corliss (2006) speak to the importance of understanding agency systems and policies:

> *Knowledge of the agency setting can guide you in developing your skills as a helper [and group leader]. Furthermore, understanding your agency setting is crucial if you are to be successful in working cooperatively with others and fitting in with the agency's mission and goals. (p. 40)*

Helpers are encouraged to learn about the nuances and intricacies of their agency's systems. Not only is learning about the agency's policies, practices, strengths, and limitations helpful in creating an environment where learning is maximized, but it can also be essential in ensuring that agency support and cooperation exist with regard to group work.

The process of learning about the agency we work in enhances our ability to develop adaptive coping strategies to deal with various facets of agency life, such as rules and regulations and personnel issues. This knowledge might also enrich our ability to interact with other professionals at various levels, including management, that will allow us to optimize our professional role within the agency setting.

Similarly, understanding the many types of client populations seen within agency settings is important in designing programs and treatment modalities tailored to meet their specific needs. According to Toseland and Rivas (2009), "Diversity can be based on a variety of characteristics, such as race, ethnicity, culture, national origin, religion, social class, gender, sexual orientation, and disability" (p. 128). We elaborate on these and other areas of diversity in hopes of encouraging a diversity-sensitive approach.

Human Service Agencies: General Functions

In the text, the term *human service agency* will be used interchangeably with that of *human service organization*, as this is consistent with the literature. As the term implies, "the focus here is on agencies whose primary function is to meet the emotional, social, family, educational, psychological, and basic welfare needs of individuals, family, and groups" (Kanel, 2008, p. 330). According to Meenaghan and Gibbons (2000):

> *In the social service world, agencies are specific devices created in different community settings to assist people and groups in a variety of ways—to protect children, to provide families with needed support, to develop appropriate and necessary benefits for the elderly, and so on. Different people have figured out what services certain types of people need and what specific helping groups can or should offer, as a result a variety of programs have become routinized. (p. 25)*

Bragger and Halloway (1978) define human service organizations as "the vast array of formal organizations that have as their stated purpose enhancement of the social, emotional, physical, and/or intellectual well-being for some component of the population" (p. 2). Lauffer (1984) views organizations as "purposeful social units; that is, they are deliberately constructed to achieve certain goals or to perform tasks and conduct programs that might not be as effectively or efficiently performed by individuals or informal groups" (p. 14). Kanel (2008) defines an agency "as an organization that exists to achieve various goals and usually provides services directly or indirectly to the community. The functioning of an agency is usually organized through the establishment of positions that work together to provide services" (p. 330). Alle-Corliss and Alle-Corliss (2006) summarize:

> *Overall, organizations consist of many individuals who perform specified roles in an effort to provide needed services to certain populations in the community. Certain positions such as manager, line worker, and support staff organize the functioning of the agency. These employees make a*

coordinated effort to work together and integrate services in a way that is supportive to all. (p. 43)

Woodside and McClam (2009) note: "Many human services are provided within the context of an agency or organization in a community or a geographic area. This context or environment for human service delivery is important to those who work within its structure and boundaries" (p. 223).

We concur with the assertion that it is important to understand this context in order to be able to "assist clients, to deliver effective services, and to develop needed policies and services. . . . Agencies and organizations set the parameters or boundaries of the work of their employees" (Woodside & McClam, 2009, p. 223).

Systems Theory

Systems theory is also useful for understanding interrelationships within agencies and organizations. Viewing an agency as a system is well documented in the literature (Alle-Corliss & Alle-Corliss, 2006; Brill & Levine, 2002; Neukrug, 2004; Sweitzer & King, 2009; Woodside & McClam, 2009). Sweitzer and King (2009) define a system as "a group of people with common purpose who are interconnected such that no one person's actions or reactions can be fully understood without also understanding the influence on that person of everyone else in the system" (p. 133). Brill and Levine (2002) describe a system as

a whole made up of interrelated parts. The parts exist in a state of balance, and when change takes place within one, there is a compensatory change within the other parts. Systems become more complex and effective by constant exchange of both energy and information within their environment. . . . A system is not only made up of interrelated parts, but is itself an interrelated part of a larger system. (p. 74)

As implied in this quote, each system or agency is part of a larger system, yet most agencies can also be broken down into smaller subsystems. An example presented by Sweitzer and King (2009) is that of a family service center, which "can be broken down into various programs it runs. However, it is also part of a system of service providers in the city or town in which it operates. An external examines the relationships between a system and other related systems" (p. 133).

Agency Mission, Goals, Objectives, and Values

It is important to learn about the agency's mission, goals, and objectives, as they are all influential in determining overall agency functioning. Kiser (2008) asserts that "a clear statement of an organization's mission, objectives, goals and strategies is central to its efficient functioning" (p. 46). Sweitzer and King (2009) note that "the mission, goals, and values of an organization tell you in an official and explicit way what that organization is all about and what makes it distinctive" (p. 133).

Woodside and McClam (2009) suggest locating the agency's "mission statement," as it usually "communicates the purpose of the agency by summarizing its guiding principles" (p. 224). It is often in this "mission statement" that such important facts as the population served, the broad goals of the agency, the type and sources of funding, the values that impact decision making, the agency structure, and the agency's priorities are detailed (Kiser, 2008; Lewis, Lewis, Packard, & Souflee, 2006). In a sense, the agency's identity is reflected in this statement, which "also conveys important information, directly or indirectly, about the agency's philosophy of helping and the values that underpin its efforts" (Kiser, 2008, p. 46).

Most agencies have a formal written policy manual where this mission statement is readily found. Often this statement is well known to both the staff and clientele served, yet sometimes this statement is vague and not well documented; much hinges on who actually authored the mission statement. Sweitzer and King (2009) share that "there will most likely be greater investment and awareness of mission statements that were arrived at collaboratively, as opposed to those created by one or two people and then handed down" (p. 135). Interestingly, learning how the mission statement actually came about can provide helpful information about formal and informal aspects of agency functioning.

Equally as important is learning about agency goals and objectives, which tend to be more specific than a mission statement in spelling out the "what" and "how." Goals are general desired outcomes the agency is attempting to accomplish; objectives are more specific and measurable targets. "Objectives are written or discussed in more specific, measurable language and are effective in focusing and directing more immediate efforts" (Kiser, 2008, p. 47).

As with the mission statement, there will be variations on how goals and objectives are presented; on one end of the continuum are agencies where goals and objectives are explicitly written; at the other end are those agencies where goals and objectives are unwritten and informal in nature.

Generally, when an agency is clear about its purpose and direction, there is a greater likelihood that it will be more successful in reaching its target. Specific strategies can be employed toward this end. Specialized programs, services, and activities can be planned, designed, and implemented to accomplish these goals and objectives (Weiner, 1990). "The[se] strategies include not only the services and programs directed toward clients but also such behind-the-scenes administrative efforts as supervision, fund raising, staff training, and continuing education" (Kiser, 2008, p. 47).

Strategies used by agencies will vary greatly, even if similar goals and objectives are pursued. For instance, let us assume that two agencies have identified a goal of reducing no-show rates for intakes. The first agency may decide to double-book clients; the latter may develop a more detailed screening process, such as an orientation group that clients must attend in order to be scheduled for intake appointments. The difference in strategies may be in large part due to different ideas and philosophies within each agency about how to reach set goals.

Values held by both line staff and management will have an impact on which strategies will be chosen. Morales and Sheafor (1995) note that the operational aspects of human services are affected by values. Alle-Corliss and Alle-Corliss (2006) concur:

> *Values are all important: Much of professional helping consists of making decisions based on values. . . . Decisions about the how, when, and why of service delivery are often motivated by the values of administrators, funding sources, and practitioners. (p. 15)*

Being aware of the different individuals involved in planning and service delivery and their respective values is important in gaining an overall understanding of the agency, its goals and objectives, and the specific strategies it employs. Value conflicts between upper management and line staff, for instance, are also important to note, as these may impact service delivery, directly or indirectly. Meenaghan and Gibbons (2000) note that "practice can be shaped in two major directions. First, the practitioner as a potential actor can be tightly constrained by existing organizational rules and guidelines. . . . Second, organizations can be committed to certain goals that encourage practitioners to expand existing service responses" (p. 23).

Agency Structure: Formal and Informal

Knowledge of how the agency is structured, both formally and informally, is also important in being able to successfully engage in treatment planning and implementation. Basically, it is the structure of an agency that determines how it will accomplish its goals (Bolman & Deal, 2003). In terms of developing groups, the more information one has regarding the agency structure, the easier it will be to seek the appropriate support and guidance.

Formal Organizational Structure

Since the human services field is so broad, it would be unrealistic for any one agency or organization to provide comprehensive services to everyone in need. For this reason, many different types of agencies exist to meet the divergent needs of varying populations. In most of these agencies, "formal structures and policies have been developed to ensure uniformity and continuity in the delivery of services . . . [and] policies and procedures are spelled out in some formal manner" (Alle-Corliss & Alle-Corliss, 2006, p. 53). Typically, agencies have a written formal agency policy and procedures manual that outlines rules, regulations, and procedures. It is important to be aware of what is spelled out in this manual in order to understand the standards of practice of a particular agency. Likewise, it is essential to understand the ramifications of not following protocol. In most cases, the policies and procedures identified in the agency manual are meant to serve as guiding principles for practice.

Most agencies also have formal organizational structures that specify lines of command and are intended to promote cohesiveness and efficiency. According to Woodside and McClam (2009), learning about how an agency is organized is another way to understand the agency and its purpose: "This is the structure of the agency, and it refers to the relationships among the people who work there and the departments to which they are assigned" (p. 225). Hansenfeld (1983) believes that most organizations establish an internal structure that defines the authority of each person and the mechanisms of coordination among them. The Weberian view of how organizations are structured describes the hierarchical distribution of power and authority, according to which responsibilities and operating decisions are delegated to different members of the organization (Alle-Corliss & Alle-Corliss, 2006; Weber, 1946). For instance, in a mental health agency, the typing is given to the secretary, the child abuse report to the social welfare worker, the suicide crisis calls to an on-duty clinician, and the budget issues to the administrator. As such, "roles and positions become specialized and the organization's activities formalized and standardized" (Alle-Corliss & Alle-Corliss, 2006, p. 54).

This chain of command "refers to the layers of authority in an agency" with those at the top of the chain typically in "control of resources and actions" (Woodside and McClam, 2009, p. 226). Although not always true, in most agencies, the lines of authority emerge from the top. The next excerpt about structures within agency environments illustrates this point perfectly.

> *For some agencies, the chain of command is hierarchical and with defined responsibilities and accountability from top to bottom. Each person is accountable for those under his or her supervision. Other agencies have a flatter chain of command. This means that there are fewer layers of authority from top to bottom so that decision making is more of a shared responsibility. (Woodside & McClam, 2009, p. 226).*

Sweitzer and King (2009) concur in the view that there are two basic elements of organizational structure: division of responsibilities and coordination of work. A simplistic example of typical hierarchical distribution of power found in many nonprofit agencies, outpatient, and mental health agencies is:

Board of directors
Administrative director
Clinical director
Supervisors
Clinical staff
Support staff

Most agency policy and procedure manuals use an organizational chart. Such charts have been identified in literature as valuable tools in better understanding the structure of an agency system. A typical organizational chart "identifies by job title the various positions in the agency and reflects who reports to whom within the system. The organizational chart conveys information about how the agency is organized to accomplish its work" (Kiser, 2008, p. 49). Sweitzer and King (2009) note as well that "the authority structure of an organization defines the chain of command, and this chain is visible in the organizational chart. . . . An organizational chart also give you an easy view of the length and complexity of the chain of command" (p. 141). Logically, the larger and more traditional an agency system is, the more likely it is to be more bureaucratic with a pyramid-type chart with a vertical organization. In contrast, smaller agencies, as well as "those with less traditional nonhierarchical management philosophies," are likely to be organized in a more horizontal than vertical manner. "These organizations use more peer supervision and collaborative methods of organizing and conducting their work" (Kiser, 2008, p. 49).

Alle-Corliss and Alle-Corliss (2006) encourage the use of organizational charting in learning more about:

- Formal hierarchical dimensions
- Formal relationships between positions
- Issues of independence
- Areas of potential conflicts
- Communication and work flow
- Organizational setup

Informal Agency Structure

Because we do not live in an ideal world, it is also important to understand the informal structure that exists in many agencies. Sometimes real life does not match the formal and official organizational structure. Kiser (2008) notes that "the patterns of communication, relationships, and influences that emerge in the day-to-day structure of the agency are referred to as its informal organizational structure" (p. 50). Alle-Corliss and Alle-Corliss (2006) echo this: "Informal agency structure includes all the policies, rules, and norms that are unspoken and unwritten, yet clearly govern the behavior of workers" (p. 54). Certainly, the more similar the formal and informal structures are, the greater the likelihood that the organization will function more effectively (Ethers, Austin, & Prothero, 1976; Halley, Kopp, & Austin, 1998; Kiser, 2008; Scott & Lynton, 1952).

In order to be successful working in an agency setting, it is essential to be knowledgeable about both formal and informal aspects of agency life. Learning about formal policies helps guide one in procedural issues, while learning about, informal structure assists in the development of relationships with key people in the agency. Daily interactions with staff, information seeking, and keen observational skills are the best sources of this critical information. When considering soliciting support for an existing group or funding for a proposed group program, knowledge about the agency's informal structure is just as important as knowledge about its formal organization.

In addition to informal structure, it is important to identify informal groups within an agency. Since informal groups are inevitable in most organizations and often are influential as well, it is important to understand their functions and personalities. It is important to take time to understand the actual or real agency structure by learning existing communication patterns, formal and informal roles and norms, the existence of cliques, management style, and awareness of any efforts to encourage staff development (Alle-Corliss & Alle-Corliss, 2006; Baird, 2002; Faiver, Eisengart, & Collona, 2004; Kiser, 2008; Royse, Dhooper, & Rompf, 1999; Sweitzer & King, 2009). Information about any of these factors can help in navigating within the agency system. Kiser (2008) suggests that "your ability to 'fit in' with a particular agency depends in part on your ability to discern and follow the currents and crosscurrents of its formal and informal operations" (p. 50). Similarly, Alle-Corliss and Alle-Corliss (2006) encourage asking questions that will result in better understanding the formal and informal aspects of the agency: "The search for answers will expose you to the structure (formal and informal) of the agency and help you recognize early on who you can trust, learn from, and develop a supportive relationship with" (p. 56). In all, this information can be useful in "surviving" within the agency and in determining the most strategic ways to plan and implement needed services, including groups.

A very important part of understanding the informal aspects of an agency setting is considering the diversity that exists among coworkers. There will undoubtedly be a great variety of personalities within an agency; differences in style and theoretical orientations are also to be expected. Taking time to recognize, accept, and respect these differences will allow for a more positive work environment. Ideally, learning to work through possible conflicts resulting from these differences is preferable to becoming resistant and closed off to any cooperative interplay.

Meenaghan and Gibbons (2000) discuss the role of organizational culture, which "simply means shared or prevailing values and norms that guide the behavior of members or a group and that provide a context and perspective for their aspirations and expectations. Culture, as an idea, can thus be applied to very small systems—families, groups, and

Table 5.1 Types of Organizational Cultures

1. ***Humanistic helpful culture.*** Encourages active participation in the organization. People are expected to help each other, to grow, and to invest their time and energy in each other.
2. ***Affiliative culture.*** Emphasizes a network of positive relationships among people. Positive behavior in this culture means friendliness, expression of feelings, and recognition of the group's needs.
3. ***Approval culture.*** Stresses avoidance of conflict or even strong dissonance. People actively seek acceptance from others and feel the need to be liked.
4. ***Conventional culture.*** Emphasizes tradition and strong commitment to long-standing patterns. The structure stresses conformity and adherence to rules.
5. ***Dependent culture.*** Stresses the centrality of a few leaders within a vertical hierarchy. Participation is not promoted, and superiors are consulted before decisions are made.
6. ***Avoidant culture.*** Highlights the need to not fail or make mistakes. When people make errors, they shift responsibility to others for fear of being punished.
7. ***Oppositional culture.*** Emphasizes the rejection of ideas and innovation. People's status is often tied to their criticism of ideas and others.
8. ***Power culture.*** Stresses nonparticipation by most people. Certain positions are key, inasmuch as they control those below them while giving the few positions above major attention.
9. ***Competitive culture.*** Stresses people's relative performance. Rewards accrue to performance winners, and people see themselves as working against each other.
10. ***Competence culture.*** Accents a relentless need to do everything, everything well, and everything on time. People are expected to do extra work, show persistence, and adhere to the structure.
11. ***Achievement culture.*** Emphasizes doing things well and promotes people who define their own goals related to organizational goals. Energy is focused within the organization and its members.
12. ***Self-actualization culture.*** Accents creativity, uniqueness, and doing routine activities in out-standing ways. People are expected to grow as individuals, enjoy their work, and initiate new activities or meet new challenges.

Source: Adapted from McGregor (1960); Meenaghan & Gibbons (2000).

organizations" (p. 32). According to Schein (1985), human service organizations are now better understood because of cultural analysis. In 1960, McGregor examined the topics of organizational perspective and atmosphere and found that all organizations, especially in human services, are defined by how they stress two particular considerations: task and interpersonal support for staff. In 1989, McGregor's work was expanded by the notion suggesting that organizations that embody and reflect cultural properties can be categorized into one or more of 12 cultural types (see Table 5.1).

Resources: Funding

Learning about the funding sources of a particular agency is helpful in better understanding the agency and is essential to planning and service delivery. Finding out about the annual budget and how it is broken down into various categories is key. "Funding, of course, provides the under-pinning for the work and sets crucial parameters. . . . It is also important to know how the budget is set, who must approve it, and how changes are negotiated" (Sweitzer & King, 2009, p. 133, 137). Agencies are often categorized by their funding sources, with three specific agency types identified as: (1) public or governmental agencies, (2) private nonprofit agencies, and (3) private for-profit agencies (Alle-Corliss & Alle-Corliss, 2006; Kanel, 2008; Kiser, 2008; Sweitzer & King, 2009; Woodside & McClam, 2009).

Public or Governmental Agencies
Public agencies are typically governmental entities (federal, state, re-gional, county, municipal, and city) whose main purpose is to provide services to designated target areas. Examples of public agencies include: social welfare or department of social services, mental health, correc-tional, health centers, senior agencies, and schools and other educational agencies. Funding for public agencies comes from tax revenues at the federal, state, and/or local level and/or other governmental funding sources, such as foundation support or grant money. In most cases, public agencies are accountable to the specified legislative bodies that determine their budget. Kanel (2008) notes that since most public or governmental agencies are very large, a highly structured approach to organizing the many services offered is necessary. Because of this need,

> *most government-run human service agencies operate under a classic bureaucratic model . . . [that] allows for efficiency and achievement of organizational goals. This structured approach emphasizes task specializa-tion and matching individual workers to appropriate positions. Manage-ment must ensure that workers understand their roles and must maintain worker morale for the good of the organization. (p. 334)*

As noted, public agencies tend to be large and operate in a vertical authority structure, which is typically complex and rule driven; there are many procedures to follow and a great deal of additional paperwork (Alle-Corliss & Alle-Corliss, 2006; Birkenmaier & Berg-Weger, 2007; Sweitzer & King, 2009).

Negative aspects of working in a bureaucratic system include "their devotion to routine, inflexible rules, red tape, procrastination, and reluctance to assume responsibility or to experiment" (Alle-Corliss & Alle-Corliss, 2006, p. 40). "Mandatory paperwork, accountability, hier-archy, and reluctance to modify programs" are additional criticisms

(Kanel, 2008, p. 334). Despite these drawbacks, public or governmental agencies are generally stable, pay well, and have good benefits, such as health insurance, sick leave, and vacation pay. Furthermore, there is often a well-organized hierarchy in place, and often the services offered are the only ones available to target populations. Without many public-run agencies in place, many client populations would not have a place to seek needed services.

Private Nonprofit Agencies

Private nonprofit agencies also provide services to those in need. As with public agencies, these agencies may be structured in a bureaucratic manner. They usually are governed by an elected volunteer board of directors and employ both professional and volunteer staff to provide services to clients in the community (Alle-Corliss & Alle-Corliss, 2006; Kramer, 1981). Also, "some nonprofit agencies deal with clients who receive direct [face-to-face] services from the agency itself. Other agencies provide an arena for fund-raising and community outreach and education," as seen in United Way, the American Red Cross, Easter Seals, and the American Heart Association (Kanel, 2008, p. 337). These agencies provide the community with needed education and distribute money they have raised to direct-service organizations.

Many private nonprofit agencies are governed by the human relations model, which differs greatly from the bureaucratic model, as it is more casual and client focused. During the 1960s and 1970s, the human relations model became an alternative method of providing services to those who were resistant to government policy and philosophies. The focus of this model is "more on client needs and program development rather than on numbers and accountability" (Kanel, 2008, p. 338). Since donations and fundraising events flourished during the 1960s, 1970s, and 1980s, and many professional services were provided by volunteers, the number of private nonprofit agencies grew. During the 1990s and 2000s, some changes in funding occurred; there was more reliance on special grants and funding through government programs. As a result, more paid professional staff were hired, and the infrastructure naturally became more complex and policy driven (Brueggermann, 1996; Kanel, 2008; McAdam, 1986; Weinstein, 1994).

Funding for these private nonprofit organizations is primarily from "private sources, such as religious organizations, foundations, individual contributions, grants, and fund-raising proceeds" (Kiser, 2008, p. 51). Additionally, federal, state, and local revenues may be provided through grants for specific initiatives. Ortiz (1995) cites cases where the government purchases services from these private agencies that are in the form of contracts. Woodside and McClam (2009) add that "the distinction between public and not-for-profit [nonprofit] agencies is not always clear because not-for-profit [nonprofit] agencies are increasingly providing services for public agencies on a contractual basis" (p. 227). The topic of revenues is important to discuss here. *Revenues* refers to the funding an agency receives from four primary sources: (1) federal, state, and local governments; (2) grants and contracts; (3) fees; and (4) donations. In many instances, a nonprofit agency may receive funding from a few if not all of these sources.

Private nonprofit agencies often feel a certain amount of economic stress because their funding comes from a variety of sources and requires them to be accountable to a variety of entities. Others might consider having multiple funding sources as a plus, as the organization does not depend solely on one source of income (Alle-Corliss & Alle-Corliss, 2006; Birkenmaier & Berg-Weger, 2007; Sweitzer & King, 2009).

As with public agencies, there are both advantages and disadvantages to private nonprofit agencies. As we have noted, the downside for most private nonprofit agencies is the instability of funding and the tendency to pay lower salaries. On the positive side, pluses include:

- Increased flexibility in hiring community-college- and bachelor-level human service workers
- A more informal work environment that emphasizes program development and client needs
- Increased autonomy and flexibility in work hours
- Increased opportunity to give back to the community
- Increased job satisfaction by being able to partake in the helping profession that possesses altruistic benefits
- Ability to work in a professional capacity with others who are equally motivated to helping

Many private nonprofit agencies exist today, including:

- Family service agencies that provide crisis intervention, parenting classes, counseling, respite care for the elderly, teen programs, and anger management groups
- American Red Cross and the United Way
- Agencies such that deal with social and child welfare concerns, mental health needs, educational programs, and correctional issues

Staff is composed of professional, paraprofessional, nonprofessional, and volunteers whose goal is to provide needed services to the community.

Private For-Profit Agencies

In the 1990s and 2000s, reduced funding for public agencies, limited resources for private nonprofit organizations, and changing economic and political times have led to an increase in private for-profit organizations. Kiser (2008) refers to these types of organizations as "proprietary social agencies," which were "initially funded by one or more individuals who invest their personal resources into the development of the organization" (p. 52). These agencies have a dual function:

1. To provide a service: medical or mental health services, education, rehabilitation
2. To make a profit while doing so (Alle-Corliss & Alle-Corliss, 2006; Kanel, 2008; Kiser, 2008)

Private for-profit agencies typically are funded by consumer fees and contracts. The 1990s saw the advent of privatization and managed care (Goodman, Brown, & Dietz, 1992). *Privatization* is "the shifting of government responsibilities to private entities, and effectiveness in the provision of services" (Alle-Corliss & Alle-Corliss, 2006, p. 47). In the human services sector, privatization includes assigning responsibility to nonprofit entities for any of these tasks: needs assessments, funding, policy making, program development, service provision, monitoring, and evaluation. *Managed care* is "an umbrella term for heath care insurance systems that contract with a network of hospitals, clinics, and private providers who agree to accept set fees for each service or flat payments per patient. Managed care involves patient care that is not determined solely by the provider" (Burger, 2008, p. 48). Estimates suggest that today in the United States there is a noticeable increase in the percentage of group health insurance coverage that is administered through managed care organizations. This increase is in part due to an effort to lower health care costs. Additional benefits are the increased emphasis on primary prevention and early detection of problems (Neukrug, 2008, p. 307).

As noted, much like nonprofit agencies, some for-profit agencies also receive reimbursement for their services from state, federal, and/or local funds and may qualify for third-party reimbursement from medical insurance companies and clients who pay out-of-pocket for services (Garner, 1995; Kiser, 2008; Sweitzer & King, 2009; Woodside & McClam,

2009). Fees for services provided by private agencies are generally higher than those of public or nonprofit agencies.

Examples of private for-profit agencies include private inpatient mental health and substance abuse facilities, educational institutions, nursing homes, group homes for the mentally challenged, and rehabilitation (Barker, 1996). Private mental health practitioners fit this category as well. Sweitzer and King (2009) stress that in this case, "the source of funding has great power and influence over the organization, since a formal diagnosis is required before treatment is authorized by insurance companies (p. 139). The last type of private agencies we will mention is perhaps the most widely used: health maintenance organizations (HMOs) (Kanel, 2008, p. 10). In the early 1900s, HMOs emerged with the main focus on keeping families healthy and providing early interventions and preventive care. The passage of the Health Maintenance Act of 1973 lead to an increase in HMOs, which began to be considered instrumental in maintaining health versus a system only for treating illnesses (DeLeon, Uyeda, & Welch, 1985). Enrollees in HMOs pay a prepaid, fixed payment for specific health and psychiatric services. HMOs often are criticized for their goal of seeking a profit by keeping their enrollees healthy in order to limit their use of the various health services to which their payments entitle them. Also, some physicians and mental health practitioners who work for HMOs feel

> *their decisions about who needs services and for how long are being micromanaged by HMO's. The policies mandated by an HMO often reduce the autonomy by which many mental health workers typically practice. Because people pay less for HMO mental health services, private practitioners may feel in competition with HMO's. (Kanel, 2008, p. 223)*

Benefits of HMOs include:

- Successful treatment of multineed clients by mental health practitioners
- Treatment of substance abuse
- Provision of educational services
- Use of a multidisciplinary team model
- A smoother referral process
- Use of more effective, brief, cost-efficient treatment modalities
- Comprehensive services that often are centrally located
- Brief, cost-effective treatment

Specific funding for HMOs is often split among client copayments, payments by insurance from a client's place of employment, and some third-party payments from Medicare and Medicaid.

Other Resources

In addition to available funding, agencies may have other types of resources, such as "buildings, land, staff, and short-term goods like equipment, supplies and . . . the skills and talents of the employees of the organization [such as] artistic abilities, physical strength, creativity, fund-raising ability, and a talent for advocacy" (Woodside & McClam, 2009, p. 228). Human resources are perhaps the most valuable in the sense that most helping occurs on a more personal level.

Special Issues

Legal and Political Issues

Recognition of the legal and political issues that may be at play within the agency is vital to successful interactions with both coworkers and administrators. Kerson (1994) underscores this in his view that the agency's legal, social, and political contexts strongly influence the overall functioning of that agency. On a macro level, it is important to understand the particular social policy issues that may be present. *Social policy* is "a set of carefully chosen guidelines that steer present and future decisions" regarding the well-being of individuals within a particular environment (Halley et al., 1998, p. 97). Kiser (2008) asserts that "because 'social policy' guides program and service development, existing social policy affects how human service professionals intervene with clients and address human problems" (p. 62). Since many of the issues tied to social policy may seem out of the scope of an individual practitioner, it is easy to dismiss them. We encourage the opposite. Time is well spent in learning about how practice and policy within an organization are tied to legal, social, and political forces at the local, state, and federal levels.

Equally important, although less formalized, are the attitudes, values, and opinions prevalent within the given agency. Sometimes these views have a major impact on which programs are implemented and which are not; also, they often set a tone within the agency that can increase or reduce morale. Becoming aware of organizational politics is key to success in practice and program development. By viewing the agency through the political frame, it becomes easier to see how agencies are made up of different coalitions with differing agendas (Bolman & Deal, 2003). By looking through this lens, one can also see how decisions about funding are made and the realties about the actual power and influence within an agency. Alle-Corliss and Alle-Corliss (2006) suggest that a great deal can be learned about an agency's formal and informal structure and politics through observation and inquisitiveness: "Observing how workers interact with each other, as well as with the administration and upper management, can give you insights into the functioning of the organization" (p. 55).

Community Needs

In addition to learning about the agency environment, it is equally as important to learn about the community in which the agency operates and the resources that exist. Since "agencies and communities are dynamic, constantly sifting in response to social, political and economic change," it is important to be aware of these aspects as well (Woodside & McClam, 2009, p. 223). We have already noted the importance of social policy and its connection to the community. Becoming aware of the many ways the community impacts both direct and indirect practice is also necessary. For instance, learning about the environment in which the agency exists leads to a better understanding of how it operates, the services it provides, the clients it serves, and the professionals it employs.

Interacting with other professionals within the community is important in learning about community resources (and what other services are offered), in making connections, and in developing support systems that can help with networking. The referral process is enhanced when practitioners are aware of resources that exist within and outside of the agency. Referrals are most successful when there is a positive relationship between the referring human service professional and other professionals. Human service agencies are said to "form an interdependent web of support and cooperation with one another" (Kiser, 2008, p. 53). It is important to view conflict that exists among agencies that are competing for the same resources or clients as natural and predictable and to encourage a positive resolution. Brueggemann (2006) believes that agencies that have a strong history of working together are better able to identify the sources of conflict and resolve them productively.

Also critical is determining how much the agency staff connects with the community. It has been found advantageous to have agency staff become part of the communities where they are located. "This means offering services within the context of client-identified needs; anticipating reactions to differences in race, ethnicity, attitudes, and roles represented by human service professionals; and planning for interactions among clients and helpers" (Woodside & McClam, 2009, p. 228).

Since "capturing information about your agency's community will be a multifaceted, complex task" (Kiser, 2008, p. 58), we encourage using a variety of resources, including: community needs assessments, U.S. Census reports, appropriate web sites (state and local government, special interest groups, etc.), contact with community leaders, interaction with professionals from other agencies, and direct contact with individuals residing in the community itself.

Homan (2004) is an excellent resource for those who are interested in additional information about working with communities. He offers these suggestions in getting to know one's community:

> *Get to know the basic characteristics of the people in your community. Grasp how the community functions to meet its needs. Identify unmet community needs, and understand what improvements may be needed as you go about making a difference in your community. Most important, evaluate the resources your community has on hand as well as ones it could develop. This information will help you to better gauge its capacity to work toward change. (p. 177)*

Potential Problems

Every agency has its own personality so to speak, with both strengths and limitations. Problems identified in many human service organizations include: inertia, limited information, fracturing of specialized units, and staff alienation. Meenaghan and Kilty (1993) have identified these additional problems commonly found in human services:

- *Access.* Clients may not be able to access care at all or have difficulty doing so in a timely manner.

- *Utilization.* Certain individuals may be cooled out or discouraged from receiving services and therefore less apt to utilize available services.

- *Coordination/duplication.* Several agencies may provide the same type of services and may even duplicate services. Meenaghan and Kilty (1993) note that "when organizations focus excessively on duplicate services, they are unlikely to be scanning the environments for unmet needs, changing needs, and so on" (p. 30).

- *Decision base and decision structure.* In some organizations, rational decision making may be impaired due to limited and/or inadequate data available. In other cases, the information gathered may not be used effectively in making ongoing organizational decisions, or the organization may have an incomplete decision structure.

- *Program contingencies and ongoing planning process.* Some agencies are not organized in an efficient manner and tend to respond in a reactive mode when a crisis occurs.

- *Intraorganizational staff relations.* In human service agencies, interpersonal tensions and conflicts often are assessed as individual problems. Meeneghan and Kilty (1993) add that sometimes workers or different units within an organization engage in serious conflict largely because of role ambiguity and uncertainty about their rights and responsibilities.

In order to ensure that human service organizations function at their optimal level, it is necessary to take time to determine if any of these problems exist or are likely. Efforts to improve agency functioning can occur only if problems are first identified. Then preventive and interventive measures can follow.

Diverse Client Populations

Human services are provided within agencies that often specialize in treating target populations. "Due to the specialization within the field, most agencies have a specific segment of the population as their target group" (Kiser, 2008, p. 23). In order to be the most effective in providing services, including developing and engaging in group treatment, it is essential to have a solid knowledge base of the populations most commonly served by the agency in which one works. Learning to work with diversity is a prerequisite for any human services provider.

> *For the practitioner working with different populations and a myriad of issues, the value of becoming diversity sensitive, knowledgeable, and skilled is crucial. Practice is less likely to be effective unless the helper considers the multidimensions of people's lives. (Alle-Corliss & Alle-Corliss, 1999, p. 246)*

Toseland and Rivas (2009) emphasize the importance "for leaders to develop a perspective on how to work with people whose backgrounds are different from their own" (p. 128).

In order to understand the value of learning about the many client groups one is likely to work with, we begin by discussing the multi-faceted concept of diversity. The term *diversity* has been defined in numerous ways. According to the Office for Equal Opportunity and Diversity Management (2003), *diversity* refers to many demographic variables, including age, color, disabilities, gender, national origin, race, religion, and sexual orientation. Kaiser Permanente (2004) states:

> *Diversity is a mosaic of people who bring a variety of backgrounds, styles, perspectives, values and beliefs as assets to the groups with which they interact. Diversity extends far beyond the obvious dimensions of ethnicity and gender. People are similar and different on an infinite number of dimensions. By viewing the idea of ''valuing diversity'' as something that is equally relevant to all of us, it becomes inclusive to everyone. (p. 2)*

Pedersen (2000) categorizes diverse groups by:

- Ethnographic variables (nationality, ethnicity, language, and religion)
- Demographic variables (age, gender, and place of residence [geographic location])
- Status variables (educational and socioeconomic background)
- Formal and informal affiliations

All of these views fit our perspective, since diversity not only emphasizes the importance of culture, race, and ethnicity but goes beyond by including socioeconomic status, age, gender, sexual orientation, disability status, religion or spirituality, and geographic location (Alle-Corliss & Alle-Corliss, 1999, 2006; Arredondo, 2002; Capuzzi & Gross, 2007; Lum, 2004).

Next we review each of these areas of diversity individually by presenting salient issues. Although it is beyond the scope of this chapter to provide a detailed description of each of these populations, we introduce important topics that illustrate their uniqueness. Specific treatment considerations for each group are presented in Part IV of this volume.

Diversity in the United States

Neukrug (2008) asserts that the United States is the most diverse country in the world—"a country that is truly a conglomerate of ethnic groups, races, cultures, and religions" (p. 190). Most recent statistics find that more than 30% of Americans belong to racial and ethnic minority groups, with estimates rising to 50% midway through the century (Alle-Corliss & Alle-Corliss, 2006; Capuzzi & Gross, 2007; Hull & Kirst-Ashman, 2004; Lum, 2004; Neukrug, 2008; U.S. Census Bureau, 2004). Additionally, the U.S. 2000 census reported that 13% of the population were age 65 and older, and 20% were identified as disabled (Capuzzi & Gross, 2007; U.S. Census Bureau, 2004). Other estimates indicate that up to 15% of the population has been identified as gay, lesbian, or bisexual; this of course does not account for the many who are unreported. Capuzzi and Gross (2007) note that "these numbers, coupled with the relatively low status and power of women in U.S. society, indicate that understanding diversity and working toward social justice are major issues facing this society" (p. 49). Neukrug (2004) has found that Americans are becoming more sensitive to special groups, "including the physically challenged, older persons, the homeless and the poor, individuals who are HIV positive, and the mentally ill" (p. 136). In all, the changing demographics and views in the United States makes it increasingly important to become more diversity sensitive.

Culture, Race, and Ethnicity

The most recognized areas of diversity involve culture, race, and ethnicity. Understanding the differences among these three terms is essential. *Culture* refers to "a learned worldview or paradigm by a population or group and transmitted socially that influences values, beliefs, customs, and behaviors, and is reflected in the language, dress, food, materials, and social institutions of a group" (Burchum, 2002, p. 7). Neukrug (2004) provides a simpler view: Culture embodies the "common values, norms, and behavior, symbols, language, and common life patterns that people learn and share with one another" (p. 194).

Race refers to those who have a common set of physical characteristics that is believed to be of the same ethnic group. Kanel (2008) and Schaefer (1988) note that the term *racial group* is often used to classify people according to their outward appearance, taking into account skin color, eye shape and color, hair type, facial characteristics, and body type. In today's world, where interracial marriage is common, it is becoming more difficult to pinpoint the specific race a person belongs to. Also, it appears that being identified solely by race is becoming less common.

Ethnicity is defined as "characteristics of people that distinguish them from others on the basis of religion, race, or national or cultural group" (Brill & Levine 2002, p. 249). In essence, an ethnic group shares some common ground, such as religious beliefs or practices, language, historical continuity, and common ancestry or place of origin (Devore & Schlesinger, 1995). Kanel (2008) adds that ethnic groups also share "traditions about parenting and marriage, types of food and the ways in which food is prepared, values about family and home, and so forth" (p. 143). Since each race is made up of many ethnic groups, there are more ethnic groups than races. For instance, *Latinos* might include Mexicans, Cubans, Puerto Ricans, and so on, while *Asians* might include Chinese, Japanese, Hawaiian, Vietnamese, and others. Similarly, Christians, Catholics, and Muslims are different ethnic groups to which many different races belong.

Becoming Diversity Sensitive

In order to become diversity sensitive, human services providers must understand and respect those that are different from them. Capuzzi and Gross (2007) highlight the need for practitioners to recognize the impact of cultural differences on client life experiences, client-helper relationships, and the helping process.

Sadly, counseling and other forms of helping "are not working for a good segment of our population" (Neukrug, 2002, p. 136). Various authors (Alle-Corliss & Alle-Corliss, 1999; Lum, 2004; Neukrug, 2004; Sue & Sue, 2008) have identified possible reasons for this fact:

- The melting pot myth, which perpetuates the notion of the blending of cultural diversity
- Incongruent expectations about the helping relationship, as seen in differences between Western and Eastern philosophies about individuality and expression of feelings
- Lack of understanding of social forces and influences that impact client populations
- Ethnocentric worldview whereby helpers view their norms and values as absolute and a standard against which to judge and measure all other cultures
- Ignorance of one's own racist attitudes and prejudices
- Inability to understand cultural differences in the expression of symptomatology, which often results in misdiagnosis, mistreatment, and early termination

- The unreliability of assessment and research instruments, which are often geared toward the majority culture
- Institutional racism, which permeates most systems, including agency systems
- A counseling or helping process that is not designed for clients from diverse backgrounds

Multiculturalism, which primarily focuses on ethnicity, race, and culture, has become well respected in the last few decades. According to Lee and Ramsey (2006), multicultural counseling today "takes into consideration the cultural background and individual experiences of diverse clients and how their psychosocial needs might be identified and met through counseling" (p. 5). The importance of integrating awareness, knowledge, and skills has been addressed by Sue and Sue (2008) in their description of multicultural counseling competencies. Based on these competencies, Alle-Corliss and Alle-Corliss (1999) emphasize the need for human service providers to:

- Become aware of their own biases, prejudices, and possible resistance toward becoming diversity sensitive
- Be willing to gain knowledge about the specific cultural and ethnic populations they will be working with
- Be open to developing skills necessary for effective practice with specific cultural and ethnic groups (p. 246)

Neukrug (2002) has compiled 10 basic and self-explanatory suggestions for maximizing the helping process when working with individuals from different ethnic and racial groups:

1. Encourage clients to speak their own language.
2. Learn about the cultural heritage of clients.
3. Assess a client's cultural identity.
4. Check the accuracy of the client's nonverbal expression.
5. Make use of alternate modes of communication.
6. Encourage clients to bring in culturally significant and personally relevant items.
7. Vary the helping environment.
8. Do not jump to conclusions about clients.

9. Know yourself.

10. Know appropriate skills.

We encourage readers to take into account all of these suggestions when working with any individual or group who is different from themselves. Below, we will address specific ethnic groups.

African Americans

African Americans are one of the largest minority groups in the United States today. Historically, as a group, they have suffered great discrimination since their arrival as slaves almost 400 years ago and are in fact the only group to have come to America as slaves (Hull & Kirst-Ashman, 2004; Lum, 2004, p. 80). Morales and Sheafor (1995) have described African Americans as one of "the most brutalized minority groups in the United States" (p. 276); Taylor (1994) eloquently speaks to their long-lasting plight: "Their history of servitude, followed by a prolonged period of legal discrimination, enforced segregation, and exclusion, has profoundly affected the institutional properties, integrity, and functioning of African American families and continues to influence their collective fate in the United States" (p. 12).

Even though African Americans speak English fluently, they are more readily identifiable that any other minority group due to their notably different appearance from Caucasians. Today, African Americans, despite the fact that many of their families have been in the United States since its founding and are more acculturated to mainstream values, continue to suffer from discrimination and racism (Alle-Corliss & Alle-Corliss, 1999; Hull & Kirst-Ashman, 2004; Kanel, 2008; Sue & Sue, 2008). As a group, African American families still suffer economically, earning less than White families; it has been noted they most likely have "received lower economic rewards than they would have in the absence of discrimination" (McLemore, 1994, p. 145).

Barack Obama, an African American whose father was from Kenya and whose white mother was from Kansas, was elected the nation's forty-fourth president, Tuesday, November 4, 2008, "breaking the ultimate racial barrier to become the first African American to claim the country's highest office" (*LA Times,* 2008). Despite generations of racial strife, Obama won a "smashing electoral victory" with his "multiracial and multiethnic coalition. His victory was a leap in the march toward equality. When Obama was born, people with his skin color could not vote in parts of America, and many were killed for trying" (*LA Times,* 2008). Despite this triumph, racism continues to exist, as many

Americans continue to hold negative attitudes toward African Americans. "African Americans often feel singled out by police, judges, and others in authority. Unfortunately, their perceptions are often true because institutionalized racism may still exist" (Kanel, 2008, p. 149).

When working with African Americans, practitioners of different ethnic backgrounds must consider all of these issues, as they may influence the helping relationship. Helpers are encouraged to take on a peer-collaborator role where there is mutual respect and mutual sharing of information instead of using an authoritarian stance. Communication patterns, family experiences, different helping styles, and macrolevel approaches to intervention are important to consider as well. Helpers must also consider the reasons from referrals and explore the multiple problems African Americans face as a group. Emphasis should be on empowerment so their clients can be helped to achieve a sense of control over their lives. Finally, the role of religion, spirituality, music, and African heritage is important to consider in developing a sound treatment plan (Alle-Corliss & Alle-Corliss, 1999).

Helpers must personalize their approach to meet the specific needs of the individual client. Similarly, helpers must not pass judgment without taking time to understand deeper issues. It is important to be sensitive to in-group diversity so as to not quickly label all African Americans the same. Kanel (2008) stresses the importance of approaching "each client as an individual and to be culturally sensitive to a client's needs. The reality of racism must always be acknowledged but never assumed" (p. 149).

Arab Americans

Arab Americans, a growing ethnic group in the United States, vary in languages spoken and religious beliefs. Nonetheless, they often share common cultural traditions of the Middle East (Kanel, 2008). After the terrorist attacks of September 11, 2001, many people from the Middle East are often associated with this negative event and unfairly judged and discriminated against. Another common myth is that "all Arabs are Muslim," when in fact recent statistics show that 42% are Catholic, 23% Orthodox Christian, 23% Muslim, and 12% Protestant (Zogby, 2001). It is important to pay attention to these statistics and not make erroneous assumptions. Equally critical is the need to consider clients' religious beliefs during the helping process; because of some clients' deep religious beliefs, helping is more effective when it is supported by their religious leaders (Nassar-McMillan & Hakim Larson, 2003). Similarly, it is important to elicit the support of community leaders; this fits with the collectivist emphasis of Middle Eastern culture, which values community acceptance. Mistrust of American human service workers that are not part of the Arab community exists and must be considered in providing human services (Nassar-McMillan, 1999).

Understanding the many facets of communication is essential when working with different cultures. Issues of personal space (proxemics), bodily movements (kinesics), and vocal cues and volume (paralanguage) may differ greatly from one culture to another and must be taken into consideration. For instance, in the Arab American culture, talking with a person dictates a much closer stance than is normally comfortable for Euro-Americans (Jensen, 1985; Nydell, 1996). Volume and intensity of speech also differ. According to Sue & Sue (2008), "Many Arabs like to be bathed in sound" and may view people in the United States as more soft-spoken (p. 166). Attention to the context of how messages are communicated is also important. It has been noted that "a normal-stressed 'no' by a U.S. American may be interpreted by an Arab as a 'yes'. A real negation in Arab culture would be stressed much more emphatically" (Sue & Sue, 2008, p. 167).

In terms of family and mental health services, it has been noted that physicians, priests, fortune-tellers, or other healers traditionally are most respected and trusted by the Arab community (Al-Krenawi & Grahma, 2000; Loza, 2001). Al-Abdul-Jabbar and Al-Issa (2000) suggest that Arab Americans will be more responsive to efforts by practitioners who spend time building rapport on a personal level versus engaging in exploring their issues and making interpretations. Last, when working with Arab Americans, it is crucial to understand the traditional makeup of the family system and respect the patriarchal position of male family members (Abudabeeh & Aseel, 1999; Nydell, 1987). According to Kanel (2008, p. 148), "A multisystem approach that involves religious leaders, medical professionals, family members, and social services is the most effective way to work with this population. Traditional models must be modified to allow flexibility around timeframe, place of service, and methods of confrontation."

Asian Americans

The term *Asian Americans* commonly refers to Chinese, Korean, Japanese, Vietnamese, Thais, and Pacific Island persons (Hawaiians, Guamanians, Filipinos, and Samoans) (Alle-Corliss & Alle-Corliss, 1999, p. 206). It is important to not generalize; each group has its own unique language, history, culture and religion, and appearance. Despite their differences, they share many of the same stressors of other minority groups and are homogeneous in their experiences in this country. Examples include their struggles with immigration and assimilation and their experience with exploitation, racism, discrimination, and oppression (Murase, 1977). Two historical examples that come to mind are the perils faced by Chinese Americans and Japanese Americans.

Chinese Americans were the first Asian minority group to arrive in the United States during the building of the cross-continental railroad. They were exploited for their labor and subjected to many restrictions and negative stereotypes (Dower, 1986; Miller, 1969; Saxton, 1971; Taylor, 1994). They were also considered "yellow peril" and criticized for their willingness to work long hours for low pay, which threatened the livelihood of white working men (Taylor, 1994, p. 115).

Japanese Americans immigrated at the turn of the twentieth century at which time they were restricted by many laws that limited their numbers and participation in certain occupations and agricultural pursuits. "Picture brides"and the label of "model minority" illustrates how Japanese women were exploited and how this group was stereotyped. Furthermore, economic discrimination is noted in the discrepancy between what a Japanese American makes compared to a White American (Kitano, 1981).

In regard to human services, Kanel (2008) suggests that "while it is important to not stereotype, it is helpful to look at recent studies of cultural variations when first working with someone from a culture different from one's own" (p. 147). For instance, Uba (1994) reports on a study of communication styles that suggests many Asian Americans are apt to be less expressive and more restrained in their nonverbal behaviors. Other findings by Kim, Atkinson, and Umemoto (2001) and Hsu, Tseng, Ashton, McDermott, and Char (1985) suggest that emotional self-control is highly valued and considered a sign of strength within the Asian American culture. Since these behaviors differ greatly from Western emphasis on being open and direct, it is essential for the practitioner to be sensitive and not judge an Asian client based on different communication styles.

European American Culture

American cultures have been influenced by many others, notably by Englishmen who were instrumental in building America. Other immigrants from Germany, the Netherlands, France, Italy, and northern European countries also were significant contributors to the early American culture. Because they shared similar values and religious beliefs, there was less disharmony. Protestantism prevailed initially until

Irish Catholic immigrants arrived in the 1880s, at which time conflict arose. As more immigrants from different parts of Europe immigrated, discrimination based on ethnicity and race grew.

Eventually, immigrants from all the various countries that came to the United States in the early nineteenth century "melted" together into what has become known as a *melting pot* where most Americans have assimilated according to the norms established by the Founding Fathers (Kanel, 2008, p. 143).

American culture is based on the creed that every individual has a right to "the pursuit of happiness" and to live independently. Freedom of speech, freedom of religion, and access to equal rights is supposed to be a given, and competition and individuality is encouraged. In the 20th century, the influx of immigrants from all over the world to the United States grew dramatically. As earlier, one-third of the population in the United States today is composed of racial and ethnic minorities, and that figure is expected to rise to 50% by 2050 (Neukrug, 2002). During the last few decades, we have seen a change in the traditional melting pot aspect of assimilating. Today, there is a tendency toward a "culturally pluralistic society" that is "made up of diverse ethnic groups, each preserving its own traditions and culture but also loyal to the nation as a whole" (Brill & Levine, 2002, p. 126). According to Lum (2004), a "realistic view of cultural pluralism recognizes the right of multicultural groups to coexist as recognized entities within a larger society that tolerates and encourages multiple cultures" (p. 99). American human service workers must be sensitive to other cultures and the fact that their norms, values, and traditions may differ. Acceptance and respect are key in working with clients who may view change and treatment in a different manner. It is important to assess if and how much an individual has acculturated, as is understanding the client's family and its level of acculturation and assimilation.

Latinos, Hispanics, and Chicanos

Latinos are one of the fastest-growing minority populations in United States today, second only to African Americans (Taylor, 1994). Latinos are a very diverse and heterogeneous group that includes Mexican Americans, Puerto Ricans, Cubans, and others from Central and South America. Even though all share the Spanish language, dialects may vary, and they are often very different in terms of culture, political views, and migration status. Puerto Ricans hold dual citizenship as Puerto Rican and American; many Cubans came to escape the communist regime of Castro; and many Mexicans, El Salvadorians, and Guatemalans have entered the United States illegally in search of employment and a better way of life.

Historically, some Latinos, such as Mexican Americans, have had their homeland incorporated into the United States. Other Latinos emigrated from their countries of origin: some came voluntarily, others left to escape war and famine, and still others came as political refugees. Undocumented immigrants who enter this country illegally are subject to increased discrimination and exploitation. Morales and Sheafor (1995) believe that undocumented immigrants are often convenient scapegoats when economic times are tough.

Regardless of the reasons for their immigration, Latinos have historically suffered from racism, discrimination, and exploitation. According to many sources, Latinos suffer from low income, unemployment, underemployment, undereducation, prejudice, poor housing, and cultural linguistic barriers much more than other minority groups (Alle-Corliss & Alle-Corliss, 1999, p. 268). As a result of these conditions, there has been a rise in alcoholism, substance abuse, juvenile delinquency, and gangs, and a higher percentage of imprisonment in the adult population. Unfortunately, as discussed by Morales and Sheafor (1995, p. 277), these conditions tend to perpetuate racist views and discriminatory behaviors.

Although differences certainly exist among many Latino subgroups, similarities are also present. For instance, many Latinos continue to speak Spanish at home and use very little English. The concept of *familism* prevails in that the family is very important, harmony is encouraged, and divorce is discouraged. Latina females are encouraged to be self-sacrificing by placing the needs of everyone else above their own; this is known as *marianisma*. Additionally, the *atague de nervios*, which is translated as "a nervous attack," has been well documented in the literature (Kanel, 2008; Koss-Chioino, 1999; Liebowitz et al., 1994) as a common psychological disorder experienced by women from various Latino ethnic groups. Viewed as a clinical syndrome where symptoms of Depressive Disorder, Panic Disorder, and Generalized Anxiety Disorder are seen together, this condition is often connected to family conflict. Kanel (2008) "hypothesized that instead of confronting family conflicts directly as mainstream American culture encourages, Latinos manifest this syndrome as a way to cope with conflicts without having to confront family members directly, thereby safeguarding family harmony" (p. 146). Other possible dynamics at play could be that the individual women suffering from this condition are the identified patients, are seeking attention through illness, or have guilt-inducing motives.

Active listening is very important in working with Latino families. Recognizing how culture influences clients' needs and taking time to explore treatment options that do not impose conflicting values onto the client is vital in remaining culturally sensitive. When mainstream values are in opposition with traditional ones, it may be necessary to educate Latino clients about these cultural conflicts. This is especially necessary when the mainstream culture considers a certain behavior of another culture morally unacceptable or even illegal; some Latino families use corporal punishment as a parenting technique, although the American perception considers this punishment child abuse. In lieu of harsh and punitive reactions, using sensitivity in working with these types of conflicts will go a long way in building trust and open communication within the families and cultural group. It is also important to pay attention to family centering, parental roles, communication patterns, and bilingualism when working with the Latino culture. Ultimately, practitioners who are open to developing unique intervention styles geared to the specific culture and family dynamics at play will likely be the most successful in their treatment.

In order to develop culturally appropriate and sensitive treatment interventions when working with Lanino clients, providers must consider various ethnically significant features that include national origin, language, family names, religion, racial ascription, and immigration or citizenship status. It is essential to keep in mind the diversity among Latinos and not assume that because they are placed in one category, they all share the same cultural traits. Castex (1994) encourages practitioners not only to value but also to expect diversity in a group: "This view conditions exceptions and encourages development of strategies that avoid stereotypes when addressing the needs of the client" (p. 290).

Sensitivity on the part of the helper to realistic fears clients might have on revealing their immigration status is necessary in being able to foster trust. When working with an immigrant population, it is necessary to become familiar with current immigration regulations as well as sociopolitical issues tied to their country of origin. Likewise, sensitivity to their economic, social, and emotional struggles is important. Poverty, low income, single-parent families, and a very young demographic profile characterizes the life of many Latinos. Taking time to assess how each client is individually affected is helpful in both assessment and treatment endeavors.

Native Americans

Native Americans are not immigrants; their plight began when their land was conquered by Americans. History reveals that as an ethnic group,

Native Americans have been subjected to both overt and subtle forms of discrimination through the years. Accounts suggest that in the 18th century in California, Native Americans numbered about 250,000; yet by 1900, this number had dwindled to only about 10,000. This decline has been related to diseases transmitted from European settlers, dehumanizing and decimating conditions, warfare, slavelike treatment, and genocide by Whites (Daniels & Kitano, 1970; Taylor, 1994). Morales and Sheafor (1995) add that "racism toward Indians has been expressed in the lack of comprehensive, progressive federal policy over a period of many years, a lack that has severely hampered Indians' ability to move forward in the United States" (p. 272).

Five major governmental policies toward Native Americans have been identified: (1) extermination, (2) expulsion, (3) exclusion (reservations), (4) assimilation, and (5) self-determination (Berry, 1965). The first three of these policies reflect mainstream views and discriminatory practices, while the last two provide some hope, although some would question whether assimilation is a positive.

Taylor (1994) highlights the negative impact of years of maltreatment toward Native Americans:

> *Generations of exploitation and neglect have had a deleterious effect on the cultures, lifestyles, and well-being of Native Americans. Expelled from their native lands and resettled on prison-like reservations where they were prohibited from practicing native religions and other displays of Indian culture, Native Americans have experienced great difficulty in sustaining and preserving their ethnic identities. (p. 14)*

Today, although some progress has been made, Native Americans continue to suffer from poverty, lack of education, unemployment, and limited access to medical and dental healthcare, medications, and rehabilitation services (Kanel, 2008; O'Brien, 1992; Seekins, 1997). Quite alarming are the statistics presented by the Native American Research and Training Center (1995) that 4 out of every 1,000 Native American infants are born with fetal alcohol syndrome (FAS), as compared to 1 of 1,000 in the mainstream population, and higher rates of hearing and visual impairment, which are 85% preventable.

Generally, ideas about child rearing, change and intervention, medicine, and healing are different in Native American families, although there is great variation. "Some incorporate mainstream American practices into their own belief systems, whereas others—often those within the same family—prefer using traditional practices" (Kanel, 2008, p. 150; Dufort & Reed, 1995).

194 *Developing Agency Skills*

Extended families are very important to most Native Americans. When family members relocate to urban areas away from the reservation, there is risk of assimilation and loss of traditional cultural beliefs that emphasize spirituality, socialization, and language. There is obvious conflict between the tribal culture that encourages dependence and mainstream America that encourages competition and interdependence.

It may be difficult for those individuals who live with a tribe to seek services outside the tribal community. This can become a problem if services that do not exist within the reservation are needed. Also, since most human service workers are unable to speak Native languages and may not understand Native American culture, treatment may be ineffective.

Williams and Ellison (1996) emphasize the importance of practice with Native Americans that is "harmonious with the client's environment and degree of acculturation" (p. 147). Client involvement in the planning and implementation of treatment can help them feel more in control and less oppressed. Including family members and community representatives in the planning and implantation of treatment programs will ensure greater success. Since intervention strategies will likely be influenced by numerous cultural beliefs, customs, and values of the specific Native American tribe to which the client belongs, it is essential to understand these and to determine what importance they may assume in ongoing care. Being careful to consider each tribe as being unique will help prevent helpers from making inaccurate generalizations. Also, being careful to adhere to confidentiality standards is important; well-defined boundaries in terms of sharing information must be taken seriously despite tribal influence. In other words, because of confidentiality laws, Native American clients must still give written consent to tribal leaders before information about their treatment can be shared.

It is important to be sensitive and cognizant of the many obstacles Native Americans face on a daily basis that may interfere with their ability to follow through with treatment. These may include economic difficulties and lack of transportation. It is very important to be sensitive to and respectful of the various spiritual beliefs and traditional medicine practices important to clients. Remaining open to incorporating ceremony and ritual in intervention strategies and/or consulting with traditional healers can be very helpful. At times, it may even become necessary to work hand in hand with medicine men and shamans. At the very least, it is important to learn about their practices and respect their importance to clients. Similarly, fostering the belief of restoring spiritual balance in their lives is key; interventions aimed at restoring a balance between physical well-being and spiritual harmony often are most effective. This, of course, requires taking time to understand the client's definition of illness and to fit the interventions with that definition.

Recognition that many Native Americans are more present oriented than past or future oriented can be helpful in developing treatment plans that emphasize the present and existing problem-solving skills. There are some cases where "grief groups are being viewed as therapeutic resources for Indian people who are finding support and understanding in releasing the accumulated pain and sorrow that has so profoundly impacted their emotional and physical well-being" (Morales & Sheafor, 1995, p. 509). This is, however, not the norm, and care must be taken not to jump too quickly to encouraging a focus on resolution of the past.

Socioeconomic Class

A vital component of becoming diversity sensitive is determining a client's socioeconomic status (SES) and understanding how this may impact overall functioning. SES refers to the position individuals hold in society based on such factors as income, education, occupational status, and prestige of their neighborhood (Sigelman & Shaffer, 1995, p. 104). Despite the fact that the United States is one of the wealthiest nations in the world, poverty remains a major concern (Alle-Corliss & Alle-Corliss, 1999; Burger, 2008; Neukrug, 2008). Individuals and families who are considered poor lack money, resources, and possessions, and face many obstacles: "Their relative deprivation affects the style and quality of their lives; it extends beyond mere distribution of income and includes inequality in education, health care, police protections, job opportunities, legal justice, and others areas" (Burger, 2008, p. 59). People's SES has a major role in determining what opportunities and resources are available to them and how those resources might affect their ability to weather a crisis. According to Hull and Kirst-Ashman (2004):

> *Social standing in the context of family's surrounding community has huge implications regarding development of self-esteem and the ability to function effectively. It affects dreams of future accomplishments, basic opportunities, and what family members can realistically accomplish in the future. (p. 313)*

Of particular importance in the human services field is the plight of the poor and homeless. As a group, they are often discriminated against and experience disparity in the services they receive. Kanel (2008) writes: "American culture values education and wealth, so it's not surprising that those who are uneducated and poor are treated as if they are immoral or just lazy" (p. 154). Clearly, there are many reasons for poverty and many subgroups of poor. Some individuals have been poor all of their lives and may not be able to overcome the cycle of poverty. Within this group, there is a subgroup called the "deserving poor"; these are individuals who are unable to be self-supporting, such as "the aged poor, young children of poor families, some discharged mental patients, and people who are permanently disabled" (p. 59). Another subgroup includes individuals and families who are facing economic struggles due to temporary setbacks, given situational or environmental circumstances. This is of course more evident today with the downturn in the economy, which has led to a massive loss of jobs and a major decline in the housing industry. Immigrants also may fit into this group since their resources are limited when they first arrive in this country.

The homeless is another subgroup of poor that are often misunderstood. They are especially subject to negative stereotypes as being hoboes, skid row bums, or alcoholics, yet "the homeless" are a very diverse group and include:

- Runaway children
- Intact single-parent families
- Intact families with no place to live
- Poor single men and women
- Those who have minimum-pay jobs yet are unable to afford shelter
- Those with a substance abuse problem
- The deinstitutionalized mentally ill (Neukrug, 1994)

Today's homeless population is younger and less apt to find employment and often belong to a minority group. Burger (2008) notes that "the poverty rate for African Americans and Latinos is considerably higher than for whites. Women and children are also overrepresented among the ranks of the poor. In fact, the great majority of those living in poverty consist of women and children" (p. 60).

Because of the obvious diversity among the various subgroups of the poor, it has been difficult to develop satisfactory programs to help them. Programs that fit one group may not be appropriate for another (Brieland, Costin, & Atherton, 1980).

We encourage helpers to gain insight about an individual's particular SES, as this can alert them to possible stressors the person may be facing and guide them in developing appropriate interventions. Alle-Corliss and Alle-Corliss (1999) note:

> *Individuals from different socioeconomic levels may also differ in their values, socialization goals, and ultimately their view of the helping process. The helper needs to be aware of these differences and work toward helping clients at the level where they are. (p. 297)*

In working with those of a lower SES, it is important to be aware of one's own biases and to keep these in check. It is critical to be aware of "clinical cooling out" of poor people in agency settings, where the poor are discouraged from seeking further help or viewed as difficult and resistant. It is vital to be respectful and sensitive to the needs and circumstances of poor people and not make rash judgments about their situation without considering possible underlying issues. Understanding the many stressors the poor and homeless face can help us become more sensitive and affirming. Far too often, helpers talk down to the poor, overgeneralize, stereotype, and adopt a blame-the-victim philosophy—attitudes that are contrary to ethical and moral codes of the human service profession.

Geographic Location

An increasingly important area of diversity tied to SES is providing human services to those in rural areas and small towns. Woodside and McClam (2009) note that because of the progressive population decline in these areas in the past few decades, individuals living there are more

> *disadvantaged, experiencing a steady erosion in their quality of life. They are more likely to be elderly, be members of disadvantaged minorities, lack the kinds of opportunities available to metropolitan counterparts, and need the help of human service agencies and professionals. (p. 63)*

Until recently, human services to those in rural areas and small towns was limited due to geographic inaccessibility and limited availability of professionals. Barriers to providing accessible and adequate services to those in rural areas include:

- Inability to recruit and retain professional helpers
- Great geographic distances between clients and helpers
- High cost of services
- Difficulties of maintaining confidentiality
- Isolation
- Problems in coordination of care
- Stigma attached to receiving mental health or other services

Today, however, the trend is changing. Many "small towns and rural areas are attracting those who see advantages in living where there are lower crime rates, opportunities for professional advancement, and larger labor pools with lower wage expectations" (Woodside & McClam, 2009, p. 65). As a result, a focus on meeting the needs of those in these communities requires focusing on

> *creative solutions to improve options, improvisation to meet needs, collaboration with a range of other professionals and informal supports, and the building of an infrastructure to provide needed supports to rural residents and communities (Woodside & McClam, 2009, p. 64)*

Gender

As with other areas of diversity, gender issues also play a significant role in work with clients and must be taken into consideration in the helping process. Even though it is important to view clients as individuals first with their own unique and personal makeups, it remains necessary to acknowledge their gender and its possible impact on their life situation. *Gender* is defined as "the psychological, social, and cultural features and characteristics that have become strongly associated with the biological categories of female and male" (Gilbert & Schere, 1999, p. 3). There are similarities and differences between men and women, and it is important to recognize both.

Physically, men and women differ. Much has been written about the psychological differences in male-female emotional development and expression as well as the formation of a distinct gender-based identity. Socially, differences among gender also exist; communication styles, career choices, demographic patterns, and socialization itself appear variable. Often it is these differences that led to gender-role stereotypes. Moreover, many of the present-day stereotypes are rooted in early childhood experiences, when boys and girls were taught about their differences based on gender. Kanel (2008) writes that "despite these many variances in gender roles, many people still hold on to obsolete gender stereotypes" (p. 137).

There is no doubt that traditional views of men and women persist, although changes in gender-role identity continues to evolve. It is anticipated that in time, new personality styles for men and women will emerge. "In fact, some research seems to indicate that individuals who take on multiple roles, including nontraditional sex-roles, may be more satisfied in life than those who do not" (Neukrug, 1994, p. 196).

Sexism—the discriminatory behavior by one gender toward the other—has historically been experienced by women, although men may be victims as well (Ashford, Lecroy, & Lortie, 1997). Defined as "a system of beliefs and behaviors by which a group is oppressed, controlled, and exploited because of presumed gender differences," sexism can have profound effects on individuals of both genders (Anderson & Collins, 1995, p. 67). As human service providers, we must take care to work toward recognizing our own biases so as to not perpetuate this problem.

It is crucial for helpers to understand and appreciate the conse-quences of gender roles and beliefs on individual clients and their development. Practitioners are encouraged to work toward these goals:

- Becoming knowledgeable about the differences between males and females
- Developing an appreciation for and understanding of the historical aspects that underlie these gender differences
- Remaining open and willing to acknowledge the changing demographics
- Understanding the impact of these changes on each gender as well as on society in general (Alle-Corliss & Alle-Corliss, 1999, p. 284)

Women

Societal change has been great for women and for the roles they play in the home, at work, and in society in general. For instance, they make up more than half of the population, are increasingly seen in the workforce, are attending college in greater numbers, and are increasingly involved in pursuing previously male-dominated professions such as business, medicine, law, and law enforcement (Morales & Sheafor, 1995, p. 267). Women are becoming more adept at managing dual careers by working both outside and within the home, although many still remain the primary child caregivers. Despite the benefits of these changing roles, women are subject to increased stress placed on them by the demands of the many roles they fill.

> *The stress of having to be a "working" mother can be great. Working women often feel guilty at being away from their children; frustration at having to deal with work stress, child care issues, and money concerns; and sheer exhaustion from having to balance two very complex and expansive roles. . . . This stress is significantly higher for single mothers or women with additional pressures of work difficulties, marital conflicts, separation or divorce, or physical or sexual abuse. (Alle-Corliss & Alle-Corliss, 1999, p. 290)*

Women have traditionally suffered from economic exploitation, inequality, discrimination, and oppression. They are often more vulnerable overall and thus subject to economic abuse, seen in lower wages, and physical abuse, seen in domestic violence, sexism, sexual harassment, and rape. Women seek more services than men for psychological problems, such as depression, anxiety, and eating disorders, and suffer more from chronic health conditions, such as osteoporosis, diseases of the urinary systems, and death from childbearing, abortion, breast cancer, and AIDS. Older women struggle even more, as there is a greater likelihood that they will be widowed and live in poverty. The personal and social problems faced by women today can be linked directly to gender inequality and institutionalized sexism.

Effective work with women requires human service providers to understand the cultural and social context of their problems, to develop strategies that can help change their lives for the better, and to continue to work toward reducing sexism that pervades our practice (Morales & Sheafor, 1995).

When working with women, specialized knowledge about women's issues and their cultural background should be incorporated into any treatment plan or change process. Collier (1982) has identified five common problems women tend to bring to treatment that practitioners need to be aware of and able to work with:

1. Powerlessness
2. Limited behavioral and educational options
3. Anger that is often turned inward, resulting in depression
4. Inadequate communication skills
5. Failure to nurture self (pp. 57–68)

It is important to evaluate a woman's functioning at home, at work, and in the community to determine the existence of gender-role norms and discriminatory practices. Similarly, economic, legal, and social issues that impact women must be closely considered. It is critical for male and female practitioners to examine their own biases and to be able to help women with an approach that is as nonsexist and nonbiased as possible. They should focus on empowerment strategies to help women who desire help in freeing themselves from the dependent roles they have typically played. "Empowerment can take place when you remain positive, hopeful, appropriately self-disclosing, and focused on women's strengths and potential for growth and change" (Alle-Corliss & Alle-Corliss, 1999, p. 291).

Emphasis in working with women must be on helping them to build their self-confidence and self-esteem, to learn to care for themselves, to become assertive, to learn appropriate ways to handle their anger and to understand underlying dynamics, and to recognize various alternatives regarding decision-making and problem-solving skills.

Because female practitioners are often positive role models for women, they must be aware of how they present themselves; it is important to practice what clients are being taught and encouraged to do in treatment. Male practitioners can also be instrumental in helping women by remaining cognizant of their gender differences. It is important for men to continually work to ensure that traditional male-female power relationships do not prevail within treatment.

Men

Men, like women, have also experienced a change in roles that has caused them stress and conflict. A well-known book by Sam Keen, *Fire in the Belly: On Being a Man* (1991), encourages men to break free of cultural boundaries in order to reassert their masculinity and male role. Theorists postulate that

> *in childhood, boys prematurely dissociate from their mothers and enter the aggressive, competitive world. The boy desires to turn to his father but finds him emotionally distant and unavailable. The result is that his developing masculinity is defined by turning away from anything feminine. (Ashford et al., 1997, p. 438)*

In today's society, men and women are being challenged to change the stereotypic images that are intricately woven into the roles they play in their everyday lives. Conflict is natural since there will be many men and women who are comfortable with traditional male roles and resist any change. No doubt men, like women, will have to battle negativity and differences in opinion as they pursue a new male identity and role. "As helpers, we will have to be both supportive and sensitive to the specific struggles inherent in their efforts to change" (Alle-Corliss & Alle-Corliss, 1999, p. 293).

Many of the issues men face in today's society are directly tied to gender-based stereotypes evident in the "male code of conduct." Fanning and McKay (1993) address the issue of typical male stereotypes:

> *The old masculine stereotypes describes a tough, lonely man who works hard and suffers in silence. The dark side of this stereotype is the man about whom women complain about so much; the man who is violent, abusive, lustful, and untrustworthy. This typical man is a kind of zombie: un-communicative, dead inside, apparently incapable of an inner life. He is friendless, unavailable to his children, and estranged from his own father. He is almost completely out of touch with his feelings, unable to express any emotion except anger. He drinks and works too much. (p. 3)*

Sadly, this account describes so many of the stereotypes men (and women) must work to dispel. In a review of the literature, Levant (1992) has identified traditional male roles and norms that are evident in the last quote:

- Avoiding femininity
- Restrictive emotionality
- Seeking achievement and/or status
- Self-reliance
- Aggression
- Homophobia
- Nonrelational attitudes about sexuality

Clearly, many of these roles and norms persist today and reflect the messages men receive from the time they are young boys. Men typically have been the breadwinners in their family as well as the authority figures. In many families, this is changing as more women are entering the workforce and sharing more in parenting and disciplining. Some men have welcomed these changes; others have met these stressors with resistance and anger.

Men are often given double messages—"be strong and don't cry", yet "be more sensitive and emotional"—which creates confusion and communication difficulties. In some cases, men may communicate their hurt in an aggressive manner, which leads to further criticism. Alle-Corliss and Alle-Corliss (1999) capture the essence of this struggle:

> *Having seldom been encouraged to express feelings other than anger, it is not surprising that some men may not know how to acknowledge and express the range of feelings they possess. To compound this confusion further, men are typically not encouraged to seek mental health treatment as readily as women and are often unjustly criticized or humiliated when they do. (p. 294)*

Helpers need to recognize that men are also in transition and require understanding and sensitivity. A positive image of masculinity must be cultivated that helps foster men's self-respect and dismisses views of an aggressive, dominant, and disconnected manhood. Levant et al. (1992) suggest that "we must walk a fine line of crediting men for what is valuable in masculinity on one hand . . . to learn to celebrate these qualities and to be able to identify those aspects which are obsolete and dysfunctional" (p. 385).

Therapists who work with men should possess specialized knowledge of men's issues. Race, culture, and ethnicity must be considered. Since stereotypes about men directly impact their use of social services, practitioners must assess their own perceptions and biases. It is important to be sensitive to the fact that it is neither easy nor the norm for men to seek professional help. Furthermore, many practitioners may not fully challenge men to engage in the emotional work that can help them learn to articulate their feelings more easily.

Female helpers may need to be aware of their own biases about men not being capable of emotionality and protect against the belief that expressing feelings openly is a sign of dependency or weakness in a man. Women practitioners must also be careful not to give male clients double messages by verbally encouraging them to express their emotions, yet nonverbally demonstrating disapproval or discomfort when they do express hurt or anger. Male practitioners may also manifest negative stereotypes about their male clients; evidence is the tendency to diagnose men with more serious problems than they may merit.

Sexual Orientation

A diversity-sensitive practitioner is able to work effectively with gay and lesbian individuals, families, and groups. In order to be effective, non-biased, and nonjudgmental, human service providers must be aware of issues tied to sexual orientation and homosexuality, beginning with "historical views."

> *Historically the mainstream of our population has defined themselves as heterosexual . . . Only in recent years . . . has it become a little easier to acknowledge being homosexual. Americans are beginning to accept or adjust to the reality that homosexuality is indeed a sexual orientation of many in our society. (Alle-Corliss & Alle-Corliss, 1999, p. 300)*

Until recently, even in the area of psychiatry and mental health, homosexuality or bisexuality was considered a mental illness that warranted a psychiatric diagnosis of Gender Identity Disorder. More recently the *Diagnostic Statistical Manual* was the first to use this diagnosis *only* when people were confused and emotionally upset by their sexual orientation, not for those who are comfortable with their homosexuality. In recent years, both the American Psychiatric Association and the American Psychological Association view homosexuality as a sexual orientation, not an illness.

Moses and Hawkins (1982) note that *sexual orientation* refers to a person's preference for partners of the same sex, opposite sex, or both sexes for sexual and affectional relations (pp. 43–44). The desire to share affection or become life partners is as important as sexual attraction in determining sexual orientation. Also, the difference between sexual preference and sexual orientation is important in understanding advances in how homosexuality is viewed today. Alle-Corliss and Alle-Corliss (1999) note that historically, "individuals were believed to choose to live a homosexual lifestyle," thus the term *sexual preference*. Today, research findings increasingly suggest that "homosexual feelings are a basic part of the individual's psyche rather than something . . . consciously chosen, hence, the term 'sexual orientation'" (p. 301). Neukrug (1994) adds that "although it is still unclear how we obtain our sexual orientation, it appears now that sexual orientation is determined very early in life and may even be related to biological and genetic factors" (p. 197). There is still much controversy over which theoretical views take precedence; present-day views favor a mixture of both biological and psychosocial variables (Crooks & Baur, 1993; Gooren, Fliers, & Courtney, 1990).

Despite the many advances in how sexual orientation is viewed today, being homosexual in our society continues to be controversial. Heterosexism—the belief that heterosexuality is or should be the only acceptable sexual orientation—still prevails. As a result, discrimination, harassment, and acts of violence toward homosexuals persist and are encouraged by fear and hatred (Blumenfeld, 1992). Kanel (2008) agrees that

> *although society has begun to accept homosexuality in less negative ways than in years past, prejudice and discrimination are still experienced by homosexuals, bisexuals (those who are attracted sexually, emotionally, and romantically to both genders), and transgenders (those who have surgeries and live as a gender other than the one they were born with). (p. 139)*

Kanel goes on to identify those who are gay, lesbian, bisexual, and transgender as belonging to the GLBT community.

Being homosexual today often involves coping with homophobia, discrimination, and oppression. *Homophobia* is defined as the "fear and hatred of sex with a same-sex partner" (Alle-Corliss & Alle-Corliss, 1999, p. 301) or as "an irrational fear about being around, touching, and liking homosexuals" (Kanel, 2008, p. 140).

Because of the many negative stereotypes, prejudice, discrimination, and even rejection faced by homosexual individuals, "coming out" and acknowledging that one is gay or lesbian is difficult and likely to create much stress and anxiety. As a result of continued incidents of oppression and exploitation, many who are homosexual today continue to live a heterosexual lifestyle due to the "stigma and shame they fear will be placed on them should they openly acknowledge their sexual orientation. It is not uncommon for many to marry and live a heterosexual lifestyle to avoid internal and/or external pressures resulting from coming out" (Alle-Corliss & Alle-Corliss, 1999, p. 301). "Leading such a life is referred to as 'being in the closet' and often causes feelings of depression, shame, guilt and fear. They must always be vigilant and anxious about having their true sexual preference [orientation] discovered" (Kanel, 2008, p. 140).

According to Ashford et al. (1997):

> *In our society, power and privilege are structured in terms of sexual preferences, and our system has institutionalized heterosexual forms of identity. In fact, a heterosexual gender identity has been considered the*

yardstick for determining normality and has contributed to the isolation and oppression of gays, lesbians, and bisexuals. (p. 130)

Clearly, homophobic views contribute to negative labels and remain a major obstacle to accepting homosexuality within our society. Internalized oppression is an unfortunate outcome of homophobia; this in turn creates problems with low self-esteem and self-image for homosexuals. Factors that have been linked with homophobia include:

- Authoritarianism
- Highly religious views
- Relating to others with negative views toward homosexuality
- Limited or no personal contact with gay or lesbian people
- In recent years, the epidemic nature of AIDS, which many erroneously attribute to sexual practices between gay men (Herek & Berrill, 1990)

Those who belong to the GLBT community face special issues that must be understood by human service workers. Those who risk coming out about their sexual orientation are more likely to experience family rejection and hostility from friends and peers and may become victims of verbal and physical abuse by those who struggle to accept their different orientation and lifestyle. Possible outcomes of having to face any of these issues are confusion, anger, and fearfulness, which further serve to reinforce their self-doubt and perpetuate already-existing feelings of low self-esteem.

It is important to be aware of the oppression faced by many homosexual individuals; they risk being disqualified from jobs or academic programs and sometimes are violently and psychologically abused due to their homosexuality. Adolescents who are dealing with identity formation are especially at risk; they often live in a world of secrecy and fear, may experience alienation and rejection by their peer group, and may feel the pressure of cultural sanctions against intimate homosexual relations.

The high risk for depression and suicide among homosexual individuals is perhaps even more pronounced for adolescents. Other areas of high risk are "destructive alcohol and drug abuse, being victims of crime, sexual diseases including AIDS, and school dropout. This risk can be compounded if the youth is a minority" (Ashford et al., 1997, p. 349). McManus (1991) notes that gay and lesbian minorities often live within three communities: their ethnic community, the gay and lesbian community, and the majority community. Being able to balance the three can be especially difficult.

Similar to other minority groups, those from the GBLT community are vulnerable to oppression and stigmatization. Each individual copes differently; on one end of the spectrum are those who have remained invisible to avoid mistreatment, and on the other end are those who are active proponents of gay and lesbian rights; many fall in between. Despite the difficulties inherent in coming out, more and more members of this minority group are refusing to be silent and hidden. "The visibility and influence of the lesbian and gay minority will continue to grow" (Morales & Sheafor, 1995, p. 339).

Alle-Corliss and Alle-Corliss (1999) encourage helpers to "strive to respect members of this group by recognizing their individual differences and preferences. If their behavior becomes problematic and they are at risk for increased difficulties, we need to help them explore more appropriate channels, not focus on their sexual orientations as the source of these problems" (p. 302). Kanel (2008) adds that "human service agencies" are often in the position to provide counseling to the GBLT population to help them with the emotional and psychological problems they are apt to face. Legal advocates can help by investigating discriminatory practices, while support groups can provide a safe place for members to deal with the rejection and alienation related to coming out.

Practitioners must be aware of their own values and biases in order to determine if they have any homophobic tendencies. Alle-Corliss and Alle-Corliss (1999) suggest that "honest self-awareness can lead up to corrective action and minimize the risk of discrimination on our part, regardless of how subtle it may be" (p. 302). Conversely, helpers who view homosexuality as a sin and attempt to persuade clients to change their sexuality "should probably refer their clients struggling with those issues to someone else" (Kanel, 2008, p. 141).

Disabilities

Understanding and being able to work effectively with individuals with disabilities is a given for human service providers. M.S. Corey and G. Corey (2007) comment that "part of understanding diversity involves understanding how ability and disability are relevant factors in the delivery of human services" (p. 200). More than 40 million Americans are said to suffer from some type of disability (Mackelprang & Salsgiver,

1999; Stoddard, Jans, Ripple, & Kraus, 1998). That includes those with motor impairments, visual or hearing deficits, psychological disorders, cognitive disabilities, and many others (Hull & Kirst-Ashman, 2004, p. 68). Other statistics find that "approximately one-fifth of U.S. citizens have disabilities. The percentage is slightly higher among women and girls (21.3%) than among men and boys (19.8%)" who tend to live in poverty (Corsini & Wedding, 2008, p. 532).

The American with Disabilities Act (ADA) defines *disability* as a "physical or mental impairment that substantially limits one or more of the major life events of such an individual," such as "caring for oneself, performing manual tasks, walking, seeing, hearing, speaking, breathing, learning, and working" (EEOC, 1991, p. 2). Burger distinguishes *disability* from *handicap*: "Disability refers to a diagnosed condition, such as blindness, and deafness, whereas handicap refers to the consequences of the disability" (p. 84). Human service professionals face the "challenge of identifying the barriers that screen out people with disabilities" or make it unnecessarily difficult for them to find appropriate therapeutic services (Corsini & Wedding, 2008, p. 532).

Practitioners can be most helpful when they take time to recognize their own biases. "The clarity of a helper's vision can be impaired by myths, misconceptions, prejudices, and stereotypes about people with disabilities" (M.S. Corey & G. Corey, 2007, p. 200). In working with this population, it is important to recognize individuals' potential, assess their strengths and limitations, and determine barriers to service delivery along with the existence of available resources.

Maintaining a positive attitude is equally important. "Helpers' attitudes are a key factor in successfully intervening in the lives of people with disabilities. Dispelling myths and misconceptions and helping people with disabilities achieve their goals can be highly rewarding" (M.S. Corey & G. Corey, 2007, p. 200). Kanel (2008) notes that "throughout history, people with disabilities have been victims of stigma, prejudice, mistreatment, discrimination, social isolation, inferior status, and inferior services" (p. 154). M.S. Corey and G. Corey (2007) make a similar observation: "People with disabilities have to face prejudice, hostility, lack of understanding, and discrimination on the basis of their physical, emotional, or mental handicap" (p. 200). As helpers, we must work to challenge existing negative stereotypes and views faced by the population of disabled persons and strive to explore ways to provide them with necessary services.

Guidelines for working with persons with disabilities have been identified by Mackelprang and Salsgiver (1999) and Neukrug (2002):

- Be knowledgeable of the many disabling conditions.

- Assume that people are capable or potentially capable.

- Help clients acknowledge their individual disability and (if applicable) engage in the grieving process to deal with loss issues.

- Be aware of the discrimination and oppression faced by this population.

- Be knowledgeable about available referral resources.

- Be well informed on the law as it pertains to disabilities.

- Be prepared to become an advocate on many different levels.

- Include the family when appropriate.

Disabilities can be divided into various categories: developmental, physical, mental, and substance abuse. A brief discussion of each follows.

Developmental Disabilities

Developmental disabilities include intellectual deficits, previously called mentally retardation. There is a wide variation in intellectual ability within those who are deemed developmentally delayed. Developmental delays are subdivided into four groups: mild, moderate, severe, and profound retardation (Burger, 2008, p. 108). According to Larsen (2008), persons with developmental disabilities are those who have customarily been labeled as having severe to profound mental retardation. As such, these individuals typically "require ongoing, extensive support in more than one major life activity in order to participate in integrated community settings and enjoy the quality of life available to people with fewer or no disabilities" (Larsen, 2008, p. 1). Despite the range of characteristics found in this population, most suffering from severe disabilities share a few of these characteristics:

- Restricted speech or communication
- Problems in basic physical mobility
- Propensity to forget skills through disuse
- Difficulty in generalizing skills from one situation to another
- Require support in major life activities (Larsen, 2008)

Interventions will depend on how severe the individual's limitations are. "Self-care, social behavior, and basic academic and vocational skills are usually the main areas of concentration," with independence being a strong goal (Burger, 2008; Dover, 1990). Larsen (2008) goes on to suggest that education programs specifically need to incorporate various components, including domestic, leisure/recreational, community, and vocational, to meet the considerable needs of individuals with severe and/or multiple disabilities. Additionally, taking a multidisciplinary approach is essential. "Professionals such as speech and language therapists, physical and occupational therapists, and psychiatric and medical specialists need to work collectively and collaboratively to provide comprehensive services to those suffering with severe and/or multiple disabilities" (Larsen, 2008, p. 2).

Individuals with some type of learning disability may also fall into this category. Often, psycho-educational testing through the school system is able to determine the specific diagnosis and extent of the problem. Many children deemed to have some type of learning disability are accommodated by the 1973 Rehabilitation Act, 504 Accommodation Plan (Lerner, Lowenthal, & Lerner, 1995). Early interventions are preferable in preventing future long-term academic, social, and psychological problems.

Physical Disabilities

Individuals suffering from physical disabilities include those who suffer from problems with one or more major life activities such as seeing, hearing, speaking, or moving. Those who are blind, deaf, and physically impaired are usually noticeable, yet there are those with more hidden impairments, such as "arthritis, diabetes, heart and back problems, and cancer," who also are considered physically disabled (Burger, 2008, p. 84). Those with a mental illness are also considered to have a physical disability.

Mental Illness Unlike physical disabilities, mental illness is much more difficult to identify. In general, those who are considered mentally ill suffer from emotional and psychological problems and seek services from psychiatric and mental health facilities. Federal regulations define a "serious mental illness" for adults as "any diagnosable mental disorder that affects work, home, or other areas of social functioning." For those under the age of 18, mental illnesses include "any diagnosable mental disorder that severely disrupts social, academic, and emotional functioning." These definitions are fairly nebulous and subjective. A literature review finds that the prevalence of mental illness in any given year is about 30% for adults and 17% for children and adolescents and includes these conditions: anxiety disorders, serious depression, personality disorders involving maladaptive tendencies that cause distress or impaired functioning, Schizophrenia, and brain disorders of Alzheimer's disease (Burger, 2008; Comer, 1995; Regier et al., 1993).

Trends in mental health indicate that more and more individuals are seeking outpatient services for a wide range of psychological and behavioral problems. Milder conditions include parent-child and marital problems or adjustment disorders. Treatment of anxiety and depression has become commonplace; typically a combination of individual and/or group therapy together with medication management is considered the treatment of choice. Those with a more severe mental illness, such as Schizophrenia, may need additional assistance with housing, outreach, hospitalization readmission, and skills for living (Johnson, 1990).

Substance Abuse Those who misuse certain substances for the purpose of altering their mood or psychological state have been identified as substance abusers (Burger, 2008, p. 95). Substances that are abused range from alcohol to such hard drugs as heroin, amphetamines, cocaine, and barbiturates. Marijuana and prescription pain medications like Oxycontin and Vicodin are also widely abused.

Treatment for alcohol and drug addiction is based on the medical model. "The general idea is that addicts are suffering from an illness and should be treated rather than punished. . . . Abusers are victims of compulsive, self-destructive cravings and are in need of medical and psychological treatments" (Burger, 2008, p. 102). Kanel (2008) identifies common elements of brief intervention with this population:

1. Educating clients about the health risks of prolonged substance use
2. Emphasizing owning responsibility for choosing to drink
3. Encouraging reduction of substance use or abstinence
4. Providing strategies to reduce or eliminate substance use
5. Being empathic
6. Encouraging clients to be resourceful and optimistic about their ability to change

A very common resource for substance users is involvement in a 12-step program. Nowinski (2000, p. 2) notes:

The Twelve-Step facilitation (TSF) consists of a brief, structured, and manual-driven approach to facilitating early recovery from alcohol abuse/alcoholism and other drug abuse/addiction. It is intended to be implemented on an individual basis in 12 to 15 sessions and is based on behavioral, spiritual, and cognitive principles that form the core of twelve-step fellowships such as AA [and Narcotics Anonymous]. TSF is suitable for problem drinkers and other drug users and for those who are alcohol and drug dependent.

Basically, 12-step programs are a set of guiding principles for recovery from addiction, compulsion, or other behavioral problems. As summarized by the American Psychological Association (2000), such programs involve:

• Admitting that one cannot control one's addiction or compulsion
• Recognizing a greater power that can give strength
• Examining past errors with the help of a sponsor (experienced member)
• Making amends for these errors
• Learning to live a new life with a new code of behavior
• Helping others who suffer from the same addictions or compulsions

Although self-help groups such as Alcoholics Anonymous or Narcotics Anonymous have been proven to be very effective for many with substance abuse problems, they do not work for everyone. More traditional methods that include individual, family, and group counseling and psychotherapy may be necessary.

Religious/Spirituality Issues

Neukrug (2008) emphasizes that "a client's religious background and current religious beliefs may hold the key to understanding the underlying values that motivates him or her" (p. 211). For that reason, it is important to determine clients' religious backgrounds and the importance of those backgrounds in their lives, to assess their level of faith development, to become knowledgeable regarding their religious beliefs, and to become familiar with religious traditions and rituals.

Protestantism, Catholicism, Judaism, Muslim/Islam, Buddhism, and Hinduism are religions commonly practiced in our country. Atheism is also an ideology; Athiests do not believe in the existence of a god. Human service providers must become acquainted with these religions and ideologies if they hope to better understand their clients' religious views.

Along with religious beliefs, it is important to understand a client's spirituality. Some believe that "addressing spirituality within the therapy is not optional. Human beings are spiritual by nature. If spirituality has no place in therapy then we leave out this part of our humanity and are therefore incapable of serving the full needs of our clients" (Zylstra, 2006, p. 4). Some clients may not belong to any particular religion or participate in religious ceremonies, yet still may be very spiritual. It is just as important to recognize, understand, and accept a client's spirituality as any religious views they may hold.

In Closing

This chapter has focused on understanding the agency systems where mental health professionals work and the special client populations they commonly serve. Taking time to learn about both of these factors is instrumental in developing successful group treatment programs. Knowledge about the agency setting can help the group leader plan a group that will be well received and conducive to agency needs and mandates. Similarly, knowledge about diverse clients—their culture, race, ethnicity, socioeconomic class, geographic location, gender, sexual orientation, disabilities, substance abuse, and religion and spirituality— is necessary in order to tailor group treatment programs to fit their needs. Chapter 6 focuses on the ethical and legal issues of group work that are equally important to understand when developing groups in agency settings.

Ethical and Legal Issues of Group Work in Agency Settings

Basic Ethical Issues of Group Work

Ethical Considerations

Becoming knowledgeable and well grounded in ethical issues is essential for any practitioner. Ethical and legal issues, as they relate to group practice, are similar to those experienced in individual work with clients; at times, they are magnified by the group process when more than one member is present. Group practitioners must strive to become thoroughly familiar with the ethical standards of their professional specialization, to learn to make sound ethical decisions, and to be competent in applying established ethic codes to a range of ethical dilemmas they are likely to be faced with. Ethical standards related to groups are found in all professional associations, including the American Counseling Association (ACA), the American Psychological Association (APA), the National Association for Social Workers (NASW), and the National Organization for Human Services (NOHS). They are also highlighted in specialized organizations, such as the American Group Psychotherapy Association (AGPA) and the Association for Specialists in Group Work (ASGW). This chapter addresses the many ethical and legal issues group practitioners are likely to face.

Ethics are constantly evolving. No doubt, helping professionals will continually be challenged by ethical issues and must therefore remain open to continuing education in this area. Professionals who lose sight of this are often those who have their licenses revoked or temporarily suspended due to a variety of ethical violations.

Practice Values and Ethics

Understanding the role of values and their relationship to ethical codes is a prerequisite to becoming adept at sound ethical decision making. In other words, in order to be able to internalize the codes and standards of group practice, it is important first to acknowledge the core values on which those standards are based. "In short, core values, the ethics codes and standards of practice, and ethical decision-making models all work together to facilitate ethical practice in group work" (Page & Jencius, 2009, p. 5).

Core and Key Values
According to Kitchener (1984); Meara, Schmidt, and Day (1996); and Page and Jencius (2009), there are several primary core values important for group practitioners to understand and internalize. These include:

- *Beneficence*, which relates to practicing in a way that benefits group members and the group as a whole. Any actions made as a group leader in planning, leading, and processing must be made for the good of each member and the greater good of the group as a whole.
- *Nonmaleficence*, which refers to resisting to act in any way that is considered intentionally or unintentionally harmful to members or the group as a whole.
- *Justice* for each group member, which is reflected in treating all members with equity and fairness, regardless of their differences.
- *Autonomy*, which relates to respecting group members' independence, freedom of choice, and self-determination.
- *Veracity*, which refers to always being honest and truthful. Honesty is important in disclosure and offering feedback to members as well as in being open and receiving honest disclosure and feedback from other members.
- *Fidelity*, which involves being responsible, honorable, and trustworthy. Through modeling fidelity, a leader can build trust and loyalty in group members and encourage their similar behavior. When leaders model a commitment to the group, members are more likely to feel a similar level of commitment.

Additional key values that have been identified by Toseland and Rivas (2009) are:

- *Respect and dignity*, which refers to valuing each member's worth and contributions to the group.
- *Solidarity and mutual aid*, which relates to acknowledging the power and promise of relationships that are instrumental in assisting members to grow and develop; helping them heal; satisfying their needs for human contact and connectedness; and providing a sense of unity and community.
- *Empowerment*, which involves encouraging members to utilize the power of the group in improving their self-esteem and their ability to help themselves, and in making a difference in their communities.
- *Understanding, respect, and camaraderie* among people from diverse backgrounds, which refers to honoring the ability of groups to help enrich members by acquainting them with people from other backgrounds. Through the life of a group, members often grow to respect and appreciate one another.

It is important to remember that as practitioners, we are not perfect, yet we must continually strive to apply these core values.

Group Work Values
Toseland and Rivas (2009, p. 7) also identify these "group work values":

- *Diversity*, given the involvement of individuals who differ in ethnicities, national origin, creed, and social class in the group.
- *Participatory democracy*, whereby members work cooperatively and engage in mutual decision making among members.
- *Individual initiative*, which is viewed as very important within the group.
- *Freedom and autonomy*, regarding participating and possessing the right to be involved in the decision-making process of the group.
- *High individualization* in the group, which allows unique concerns of each member to be addressed.

Certainly, all of these values are important in any aspect of the helping profession, yet they are of central importance in group work. It is important for group practitioners to internalize, practice, and model these core values in group sessions, "thereby encouraging members to incorporate these values into their own behavior patterns" (Page &

Jencius, 2009, p. 7). When leaders incorporate core values as a foundation for group process, they establish the unique growth-producing experience that we call group counseling.

Personal Values

The leader's values play a critical role in how he or she will proceed, since people's values are a fundamental part of who they are and they inevitably influence the way they lead a group. Brill (1990) states: "Values and standards are internalized and emotion laden, and have become so much a part of one's attitudes, feelings, thinking, and behaving that one is often unaware of their existence" (pp. 24–25). M.S. Corey and G. Corey (2006) suggest: "You can increase your effectiveness as a leader by becoming aware of the values you hold and the subtle and direct ways you might influence group members" (p. 77). The ACA's ethical standard A.5.b corroborates the importance of value awareness: "Counselors [group leaders] are aware of their own values, attitudes, beliefs, and behaviors and how these apply in a diverse society, and avoid imposing their values on clients." Helpers may be tempted to influence, push, or indoctrinate group members toward their own values; sometimes we do so just by our interactions with clients. Often group members seek help because of a value conflict; thus they are prime candidates to be swayed by group leaders. Group members may be more vulnerable to the influence of an authority figure. Part of the group leader's role may be to help clients understand their values and how they may impact their goals and decisions. This does not mean, however, that the group leader should tell clients how to proceed based on their own values. "Allowing inappropriate intrusion of one's values into practice settings is ethically unacceptable and unprofessional" (Alle-Corliss & Alle-Corliss, 2006, p. 22). Ideally, helpers and group leaders "can help clients search out alternative value systems and openly indicate when their own biases may unduly influence a client" (Nugent, 1990, p. 263).

We concur with G. Corey's (2004) belief that

> as group leader, when you impose your values, you are showing disrespect for the members' integrity. Expecting members to adopt your value system gives them the message that they are incapable of discovering a meaningful set of values and acting on them by themselves. When you expose your values, in contrast, members are free to test their own thinking against the background of your beliefs, but they can still make their own choices without being burdened with guilt that they are not meeting your expectations. (p. 66)

Clearly, it is important for any helper, including group leaders, to be aware of their values and remain objective when working with clients whose values differ. Typical value conflicts that helping professionals must be aware of include those tied to family issues, gender roles, religion, abortion, sexuality, sexual orientation, AIDS, and cultural and racial identity. Although it is inevitable for value conflicts to enter into the therapeutic relationship, it is possible to be cognizant of them and to strive to work through them. In cases where a group practitioner's values differ greatly from those of clients, coworkers, or agency, effective treatment can still be rendered, provided the helper is open and aware. If value conflicts are too great, however, referrals or transfers are recommended. Care must be taken, however, in examining the reasons for a referral to ensure that it is ethically appropriate. Alle-Corliss and Alle-Corliss (2006) suggest that

> *helpers need to carefully examine their reasons for referring and to ask themselves if the referral is appropriate. Will the referral benefit the client or the helper? Simply because one does not like a client or is uncomfortable with a person is not a sufficient reason to refer that person to another helper. Some clients may take the referral personally and may be offended and hurt. Informing clients about such referrals needs to be handled sensitively. (p. 22)*

Group Membership

Client Rights

Group leaders must be aware of and respect the rights of group participants. Informed consent, involuntary membership, freedom to withdraw from a group, freedom from coercion and undue pressure, and the right to confidentiality are the most common client rights.

Informed Consent
Informed consent is the "cornerstone of group therapy. It is an agreement between the therapist and group member that is a foundation for the member's constructive work within the group" (Brabender, Fallon, & Smolar, 2004, p. 188). Informed consent requires helpers to disclose to their clients relevant information about the treatment they are pursuing. "Informed consent involves the client's right to know the purpose and nature of all aspects of client involvement with the helper and within the helping relationship" (Neukrug, 2002, p. 162). This type

of disclosure can help clients to make informed decisions about entering and remaining in treatment and ultimately ensures their rights to self-determination and autonomy and promotes respect for them and their desires.

Even though informed consent is considered a singular term, each component must be considered separately. *Informed* relates to the clients' right of being informed of all of the crucial aspects associated with treatment, specifically group treatment. *Consent* applies to the agreement by members entering treatment to participate in the group.

Facets of informed consent and how they relate to group practice are discussed next. These are divided into pregroup disclosures and clients' rights during the group.

Pregroup Disclosures

Informing Clients about Helper's Role, Qualifications, and Experience:
- Provide a statement describing the education, training, and qualifications of the group leader(s).

Informing Clients about Services to be Rendered:
- Provide a clear statement regarding the nature and purpose of the group.
- Provide a description of the group format, procedures, and ground rules.
- Provide a description of the leader's theoretical orientation.
- Engage in an initial interview to determine whether this particular group with this particular leader is appropriate to their needs at this time.
- Allow members an opportunity to seek information about the group, to pose questions, and to explore concerns.
- Engage in a discussion of ways the group process may or may not be congruent with the cultural beliefs and values of group members.
- Engage in a discussion of the rights and responsibilities of group members.

Providing Clients with Information Regarding Goals, Limitations, and Potential Risks of Treatment:
- Provide information about the length of group, frequency and duration of meetings, group goals, and techniques being employed.

- Offer information about the psychological risks involved in group participation.
- Offer clarification of what services can and cannot be provided within the group.
- Provide assistance in developing personal goals.
- Provide a clear understanding of the division of responsibility between leader and participants.
- Inform members about how the group will affect them both during the session and while they are living in their daily lives.

Ensuring that Clients Understand the Fees and Billing Arrangements:
- Provide information concerning fees and expenses including fees for a follow-up session.

Informing Clients about Their Rights to Obtain Case Records:
- Provide clients with accurate information regarding their right to obtain case records.

Allowing Clients to Participate in Developing the Treatment Plan:
- Providing clients with an opportunity to participate in their treatment planning encourages a cooperative atmosphere, enhances the helper-client relationship, and facilitates evaluation of the treatment strategies used.

Informing Clients about Their Right to Refuse Any Recommended Services:
- Inform clients that it is their choice to continue in treatment.

Providing Clients with Clear and Specific Information about Their Rights to Confidentiality:
- Educate clients about confidentiality and engage in a discussion of clients' rights to confidentiality and the importance of confidentiality being honored outside of the group.

Discuss the Exceptions to Confidentiality:
- Provide knowledge of the circumstances in which confidentiality must be broken because of legal, ethical, or professional reasons.

Informing Clients Regarding the Need for Their Written Consent Before Releasing Client Records/Information:

- Inform clients that as a right of privacy, they must sign a release before client records or information can be released.

Clients' Rights During the Group

- Inform clients about what is expected of them.
- Give notice of any research involving the group and of any audio- or videotaping of group sessions.
- Inform clients of their rights to stop any recording if it restricts member participation.
- Assist clients in translating group learning into action in everyday life.
- Provide opportunities for review and evaluation of group, and prepare for closure by discussing any unfinished business.
- Provide crisis intervention or referral for such if a crisis should arise as a direct result of participation in the group.
- Exercise the use of reasonable safeguards in minimizing the potential risks of group.
- Respect client privacy and degree of disclosure.
- Observe confidentiality on behalf of group leader and members.
- Members should be free from having values imposed by the leader and other group members.
- Enforce values of dignity and respect.

Benefits of Informed Consent As we have seen, informed consent is an important client right and an ethical and legal requirement. In addition, providing informed consent is considered an integral part of the therapeutic process, regardless of the professional role or theoretical framework being used. Establishment of trust is more likely when helpers provide informed consent. Informing clients about the services to be rendered fosters the development of a trusting relationship. "It demonstrates respect for [clients'] their ability to make informed choices and encourages them to entrust you with their confidence" (Alle-Corliss & Alle-Corliss, 2006, p. 163). The act of educating clients about their rights and responsibilities also serves to empower them and to promote their active cooperation in their own treatment.

During the process of informing clients about their rights, helpers may discover possible problem areas. For instance, when discussing the issue of confidentiality and legal exceptions, clients who struggle with some form of abuse may become anxious or may prematurely exit from treatment. Being observant and alert to signs of possible conflicts or areas of difficulty is important. It is also suggested to begin early exploration of such areas and provide education regarding possible treatments.

Agency Responses to Informed Consent Depending on the types of services provided, what agencies are required to disclose varies. "Agencies require different levels of disclosure; some agencies may be rigid about these policies, whereas others may be indifferent or even unaware of the disclosure requirements" (Alle-Corliss & Alle-Corliss, 2006, p. 163). Formal policies and procedures exist in many agencies, with standardized forms for clients to sign as well as informative brochures and pamphlets. More informal ways of providing informed consent also exist in some agencies. To learn how informed consent is dealt with at a particular agency, directly ask professionals there how they handle these issues.

Involuntary Membership
Involvement in any type of treatment, including group therapy, is most beneficial when it is voluntary. Mandated or involuntary treatment is more complicated and requires special care. According to G. Corey (2004, p. 58), in cases where participation in treatment is mandatory, the issue of informed consent is especially important. Group leaders must make a concerted effort to fully inform involuntary members about the nature and goals of the group, the procedures that are likely to be used, their client rights and responsibilities, the limits of confidentiality, and the impact their participation will likely have on decisions made about them outside of the group.

Involuntary group clients are those who are pressured or required to be involved in group treatment for various reasons. Some enter treatment "in lieu of some worse punishment such as going to jail, losing a license, or as a condition of probation"; others may be "forced into a group by a school system, a therapeutic community, or some other entity with the notion that it will do them some good to participate" (Toseland & Rivas, 2009, p. 211). Alle-Corliss and Alle-Corliss (2006) describe involuntary clients as those "who do not voluntarily seek the services of the helper but are court ordered, coerced by parents or spouse, or manipulated by threats of divorce by the spouse or of grounding by the parents" (p. 232).

Subtle pressure to be treated in a group may also exist, since group treatment is becoming the modality of choice for many mental health facilities and health maintenance organizations due to cost considerations; clients may be encouraged to participate in group versus individual treatment.

Clearly, clients who resist entering treatment create a difficult and sometimes awkward situation for the group leader. In working with involuntary clients, it is important to begin by assessing their readiness for change. Using the five part model of change—(1) precontemplation, (2) contemplation, (3) preparation, (4) action, and (5) maintenance— proposed by Prochaska, DiClimente, and Norcross (1992) is helpful in determining where the client is on the continuum. Toseland and Rivas (2009) suggest that helpers can better assess where each group member is on this continuum by asking members from the start how they feel about attending the group and what they hope to get out of it. It is important to use reflective and skillful listening in order to better understand how group members feel, all the while taking care to not be judgmental, critical, or blaming (Miller & Rollnick, 2002).

Many times involuntary group members initially manifest their resistance by expressing hostility toward the group leader and/or group members (Rooney & Chovanec, 2004). Brill (1990) adds that in addition to hostile behavior, clients may express their resistance through indifference or apathy or by pretending acceptance. Any of these situations pose difficulties for the group leader. It is important to not be put off by any forms of client resistance; instead, group leaders must make an effort to understand the resistance. It is important for group leaders to convey to members that they understand their feelings of being pressured or coerced to be in the group and thus their hesitation to commit to it. Group leaders should be accepting and strive to develop a respect for resistance, as it may serve a valuable purpose. Certainly it is vital to explore the significance of the resistance and its inherent dynamics, to work toward developing a trusting relationship, to address the resistance directly and empathetically, and to be flexible, creative, and willing to work with the resistance.

Far too often group leaders erroneously assume that mandatory groups will be composed of unmotivated clients and that client resistances are difficult to treat. Group leaders who hold these assumptions have difficulty in being successful. M.S. and G. Corey (2006) suggest that "this belief is bound to have a negative effect on group members. . . . any initial distrust must be treated with respect as this can be the very material for exploration that leads to increased trust. Sometimes people who are mandated to attend groups make significant changes in their lives" (p. 68).

Freedom to Withdraw from Group

It is important that group members be informed about group "policies regarding attendance, commitment to remaining in group for a predetermined number of sessions, and leaving a particular session if they do not like what is going on in the group" (M.S. Corey & G. Corey, 2006, p. 68). We concur that the leader's attitudes and policies regarding members' rights to leave a group must be spelled out at a preliminary session (G. Corey, Schneider-Corey, Callanan, and Russell, 2004). Forcing a group member to stay in a group is not ethical or therapeutic. It is also not conducive to group process to encourage members to have the freedom to leave whenever they choose. Since the premature departure of a group member can impact both the person who is leaving and the trust and cohesion among remaining group members, it is important to discuss early departure at the onset of treatment. The leader should discuss his or her attitudes and polices regarding leaving the group in the initial group session. Despite these efforts, there will be times when a group member will want to terminate treatment prematurely. Ideally, it is important to encourage group members to verbalize any doubts or concerns they may have about participating in the group rather than keeping these reactions to themselves. Group members need to know that the best way to work through interpersonal conflicts or dissatisfaction with a group is to remain an active participant. "With a commitment to discuss the factors related to leaving, there is an opportunity for everyone concerned to express and explore unfinished business" (M. S. Corey & G. Corey, 2006, p. 69). In the event that a group member chooses to leave without warning, the group leader should encourage the group to process their feelings openly during the next group session.

Psychological Risks for Members

Because groups can be powerful impetuses for change, there is always the potential for certain psychological risks for members (Brabender et al., 2004; G. Corey, 2004; G. Corey et al., 2007; M.S. Corey & G. Corey, 2006; Toseland & Rivas, 2009). Merely going to a group can by risky, as members usually undergo some change, which is bound to affect themselves as well as others in their lives. G. Corey (2004, p. 62) cites "life changes that cause disruption, hostile and destructive confrontations, scapegoating, and harmful socializing among members" as possible risks. Other examples include misuse of self-disclosure, heightened awareness of unpleasant events from their past, or the desire to make decisions that could lead to stressful consequences, such as getting a divorce. Brabender et al. (2004) detail these areas as potential risks:

- Experiencing discomfort in the group sessions that extends to life outside the group: "Depending upon the goals and processes of the group, members may have negative reactions associated with receiving constructive feedback, recognizing certain psychological elements within themselves, or facing difficult behavioral tasks" (p. 189).

- Failing to benefit from the group: "Not every member benefits and the entering member should be helped to understand that no guarantee of his or her progress can be made" (p. 189).

- Breach of member confidentiality by another member who shares information outside of the group: "Members often fail to think through the possible consequences sufficiently to recognize that they could be very serious" (p. 189).

- Breach of confidentiality that is covered in exceptions to confidentiality: for example, when there is a need to make an abuse report (child, dependent adult care, or elder) as a mandated report, when there is a risk of harm to self or others, when a client is gravely disabled, or when some form of privilege is necessary.

These are only a few of the potential psychological risks of involvement in group treatment; surely there are many more. Ethically, it is the responsibility of the group leader to address these potential risks with prospective new members, preferably during the screening interview and at the initial session during the orientation phase. The various codes of ethics substantiate the need to inform group members of potential risks. The ACA's ethical standard A.9.b (1995) says that "in a group setting, counselors take reasonable precautions to protect clients from physical and psychological trauma," precautions that include discussing potential life changes and advantages and disadvantages of group involvement.

It is a given that participation in any type of group involves some risk. Group leaders must be ethically responsible to ensure that their prospective group members are aware of the potential risks of group treatment and must take every precaution again them. Ultimately, however, some risk may be necessary for meaningful life learning.

Confidentiality

Confidentiality has been called a keystone condition or central ethical issue in group counseling and is considered an essential condition for effective group work. Confidentiality issues are especially important in group work. "The leader must not only keep the confidences of members but must also encourage that members maintain confidentiality between one another. Mistrust and betrayal are likely repercussions when confidentiality is violated" (Alle-Corliss & Alle-Corliss, 1999, p. 193). Jacobs, Masson, and Harvill (2006) note that "there are two issues regarding confidentiality that any group leader should understand: the leader's ethical responsibility for keeping material confidential and the leader's lack of total control regarding members' keeping matters confidential" (p. 437). Because of this reality, it is important for group leaders to create the conditions in which confidentiality is likely to be maintained among members. The Code of Ethics and Standards of Practice (ACA, 1995) confirms the importance of confidentiality in group work:

> *In group work, counselors [group leaders] clearly define confidentiality and the parameters for the specific group being entered, explain its importance, and discuss the difficulties related to confidentiality involved in group work. The fact that confidentiality cannot be guaranteed is clearly communicated to group members. (B.2.a)*

Brabender et al. (2004) contend that confidentiality must be preserved "in order to safeguard each member's right to privacy and to enable the delivery of an effective therapeutic experience." They also encourage establishing expectations and consequences that involve outlining "in very concrete terms what is meant by the requirement of confidentiality" (p. 184). In addition to emphasizing not to share group content outside of the group, members must also be informed to not disclose group members' identities (Luepker, 2003).

The various consequences of breaching confidentiality are also important to address at the onset. M.S. and G. Corey (2006) have found that "generally, members do not violate confidentiality when they talk about what they learned in group sessions. But they are likely to breach confidentiality when they talk about how they acquired insights or how they actually interacted in a group" (pp. 72–73). The best way to prevent any such breach is to continually stress the importance of confidentiality during group sessions and to discuss the subject whenever it seems necessary. Furthermore, reinforcing confidentiality helps build a trusting group environment.

Limits to confidentiality must be specified at the outset of the group. These legally mandated disclosures are commonly referred to as exceptions to confidentiality and vary from state to state and even county to county. Common exceptions whereby group leaders are able to breach confidentiality include:

- Physical or sexual abuse of children, the elderly, and dependent adults (mandated reporting laws)
- Cases of potential harm to self, possibly requiring hospitalization for an involuntary 72-hour hold (5150)
- Cases of potential harm to others that may require use of the Tarasoff law that requires helpers to warn the intended victim
- Gravely disabled individuals who may need to be involuntarily hospitalized for a 72-hour hold (5150)
- Court orders and subpoenas requesting client information
- Client waivers of confidentiality
- Supervision and consultation
- Permissible reporting of emotional abuse and spousal abuse
- Reporting of AIDS when deemed necessary

The ACA's Code of Ethics (1995) discusses these exceptions to confidentiality:

> *The general requirement that counselors keep information confidential does not apply when disclosure is required to prevent clear and imminent danger to the client or others or when legal requirements demand that confidential information be revealed. Counselors consult with other professionals when in doubt as to the validity of an exception. (B.1.c)*

It is important for group leaders to be knowledgeable about their legal rights and which situations may fall under the category of exceptions. Every situation is unique and must be judged on an individual basis. Woodside and McClam (1994) write, "Agency guidelines, the profession's code of ethics, and laws of the state in which one practices are important considerations in the delivery of services" (p. 260).

Need for Proper Screening

The importance of thorough screening has been emphasized in an earlier chapter. Here we wish to mention screening as an ethical issue. Proper screening is necessary to avoid potential physical and psychological risks for everyone in the group. If the leader has valid concerns about accepting a particular group member, it would be unethical to allow the person to participate in the group without further evaluation. Proper screening requires careful preparation by the leader(s) and sound assessment skills. In some instances, specific screening questions are asked to screen out those who may not be ready or may not be appropriate for the group.

Group Preparation
As we have seen, preparing group members for group work is part of informed consent. When group leaders take time to provide group members with information about the group, they are acting ethically. Conversely, when group leaders neglect to discuss in any depth relevant information about the group's purpose and process, there is greater likelihood that members will feel unclear about the group. At the very least, group members may feel uninvolved in the process, which can adversely affect the direction of the group. In more severe cases, group members may feel upset that they were not properly prepared for the intensity of the group or were not informed about group expectations. Perhaps they feel they were misled or were not ready to disclose or to hear others disclose certain feelings. Of course, the group leader cannot predict everything that will transpire in a group, but taking time to prepare the group as much as possible sets a positive tone and facilitates open dialogue among members and the leader throughout the group.

Ethical Use of Exercises and Techniques
Therapeutic exercises are common to group work and can be very effective. However, when there is little preparation or expertise in using certain exercises, harmful effects are the result. Jacobs et al. (2006) suggest: "Leaders should keep several ethical considerations in mind when using structured activities or exercises during a group session. Most ethical problems involving exercises result from a lack of expertise or sensitivity on the part of the leader" (p. 438). For instance, it is unethical for inexperienced group leaders to use certain exercises that elicit overwhelming emotions in the group. This is a clear example of unethical behavior as is any situation in which leaders go beyond their skill level.

Jacobs et al. (2006) have identified these examples of operating without adequate skills and thereby acting unethically:

- Not preparing group members about what they are to experience, including disclosing potential risks, if they are to participate in a group exercise

- Leader placing undue pressure on a member to participate in an exercise he or she is not open to
- Encouraging an exercise on death, such as writing one's own epitaph, and then not being able to deal with the resultant pain and other emotions
- Conducting an exercise that relates to guilt and shame and not being able to properly deal with various memories that surface, including incest, child abuse, affairs, and the like
- Engaging in a feedback exercise whereby the leader allows a member to be psychologically attacked by the other group members
- Continuing to demand group member participation when members are not receptive
- Manipulating clients into revealing something personal they are not ready to share in the group setting
- Encouraging use of exercises that result in disclosure of heavy emotional material without planning for time after to process feelings; "unzipping members and leaving them hanging" (p. 438)

Group leaders must exercise caution regarding the use of exercises and techniques within the group. When therapeutic methods have a potential to be experienced intensely, it is important to exercise caution in their use. Group leaders must be prepared to manage any powerful reactions that certain role-playing activities can trigger. A general rule of thumb is to consider using techniques that are likely to elicit powerful emotions only with those group members with whom trust has been established, who have been properly prepared, and who are open and willing to participate. Also, being careful to tailor exercises to deal with specific group member situations in a group is preferable to the random use of exercises and techniques. Experience and proper supervision is essential. Being knowledgeable about how theory guides practice is important. G. Corey (2004) notes that "theories give rise to many therapeutic strategies and techniques. Such techniques are a means to increase awareness, to accomplish change, or to promote exploration and interaction. They can certainly be used ethically and therapeutically, yet they can also be misused" (p. 68).

Taking care to ensure that group members avoid undue pressure is certainly ethically indicated. G. Corey et al. (2004) and Corey,

Schneider-Corey, and Callanan (2007) describe five areas of undue pressure to be cautious of:

1. Freedom not to participate
2. Pressure from other members
3. Misuse of confrontational techniques
4. Forced touching
5. Inappropriate catharsis

In the first area, the "freedom not to participate," it is important to convey to group members that they need not participate in exercises they are uncomfortable with. Often group members feel they must participate to be accepted. They feel pressured even though they are told it is okay not to participate. Group leaders must genuinely convey acceptance to members when discussing their feelings about participation. When a group leader believes an individual member would benefit by group involvement, it is the leader's task to achieve a balance between appropriate challenge and undue pressure or unethical coercion. Leaders must remain alert to the subtle differences that may exist.

Certainly the group's makeup and purpose as well as the client-therapist relationship will have an impact on how much a leader will consider healthy challenging. We concur with views of G. Corey et al. (2004):

> *The more trust you have established with group members, and the more cohesive the group, the more you can challenge these members. The ethical issue centers on having a basic respect for working with material that is already present and, even more important, a basic respect for the client's decisions about what to explore and how far to go with it. (p. 32)*

Regarding pressure from other members, at times group members feel undue pressure from other members to participate in exercises or to disclose more than they are comfortable with. It is the group leader's ethical obligation to respond to the undue peer pressure on a group member. This is especially essential when the leader has assured the group that no one will be coerced into making disclosures or participating in activities. The leader must remain attentive to both overt and subtle clues regarding peer pressure and find appropriate ways to intervene.

The third area of undue pressure is misuse of confrontational techniques, which relates to the abuse of power by group leaders who use inappropriate techniques. Some leaders may misuse their power by directing techniques at a particular member; doing so is unwarranted and unethical.

Forced touching is definitely a major violation of ethical codes. Sometimes members may touch to show physical intimacy, or a leader may be in a position to touch a member during an exercise. Care must always be used and a clear rationale must be present. If possible, the group leader could introduce the topic for discussion within the group so that members are assured that their personal privacy will not be invaded.

Likewise, inappropriate catharsis is clearly unethical. There will be times when catharsis or venting is appropriate. Other times such intense emotional venting may not be acceptable or therapeutic. It is important to clarify whether catharsis is used to fulfill the leader's own needs or those of the clients. Furthermore, it is important to determine if a client is psychologically able to tolerate such catharsis, if the group leader is sufficiently qualified and experienced, and if the group as a whole is okay with this.

Use of Multiple Treatments

Many times clients are involved in more than one type of treatment. For instance, a client may be receiving individual therapy and be involved in group treatment simultaneously. Certainly "clients can benefit from participation in treatment modalities simultaneously with the group therapy experience [yet] such participation in multiple treatments creates the need for the coordination of each component" (Brabender et al., 2004, p. 191). It is important for practitioners to carefully conceptualize whether, how, and what information will be shared and how this will be explained to the client. Also, the consideration of referrals and how they will be made is necessary to address. Clients must authorize the release of any information necessary to make the referral. In all cases, the practitioner must be open to discussing all relevant alternatives to any and all treatment modalities.

Using Physical Techniques

Perhaps even more potentially problematic than other areas is the use of physical techniques in group sessions. Generally, because of the potential for physical and psychological harm and misuse, physical techniques are discouraged. Group leaders who consider introducing physical

Table 6.1 **Guidelines for Ethical Use of Techniques**

1. Work therapeutically with emotional issues that members themselves initiate. Sometimes group leaders may find it therapeutic to encourage experiencing feelings that are hidden or only beginning to emerge; members must be willing and open to do this.
2. Do not use techniques solely to stir up emotions. It is important to have a rationale underlying the use of any technique.
3. Use techniques to foster the client's self-exploration and self-understanding.
4. Use techniques to help group members, not to cover up the group leader's discomfort or incompetence.
5. It is inappropriate to use a technique, such as the "empty chair" technique, that serves to deter a member's possible confrontation toward the therapist.
6. It is unacceptable to use techniques to avoid dealing with the group leader's fears of exploring certain themes. The leader must deal with any countertransference issues in supervision.
7. Introduce techniques in a sensitive manner. Reconsider using a technique when individual group members or the group as a whole are not emotionally ready to partake in the exercise.
8. Timing is important. Engaging an exercise at the end of the session is dangerous, as is suggesting an exercise when other issues and concerns should be addressed first.
9. Do not continue to use techniques that have proven ineffective.
10. Intervene when a group member is being pressured to participate in an exercise he or she is not ready or willing to engage in.
11. Remain diversity sensitive in considering techniques to be used.

Source: Adapted from Brabender et al. (2004); G. Corey (2004); G. Corey et al. (2004); G. Corey et al. (2007); M.S. and G. Corey (2006); Jacobs et al. (2006); Toseland and Rivas (2009); Zastrow (2009).

techniques must have appropriate training, must be experienced enough to understand the group process, and must be aware of possible consequences. G. Corey et al. (2004) note that "in using techniques, the central ethical issue is the competence of the leader" (p. 36). They further highlight the importance of the group leader being familiar enough with the group member to determine if it is therapeutically appropriate to engage in physical techniques. Table 6.1 presents 11 guidelines for ethical use of various techniques.

Group Leadership

Leaders play a vital role in determining the outcome of the groups they lead. In fact, it has been noted that "the leader's character, personal qualities, and philosophy of life are more important than any technique for facilitating the group process" (G. Corey et al., 2004, p. 24). It is recommended that group leaders learn to "pay attention to themselves" in order to monitor their own experiences in the group and to recognize the impact of their presence. Being able to trust one's hunches and take healthy risks in trying out new exercises with the group is also encouraged. Similarly, group leaders who are open to modeling within the group set a positive example that encourages openness.

Ethically, group leaders must also be aware of their motivations and be clear about their theoretical stance. Group leaders who are unaware of their motivations may misuse group techniques, such as applying pressure on clients to perform in certain ways, striving to impress clients, attempting to steer clients away from exploring feelings and issues that they may find personally threatening, and stirring up emotions through the use of confrontational techniques.

Skilled and savvy group leaders may appear superhuman. Group members may tend to "attribute exaggerated power and wisdom" to them, resulting in a "temptation for leaders to be seduced by this" (G. Corey et al., 2004, p. 28). Leaders can avoid this by remaining self-aware and by routinely explaining the purpose of a suggested technique to clients. Leaders who are aware of the therapeutic rationale for the techniques they use are less likely to misuse them.

Adequate Training for Group Leader(s)

Determining Competence Level

Since effective group leadership requires a skilled practitioner, it is important for group leaders to be continually aware of their level of competence. According to M.S. and G. Corey (2006): "Competence is one of the major ethical issues in group work. . . . It is essential for leaders to recognize the boundaries of their competence and to restrict themselves to working only with those groups for which their training and experience have properly prepared them" (p. 85). Different groups and client populations will require different leadership skills. A leader who is skilled in providing psychoeducational groups may not feel as comfortable in conducting a psychodynamic process group. Likewise, working with children and adolescents is not the same as working with adult anger management groups, chemical dependency, or elderly clients. Because of the many facets involved, group leaders may need specific training and supervised experience for each specialized type of group they intend to lead. Besides formal education at the bachelor's, master's, or doctoral levels, many group leaders may also be required to take a variety of specialized group therapy training workshops.

Leader Preparation

According to Jacobs et al. (2006), "the fundamental ethical principle for leading groups" is found in ASGW's "Best Practice Guidelines" (1998): "Group counselors [leaders] do not attempt any technique unless thoroughly trained in its use or under supervision by a counselor [leader] familiar with the intervention" (p. 434). Simply said, it is unethical to lead a group, especially a therapy group, without the proper qualifications and preparation. The ASGW (1998) suggests these ways for group leaders to enhance their level of competence:

- Remain current and increase your knowledge and skill competencies through activities such as continuing education, consultation, supervision, and participation in personal and professional developmental activities.
- Be open to getting professional assistance for your own personal problems or conflicts that may impair your professional judgment or ability to facilitate a group.
- Utilize consultation and supervision to ensure effective practice when you are working with a group for which you need to acquire more knowledge and skill competencies.

Page and Jencius (2009) offer additional suggestions:

- Consider your designated scope of practice. The scope of practice for each type and level of licensure is important for every group leader to assess.
- Consider your experience and expertise: Evaluate your experience on the topic that is the group focus and your experience leading such a group. If you do not have the necessary skills, begin by coleading.
- Secure clinical supervision with a supervisor with experience in leading groups.
- Read up on the topic of the group you are interested in conducting. Texts, journal articles, or credible Internet sites are all areas from which to enrich your learning.

Gaining knowledge regarding the theory or therories being used, the subject matter or group topic, and the client population are all necessary to be effective in group leading. "It is unethical to lead a group without having a good grasp of the material being discussed" or familiarity with issues that may be unique to the members due to their diverse backgrounds (Jacobs et al., 2006, p. 434). We elaborate on diversity issues in a later section.

Professional Training Standards for Group Counselors
Specific training standards for group leaders has been expanded in ASGW's (2000) "Professional Standards for the Training of Group Workers," which covers three areas of competencies: knowledge competencies, skill competencies, and core group work specialization.

The area of knowledge competencies includes: leader identification of strengths, weaknesses, and values; knowledge of group stages and development, therapeutic factors, and group member roles and behaviors; and awareness of the importance of evaluation and ethical and legal issues specific to group work.

The area of skill competencies consists of the ability to open and close group sessions, to model appropriate behaviors for group members, to engage in appropriate self-disclosure, to give and receive constructive feedback, to assist members in attributing meaning to their experience and integrating and applying learning from the group experience, and to be competent in applying ethical standards in group practice.

CORE group work specializations include: task and work groups, psychoeducational groups, group counseling, and group psychotherapy. Training in all these four areas is ideal. Many group leaders will not have the opportunity or will not choose to receive added instruction in group practice. We suggest, if possible, that both new and seasoned group leaders seek any additional training possible. Those training to be group leaders would greatly benefit by engaging in their own personal therapy, participating in group counseling or a personal growth/self-exploration group, and partaking in an experiential training and supervision group.

Ethical Issues in Training Group Counselors
Combining experiential and didactic training methods is considered controversial since ethical issues related to the training and preparation of group leaders are involved. Although many (G. Corey, 2004; M.S. Corey & G. Corey, 2006; G. Corey et al., 2007; Markus & King, 2003; Stockton, Morran, & Krieger, 2004) in the field find that participating in an experiential growth process group is necessary, four ethical issues must be taken into consideration:

1. Group leader trainees have the right to be informed about the specific nature of course and program requirements.

2. They must be open to self-exploration and to dealing with interpersonal issues in a group setting.

3. They must be ready to receive and to offer constructive feedback to
other group members.

4. The management of multiple roles by the trainer, who may also be
the group facilitator, evaluator, and supervisor, poses issues tied to
boundaries and power.

Recognizing these potential ethical pitfalls is critical when considering entering a training program.

Ethical Considerations for Group Leaders

Dual Relationships

In group work, dual relationships arise when the group leader mixes
professional and personal relationships with a group member or members. Jacobs et al. (2006) define a dual relationship for group work "as a
relationship that exists in addition to the therapeutic relationship established between the leader and the members" (p. 436). Welfel (2002)
adds, "Whenever [helpers] have other connections with a client in
addition to the therapist-client relationship, a dual or a multiple relationship exists" (p. 155).

Although many dual relationships may not be harmful in and of
themselves or may be completely avoidable, they can still pose a
boundary breakdown and be viewed as unethical. It is generally believed
that group leaders should honor the boundary between the professional
and personal lives of the helper and client (Alle-Corliss & Alle-Corliss,
2006; Corey & Herlihy, 1997; Cormier & Hackney, 2005; Welfel, 2002).
The codes of ethics of all helping professionals recommend refraining
from dual- or multiple-role relationships when possible. The literature
identifies three basic reasons that justify our view that dual relationships
can be problematic and potentially unethical:

1. A dual relationship may suggest that the practitioner/therapist is
vulnerable to other interests that compete with promoting the
welfare of the client.

2. When a practitioner/therapist has another role in the client's life,
the client may become confused.

3. A power differential is said to exist in all helping relationships, with the practitioner/therapist holding more power than the client. "The client who feels powerless may feel coerced to participate in a dual- or multiple-role relationship" (Cormier & Hackney, 2005, p. 177–178).

Ultimately it is important to determine if the social relationship is interfering with the therapeutic relationship. The ACA (1995) code of ethics says this about dual relationships:

> *Counselors [group leaders] are aware of their influential positions with respect to clients, and they avoid exploiting the trust and dependency of clients. Counselors [group leaders] make every effort to avoid dual relationships with clients that could impair professional judgment or increase the risk of harm to clients. When dual relationships cannot be avoided, counselors [group leaders] take appropriate professional precautions such as informed consent, consultation, supervision, and documentation to ensure that judgment is not impaired and no exploitation occurs. (A.6.a)*

The ethical standards and codes of ethics of social workers and human service providers propose similar stipulations. The NASW code of ethics (1999) states:

> *Social workers should not engage in dual or multiple relationships with clients or former clients in which there is a risk of exploitation or potential harm to the client. In instances when dual or multiple relationships are unavoidable, social workers should take steps to protect clients and are responsible for setting clear, appropriate, and culturally sensitive boundaries. (1.06.c)*

The National Organization of Human Service Educators (NOHSE) ethical standards of 2000 emphasize the power and status differential that exists between clients and helpers:

> *Human service professionals are aware that in their relationships with clients power and status are unequal. Therefore they recognize that dual or multiple relationships may increase the risk of harm to, or exploitation of, clients, and may impair their professional judgment. However, in some communities and situations it may not be feasible to avoid social or other nonprofessional contact with clients. Human service professionals support*

the trust implicit in the helping relationship by avoiding dual relationships
that may impair professional judgment, increase the risk of harm to clients
or lead to exploitation. (p. 2)

A theme that runs through all of these codes is the concern that the group leader could potentially harm a client while engaging in a dual relationship, especially if there is sexual contact. Helpers of any type must avoid, without exception, sexual relationships with their clients. Leslie (1993) asserts that any exploitation of a sexual nature is prohibited with a client, a client's spouse, or a client's partner.

Additional types of dual relationships that should be avoided "include, but are not limited to, familial, social, financial, business, or close personal relationship with clients" (Alle-Corliss & Alle-Corliss, 2006, p. 211). Nonsexual dual or multiple relationships that could be problematic in individual and group treatment include:

- Accepting a friend or relative as a client/group member
- Providing treatment to an employee
- Employing a client/group member
- Going into business with a current and/or former client/group member
- Providing treatment to a student and/or supervisee
- Allowing a client/group member to enroll in a course taught by the helper/group leader
- Inviting a client/group member to a party or going to a social event with the client/group member
- Selling something to the client/group member (Welfel, 2002, p. 165)

Certainly these examples are not as severe as sexual intimacy. Nonetheless, the inherent danger in engaging in any of these types of relationships is the professional's impaired objectivity and judgment that would likely result from the blending of the two types of relationships. Jacobs et al. (2006, p. 436) agree: "Any dual relationship should be entered with caution, and any exploitative dual relationship is unethical and should be avoided."

An example of a different kind of dual relationship exists when the group leader treats a group member in individual counseling. There are differing opinions about this being ethical; some believe group leaders should not conduct individual counseling with members of their therapy groups, while others feel it is advisable if it is in the best interests of the client. Jacobs et al. (2006, p. 436) believe that if individual therapy "aids in the client's improvement, then it should be seen as a valuable tool in the therapeutic process." In fact, "many times groups are formed as a result of clients being in individual counseling with the leader and the leader deciding that a group would be beneficial."

Sometimes boundaries are not as clear and can easily be crossed. When encountering these gray areas, it is important to be mindful and self-aware. The risk of entering a dual relationship increases when group leaders play many roles that overlap. Guidelines for minimizing the risks involved in dual relationships are:

- Set healthy boundaries from the outset.
- Discuss with clients any potentially problematic relationship.
- Seek consultation and/or supervision.
- Make a referral when indicated.
- Fully inform clients about any potential risks.
- Disclose and clarify areas of concern.
- Consult with other professionals periodically if you are engaged in dual relationships.
- Document discussions about any dual relationships and relevant steps.

Socializing among Group Members

Another ethical issue relates to whether socializing among group members hinders or facilitates the group process. G. Corey (2004) considers that problems arise when members form cliques and gossip about others in the group or when hidden agendas appear. Yalom (1995, 2005) agrees that out-of-group socialization that interferes with the group process can be counterproductive and should be discouraged. In order to prevent inappropriate and counterproductive socialization among group members, the issue must be discussed during the orientation, at the initial session, and regularly thereafter. During orientation to group, the issue of forming cliques must be addressed as a potentially destructive behavior that can negatively impact group process.

Making Referrals

The leader's role in making referrals is also an ethical responsibility that should be considered carefully. Group treatment can open clients up emotionally, and it would be unwise to leave them hanging without follow-up. Leaders must be able to determine when referrals are needed and be aware of follow-up treatment possibilities. It is a possibility for group members to be seen by the group leader or referred to other therapists. "Follow-up is important because very often in therapy groups, members need additional individual, group, or family counseling. Too often, this ethical standard is violated in that no follow-up treatment is outlined" (Jacobs et al., 2006, p. 439).

Ethics and Technology

Advances in technology have skyrocketed in the last decade. Issues tied to confidentiality and privacy are more challenging today because of answering machines, cell phones, pagers, fax machines, and e-mails. Online counseling, chat rooms, computer files and networks, laptop computer security, and technical failure and computer viruses are additional examples tied to technology that can impact both confidentiality and treatment.

Technology and Safeguarding Confidentiality

In today's high-tech world, it is essential to find ways to safeguard client confidentiality and privacy and to "ensure that all mediums used are appropriate and quality controlled" (Alle-Corliss & Alle-Corliss, 2006, p. 168). The inappropriate use of technology can lead to the violation of a client's rights. For instance, the use of telephones, answering machines, voice mail, pagers, faxes, cellular phones, and e-mail can present a number of potential ethical problems regarding the protection of client privacy.

It is important to consider different types of technology-related scenarios and issues where problems may arise. Some of those identified include:

- Misdirected e-mail accidentally read by third parties
- Family members eavesdropping on telephone calls
- Family members (or network administrators) gaining access to clinical e-mail

- Snoopers (or neighbors) intercepting cell or cordless phone conversations
- Hackers uploading e-mail or listening in on PC-based videoconferences
- Misrepresentation by e-clients
- E-mail communication that includes documentation of extensive clinical records (NASW, 2004)

DeAngelis (NASW, 2004, p. 3) emphasizes that "for every technology there are pitfalls involving matters of confidentiality and privacy. Without appropriate safeguards, unwanted third parties can gain illegal access to confidential records." Because of the potential hazards of modern technology, much care must be taken when using various forms of common technology. Because it is fairly simple to unintentionally breach client confidentiality using these mediums, it is necessary to discuss these potential problems regarding technology and privacy during the informed consent process. "Electronic record keeping and online counseling are especially at risk of misuse if precautions are not taken. Practitioners must take special care in using computers in these areas and remain abreast of all the relevant ethical and legal guidelines that apply" (Alle-Corliss & Alle-Corliss, 2006, p. 168). Next, we briefly discuss the most commonly used technologies.

Telephone and Answering Machines

There is concern about maintaining confidentiality when returning a phone call or calling to cancel an appointment and there is a need to identify oneself. Group leaders need to call to schedule a screening interview or to invite the client to become a group member. Remley and Herlihy (2001) suggest adhering to these guidelines:

- Refrain from acknowledging that clients are receiving services, and do not give out information regarding clients to unknown callers.
- Ensure that you are actually communicating with the intended person when you make or receive calls where confidential information may be discussed.
- Abstain from making any comments you would not want your client to hear or that you would not want to repeat in legal proceedings.
- Do not allow unauthorized persons to hear answering machine messages in your office while they are being left or retrieved.

- Do not leave personal messages on an answering machine unless you have arranged to do so with your client. Be aware that another family member may retrieve the message left for your client.

Cellular Phones

Cell phones are widely used by clients and helpers alike. Because privacy is often compromised when talking on a cell phone, assume that the client may not be in a private place. Also, be aware that your conversation may be intercepted by someone who is unauthorized. Do not mention information that might identify a client or otherwise compromise confidentiality.

Interest in "texting" using cellular phones is mounting. Dangers in texting are only now beginning to surface. Toseland and Rivas (2009) warn that "group leaders may respond too quickly to text messages with little context or background" (p. 177). We recommend that practitioners, including group leaders, be cautious about responding via text message, as there is no guarantee of who will have access to it. Also, there must be a thorough understanding of relevant client issues before any response via text message is sent.

Pagers

Caution must be exercised when retrieving a message using a pager. In sending a pager message to a client, practitioners must be careful to ensure client privacy by exercising the same caution that would be used if leaving messages on answering machines or voice mail.

Fax Machines

Since faxes are commonly used to transmit information to or about a client, it is important to always double-check if the number is correct and to ensure that the person for whom the fax is intended is present to personally retrieve the fax. Calling before sending the fax is suggested, especially if the fax machine at the receiving site is in a common area.

Electronic Mail

Even though use of e-mails is commonplace, they can be accessed by people other than their intended recipients, and thus privacy is not guaranteed. "Since there is no reasonable expectation of confidentiality for e-mail, clients need to have input regarding how they want communication to be handled so that their privacy is protected" (M.S. Corey & G. Corey, 2004, p. 235). To avoid a breach of confidentiality, ensure that clients have given their consent for e-mail use and are aware of the inherent security risks in e-mail transmission, consider encoding identifying information and deleting client identifying information if necessary, assess the security of the e-mail reception site, and make certain there is password protection at the directory level.

Electronic Communication/Record Keeping

Using computers to generate progress notes is increasingly becoming the primary mode of record keeping. It is important for helpers to maintain appropriate confidentiality in creating, storing, accessing, transferring, and disposing of treatment records. Codes of ethics of all helping professionals require that helpers ensure confidentiality and privacy of all information transmitted through electronic or computer technology. It is recommended that group leaders take time to discuss potential problems related to technology with their clients during the informed consent process. Creating an open dialogue in this matter can lead helpers and clients to take preventive measures to avoid any unnecessary and illegal breaches of confidentiality.

Use of Chat Rooms

The use of chat rooms is increasing. However, since chat rooms are typically not confidential, it is not recommended to use the Internet as a forum to discuss clients unless a special provision to ensure confidentiality is arranged, written client permission is secured, and information that may be used to identify the client is excluded from all dialogue.

Laptop Computer Security

Because the use of laptops by both clients and helpers has increased, it is important to ensure that the security of the client information stored in these portable computers is not compromised. Since laptops are more vulnerable to loss, theft, and damage, we recommend these precautions:

- Using a nonidentifying bag or carrying case for transporting
- Installing a code entry password and an encryption program
- Backing up data frequently onto a diskette
- Using a locking cable when outside the home or office

Technical Failure and Viruses

Because of the ever-present risk of technical failure and computer viruses, the internal security of files must be safeguarded by installing an antiviral program on any computer that will be used for inputting client data, by saving all files from the hard drive to a backup flashdrive or CDs, and by making backup copies of either of these if they are the main source of data storage.

Online Counseling
Online counseling for both individual and group counseling is growing in popularity, despite potential legal and ethical problems. Potential ethical concerns regarding online treatment identified in the literature (Alle-Corliss & Alle-Corliss, 2006; Brabender et al., 2004; Franz and MacCartie, 1999; NASW, 2004) include:

- Validating the identity of both the therapist and the client
- Supplying proof of the therapist's professional credentials
- Securing permission for counseling minors
- Ensuring client confidentiality
- Providing for emergency counseling services
- Verifying that liability insurance covers the client's geographical location
- Determining the appropriateness of online counseling for the client population
- Developing a protocol for online technical failures, legal jurisdiction, and technical competence of the therapist

Since Internet group therapy takes place online, it is difficult to guarantee client privacy and confidentiality. Also, individuals cannot be reliably identified over the Internet, and individuals other than clients can pose as clients.

Virtual Groups
Virtual groups are those where clients/group members do not meet face to face, but over the telephone or through the Internet. Toseland and Rivas (2009) cite the following reasons why virtual groups are considered important alternatives to face-to-face groups. Clients may not be able to meet face to face due to:

- Debilitating illnesses or physical deterrents
- Transportation, distance, and costs that pose barriers
- Preference for non–face-to-face contact due to stigmatizing concerns, high social anxiety, and/or hectic schedules and time constraints

Recent research suggests that virtual groups are quite therapeutic and cohesive in some situations (McKenna, Green, & Gleason, 2002; Postmes, Spears, & Lea, 1999; Postmes, Spears, Sakhel, & deGroot, 2001; Toseland & Rivas, 2009). Clients feel less distracted by visual cues and are better able to focus more on the core interests and values that were initial motivations for group involvement. Diversity issues, such as skin color, socioeconomic status, gender, and sexual orientation, are less of a concern to members than their shared issues. Bonding and compliance with group norms are more likely to be followed when members are able to identify with the issues that led to their involvement in the group.

Despite these advantages, there are serious concerns about both telephone and online virtual groups. The risk of breaching confidentiality is great, and it is difficult to ensure that group membership remains constant.

Teleconferencing or Conference Calls

Teleconferencing or conference calls have become common ways to communicate with a number of individuals at once. Research on use of telephone support groups for clients who are disabled has been very positive. Toseland and Rivas (2009, p. 178) have detailed advantages and disadvantages that provide a comprehensive view of this form of communication (see Table 6.2).

Group leaders using the phone must be particularly attentive to tone of voice, inflection, and silence. Schopler, Galinsky, and Abell (1977) recommend:

- Having members identify themselves each time they communicate
- Assisting clients to prepare for frustrations such as missed cues or interruptions during group meeting times while still acknowledging the benefits of the medium
- Encouraging group members to clarify statements and to give clear feedback to one another
- Continually assessing members' emotional reactions and making these clear to all group members.

Because of the nature of the medium, group leaders generally must be more active and directive. Ideally, it is also recommended for group leaders to meet with each member of the telephone group at least once before the group begins. Since professional standards for delivering

Table 6.2 **Advantages and Disadvantages of Telephone Groups**

Advantages of Telephone Groups

- Convenience and accessibility of meeting in one's own home
- Reduced time needed to participate, because there is no travel time
- Reduction of stigma because of greater privacy
- Ability to reach persons living in rural areas and those who lack transportation
- Ability to reach people who are homebound or caring for someone who cannot be left alone
- Greater willingness to share issues that might be taboo in in-person groups

Disadvantages of Telephone Groups

- Cost
- Difficulties in assessing members' needs and the impact of interactions without the benefit of facial expressions and other nonverbal cues
- Difficulty of including members with hearing problems
- Distortions caused by technological problems, call waiting, or background noises from other persons in the household
- Concerns about confidentiality because of a lack of privacy within callers' households
- Changes in group dynamics caused by the lack of visual and nonverbal clues
- The difficulty of using program activities, flip charts, and other visual media
- Expressions of hostility or insensitivity that can sometimes be greater when members are not meeting face to face

telephone services remain limited, caution must be taken in using this type of technology (Glueckauf, Pickett, Ketterson, Loomis, & Rozensky, 2003; Maheu, Whitten, & Allen, 2001; Nickelson, 2000; Toseland & Rivas, 2009).

Computer-Mediated Groups: Online Services

Santhiveeran (1998) has identified four ways that computer-mediated groups can be formed through the Internet: (1) chat rooms, (2) bulletin boards, (3) e-mail, and (4) Listservs.

Chat rooms are considered virtual spaces that are open during specific time periods. Group members are able to post messages and receive feedback interactively in a short time period.

Bulletin boards are typically always open and enable group members to post messages that can be answered at any time.

E-mails allow group members to write messages to particular individual(s) who may respond at any time.

Listservs allow group members to present and receive information and news. Group meetings occur in real time, as everyone participates at the same time and the discussion is interactive.

Group leaders conducting an *online group* often have two roles as coordinator and/or consultant: "A group therapist may share his or her knowledge of interpersonal behavior and group dynamics on a web page or respond to questions about relationships" (Brabender et al., 2004, p. 194). Group leaders may face difficulties with role clarity, in that group members may not recognize the leader as a coordinator or consultant and/or may misconstrue the leader's role as one of personal psychotherapist (Humphreys, Winzelberg, & Klaw, 2000). Furthermore, since membership can fluctuate rapidly in online groups, it is often difficult for the professional to know who has entered the system and when (Weinberg, 2001). There are special case management issues due to the wider geographic area from which group members are drawn. Essentially, the greater this area, "the greater the therapist's domain of responsibility. [Furthermore], if a member is from a geographic area other than the therapist's, the therapist may need to know the mental health resources in that member's area in order to respond appropriately and promptly to any emergencies" (Brabender et al., 2004, p. 196).

Three safeguards that might minimize these difficulties include:

1. Group leaders must continually clarify their role.
2. Group leaders must avoid individual personal interactions with group members.
3. Group leaders must use a "separate e-mail account for participation in an online group so that the professional will not mistake a listserve member's message for that of a party with whom the group leader does have an individual relationship" (Brabender et al., 2004, p. 195).

Despite the obvious concerns, online groups, which are plentiful on the Internet, are thought to serve useful functions for many people (Page, 2004). Brabender (2002) suggests that those who use technology are venturing into "territory that is relatively uncharted from a legal and ethical perspective" (p. 274) and recommends that group workers first identify possible ethical dilemmas to systematically address any ethical and legal issues. Since research on the effectiveness of online groups is still scant, more data should be collected. Chang and Yeh (2003) note that "online groups are not . . . equivalent to face-to-face group psychotherapy, and there is no evidence to date that online groups are effective in fostering change. In fact, research examining the effectiveness of online groups in comparison to face-to-face groups has only just begun" (p. 640).

Group leaders conducting online groups are encouraged to take the following precautions:

- Obtain information and follow professional, ethical, and legal standards of practice.
- Be conscious of cultural considerations that may apply to the client's geographical location.
- Provide clients with addresses of all appropriate professional and registering associations related to the field of practice.
- Obtain written consent from the legal guardians of minors prior to engaging in Web counseling.
- Implement an identification system between client and therapist, such as the use of a code word or graphic.
- Supply a reference to an appropriate professional who can provide emergency counseling within the client's geographical location.
- Implement an intake and assessment tool for use with Web clients.
- Identify those issues that may not be appropriate for online counseling (e.g., suicidality, psychiatric disorders).
- Develop and discuss preplanned communication strategies with the client in the event of online technical problems. (Alle-Corliss & Alle-Corliss, 2006, pp. 169–170; Franz et al., 1999, p. 7).

Other Online Services
Quality of information and services that are received during virtual groups may not be professionally sanctioned (Bowman & Bowman, 1998). Toseland and Rivas (2009) warn that "information shared on the Internet is not subject to the same standards as information printed in scientific journals" (p. 177). Care must be taken to ensure that information from the Internet is credible and appropriately used. Some group members may read about a treatment or a diagnosis and quickly apply it to themselves or others without proper supervision or professional involvement.

Another concern about using online services is the fact that counseling and support may be provided by individuals without professional degrees who have not agreed to abide by the professional standards of accrediting bodies.

Maintenance of Skills: Technology and Training
Exposure to advancing technology in the helping field is a given. Ethically, all helpers, including group leaders, must make every effort to seek

out adequate training and to develop the necessary skills to use new forms of technology effectively. Specific to the computer, Alle-Corliss and Alle-Corliss (2006) write:

> It is incumbent upon individual therapists to seek out adequate training and develop necessary experience to use the computer effectively. This entails ensuring a good working knowledge of the computer, including its software programs, securing support services necessary to protect file security in the event of a technical problem, upgrading computer training skills in keeping with advances in technologies, and staying apprized of the use of technologies in the context of the code of ethics and the technology guidelines of their respective profession. (p. 170)

Learning new skills and keeping up with advances is critical. In regard to group work, group leaders must be familiar with the legal and ethical issues tied to online counseling and other services provided by the Internet. We advocate that group work practitioners be open to the use of technology in group settings only if they are receptive to seeking ongoing training and supervision. McMinn, Buchanan, Ellens, and Ryan (1999) go a step further to propose that graduate training programs and continuing education programs for all helping professionals provide specific instruction in appropriate technological applications for professional practice. Table 6.3 presents a list of considerations for practitioners who use computer technology.

Table 6.3   Considerations for Practitioners Using Computer Technology

- Provide clients with full disclosure of the possible benefits and risks.
- Use comprehensive assessment tools along with a statement of how important it is for the client to be forthright in completing any questionnaires, forms, and so on.
- Provide clients with specifics on confidentiality and disclosure of safeguards.
- Secure emergency contact information from the client and develop a clear emergency plan in case online communication is interrupted.
- Consult the code of ethics of the profession to ensure compliance with issues pertaining to confidentiality, privacy, informed consent, conflict of interest, misrepresentation of credentials, and more.
- Consult state licensing provisions to check for applicable statutory regulations.
- If necessary, consult a malpractice/risk management attorney to learn more about existing standards of care, malpractice issues, and more.
- Review the codes of conduct for online services from relevant associations of online professionals and healthcare organizations.

Source: Adapted from Alle-Corliss and Alle-Corliss (2006), p. 171.

Diversity Issues

Remaining diversity sensitive is also an important ethical consideration when working in a group setting. Because groups are often made of culturally diverse client populations, it is important to use techniques that are appropriate with their diverse backgrounds. Common techniques that encourage self-disclosure, sharing private matters, expressing deeper emotions, practicing assertion skills, and engaging in confrontation may not be appropriate with certain clients. Careful assessment and planning can prevent misuse of techniques that are considered diversity insensitive. The ASGW (1998) "Best Practice Guidelines" emphasizes the ethical need to recognize the role of diversity in group practice:

> Group workers practice with broad sensitivity to client differences including but not limited to ethnic, gender, religious, sexual, psychological maturity, economic class, family history, physical characteristics or limitations, and geographic location. Group workers continuously seek information regarding the cultural issues of the diverse population with whom they are working both by interaction with participants and from using outside resources. (B.8)

Certainly there is a great need for a multicultural perspective in our pluralistic and culturally diverse society. In group practice, remaining respectful of others and their differences is critical in developing rapport and trust. Learning effective strategies that promote an understanding and appreciation of the various areas of diversity, such as culture, ethnicity, race, gender, class, religion, and sexual orientation, is equally as vital. Multicultural counseling/therapy has been defined

> As both a helping role and process that uses modalities and defines goals consistent with the life experiences and cultural values of clients, recognizes client identities to include individual, group, and universal dimensions, advocates the use of universal and culture-specific strategies and roles in the helping process, and balances the importance of individualism and collectivism in the assessment, diagnosis, and treatment of client and client systems. (Sue & Torino, 2005, p. 3)

Based on this definition, several important implications for counseling practice have been identified:

- The *helping role and process* must meet the specific needs of the client populations being served. To do so, counselors may need to broaden their role and expand their repertoire of skills. For instance, in some cultures, a more passive and objective helper is preferred; in other cultures, effective helpers also play the role of teacher, consultant, and advocate.

- Modalities used and goals set must be *consistent with life experiences and cultural values* of the population being served.

- Help in a manner that recognizes the totality of a person's identity by taking into account *individual (unique), group, and universal dimensions of their existence.*

- Use *culture-specific strategies* with different ethnic/minority groups that are best suited to their needs and views of helping while remaining aware that certain strategies are *universally* accepted.

- Respect both *individualism and collectivism* in working with diverse cultures. Balance the individualistic approach with a collectivistic reality that acknowledges the role of family, significant others, community, and culture.

- Be open to working both with the *individual client and client systems* as the need mandates. Typically when clients experience problems in their environment due to differences in race, culture, ethnicity, gender, or sexual orientation, it is important to shift the focus to altering client systems rather than only working with individual clients.

In line with these implications for practice, the literature identifies three main components to becoming culturally competent practitioners:

1. *Being aware of one's own assumptions, values, and biases*
   - Knowing about our own cultural heritage and valuing and respecting differences
   - Being aware of our own values and biases and how they might impact minority clients
   - Being comfortable with differences regarding race and beliefs between you and your clients
   - Being sensitivity to the need to refer a minority client to a helper of the client's own race/culture or to another helper when appropriate
   - Acknowledging our own racist attitudes, beliefs, and feelings when they are present

The ASGW "Principles for Diversity Competent Group Workers" (1998) reinforces the importance of self-awareness: "Diversity-competent group workers demonstrate increased awareness of how their own race, ethnicity, culture, gender, SES, sexual orientation, abilities, and religion and spiritual beliefs are impacted by their own experience and histories, which in turn influence group process and dynamics" (I.A.3).

2. *Understanding the worldview of one's culturally diverse clients*
   - Being knowledgeable and informed about the particular group one will be working with
   - Understanding how the sociopolitical system of the United States operates with respect to its treatment of minorities
   - Being aware of the institutional barriers that prevent minorities from seeking assistance
3. *Developing appropriate intervention strategies and needs*
   - Using a multitude of response modalities
   - Communicating skillfully; considering that communication patterns differ from one culture to the next
   - Intervening within institutions on behalf of clients when appropriate
   - Knowing our helping style, limitations, and the likely impact of these on our clients

As group practitioners, it is important to understand the cultural values of our clients in order to select interventions that are congruent with their worldviews. Many times culture influences, values, decisions, and actions of all group members determine what types of problems are brought into group therapy. Each person and cultural group brings its own experiences and expectations into treatment. Helpers should attempt to understand the particulars of each group to ensure that appropriate treatment will follow. All these considerations underscore the need for helpers to become diversity sensitive.

DeLucia-Waack (1996) advocates similar considerations for group practitioners working in today's multicultural world. She encourages being open to modifying theories and techniques of group work to different cultures in ways that are congruent with cultural beliefs and behaviors and to revising theory and practice of group work so that it makes full use of the diversity among members as a way to facilitate change and growth.

In order to achieve these mandates, G. Corey (2004) suggests that "group counselors must be willing and able to challenge the culturally encapsulated view of a group's structure, goals, and techniques, and practice" and to reexamine the "underlying culturally learned assumptions of all the major theories in light of their appropriateness in a multicultural context" (p. 14). Ivey, Pedersen, and Ivey (2001) discuss the premise behind *multicultural intentionality,* which basically encourages helpers to alter their approach when it comes to working in group settings. No longer can client problems be explored only by looking internally; an external focus is just as important. Helpers must expand their knowledge of issues pertaining to gender, sexual orientation, degree of physical and emotional ability, spirituality, and socioeconomic status that are also likely to impact individual group members.

A helpful framework to systematically consider complex cultural influences in group counseling is the ADDRESSING model (Hays, 2001), which recognizes nine dimensions that can be used to better understand an individual client's identity.

A   Age and generational influence

D   Developmental and acquired

D   Disability

R   Religion

E   Ethnicity/trace

S   Socioeconomic status

S   Sexual orientation

I   Indigenous heritage

N   National origin

G   Gender

In Chapter 5, we discussed many of these dimensions in the context of diverse client populations. Here we wish to emphasize considering these dimensions in relation to group work. Since many groups today are heterogeneous, it is essential to acknowledge and understand the various areas of diversity represented within the group. Brabender et al. (2004) also suggest that group therapists use this system to develop a greater awareness of their own personal worldviews. By identifying which cultural factors apply to each group member, "therapists can understand (1) themselves more fully; (2) themselves in relation to the group members; (3) each member more fully; and (4) each member in relation to one another" (p. 207).

Becoming a skilled group practitioner who is also diversity sensitive requires work on many different levels. The group leader must be aware of the content of what each group member is saying, of the context of their culture, of how this impacts these issues, of the connection between helpers and group members, and of the relationships among members themselves, all the while paying attention to group process, to the use of culturally appropriate group techniques and strategies, and to the pursuit of goal attainment. Hays (2001) offers 12 culturally responsive interventions that therapists can implement when engaging in group work with clients from diverse backgrounds. For more detailed information, please refer to Hays (2001), *Addressing Cultural Complexities in Practice: A Framework for Clinicians and Counselors.*

Becoming knowledgeable and skilled when working with diverse populations also requires familiarizing oneself with resources on diversity including professional ethical codes, principles, and guidelines. It is necessary to be open to seeking consultation and training on a continual basis and to remain respectful of others who are different from oneself.

Potential Ethical Dilemmas

There will always be ethical dilemmas in working with others, regardless of what type of treatment is being rendered. Ethical dilemmas may be magnified in group work, given that more individuals are involved. Next we present several potential ethical dilemmas that require careful consideration:

- Several group members socialize outside of the group. Cliques form during group that are carried outside of the group. How should this be handled?

- The group leader is asked to join group members in a social gathering outside of group. Should the group leader consider this? If so, why? If not, why not?

- A group member is a financial advisor and offers group members and group leader a rate cut if they hire him. How should the group leader proceed? Even if the group leader does not accept the offer, would it be okay for group members to do so?

- The group leader uses a group exercise that is too intense for the group members to handle. There is no preparation for the exercises and no closure. How should this be dealt with?

- Family members or friends want to join a group together. Could this pose potential difficulties?
- Coleaders in a group become intimately involved outside of the group. Is this appropriate? What might some ramifications be?

Agency-Related Ethical Issues

Group leaders must be aware of potential agency-related ethical difficulties. These situations should be considered:

- Is the group appropriate for the agency setting? For instance, what about conducting a substance abuse group in a child care agency? Or what if the group members become too upset (as in an anger management group), and the agency is not equipped to handle this?
- Are clients properly served by the group modality? It is important to review the purpose of the group itself. What if the group is developed solely to meet productivity needs, for staff to gain experience, or primarily due to client interests? Are these reasons sufficient to warrant a specific group?
- Are the time and location of the group conducive to client needs? What about offering a children's group at a counseling center in the middle of the school day? Or how about scheduling a night group at an inconvenient location that is far away and secluded?
- What if the agency needs to develop an intense Dialectical Behavior Therapy (DBT) depression group, and the only staff member available to follow through has limited experience? Would it be appropriate for a novice clinician to lead such an intense group alone?
- The agency assigns two therapists to colead a series of groups, yet they are very different in style, orientation, and approach and are not pleased to be working together. Is it a good idea for them to work together?

Challenges of Agency Work

A last ethical issue that human service practitioners, including group leaders, must be cognizant of are three challenges of day-to-day work in human service agency settings: personal, organizational, and environmental. Professionals in other fields are also as likely to face these same challenges.

Those who work in the helping field face many personal challenges. Personal involvement allows helpers to understand others' pain and struggles as well as their joys and excitement. This ability to empathize contributes to the development of trust and rapport with clients and allows helpers to enter their world. Sometimes through our work, we are exposed to many injustices and tragedies of life, which can be disconcerting. Fears and anxieties are natural, especially when facing new experiences or taking on a new role, such as becoming a group leader. Other challenges include knowing the difference between caretaking and rescuing, recognizing transference and countertransference, and being able to work with resistant and difficult clients. Organizational challenges include understanding the organization or agency system, being aware of organizational limitations, and fitting in. Learning to work with other organizations and the community can also be challenging. Environmental challenges include understanding both fiscal and political realities that impact agency life. Also, we have already discussed the challenges of using new technology and the impact of the Internet on human services. Coping strategies to deal with these various challenges include maintaining open communication, being flexible and patient, and avoiding negativity.

Guidelines for Ethical Group Work Practice

Professional organizations specifically address ethical issues in group work. We list names of several of these we have found invaluable:

- American Group Psychotherapy Association (AGPA): http://www. agpa.org/guidelines/index.html. This site offers "Practice Guidelines for Group Psychotherapy."

- American Society of Group Psychotherapy and Psychodrama (ASGPP): http://www.asgpp.org/

- Association for the Advancement of Social Work with Groups Inc. (AASWG): http://www.aaswg.org/. This international professional organization has proposed "Standards for Social Work Practice with Groups" Specifically at: http://www.aaswg.org/webfm_send/4

- Association for Specialists in Group Work (ASGW): http://www. asgw.org/. This web site produced three sets of very useful standards:

1. "Best Practice Guidelines": http://www.asgw.org/PDF/Best_Practices.pdf
2. "Principles for Diversity-Competent Group Workers": http://www.asgw.org/PDF/Principles_for_Diversity.pdf
3. "Professional Standards for the Training of Group Workers": http://www.asgw.org/PDF/training_standards.pdf

Along with these, the professional codes of ethics for human services educators, counselors, psychologists, and social workers all address ethical issues tied to group work:

- American Counseling Association (2002): "Code of Ethics and Standards of Practice," available at http://www.counseling.org/Resources/codeofethics/TP/Home/CT2.aspx
- American Psychological Association (2002): "Ethical Principles for Psychologists and Code of Conduct," available at http://www.apa.org/ethics/code2002.html
- National Association of Social Workers (2004): "Code of Ethics," available at http://www.socialworkers.org/pubs/code/code.asp
- National Organization for Human Services (2004): "Ethical Standards of Human Service," available at http://www.nationalhumanservices.org/ethical-standards-of-human-service-professionals

In Closing

This chapter has explored the many ethical and legal issues relevant to group work practice. We have discussed practice and personal values and their relationship to group work. Issues tied to group membership including client rights and informed consent were detailed. Discussions regarding pregroup disclosures, clients' rights during the group, and psychological risks for members were presented to help group leaders be well prepared. The important issue of confidentiality was examined. Appropriate use of techniques was reviewed in detail, as was group leadership and dual relationships. The issue of safeguarding confidentiality and the use of technology was expanded, given the highly technological world in which we live. Diversity as it relates to ethics was also discussed in hopes of orienting group leaders to the importance of being culturally competent. Chapter 7 focuses on specifics of developing groups within agency settings.

How to Engage in Successful Group Practice within an Agency

7

Chapter

Learning to work in agency settings and adequately providing group treatment services is essential for human service practitioners. In addition to developing clinical skills and engaging in specialized training of group process and practice, human service workers are most successful if they learn to work within various agency systems. Such success is more likely if there is an understanding of the agency structure, policies, history, formal and informal organizational lines, client demographics, and existing needs. Strategically and positively maximizing the available resources leads to the optimal goal of providing effective, quality group treatment.

In this chapter we elaborate on our model for group planning and implementation that contains salient issues key to the success of group practice within agency settings: preliminary considerations, group planning, group formation, group implementation, and group evaluation. This model is based on information gathered from our own experience of conducting groups within a variety of agency settings and from a literature review (M.S. Corey & G. Corey, 2004; Page & Jencius, 2009; Toseland & Rivas, 1984, 2009).

Contemplation

Preliminary Considerations

The actual implementation of a group begins with initial contemplation on the part of the group leader. Common questions such as "Why group treatment?" "Who is involved?" and "What are motivating factors?" are considered during this phase. Let us explore these questions further.

It is essential to determine who is primarily responsible for proposing the specific group and why. Toseland and Rivas (2009) note that "the purpose of a group can frequently be clarified by considering how the idea for establishing it was generated. The idea may have come from several sources, such as the group worker, agency staff member, potential clients, or the larger community" (p. 154). Page and Jencius (2009) add that in most settings, groups are formed in response to client need, agency need, and/or leader interest.

Whether the group proposal is agency directed, staff/clinician directed, member (client) directed, community directed, or a combination of these makes a difference in both the development and delivery of group services.

Agency-Directed Groups

Often groups are mandated by the agency administration for a variety of reasons. In today's turbulent economic climate, funding pressures to develop more cost-effective services and increase productivity are common motivators. Similarly, access concerns are important factors in encouraging group development, since groups allow the treatment of more clients at regular intervals than individual therapy.

When staff members are open to developing and leading more groups as directed by management, a win-win situation is likely to exist. However, when resistance exists with administrative personnel or line staff, problems are more possible. Various reasons for staff resistance include:

- Fear of being more vulnerable than when engaging in one-to-one work
- Fear of incompetence, as designated leader(s) may not feel adequately trained or prepared to lead specific groups
- Discomfort with group modality or preference for other type of treatment intervention(s)
- Lack of motivation or support to do groups
- Lack of faith in the group process or in the appropriateness of using group modality to address client needs
- Adjustment difficulties due to a need to adapt to the different qualities of group process and the changing relationship with clients
- Anger at the system for imposing group on staff and/or clients

In order for a successful group outcome, it is important to assess if any of these issues exist and if so, to address them.

Example: The child therapists in a clinic did not believe in groups for children and were angry at the agency for mandating children's groups.

Staff/Clinician-Directed Proposals

When clinical staff themselves direct group treatment, the likelihood of a positive outcome is greater, since motivations are more personal. The decision to begin a group is often the product of the group leader's interest and/or personal experience. Clearly, when staff members are invested in the process, the possibility for success is greater.

Example: Two clinicians coleading a chronic pain management group were not only encouraged by the agency but also felt motivated to work together, given their common styles.

Client-Directed Groups

There are times when groups are developed primarily due to member need and demand. Usually when this is the case, membership is sound. Likewise, motivation is often high when clients themselves have been influential in the group becoming a reality.

Example: A women's sexual abuse survivor support group was born out of a need voiced by individual clients.

Community-Directed Groups

Community demands for a specific group may be an impetus for agencies to follow through with group implementation. Not only does this create goodwill with other community agencies, but it can also respond to community needs for additional services.

Example: Community programs often encourage both teen and adult anger management programs.

Combination of Reasons

A combination of reasons is probably the impetus for the establishment of most groups: agency, community, client, or staff and client. These groups are often the most successful since various individuals are involved in their development.

History of Group Treatment within an Agency

The history of group treatment within the particular agency sponsoring the group is important to assess, as it provides valuable information about the viability of groups at that location and their past experience. Questions that might prove beneficial include:

- Have groups existed before? If so, who led them? What was the outcome?
- Were they considered effective?
- What was the reputation of both the group and group leader(s) within the agency, among the clients, and in the community at large?
- If no group treatment has ever been provided within the agency, what are the prevailing views? Are there fears or stereotypes? Are there any conflicts?
- How would group treatment fit into this agency?

The type of agency, type of group, and agency strengths and limitations are also important to consider in group planning.

Type of Agency Setting
The type of agency—nonprofit, public, or for-profit—can also have an impact on group development, implementation, and treatment success.

Nonprofit (Voluntary) Agency These types of agencies are essentially bureaucratic in structure, governed by an elected volunteer board of directors and employing professional or volunteer staff to provide a continuing service to a clientele in the community.
Examples: Family Services, United Way, and the Salvation Army.

Public (Governmental) Agencies The main purpose of governmental entities—federal, state, regional, county, and city—is to provide services to designated target populations. These agencies fluctuate in regard to funding, given their reliance on governmental aid.
Examples: County mental health centers and drug rehabilitation programs.

For-Profit (Commercial/Private) Agencies The number of for-profit organizations has increased dramatically, given the reduced funding for public agencies, the limited resources for voluntary agencies, and the changing political and economic times. Known as proprietary agencies, they have a dual function to provide services and to make a profit while doing so. Because they compete with public and nonprofit agencies, there is often much controversy over for-profit agencies. Some believe that such agencies focus primarily on the profit motive, not the clientele they are supposed to be serving.

Examples: Employee Assistance Programs (EAPs), managed care, health maintenance organizations (Kaiser, Cigna, FHP), private corporations, and service agencies.

Assessing Agency Strengths and Limitations

An assessment of the agency's strengths and limitations provides the group leader with critical information that can also help guide group development. Clearly, if more limitations than strengths exist, this fact might suggest potential problems that must be carefully explored and dealt with before a group is implemented. Strengths can be emphasized and efforts can be made to reduce existing limitations if they are discovered early on in the process.

Type of Group

Groups are extremely diverse and often are developed for different reasons. Determining what type of group is being considered can be extremely helpful in planning and implementation. A partial list of the many types of groups commonly conducted in agency settings today follows:

- Guidance/psychoeducational
- Counseling/interpersonal problem solving
- Psychotherapy/personality reconstruction
- Task/work groups
- Support groups
- Brief groups
- Self-help groups

- Recreational skill building
- Medication

Exploring Group Possibilities

At times, deciding on what groups are realistic within the particular type of agency setting is not an easy endeavor. In this case, it may be necessary to explore what type of group best matches agency and client needs as well as to determine if available staff is appropriately trained and willing to lead designated groups. When the agency, clients, and staff are all in favor of a specific group, there is a great possibility that it will become a reality. Conversely, when proposed groups do not have the necessary support, their viability is questionable.

Existence of Ongoing Groups

In determining which groups might be viable, it may be helpful to consider what other groups the agency currently is offering. Examination of the response and outcome of these groups is apt to yield useful information about what has worked and what has not.

Group Planning

Sound group planning is the foundation for an effective group. G. Corey (2004) notes: "If you want a group to be successful, you need to devote considerable time to planning" (p. 80). In contrast, "many groups are not successful due to too little emphasis on pre-group planning" (Jacobs, Masson, & Harvill, 2006, p. 64). Schneider-Corey and Corey (2007) write about this "pre-group stage" that "consists of all the factors involved in the formation of a group." They encourage giving careful thought to planning in order to lay a solid foundation: "Before the group ever meets as a group, the leader will have designed a proposal for a group, attracted members, and screened and selected members for the group" (p. 338). According to Zastrow (2009):

> The process of establishing and conducting groups varies significantly, depending on the type of group and the specific purposes to be achieved. However, for a group to reach its maximum potential, there are still some unifying or common elements to be addressed prior to establishing the group. (p. 10)

Various models for group planning exist, and we have incorporated steps from several of them (M.S. Corey & G. Corey, 2006; Toseland & Rivas, 2009; Zastrow, 2009), including:

- Establishing a group purpose
- Discerning potential group sponsorship and membership: assessing potential sponsorship and existing support; potential membership and availability of group members. Are members voluntary or nonvoluntary?
- Available resources: Are there available resources, adequate location/space for group, safety issues, time factors, and appropriate staffing?

Establishing a Group Purpose

A very first step in planning for a group is for the leaders to consider why they are forming the group and what general objectives best fit the identified purpose. Zastrow (2009) emphasizes the importance of carefully considering group objectives in order to select appropriate members. He notes: "It is essential that the objectives or purposes of each group be established at the beginning because they have a significant impact on the process of membership selection and other aspects of functioning" (p. 11).

A statement of purpose is needed that is broad enough to encompass various individual goals yet specific enough to define the common nature of the group's work. The statement should contain specifics about the reasons the group is being formed, about the group process, and about the range of individual goals the group is likely to consider. "Being clear about the purpose of the group is perhaps the most important group leadership concept to be learned. . . . *Clarity of purpose* helps the leader keep the members on course by suggesting relevant activities, asking relevant questions, and cutting off irrelevant discussions" (Jacobs et al., 2006, p. 51). A well-thought-out proposal helps convince prospective members and administrators of the value of a specific group program. Such a statement can serve to help prospective members decide if the group fits their needs and can satisfy administrators whose approval is needed. A detailed group proposal has been found to be especially useful in planning a group. "Such a proposal serves as a means of clarifying the rationale for the group, taking into consideration its potential members, the group as a whole, the sponsoring organization, worker activities, and the meeting environment" (Reid, 1997, p. 168).

This proposal is much like a preliminary plan from which to begin. Logically, the more specific the proposal, the more likely the desired outcome.

Relevance of purpose (for the members) is important as well. Buy-in by group members makes sense. In contrast, when members have little or no interest in the group, it is less likely to be productive. Buy-in becomes a challenge for group leaders who attempt to conduct a group with nonvoluntary clients, such as anger management or DUI (driving under the influence) groups.

M.S. Corey and G. Corey (2006) have identified the five general areas to consider in developing a group proposal:

1. *Rationale*: Is the purpose clear and justifiable?
2. *Objectives*: Are the objectives clear, specific, measurable, and attainable within the specified time?
3. *Practical considerations*: Is the membership defined? Are meeting times, frequency of meetings, and duration of the group reasonable?
4. *Procedures*: Are specific procedures defined and appropriate to objectives? Are these procedures appropriate and realistic for use with group?
5. *Evaluation*: Are evaluation strategies in place? Are these evaluation measures objective, practical, and relevant (pp. 107–108)?

Page and Jencius (2009) suggest including three key ingredients in a group proposal:

1. Group information, including a brief description of the target population, a statement of the group's purpose, the meeting site, and a cost estimate
2. A proposed advertisement
3. A screening plan (pp. 21–22)

If the proposal is slipshod, problems are more apt to surface as the group develops. We concur with G. Corey, Schneider-Corey, Callanan, and Russell (2004), who believe that "when the goals are vague, neither the administrator nor potential members will be likely to receive the idea for a group enthusiastically" (p. 41). Jacobs et al. (2006) suggest that when the objectives are not well defined or the leader does not follow through with stated objectives, the group is likely to be "confusing, boring, or unproductive" (p. 52). "Gathering information about the members' needs, deciding which needs can be met by the group, and then conceptualizing the kind of group that will ideally meet those needs clarifies the purpose for the leader" (p. 54).

Preparing a written proposal can be especially important for several reasons: It can help in obtaining agency sponsorship and funding from various sources, it can inform potential members about the specifics of the group, and it can assist the group leader in actually preparing for group sessions (Toseland & Rivas, 2009, p. 181).

G. Corey et al. (2004) suggest considering these points in preparing a written proposal:

- Leader's qualifications and background experience
- Type of group and its structure
- Major functions of group leader
- Usefulness, purpose, and value of group
- Potential membership of group
- Likely group goals
- Location and length of group
- Diversity sensitivity
- Accessibility for physically challenged
- Ensured confidentiality
- Expected topics of discussion
- Potential dangers and risks of group participation
- Evaluation and assessment procedures
- Follow-up procedures to consolidate learning and growth

Discerning Potential Group Sponsorship and Membership

The agency and its clients are naturally linked together. Therefore, in group planning, it is important to consider the agency where the group is to meet and the potential types of members available. Presenting a clear and well-written group proposal to administrators and staff is the first step in translating ideas into action.

Assessing Potential Sponsorship/Existing Support

It is important to consider the degree of support the sponsoring agency will provide. Toseland and Rivas (2009) contend that "agency sponsorship determines the level of support and resources available to the group" (p. 155). The mission, goals, objectives, and resources of the organization are additional elements that are important in determining potential sponsorship. Wilson and Ryland (1980) suggest that "whatever is defined as the purpose of the agency has a direct bearing on the decision-making process within the agency's constituent groups" (p. 172). Toseland and Rivas (2009) add:

> *Treatment groups rely on agency administrators and staff for sanctions, financial support, member referrals, and physical facilities. Similarly, task groups are intrinsically linked to the functioning of their sponsoring agencies and must continually refer to the agency's mission, bylaws, and policies for clarification of their task, charge, and mandate. (p. 155)*

Considering the level of support within the organization is important in evaluating how and if sufficient support exists to proceed with group development. Sometimes groups sound great in theory, yet when specifics are presented, the initial support may wane, and plans to proceed with the group may be halted. In determining if support is likely, it is wise to consider the actual costs and benefits of the specific group within the agency. Naturally, if the value and worth of the group outweigh the potential expenses, sponsorship is more plausible. When the group is too costly and labor intensive, an agency may reconsider its backing.

Determining whether there is a fit between the agency policies and goals and the purpose of the group is also important before attempting to form a group. When this fit is not considered, conflicts may arise within the agency that can have a serious impact on group formation. "The proposed group should fit within the overall operating goals of the organization. If the group represents a new form of service or suggests a problem area or a population that has not been the focus of the potential sponsor, the worker will have to be prepared to justify the request to begin a group" (Toseland & Rivas, 2009, p. 155). In order to engage successfully in group practice within an agency, it is essential to work within the system and to take time to educate fellow staff members about the benefits and possible limitations of particular groups for their clients. It is helpful to poll agency staff before a group is considered to see if there is a need. It is preferable to let staff know about a group one plans on conducting, to share exclusion criteria, and to solicit referrals.

Last, it is important to consider the political and power issues that may be at play within the sponsoring agency. Learning about these issues will likely require time and careful observation of both formal and informal norms at play within the agency and existing political realities. Attitudes of coworkers and administrators can provide a clue about their likely support. "To get a group off the ground, you need to negotiate sensitively with the staff of the institution involved. In all [agencies], power issues and political realities play a role" (M.S. Corey & G. Corey, 2006, p. 108). Years ago, for example, when ideas for a men's group were being considered, one clinician in the agency we worked in commented, "You can't have a group with men!" Fortunately, other staff were supportive, and the group eventually materialized. In fact, it became an ongoing open-ended group that existed for many years with a core group of members who were very loyal and involved in the group process.

Besides internal forces, it is important to consider the community support. Toseland and Rivas (2009) suggest assessing "the level of community need for the group and the level of community interest in the group" (p. 155). Abramson (1983) agrees that identifying key areas of interest and the perceived need within the entire organizational community is essential. Sometimes groups that are of interest to particular staff members may not be valued by the community and therefore are less favored.

To summarize, three areas of support that are important to consider are administrative, staff, and community. Response to the questions in Table 7.1 will help one to decide whether a specific group is likely to succeed.

If there are too many negative responses, group leaders should reconsider their group, work harder to gather support from staff, or explore a different approach to their group proposal. It is important to be persistent and assertive.

Assessing Potential Membership
"The assessment of potential membership helps the worker make an early estimate of the group's potential viability" (Toseland & Rivas, 2009, p. 154). Assessing potential membership early on in the process is pivotal. Although assessment at this stage is more basic and limited than during the screening interview, it is still valuable in alerting the leader to the possible viability of the group. Certainly it is important to determine whether a sufficient number of members are available to justify a specific group. Sometimes practitioners may have a sound group

Table 7.1 **Types of Support for Group Development**

Administrative Support
- Do administrators value the group process?
- Do they allow for specialized training of group leaders?
- Do they provide sufficient time for group preparation and screening of prospective group members?
- Is additional support available when needed?
- Will resources be available to undertake/perform the group?

Staff Support
- Are staff members receptive to group development and to providing appropriate referrals?
- Is there staff resistance and negativity?
- Have the possible reasons for resistance been considered?
- Are there fears of vulnerability and lack of experience?
- Is there discomfort with group modality?
- Is there a lack of motivation and faith in groups?
- Are there adjustment difficulties?
- Is there anger at the system for imposing group modality?

Community Support/Resources
- Is the community aware of the agency and its interest in group development?
- What is the history of agency and community relations?
- What is the current relationship like?
- Is the community receptive and supportive?
- Are community referrals anticipated? What might be some potential problems?

proposal, yet the potential membership is lacking, given the existing agency clientele.

Very basic to assessing potential membership of a new group is examining the extent of the problem and the need for a new group service. For instance, if the group addresses a common problem, such as parenting effectiveness, will group members agree on the purpose of the group? It is also important to consider the differences (cultural, demographic, etc.) and commonalities among group members as well as the potential benefits and limitations of the group.

Key questions to consider include: Are there enough clients who meet the criteria for the group being proposed? Are clients genuinely interested, or are they feeling pressure to participate or have no other options from which to choose?

Availability of Group Members: Voluntary or Nonvoluntary

Whether members are voluntary or nonvoluntary can have a major impact on the group itself. Voluntary participation in group work eliminates the pressure leaders may experience in keeping members. Yalom

(2005) and many others (G. Corey, 2004; Gladding, 2004; Jacobs et al., 2006) maintain that motivation to be in the group is directly connected to positive outcomes. There are many instances when group participation is mandated; courts, correctional institutions, residential treatment centers, and schools are common settings where members are nonvoluntary. Leaders who are realistic and prepared for the possible negative attitude of mandated group members can better plan to deal with their resistance. G. Corey (2004) suggests that group leaders need to learn to accept that groups can work with involuntary members "rather than hold to the position that they can be effective only with a voluntary population" (pp. 83–84). He goes on to suggest:

> *By presenting the group experience in a favorable light, the leader can help involuntary members see the potential benefits of the experience and the change of productive work taking place will be increased. The key to successful participation lies in thorough member orientation and preparation and in the leader's belief that the group process has something to offer to these prospective members. (p. 84)*

Available Resources

Along with a strong group proposal, adequate sponsorship, and sufficient membership, it is important to determine if there are available resources to proceed. The need for resources varies depending on the nature of the group and the type of agency. For instance, a children's group might require art materials, snacks, and prizes. Some groups may require specialized readings. Anxiety and depression groups, for example, may emphasize cognitive-behavioral therapy techniques and encourage the use of a text or written material. There is no problem when the agency and/or group members are able to furnish these resources; when this is not the case, the group may need to be reevaluated. At times group leaders are oblivious to the gap between ideal versus actual resources. Care must be taken to consider these issues early on in order to reduce future complications.

Adequate Location/Space for Group

The physical setting or location where the group is to meet has a marked effect on the behavior of group members and the group performance. Gladding (2004) believes that the setting can be either an asset or a liability. Toseland and Rivas (1984) assert:

The size, space, seating arrangements, furnishings, and atmosphere should all be considered when preparing for a place for the group to meet. Difficulties encountered in early meetings, inappropriate behavior by members, and unanticipated problems in the development of the group can sometimes result from inadequate attention to these aspects of a group's physical environment. (pp. 134–135)

Brabender, Fallon, and Smolar (2004) emphasize the importance of using a room that "safeguards the confidentiality of communications made in the room and protects the group from intrusions from the outside" (p. 79). Securing a setting that is private is important in treatment groups where intense emotional issues are discussed. Members need to be assured that their conversations will not be overheard in adjoining rooms.

In addition to privacy, the meeting place should be attractive and allow for face-to-face interaction. G. Corey (2004) cautions that "a poor setting can set a negative tone that will adversely affect the cohesion of the group, so every effort should be made to secure a meeting place that will facilitate in-depth work" (p. 84).

Brabender et al. (2004) also believe group leaders need to attend to such aspects of the physical environment as the configuration of the chairs, level of illumination, size of the room, noise level, and temperature. For instance, placing chairs in a circle and at a comfortable distance allows everyone personal space and the ability to see each other. Room size, either too small or too large, can create problems. Lighting is important; illumination that is either too bright or too dim can hinder participation. A noise level that is too great can be a distraction. The temperature of the room—either too cold or too hot—can influence participation.

Member access is equally as important as room size and atmosphere. Toseland and Rivas (2009) highlight the potential of success when a group is conducted in a space that "is accessible to all possible members" (p. 30). Members should be able to get to and from the group meeting site without difficulty, whether they travel by public transportation or drive themselves. Parking must be ample, and the site must be wheelchair accessible.

Time availability is a simple matter that is often overlooked. Group leaders must ensure that the designated location is available at the specified time. In many agencies, afternoon and evening groups are popular, and space for additional groups may not exist. The group site should be free well before and after the actual group meeting to ensure time for preparation and cleanup.

Safety Issues
Safety needs are always important, especially in cases where the group process may become intense and/or where group members have a history of dangerous and violent behavior. Issues related to harm to self or others should always be anticipated, and security and available supervision must be present. Taking care to ensure that safety precautions are in place allows the group to proceed more freely and the leader to feel more secure.

Time Factors
Deciding on a time of day that would be best for the majority of the members is important. Often when the meeting time is either right after lunch or too late in the day, members are likely to be low energy and sleepy. It is important to consider a time that is conducive to member availability. Sometimes leaders offer a group at a time that fits their needs or those of the agency but neglect to consider whether potential members can attend at the designated time. For instance, when members work a traditional nine-to-five job, a group offered during the day may not be feasible or sensitive. Some leaders may believe that group members must simply ask their employer for time off to attend, but this may not be realistic.

Appropriate Staffing
Care must be taken to ensure that there is appropriate staffing. It is important to ascertain if the group leader is adequately trained or qualified to engage in group work in general. In some cases, groups may require more seasoned leadership and/or coleaders in order to meet the therapeutic needs of the individual group members.

When working in agency settings, it is also important to ensure that ancillary staff is available. For instance, receptionists may be needed to check in clients and to direct them to the group site.

Group Formation

Recruitment of Members and Selection Process

When all the aspects of group planning have been completed, it is time to begin advertising and recruiting potential group members. Burger (2008), G. Corey (2004), M.S. Corey and G. Corey (2006), Page and Jencius (2009), and Toseland and Rivas (2009) all believe that how a group is announced or advertised is important. The manner in which the group is announced influences both the way it is received by potential members and the type of individuals it will attract.

Recruiting Members/Attracting Members

Sound recruiting methods are essential in ensuring that a proposed group can actually become a reality. Recruitment is meaningless, however, if the pool of potential members is insufficient. It is important to explore sources for group referrals from within the agency and from the outside. Toseland and Rivas (2009) note that "recruitment procedures should ensure an adequate number of potential members for the group" (p. 160).

In an ideal world, group leaders make personal contact with potential members. However, since this is sometimes unrealistic, other types of recruitment may be necessary. The use of multiple approaches such as presentations, posters, agency announcements, e-mails, newspaper articles, flyers, web sites, and staff referrals is most helpful. The group leader is ultimately responsible to become "familiar with the resources in the community and to educate referral sources" (Corey, Schneider, Callanan, & Russell, 2004, p. 47). Successful recruitment exists when group leaders are knowledgeable about sources from which potential members can be identified and referred to the group. Group members usually are recruited from within the agency, from other organizations, or from the community. Some specific examples of key contacts for referrals include colleagues, clinic directors, teachers and professors, physicians, ministers, school counselors, psychologists, and social workers.

The Association for Specialists in Group Work (ASGW) (1998) advocates providing prospective members with access to information about the group that includes:

- Statement of goals and purposes, policies, and procedures
- Expectations
- Rights and responsibilities
- Ground rules regarding confidentiality and out-of-group contact
- Techniques and procedures that may be used
- Information about the leader's education, training, and qualifications
- Fees and time parameters
- Potential consequences of group participation

Whatever information is provided should be accurate and should present a realistic view of the group. Page and Jencius (2009) emphasize the need to recognize that truth in advertising affects not only the leader's reputation and credibility but also that of the agency that sponsors the group.

Selection Process: Screening Group Members

The process by which group members are selected is formally known as screening. Page and Jencius (2009) find that "in a sense, a specific and carefully worded advertisement is actually the first step in the screening process, because it appeals to a subgroup of people who might be interested in the group and does not appeal to others" (p. 33).

The best candidates for a group are those who would benefit most. Brabender et al. (2004) believe that "the quintessential criterion for including a member in a therapy group is that the member's goals are compatible with the goals of the group" (p. 61). According to ASGW (1991), "insofar as possible, the counselor selects group members whose needs and goals are compatible with the goals of the group, who will not impede the group process, and whose well-being will not be jeopardized by the group experience" (p. 2.)

A very basic yet very important criterion to consider is the appropriateness of group members. Too often, when compatibility is ignored, a group forms with members who are ambivalent or who are not appropriate for or emotionally ready to engage in group process. To prevent this, it is essential to establish inclusion and exclusion criteria. Brabender et al. (2004) and Page and Jencius (2009) identify these exclusion and inclusion criteria and group screening guidelines:

Inclusion
- Compatible with goal
- Fits group composition
- Able to use group process
- Motivated and open
- Genuinely interested
- Likely to benefit from group participation
- Able to contract to be in group
- Will honor confidentiality
- Meets appropriate developmental level for group

Exclusion

- Unwilling or unmotivated to participate
- No true interest in making genuine changes
- Unable to commit to all groups sessions
- Presents with history of dropping out of groups
- Extremely high level of distress
- Noncompliant with rules, may impede progress
- Unable to connect and interact
- Limited cognitively
- Not directly concerned with group purpose
- Unable to commit to confidentiality
- Presents at a different developmental level from other potential members

In-person screening interviews are ideal, as they allow for direct observation of potential group members. Verbal and nonverbal communication can be observed and the suitability of group candidates more easily be assessed. It is important to engage in a thorough screening process and to not succumb to any pressures to begin a group hastily. "Careful screening will lessen the psychological risks of inappropriate participation in a group" (G. Corey, 2004, p. 81). Group leaders would also be wise to attend to their gut-level feelings and to trust their intuition in determining which clients are appropriate and which are not.

During the screening process, it is important to consider diversity issues. In fact, it is suggested that group leaders attempt to balance diversity and individual characteristics of potential group members (DeLucia-Waack, 1996). Recruitment should be of individuals who share common experiences but who are also diverse in some way. Creating a diverse group affords members the opportunity to dispel myths, stereotypes, and misconceptions about those who are different from themselves.

It is recommended that screening be a two-way process. We advocate affording potential group members the opportunity for an individual screening interview to ask questions that will help them determine if the group is right for them. Far too often, however, this opportunity is not feasible. Nonetheless, group leaders can advocate that prospective clients be proactive in determining if the group is appropriate for them. Introducing confidentiality at this time is optimum. When prospective members learn about the various aspects of confidentiality along with the limitations, they may feel more comfortable with the idea of sharing. Corey, Callanan, & Russell (2004) note: "Group participants are not going to reveal themselves in meaningful ways unless they feel quite sure that they can trust both you and the other members to respect what they share" (p. 13).

Alternatives to in-person screening procedures are group screening sessions, which can be just as helpful. Brabender et al. (2004) agree that group screenings provide helpful information concerning a member's capacity to benefit from group therapy, since behavior within the small group can be directly observed. Sometimes no screening occurs, and leaders must choose members based on their diagnosis or simply through referrals. When care is taken in choosing group members, group leaders are likely to feel more empowered and hopeful. Simply said, screening is "not a highly objective and scientific process, but a device for getting together the best clientele for a given group" (M.S. Corey & G. Corey, 2006, p. 116).

G. Corey et al. (2004) suggest asking prospective members these questions to determine their readiness for the group:

1. *Why do you want to join the group?*

2. *Have you participated in a group or in individual therapy before? What was that experience like for you?*

3. *Do you understand the purpose and nature of this group?*

4. *Do you have any fears about joining this group?*

5. *How ready are you to take a critical look at your life or address a particular problem you are facing?*

6. *What are some specific personal concerns that you would most like to explore?*

7. *What would you hope to get from this group?*

8. *What do you want to know about me (p. 48)?*

Once the screening process is complete, group leaders must determine if prospective members are suitable for a given group and must inform members of their decision. At times, this requires notifying candidates that they may not be appropriate for the group. Ethically, it is important to cite reasons for the decision and to offer more appropriate referrals. Such referrals may be difficult to make. "It is a delicate matter to ensure that the person being referred to another source of help does not feel pushed away or does not feel pathologized" (Page & Jencius, 2009, p. 33). It is recommended to "express caring and hope and to listen carefully to what services the person desires" and to provide several referrals and hotline numbers (p. 33).

Group Composition

Typically, group membership is determined according to a set of established criteria that is decided on prior to the establishment of the group. Brabender et al. (2004) suggest that the group leader "have a picture of the overall composition of the group. This picture encompasses an idea of the extent to which members will be variable from one another on important dimensions related to the group's functioning" (p. 62). Many group theorists recommend that individual members share their views on group purpose and some personal characteristics, while coping skills, life experiences, and expertise can be different. Alle-Corliss and Alle-Corliss (1999) add that group leaders need to decide on the question of homogeneity versus heterogeneity in the composition equation as well as assess the potential compatibility of members. Henry (1992) suggests that members be compatible in terms of their "needs and behaviors, similarity of problems, range of tolerance for deviance from behavioral norms, cultural and other characteristics and skills related to the purpose of the group. The aim is to assemble a configuration of persons with the potential to coalesce and function as an entity" (p. 5).

Yalom (1995) believes that homogeneity of members is tied to the cohesion theory, which proposes that "attraction to the group is the interviewing variable critical to outcome, and that the paramount aim should be to assemble a cohesive, compatible group" (p. 662). Yalom's argument for heterogeneity is based on the social microcosm theory, which

> *postulates that because the group is regarded as a miniature social universe in which members are urged to develop new methods or interpersonal interaction, the group should be heterogeneous in order to maximize learning opportunities. It should resemble real social universe by being composed of individuals of different sexes, professions, ages, and socio-economic and educational levels. In other words, it should be a demographic assortment. (p. 277)*

Forming the Group

In forming a group, certain practical concerns need to be addressed, including group size, frequency and duration of sessions, length of group, and whether the group is open or closed.

Group Size

During preplanning stages of the group, it is important to decide how large or small the group will be. Several factors go into this decision, including age of clients, type of group, problems to be explored, and leaders' experience (Alle-Corliss & Alle-Corliss, 1999, p. 192). Betcher and Maple (1985) also believe that size "depends on the objectives of the group and the attributes of its members" (p. 190). It is generally felt that large groups are less able to focus on individual needs of members; thus, groups of 6 to 8 members is the norm. There is no optimal size for a group, yet a general rule of thumb is that more intense therapeutic groups are best when smaller, whereas psychoeducational groups may do well with more (10 to 12) members. G. Corey (2001) believes that "in general, the group should have enough people to afford ample interaction so it doesn't drag and yet be small enough to give everyone a chance to participate frequently without . . . losing the sense of 'group'" (p. 93). Toseland and Rivas (2009) encourage the group leader "to consider the advantages and disadvantages inherent in different group sizes" (p. 167). They identify these benefits for large and small groups:

Large Groups

- Present more ideas, skills, and resources to members
- Capable of handling more complex tasks
- Offer members more potential for learning through role models
- Afford members with more potential support, feedback, and friendship
- Allow members occasionally to withdraw and reflect on their participation
- Help to ensure that there will be enough members for meaningful interaction even if some members fail to attend

Small Groups

- Offer members with a greater level of individualized attention
- Facilitate closer face-to-face interaction

- Give less opportunity for the formation of harmful subgroups
- Provide fewer opportunities for members to withdraw from participation
- Allow for easier management by the worker
- Tend to have more informal operating procedures
- Offer more opportunities for achieving cohesiveness
- Can achieve consensus more easily (p. 168)

Frequency and Duration of Sessions
Calculating the time allotted for each group session may seem insignificant, yet this estimation can be instrumental in determining how well the group functions. When sessions are too short, members may feel unheard or cut off; this can lead to a sense of frustration and a feeling of apathy regarding the group. Conversely, when too much time is allotted, the focus may be lost.

Specifying how long each session will last requires consideration of the group purpose and composition and the type of setting. A good rule of thumb is if the sessions are found to be too boring, the frequency is too great, and when each session seems like the first, the frequency is too limited (Jacobs et al., 2006).

Similar to determining the length of each session is deciding how often the group will meet. Once again, the purpose and composition of the group and the type of setting are factors important to consider (Alle-Corliss & Alle-Corliss, 1999). For instance, group members in an inpatient setting, such as a hospital, chemical dependency program or group home, often meet daily, whereas clients in an outpatient mental health setting may meet weekly or bimonthly.

Length of a Group
Decisions regarding the length of the group will depend on such factors as the particular agency involved, the clinician's preference, the group purpose, the time needed for skill acquisition, and the group goals. In today's world, time-limited, short-term groups are often preferred over longer-term treatment. Besides the advantage of being cost effective, short-term groups are favored when topics are more focused in nature; members appreciate the idea of making changes in a short period of time.

Open or Closed Groups
Simply put, open-ended groups admit new members after they have started; closed groups do not. The group leader will have to determine

whether group membership will be open or closed. The type of group, population, duration, and time frame of the group will, in part, factor into this decision. There are advantages and disadvantages to both.

Many long-term outpatient groups are open ended. Since in open-ended groups members join and leave periodically, an advantage is the opportunity members have to interact with a greater number of people. Open-ended groups are able to replace lost members rather quickly and maintain an optimal size. Because open-ended groups are dynamic, cohesion and continuity may be difficult to achieve. An open-ended group may not evolve through various stages, as members will always be at different places in their feelings about the group. It may be difficult to introduce new members and orient them to an already-established group. Leaders will have to be very active and structured as well as have some idea about member turnover rates. Interventions must be tailored to the length of time members may stay in group. Allowing members sufficient time at the end of each group meeting to discuss their feelings about ending the session is therapeutic.

Close-ended groups have become more popular since they are often time limited and goal oriented. "Close-ended groups, although not as flexible in size, promote more cohesiveness among group members and may be productive in helping members achieve stated goals" (Gladding, 2004, p. 260). As the group evolves, trust and comfort are easier to develop. One drawback of closed groups is not being able to add new members to add life to a group that is flat. Also, if members leave and goals are not met, the group may not end as successfully.

Leader's Attitude

The leader is instrumental in setting the tone for the group. In Chapter 2, we cited certain characteristics as being valuable for group leaders to possess. "Willingness to model" is one characteristic that highlights the importance of the leader's behaviors and attitudes in encouraging group members to work together positively. "Belief in the group process" is another trait found beneficial to the group that is reflected in the leader's attitude. Sometimes leaders feel negative about a group when members are especially difficult, when there is negative countertransference, when conflict with the coleader exists, or when they are required to lead the group.

Members' Level of Commitment

Connected to voluntary and nonvoluntary membership is the members' level of commitment. Often those members who are in some way forced to join the group are less committed. "When commitment is low, members tend to get off track, show little interest, contribute very little, display disruptive behavior, argue with the leader, or attack each other" (Jacobs et al., 2006, p. 46). Generally, when clients choose to be a part of the group, they may be more committed, may work harder in the group, and may be more cooperative.

Level of Trust

Trust can develop when both the group leader and group members are committed to being in the group and believe in the group purpose. Often, when there are too many different points of view among members or when a deep dislike exists between them, trust is less likely. Also, trust is affected when members breach confidentiality or when they are hostile with one another. As a group develops, trust often increases or decreases depending on the group's composition and interactions. It is essential for the group leader to be attentive to the group's trust level and to be alert to subtle changes. Sometimes, with appropriate interventions and planning, the trust within a group can be restored; other times, the trust level may not change.

Members' Attitude toward the Leader

Another factor that influences the trust level within a group is the members' attitude toward the leader. Logically, when a leader is well liked and respected, trust is likely to emerge. It is important to pay attention to situations when there is negativity toward the leader and to determine why. Efforts should be made to understand these reasons and to explore ways to impact group dynamics in a positive manner.

Leader's Experience in Leading Groups

Leaders who are new at group work have little experience to guide them, which can often lead to feeling nervous and making mistakes. This is normal. What is important here is for group leaders to be open about their inexperience, to learn from their mistakes, and to seek guidance and support through supervision, consultation, and additional training. Sometimes working with a more experienced coleader can be helpful.

Coleadership Harmony

When groups are co-led, it is important for a good working relationship to exist between the leaders. Good communication, a willingness to be vulnerable and open, and an ability to adjust to differences are essential skills. Coleaders who are not in sync, who have very different styles, and who are not respectful of one another will have difficulties in creating a trusting and open group environment. Cooperation among leaders fosters a sound working relationship.

Designing the Group's Environment

Three factors are related to preparing for the group environment: (1) preparing the physical environment, (2) securing financial support, and (3) securing special arrangements.

Preparing the Physical Setting We have already discussed the importance of the physical setting in ensuring the safety and growth of a group. Privacy, concentration, comfort, and intimacy are four factors related to a group's physical setting that have been shown to directly affect the interaction among members and to have a bearing on the overall composition of the group.

Securing Financial Support Support, both emotional and financial, from the sponsoring agency is essential in ensuring the success of any group. Sometimes this is not an issue, as the agency itself is promoting group treatment and supports the new idea. On other occasions, however, the agency may be leery about a specific group and reluctant to offer financial support. The group proposal should offer valid reasons why a specific group would be worthwhile to invest in.

Making sure the financial aspects are considered in group development is critical, as they can severely impact the existence of the group. Leaders should be aware of possible problems in this area and be proactive.

Special Arrangements Sanctions from the sponsoring agency are necessary in developing and leading certain types of groups. Agency administration approval must be secured to ensure that a proposed group will become a reality. Similarly, if special arrangements are needed for certain members, such as special seating, reading material with a larger font, or transportation, they should be taken care of either before the first group or soon thereafter.

Once all the pregroup issues have been considered sufficiently, it is time to begin the group.

Group Implementation

Orienting Members to the Group

Once group screening is completed and the group is formed, members need to be properly oriented. Orientation can take place during the screening process itself, during the initial group session, or at both times. Group preparation is essential in setting the foundation for a meaningful group experience. Yalom (2005) asserts that taking time to prepare new members to the group often compensates for a less than ideal group composition.

Brabender et al. (2004) believe that "preparation should fulfill two purposes: (1) to give the individual an accurate picture of the group and (2) to insure member behavior that is supportive of the group goals" (p. 69). Earlier in our discussion about attracting new members, we touched on the importance of providing prospective members with as much relevant information about the group as possible. During this phase, "it is important to explain the purpose of the group and determine group goals, and to familiarize members with the group by discussing procedures and ground rules that often contain limits of the group as well" (Alle-Corliss & Alle-Corliss, 1999, p. 192).

Orientation is an excellent time for potential group members to become acquainted; it also provides them with necessary information to "decide if they are willing to commit themselves to what would be expected of them [and is] an ideal time to focus on the clients' percep-tions, expectations, and concerns" (M.S. Corey & G. Corey, 2006, p. 119). Continuing to screen members for appropriateness is also critical during this stage. As a form of continued screening, this pregroup session is also valuable in demonstrating that certain members are inappropriate, that the original group purpose may need to be refined, or that the group composition is lacking in some way. Learning early on about any of these factors allows leader(s) to work toward refining the group and making necessary changes before the actual group gets under way.

Contracting

A contract, defined as a verbal or written agreement between the leader and members, typically occurs prior to the first session and can be either formal or informal. "The contract not only helps to clarify the purpose of the group but also helps foster commitment and a sense of responsibility in both the members and the leader. Often, contracting occurs at two levels: contracting for group procedures and contracting for individual member goals" (Alle-Corliss & Alle-Corliss, 1999, p. 193). Contracting encourages members' active participation and ownership by helping them to feel they are integrally involved in the group process.

Group Evaluation

Equally as important as the development of the group is the evaluation that takes place on the group's ending. M.S. Corey and G. Corey (2006) believe that it is essential in most settings to "devise procedures to assess the degree to which clients benefit from the group experience" (p. 124). They suggest including in the initial group proposal the procedures intended to evaluate both individual member outcomes and the outcomes of the group as a unit. Periodic evaluations can give group leaders "useful feedback about their approach to groups, as well as information on the kinds of experiences that are most helpful in meeting the goals of their members" (Jacobs et al., 2006. p. 440). Recent emphasis is on developing evidence-based practice guidelines that describe the most effective interventions for particular problems (Howard & Jenson, 2003; Roberts & Yeager, 2004; Rosen & Proctor, 2003; Toseland & Rivas, 2009).

Evaluations can be either formal or informal. An informal way to obtain information about the effectiveness of the group is simply to ask group members to evaluate their group experience. Toseland and Rivas (2009) note that "to complete a formal evaluation, a worker [group leader] might collect information systematically using preplanned measurement devices before, during, or after the group has met" (p. 400). They also detail the benefits of evaluations. Next we list some of the most important of these benefits:

- Information from evaluations can encourage group leaders to improve their leadership skills.
- Evaluations can demonstrate the usefulness of a specific group or a specific group work method to an agency, a funding source, or society.
- Evaluations allow group members and others who may be affected to express their satisfaction and dissatisfaction with a group.

- Knowledge gathered through evaluations can be shared with others who are using group methods for similar purposes and in similar situations.

- Evaluations can examine the cost-effectiveness of group work services.

- Evaluations can validate leaders and encourage them, especially when group members' issues are challenging.

Two types of evaluation measures are member-specific measures and group-specific measures. The first type is used to assess changes in attitudes and behaviors of individual clients; the second is used to assess the changes common to all members of the group, such as increased awareness, decreased anxiety, and improved personal relationships (M.S. Corey & G. Corey, 2006; Fuhriman & Burlingame, 1994).

The basic three types of evaluations include:

1. Evaluation of the changes that actually occur in members' lives
2. Evaluation by the group leader
3. Evaluation by the group members

Evaluating Changes in Group Members' Lives

There are several methods to evaluate group members' behavioral changes, including members' self-reports and more objective feedback from others in members' lives (i.e., teachers, employers, parents, spouses, friends, probation counselors, primary medical treatment staff, and individual therapists).

Jacobs et al. (2006) spell out eight specific steps that are helpful in producing data measuring the outcome:

1. *Identify the outcome goals.*
2. *Collect pregroup data.*
3. *Focus the group sessions on the desired outcome goals.*
4. *Develop an appropriate form for members to complete regarding their progress toward the established goals.*
5. *Determine whether people other than the members can be involved in evaluating outcome, and if so, obtain permission from members and contact those people.*

6. *Collect data periodically using a form.*

7. *At the end of the group, collect data using a form.*

8. *Plan for follow-up data collection by either mailing at designated intervals or using during postgroups (p. 441).*

Group Leader's Evaluation

Informal self-evaluations by group leaders are common, since it is customary for group leaders to reflect on the group experience at the end of each session and at the final group meeting. By taking time to review the group dynamics and their role in dealing with the group, group leaders are able to learn what has worked and what has not worked. Continuous evaluation allows group leaders to fine-tune techniques and enhance their leadership skills.

Jacobs et al. (2006) recommend routine questions group leaders can ask themselves after each group that include:

1. How well did I follow my plan?
2. How effectively was I able to meet the needs of individual members?
3. Did anything happen that was not anticipated? How did I handle this?
4. Could I have predicted these better?
5. What have I learned from the session that I can implement next time?
6. On a 1 to 10 scale, how would I rate my overall satisfaction with the session? Is this rating higher, lower, or the same as my rating for the last session (p. 443)?

Questions to ask when the group has completed its final session include:

1. How effective was this group?
2. Did individual members seem to benefit? Did they successfully meet their goals?
3. Was the group as a whole cohesive and responsive to the group modality?

G. Corey et al. (2004) recommend that group leaders keep a journal "to evaluate the progress of the group and to assess changes during the stages of its development" (p. 178). They suggest writing about any of these areas:

- Initial views of group? Initial reactions?
- Initial reactions to individual group members? How did any of these reactions or impressions change?
- Which members were preferable and why? Which were not?
- Feelings about leading the group? Positive or negative?
- Any unexplored personal areas that led to being stuck?
- Turning points of the group?
- Factors that contributed to success or failure of the group?
- Able to accept constructive feedback?
- Techniques used and outcome?
- Key events of each session and group as a whole?
- Dynamics of the group and relationships among members?
- Personal learning?
- Lessons learned from reactions toward specific members?

In today's fast-paced, production-oriented work environment, it may not be possible to keep so detailed a journal. We challenge leaders to find some way to reflect on their group experience nonetheless.

Members' Evaluations

It is most helpful to have members themselves evaluate the group. Informally, a group leader might ask individual members: "How did you feel about your group experience? Was it valuable? How so? If not, what might have been handled differently?" A more formal evaluation made up of a questionnaire can be given midway through the group so as to allow the group leader to make necessary changes based on members' feedback. A more comprehensive questionnaire is important to use at the end of the group as well. Carefully designed questions are essential in evaluating the outcomes of a group. Consider these questions:

- How did you most benefit from this group?
- Did you feel the group helped you meet your goals?

- Are there any activities, discussions, or topics that stood out for you?
- What did you like most (and least) about the group?
- Do you have any suggestions for how the group could have been more effective?
- Are there any things the group leader could have done differently that would have been more effective?

G. Corey et al. (2004) suggest that an evaluation form

can ask members to assess their degree of satisfaction with the group and the level of investment they had in it; to recall highlights or significant events; to specify actions they took during the group to make desired changes; to specify what techniques were most and least helpful and to suggest changes in the format; and to describe the group after some time has elapsed. (p. 177)

The member evaluation form in Table 7.2 poses important questions about the group upon ending.

Much can be learned from evaluations. M.S. Corey and G. Corey (2006) note that "the practice of building evaluation into your group programs is a useful procedure for accountability purposes, but it can also help you sharpen your leadership skills, enabling you to see more

---

Table 7.2   **Group Member Evaluation Form**

- What general effect has your group experience had on your life?
- What were the highlights of the group experience for you?
- What specific things did you become aware of about yourself, your lifestyle, your attitudes, and your relationships with others?
- What changes have you made?
- Which of the techniques used by the group leaders had the most impact on you? Which techniques had the least impact?
- What are some of your perceptions of the group leaders and their styles?
- What problems did you encounter in the outside world when you tried to carry out some of the decisions you made in the group?
- What are some of the questions you have asked yourself since the group ended?
- Did the group experience have any negative effects on you? If so, what were they?
- Is there anything about groups in general, about this group, or about how it was conducted that you find yourself viewing critically or negatively?
- How did your participation in the group affect significant people in your life?
- How might your life be different if you had not been a member of the group?
- If you had to say in a sentence or two what the group means to you, how would you respond?

Source: Adapted from G. Corey et al. (2004), p. 178.

clearly changes you might want to make in the format for future groups" (pp. 125–126). In addition to evaluations being ways for leaders to measure the effectiveness of group, they are also ways for the members to focus on what they accomplished during the group and how they benefited. Taking time to implement some form of evaluation measure into the group process is highly recommended. In fact, the ASGW (1998) "Best Practice Guidelines" offers these standards for group evaluations:

- *Group workers [leaders] process the workings of the group with themselves, group members, supervisors, and other colleagues, as appropriate. This may include assessing progress on group and member goals, leader behaviors and techniques, group dynamics and interventions, as well as developing understanding and acceptance of meaning. Processing may occur both within sessions and before and after each session, at time of termination, and later follow-up, as appropriate. (C.1)*

- *Group workers [leaders] attend to opportunities to synthesize theory and practice and to incorporate learning outcomes into ongoing groups. Group workers attend to the relationship between session dynamics and leader values, cognition and affect. (C.2)*

- *Group workers [leaders] evaluate process and outcomes. Results are used for ongoing program planning, improvement and revisions of current group and/or to contribute to professional research literature. Group workers [leaders] follow all applicable policies and standards in using group material for research and results. (C.3)*

Follow-Up

Postgroup follow-up sessions are not mandatory, although they are an excellent way to encourage that treatment goals be sustained and applied to members' individual life situations. Follow-up sessions provide group members with the opportunity to meet together for sessions after the completion of the formal group treatment program. Ideally, follow-up sessions serve to reinforce group members' commitment to maintaining changes.

Follow-up allows members to keep in touch with one another after the group has ended to determine how well they are progressing on personal and group goals. ASGW "Best Practice Guidelines" (1998) stipulates that "group workers conduct follow-up contact with group members, as appropriate, to assess outcomes or when requested by group member(s)" (C.3, p. 4).

Follow-up can be helpful to both group members and group leader(s) in assessing what they have gained from the group experience and in determining if additional referrals are necessary. In sum, follow-up sessions serve to maximize the effects of a group experience and encourage members to keep pursuing the original individual and group goals set while they were in group (Jacobs, Harvill, & Masson, 2006). It has been found that when members are aware during the termination stage of their group that a follow-up session is planned, they are more likely to continue pursuing their goals (G. Corey, 2001; Gladding, 2004).

Common Agency Barriers for Group Development

Various agency barriers may exist that, if not considered, can extinguish a group idea before it ever can become a reality. Agency demands for short-term groups may pressure group leaders to conduct a group they are either uninterested in or unequipped for. The pressure for high productivity can at times overshadow the importance of taking time to develop a group that is composed of appropriate and motivated group members. Additionally, when cost-effective treatment is a primary concern, coleadership may not be allowed, leaving some group leaders alone with a very challenging group. Despite these barriers, there are many benefits to conducting groups within an agency setting: more clients can be seen, theme-based groups are more plentiful, and there is more opportunity for practitioners to gain experience.

Small-Group Exercises for Group Work in Agency Settings

This exercise was developed to encourage practical application of the issues presented thus far regarding group work in agency settings. It is anticipated that by working in small groups, leaders will become aware of the many intricacies and facets of group work. Imagine that this exercise is part of a training on groups within an agency setting. Please form small groups with your coworkers and follow the next seven steps.

1. Randomly select a type of agency that you will assume you are working or interning in (nonprofit, public, for profit).

2. Choose a group you would be interested in conducting, you are currently conducting, or one you have been asked to do. Describe the type and purpose of this group.

3. Determine how group development is directed: agency, staff, or client directed? What possible conflicts might there be?

4. Consider if support exists within the agency for this type of group. If so, how? If not, how not? Be specific. For instance, has such a group been run before in the agency? How does the administration view the group? Does this view differ from that of the line staff? If there are conflicts, what might you do to enlist support?

5. What are available resources for this group? What is lacking? What efforts might you make to acquire needed resources?

6. What other limitations do you envision due to the specific type of agency being considered?

7. What are your strengths and weaknesses as they pertain to you as the group leader/coleader? Questions you might ask yourself to determine these areas of strength and weakness include:
   - Is this my first group leadership experience? If not, what were my other experiences like?
   - Do I feel equipped to conduct such a group, given my training and preparation?
   - Do I feel confident? Anxious? Scared? Excited? A mixture of emotions?
   - How do I feel coleading will be? How well do I relate to my coleader? Are there any problems, conflicts, or positives?
   - How do I feel I will be most effective?

Developing successful groups is an art. Table 7.3 presents a six-step process we have found to be helpful in developing groups.

Table 7.3   **Steps in Developing Groups**

Step 1. Start with an interest in a topic or theme (e.g., anger management, cognitive-behavioral therapy group, anxiety group, etc.).
Step 2. Research the topic by exploring the issues in the literature and gathering relevant statistics.
Step 3. Examine common treatment suggestions.
Step 4. Be able to answer the "Why group?" question.
Step 5. Write a group proposal with clear objectives.
Step 6. Develop an outline of sessions that highlights session-by-session goals and weekly activities.

In Closing

This chapter has focused on the practical aspects of group planning and implementation. Preliminary considerations about group development are presented. Group planning, group formation, group implementation, and group evaluation are all detailed. A small-group exercise about developing groups in agency settings is presented to encourage a practical application. The chapter ends with a step-by-step account of how to develop groups that we use in the next section.

Applying Group and Agency Skills

Part

Application of Skills: A Lifespan Approach

Considering a lifespan approach in designing groups for individuals of a certain age group has been proven very useful in group practice. Possessing knowledge of typical age-related issues is equally as important as understanding specific conditions relevant to that age category. In this last chapter, group work with children, adolescents, adults, older adults, and the medically ill will be addressed. A relevant topic for each age group, such as ADHD in working with children, will be highlighted: Issues will be discussed, treatment considerations will be identified, a group proposal will be presented, and an outline of sessions and activities will be profiled. A list of additional topics and corresponding group profiles for each age group will be listed; the details of each of these topics and groups are easily accessed through the accompanying CD-ROM.

8

Chapter

Group Work with Children

Children, because of their dependent and often defenseless status, are often the most at risk. Burger (2008) highlights the plight of many children: "Children are endangered not only by poverty but by illness, rejection, lack of understanding, the inability of parents to socialize them properly, and many other factors" (p. 67). Given that children are a high-risk group for developing both physical and emotional problems, mental health practitioners must be available to them and must be aware of any special issues they may be facing.

The number of years between early childhood and adolescence may not be long, yet vast changes and growth occur during this short span of time, given the physical, cognitive, and psychological maturation that typically take place. It is important to be aware of each child's particular stage of development and to be able to assess the developmental milestones that have been mastered and the ones yet to be conquered. Helpers must ascertain which factors in a child's life are positive and promote development, such as a stable, loving family, positive role models, a solid education, and physical and psychological health. Equally as important is the need to determine which factors may serve to impede development, such as poor prenatal care, parental addiction or mental illness, limited medical care and health care, poverty, child abuse, family violence, immigration status, learning disabilities, developmental delays, and medical and psychological disorders.

Working with children can be a very rewarding experience, yet it is also quite challenging and sometimes emotionally difficult, as children are often the most vulnerable clients for emotional, physical, and sexual abuse and exploitation. Since children have not yet developed the skills and defenses necessary to deal with life stressors, they are more likely to need our attention, guidance, and support.

From a biological perspective, prenatal care can greatly impact children and have a significant bearing on their overall development. Substance abuse, poor nutrition, and environmental circumstances for the mother can adversely influence the child. In some cases, the ill effects of poor prenatal care are subtle and difficult to establish; for example, some learning disabilities do not become evident until children enter school.

Conditions in the environment can also have a bearing on the child's health and development. Living in poverty can have far-reaching effects on a child's development; physically, these children may be prone to illness and malnutrition that likely impact their cognitive and psychological growth. Similarly, children with physical, developmental, and emotional disabilities may experience additional psychological difficulties that are directly related to their condition. For instance, children with developmental delays often face ridicule and are stigmatized by their peers. Often they must cope with frustration and low self-esteem due to their inability to function at a higher level. Children who suffer from a specific type of psychological disorder, such as Attention Deficit Hyperactivity Disorder or Asperger's syndrome, often encounter additional stress in daily living resulting from their functional impairment(s). Learning difficulties, academic problems, and a wide range of behavioral and social problems are often present as well. Ultimately, due to their overall difficulties in functioning, these children may develop strong feelings of inadequacy and/or low self-esteem. In many of these cases, specialized care is required, including individual, family, and group counseling; parent education, school interventions, and medication management.

Victims of child abuse and violent crimes also face challenges in order to overcome the negative effects of being abused or witnessing abuse. Individual children respond differently; some are able to go forward successfully despite their past others may never be able to erase the physical and emotional scars of abuse. Feelings of insecurity, depression, and anxiety may be prevalent; abuse may be repeated in their own interpersonal relationships; and in some cases, criminal behavior may become the norm.

The increase in divorce, in single-parent families, and in blended marriages subjects children to additional stress and challenges. Many are affected by bitter divorces, lengthy custody battles, and remarriages of their parents. The ability to overcome these life events depends on specific circumstances and particularly on the existence of supportive and caring significant others.

General Treatment Considerations for Working with Children

Working with children requires a special type of helper who can promote a safe and welcoming environment and easily enter the child's world. Alle-Corliss and Alle-Corliss (1999) cite these characteristics as the most desirable ones for working with children:

- Be willing to know yourself and the child within.
- Be able to be imaginative and accept the role of the child, regardless of how bizarre the child may appear initially. This requires an empathic, accepting, and understanding approach.
- Display an optimism that allows you to instill hope in the child and provide a positive role mode.
- Be aware of your own social situation and of the ways your position influences childrens' perspectives. This includes being aware of your own prejudicial views and committing to remain as objective as possible in working with others, especially those who are different.

- Take care not to make premature assumptions or judgments about a case, as this will surely influence the course and outcome of treatment. Acknowledge when you are not sure you fully understand what is going on.

- Acknowledge and recognize the child's parents and siblings. Attempt to think of them as allies who can possibly enhance the treatment outcome with the child. When this is not possible, at the very least, do not alienate them. Consider their strengths and avoid focusing only on their limitations. Respect the child's love for his or her parents and be careful not to undermine their relationship.

- Make an attempt to understand the child, to recognize his or her strengths, and to work toward emphasizing them. By conducting a good assessment, practitioners can better determine ways to successfully enter the child's work. Confidence in the use of play therapy and in cognitive and behavioral approaches is important when working with children.

- Recognize the importance of proper referrals and the transition that may be necessary for a successful follow-through. Children and their parents may need additional treatment. Ensuring that they are given proper referrals is important in the overall treatment process.

Specific Treatment Considerations

- Complete a thorough, comprehensive assessment that includes pertinent information on pregnancy and early developmental milestones. Gaining information on childhood and family history is crucial to better understand the overall world of the child.

- Acknowledge that children often live in a world of fantasy and play in the here-and-now. Be willing to enter their world rather than expecting them to enter the adult world.

- Recognize each child as a unique individual with his or her own set of values, temperaments, and issues. Make an effort to individualize their treatment as much as possible.

- Because working with children may trigger many of our own family-of-origin issues and perhaps may create countertransference reactions, it is important to remain self-aware.

- Assess if your particular style of working with children is therapeutic, and be willing to alter it if need be.

Guidelines for Group Work with Children

1. Develop a sound group proposal that clearly describes the group purpose, rationale, goals, procedures, and evaluation process.

2. Consider legal issues, such as the state laws regarding children, the policies and procedures of the agency, and the legal and ethical reporting responsibilities. For some groups, parental written consent may be required.

3. Be clear about these practical considerations:
   - Ensure that the setting is comfortable and age appropriate for children.
   - Communicate clear expectations to children; make sure they understand the ground rules.
   - Be well prepared for each session; make sure to plan an activity, as children seem to respond best to this.
   - Be open to involving parents in understanding the group process and goals. Encourage their participation to the extent that it is appropriate.

4. Pay careful attention to these areas:
   - Ensure appropriate use of self-disclosure on the helper's part.
   - Emphasize the importance of maintaining confidentiality.
   - Maintain neutrality; do not side with any child in particular.
   - Make suitable use of exercises and techniques.
   - Use sound listening skills.
   - Adequately prepare children for termination.

Attention Deficit Hyperactivity Disorder Children's Group

Issue

Attention Deficit Disorder (ADD) with hyperactivity (ADHD) is considered one of the most common childhood disorders. Conservative estimates report that 3 to 5% of school-age children, or approximately 2 million children and adolescents, suffer from this condition. Males are diagnosed more often than females. Attention Deficit Disorder constitutes chronic neurobiological conditions characterized by developmentally inappropriate attention skills, impulsivity, and in some cases, hyperactivity. According to Parsons (2007): "AD/HD is an impairing, persistent condition that can significantly affect a student's academic and social development. Children with AD/HD are prone to serious accidents and injuries, are likely to be academic underachievers, are often rejected by their peers, and typically present with lowered self-esteem" (p. 3). Longitudinal studies have found that individuals suffering from ADHD are at higher risk for academic, behavioral, and social problems across their lifespan (Barkley, 1997a; Goldstein, 1999; Weyandt, 2001).

Attention Deficit Disorder impacts children in all areas of their lives, that is, in the home, at school, and with their peers. Parents report that at home, children with ADD/ADHD may struggle in following routines and in meeting parental expectations; they may resist bedtime, refuse to eat, and/or be destructive in their play and with siblings. Outings to public places can be overwhelming for parents, as children with ADD/ADHD tend to become overstimulated when in a public environment and often struggle when asked to sit still and be quiet.

At school, teachers report that these children may be extremely restless and easily distracted and often do not complete classwork. Because of their underdeveloped attention capacity, many children miss certain valuable information presented in class, which affects their capacity to complete homework and to do well on tests and exams. Impulsivity results in children speaking aloud and out of turn, thereby disrupting the class. In the playground, they often are aggressive and have difficulty waiting their turn. Although they may be very capable academically, their poor grades and test scores do not reflect this.

In many instances, parents spend a great deal of time and energy helping their children with homework, only to learn that the child misplaced it or forgot to turn it in.

Socially, children with ADD/ADHD have difficulties making and keeping friends and experience social skills problems. Peers may consider them demanding, controlling, and out of control. They are often shunned by peer groups and sometimes act out even further as a result. Sometimes they are labeled as troublemakers, are picked on more readily, and at times are even blamed unfairly for disruptions in class, on the playground, and in their neighborhoods.

Coexisting conditions that often occur alongside the ADD include: learning disabilities (25%); behavioral disorders such as Oppositional Defiant Disorder (40 to 60%); conduct disorders (20 to 30%); and emotional problems, given the low self-esteem and depression that results from chronic problems at home, at school, and socially (Fowler, 1992; Frick & Lahey, 1991; Lerner, Lowenthal, & Lerner, 1995; McKinney, Montague, & Hocutt, 1993).

Treatment

Treatment for children suffering from ADD/ADHD encompasses a wide variety of services. Family counseling and parental education is important in helping parents and siblings understand, help, and cope with the demands of living and raising a child afflicted with this condition. Couples counseling and parenting classes specifically designed to help parents with ADD/ADHD children are becoming commonplace and have been found very helpful. Parents are said to go through a series of predictable stages of grief when faced with the fact that their child has a serious problem such as ADD/ADHD.

At school, teachers may need to implement specific classroom management techniques and to institute a behavioral reward system. Some children may need special education services as well. Understanding the law as it pertains to ADD/ADHD is important, as these children may be eligible for additional services. The Individuals with Disabilities Education Act (IDEA) passed by Congress in 1990 "guarantees all children and youth with disabilities, ages 3 to 21, the right to a free, appropriate, public education (Lerner et al., 1995, p. 39). A child with a formal diagnosis of ADD/ADHD may be eligible for special education services under Part B of IDEA, under the "other health impaired" (OHI) category, or under other disability categories, including "specific learning disabilities" (SLD) and "serious emotional disturbance" (SED). Additionally, special education services may be available under Section 504 of the Rehabilitation Act of 1973, which allows schools to institute a 504 Accommodation Plan developed in conjunction with an Individualized Educational Plan (IEP) that specifies academic and behavioral goals for the child and proposed interventions to meet these goals. Encouraging a positive parent-teacher relationship is, of course, advisable.

Individual counseling with children with ADD/ADHD can be instrumental in helping them deal with their deficits and in learning adaptive coping and social skills. Common approaches to counseling in this area consist of: (1) a dynamic approach, (2) a behavioral approach, and (3) a combination of these. The dynamic approach involves "guiding children to better understand themselves, to learn better methods of coping with stress, and to express inner feelings. Children need to recognize their conflicts, comprehend their use of defense mechanisms, and recognize their nonproductive coping strategies" (Lerner et al., 1995, p. 164).

The behavioral approach involves environmental modifications to encourage appropriate behaviors using reinforcement, punishment, extinction, and shaping. Specific behavioral therapy strategies commonly used include: consistency management, token economies, response cost, time-outs, and contingency contracting. Cognitive-behavioral modification strategies have also been found to be helpful in teaching self-monitoring, self-reinforcement, and self-instructional problem solving to children with impulse control problems (Abramowitz & O'Leary, 1991; Barkley, 1990; Dupaul, Guevremont, & Barkley, 1992; Fiore, Becker, & Nero; 1993; Haake, 1991; Lerner et al., 1995; Whalen & Henker, 1986).

Social skills training is perhaps one of the most important treatment approaches to ADD/ADHD. As noted, children with ADD/ADHD exhibit significant and persistent problems in the social arena due to their inattentive, impulsive, and hyperactive behaviors. Children with ADHD tend to be more aggressive; those without hyperactivity are more withdrawn; both are unpopular and tend to be rejected by peers, teachers, siblings, and at times, even parents. Because of their social difficulties, these children require social skills training through direct instruction, prompting, modeling, rehearsal, and reinforcement (Landaw & Moore, 1991).

Helpful strategies to help teach social skills include:

- Judging behavior through stories
- Grasping social situations through pictures
- Distinguishing reality from make-believe
- Learning to generalize to other situations
- Learning how to communicate effectively
- Developing friendships (Lerner et al., 1995, p. 144)

Medication management may be considered as a necessary adjunct to any or all of the treatments listed. Parental concerns about medications, school responsibility, and a collaborative relationship with the medicating physician are important to consider. Ultimately, multimodal plans have been found most effective, as they combine medication, effective instruction, behavior management strategies, family and child counseling or therapy, and good parenting and home management. There has been widespread support for a multimodal, multidisciplinary form of intervention when working with children who have ADD/ADHD. Intervention models found to be most comprehensive and useful encourage the promotion of appropriate behaviors and the use of ancillary support for children and parents (e.g., individual and group counseling, parenting support groups; DuPaul & Stoner, 1994; Goldstein, 1999).

Why Group?

Group counseling seems to be the most effective way of incorporating supportive, educational, cognitive-behavioral therapy with social skills training techniques that are important in the treatment of ADD/ADHD. When children with these disorders are seen on an individual basis, their problems may not be evident and therefore are difficult to treat. However, when seen in a group setting, these same children are apt to display difficulties with inattention, impulsivity, and/or hyperactivity, given the added stimulation and chances for distractibility. Group leaders can witness the problems these children are apt to face in real life and thus are better able to develop more appropriate treatment plans that target specific behaviors.

Proposed Group and Overall Objectives

Through involvement in an 8-week coed group of children ages 7 to 10, members will be helped to understand ADD/ADHD and how it impacts their school performance and social skills. The group will emphasize that the disorder by itself will not keep students from their personal, academic, or career goals, thereby setting a positive and hopeful tone. Students will learn to identify problem areas at school, at home, and with peers, and will be encouraged to work on problem-solving skills and building self-esteem.

Group Profile: Outline of Sessions
Session 1

- Introduce group purpose and ground rules.
- Help children understand ADD and ADHD: Awareness of this condition is key.
- Discourage children from using the diagnosis as an excuse for acting out or for academic problems.
- Provide hope using empowerment strategies.

   Activity: Read *Shelley, the Hyperactive Turtle* by Deborah M. Moss, and discuss any similarities they see between Shelley and themselves.

Session 2

- Discuss the concept of impulsivity: acting before thinking.
- Discuss how to maintain appropriate behaviors: Recognize appropriate versus inappropriate behaviors.
- Explain how children can catch themselves by counting to 10 or 20.

Activity: Encourage the group to discuss situations at home and at school where they are impulsive. Demonstrate impulsive behaviors through a role-play; then ask members to enact the situation again, but this time to use the counting technique to minimize an impulsive reaction.

Session 3

- Introduce problem-solving skills by discussing these questions:
  - What is the problem?
  - What are the possible solutions?
  - What is the best solution for me?
  - How do I follow through?

Activity: Begin by presenting an age-appropriate problem (e.g., a schoolmate does not want to share his lunch even though everyone else shares with him), and ask the group to use the problem-solving questions just described. Next have members identify problems of their own and take them through the problem-solving process.

Session 4

- Discuss peer relationship issues.
- Discuss why ADD and ADHD children are prone to rejection by their peers:
  - Too impulsive
  - Too immature
  - Seem out of control
- Explore positive ways to make friends.

Activity: Use a "making friends" worksheet to discuss ideas on how to make friends. Discuss as a group the qualities most people want in a friend. Role-play initiating a conversation with a potential friend.

Session 5

- Discuss school concerns children with ADD/ADHD often have. Identify problem areas and explore why school is difficult.
- Discuss listening, staying on task, following rules, and the like, and explore ways to be able to be more attentive
- Encourage asking for help (from teachers, aides, parents, etc.).
- Discuss homework: How can children become organized and structured?

Activity: Go around the group, having each member answer this question:

What is one thing that could help you do better in school?

Write the answers on the board and determine which responses are realistic avenues to pursue. (The group leader can identify areas where parents and teachers might help and share these ideas with the caregivers after group or in a special meeting.)

Session 6

- Discuss home life issues.
- Explore difficulties with parents and siblings.
- Encourage taking responsibility for their part in conflicts.

Activity: Brainstorm ways to improve relationships at home. Discuss the use of "Okay" versus "Why?" or "In a minute!"

Session 7

- Introduce self-esteem building and its importance.
- Assess the self-esteem of each member. Discuss how it is easy for the children to feel as if they are bad since they are always getting in trouble. It is important to separate the ADD/ADHD condition from the child. Emphasize that the child is not bad, only the behavior is viewed so.
- Focus on positives. Encourage children in ways to feel better about themselves.

Activity: Complete an "I AM SPECIAL BECAUSE . . . " art project that helps members to be able to identify their strengths through artwork.

Session 8

- Present concluding remarks.
- Consolidate learning: Review progress.
- Discuss feelings about ending and positively reinforce their participation.
- Address plans for the future.

Activity: Celebrate with a party that the group planned. This shows their ability to follow directions and stay on task.

Agency Considerations

An Attention Deficit Hyperactivity Disorder children's group can be conducted in public school settings, nonprofit and for-profit counseling agencies, mental health centers, or the pediatric, psychiatric, or behavioral health departments of health maintenance organizations. It is important to have a good relationship with personnel at the schools the group members attend; collaborative work is essential in education management endeavors. Similarly, it may be necessary to liaison with the child's pediatrician or psychiatrist if a medication evaluation is needed or if medication management is in place.

Additional Topics and Corresponding Group Profiles

There are many other issues relevant to working with children. For your convenience, the following topics and corresponding "Group Profiles" are addressed in depth in the accompanying CD-ROM:

- Abused Children's Group
- Anxiety Support Group for Children (Separation, Social, Phobias)
- Depression Children's Group
- Divorce Adjustment Children's Group
- Domestic Violence Children's Support Group
- Foster Care Children's Support Group

- Life and Social Skills Children's Training Group
- Children's Loss Support Group
- Nutrition (Obesity Prevention) Children's Support Group
- Preteen Support Group
- School-Based Learning Disabilities Children's Support Group

Group Work with Adolescents

Adolescence

The period of adolescence is often a very turbulent and stressful time, yet it can also be a positive and exciting period of growth and discovery. Difficulties common during this stage are often tied to identity development and the need for peer approval. For many teens, this stage is fraught with crises and stress, as noted by Carlson and Lewis (1988):

> *Adolescents are unquestionably at a vulnerable developmental stage as they attempt to navigate the difficult transition from childhood to adulthood. Any life transition holds the potential for danger or for growth, but adolescence represents probably the most crucial transition, combining a general life adventure (bidding farewell to childhood and joining the adult world) with a series of specific changes (leaving one school for another, entering the work world, learning to think differently, meeting new expectations, seeking independence from parents—even adapting to a new body). (p. 1)*

This is a stage where there is major growth, physical maturation, and hormonal challenges; thus it can be overwhelming and emotionally difficult to cope with. Problems with body image can be great, and some teens develop eating disorders. Also, adolescence is a time when some teens begin to manifest signs of a specific psychological condition, such as depression, anxiety, Bipolar Disorder, and Schizophrenia. Since these conditions can be difficult to diagnose and treat, stress for both the teens and their families can be great.

Because adolescence can be tumultuous, many teens are likely to engage in high-risk behaviors, such as illegal drug and alcohol use, driving recklessly or under the influence, entrance into gangs, involvement in criminal activities, and unprotected sex that often results in unwanted pregnancies or becoming infected with sexually transmitted diseases. Additionally, any existing family problem (i.e., divorce, family violence, unemployment) can add to their stress and possible acting out. It has been noted that "some teens react to their life difficulties through delinquent behavior [such as] running away, school suspensions, dropping out, etc. . . . The resulting legal issues when teens are arrested for criminal activity add to their already difficult situations" (Alle-Corliss & Alle-Corliss, 1999, p. 276).

General Treatment Considerations

The following general treatment considerations have been found useful in working with adolescents:

- Recognize that there is great diversity among adolescents. It can be a turbulent time for some, but a positive stage for others.
- Identity versus identity diffusion is the development task of this stage. Many adolescents will be searching for their identity, and some will act out as a result.
- Beginning individuation is also common at this stage. Some adolescents engage in rebellious behaviors as a way to separate.
- Be aware of the biological risks for some adolescents: Poor nutritional habits can lead to eating disorders, problems with dysmenorrhea in females, and obesity, prediabetes, and diabetes. Poor sleeping habits can impact energy, cognitive abilities, memory and concentration, and mood; poor self-care can cause acne and self-esteem issues.
- Psychological risks to consider include emotional issues tied to maturation. Some adolescents tend to externalize these frustrations by acting out or engaging in delinquent behaviors. Others, in turn, may internalize these pressures and become depressed (and suicidal) or use drugs and alcohol to cope.
- Social risks to consider include substance abuse and sexual acting out. Both can lead to increased problems in a variety of areas, including drug addiction, teen pregnancy, abortion, sexually transmitted diseases, and HIV/AIDS.
- Treatment must be geared to the adolescent; their perspective and specific stage of development must be taken into consideration.

Guidelines for Group Work with Adolescents

Some of the issues and challenges commonly experienced when leading adolescent groups have been well described in the literature (Alle-Corliss & Alle-Corliss, 1999; M.S. Corey & G. Corey, 2006; Rapp-Paglicci, Dulmus, & Wodarski, 2004; Zastrow & Kirst-Ashman, 2004). We summarize these next.

- Group leaders must be able to motivate adolescents to actively participate in group treatment.
- Group guidelines, purpose, and goals must be clearly outlined in a manner that adolescents can understand.
- Group leaders must be creative in working with adolescents and in keeping the group moving forward.
- Group leaders should work toward a gradual climate of trust with adolescent group members.
- Group leaders should be cognizant of appropriate use of self-disclosure.
- Group leaders should be open to work with resistance versus against it; accept that some adolescents will initially present as involuntary clients. It is important to start where group members are at, while respecting them and showing patience.
- To gain trust within the group, leaders must present themselves in a positive manner. Leaders who are caring, enthusiastic, vital, open, and direct are better able to relate to adolescent clients.
- Leading in an active manner that keeps the group process moving is essential when working with adolescent groups. If members consider sessions as slow and boring, they are likely to become distracted and uninvolved. Often, theme-related structured exercises keep the group momentum going.
- Action-oriented techniques are also important in keeping the group interesting and therapeutic. Role-plays and other Gestalt exercises are very useful but must be appropriate to the group population and topic being served.
- Ultimately, encouraging active participation from adolescent members is vital to the group process.

Depression Support Group for Teens

Issue

According to the U.S. Surgeon General's Report on Mental Health (1999), depression affects children and adolescents differently from adults. Depressed children and adolescents rarely have psychotic features, yet tend to complain more than do depressed adults about anxiety symptoms including separation anxiety, reluctance to meet people, and somatic symptoms of headaches and stomachaches (Roe-Sepowitz & Thyer, 2004, p. 78). It has been estimated that more than 30% of the adolescent population experiences depression, with one in five teens reporting a minimum of one episode of major depression by the age of 18 (McWhirter, McWhirter, McWhirter, & McWhirter, 1998). One in every eight adolescents is said to be depressed, with teenage girls more likely to suffer from depression than boys (Center for Mental Health, 1998; National Institute of Mental Health, 2000). No doubt, these reported numbers are lower than actual numbers, since many teens may who suffer from milder forms of depression do not seek treatment or are diagnosed with another condition, such as an anxiety or a conduct disorder (McCarter, Sowers, & Dulmus, 2004).

Because of the link to an increase in risk for suicide, depression in adolescents is a diagnosis that is of concern to clinicians. The Centers for Disease Control and Prevention (CDC, 1999) reports that suicide is the third-leading cause of death during the teen years. Smolowe (1995) estimates that as many as 2,000 young people commit suicide each year, and for every success, up to 350 teenagers attempt to do so. These estimates are likely low, since many suicides are not reported due to the "family's embarrassment or religious beliefs or the discomfort of the school and the community" (McWhirter et al., 1998, p. 181). Furthermore, both alcohol/drug use and reckless behavior are related to suicide ideation. Some teens who are reckless may, in fact, be courting death without acknowledging it (passive suicide). Also, many accidental deaths and drug overdoses may be unrecognized or unreported suicides. Teens who are depressed often use alcohol and drugs to cope and may act out their feelings through reckless behavior.

Vulnerable and underserved youth, such as ethnic minority children and adolescent gay and lesbian youth, are at higher risk of becoming depressed and suicidal. Risk factors that may influence the probability for adolescent depression include:

- Having a parent or other close biological relative with a mood disorder
- Having a severe stressor, such as a loss, or the divorce, marital separation, unemployment or job dissatisfaction of parents
- Having a physical disorder, such as a chronic medical condition
- Suffering through a traumatic experience
- Having low self-esteem, a sense of low self-efficacy, and a sense of helplessness and hopelessness
- Being female
- Living in poverty (Institute of Medicine, 1994)

The causes and characteristics of youth suicide are similar and can be divided into two major categories: (1) interpersonal, family, and psychosocial; and (2) interpersonal and psychological characteristics.

Interpersonal, Family, and Psychosocial Characteristics
- Loss and separation
- Dysfunctional and disintegrated families
- Poor communication skills
- Under- and overachievement

Interpersonal and Psychological Characteristics
- Hopelessness and depression
- Impulsivity and risk taking
- Loneliness
- Self-image
- Negative thinking patterns

Motivations for attempting suicide may be related to:

1. A faulty view of suicide as a form of self-punishment
2. Perverted revenge to get back at those who inflicted physical and emotional pain
3. Retaliatory abandonment to get back at those who have abandoned them (e.g., after a breakup with a girl- or boyfriend)
4. Fantasy of omnipotent mastery, which is the "desire to have absolute control of the self and others, to control life and death itself,

and to be completely autonomous" (McWhirter et al., 1998, pp. 187-188).

Warning signs of suicide include: behavioral changes, verbal messages, cognitive preoccupations, and depression. A first step in preventing suicide is to actively treat depression in the adolescent population.

Treatment

Treatment for depression in teens can take many forms, from individual and family counseling to medication management and group counseling. Cognitive-behavioral therapy (CBT) has been found to be most effective in treating depression in adolescents. Brown and Prout (1999) note that "the primary behavioral treatment for depressive disorders involves the reinforcement of socially appropriate behaviors and the heightening of the potency of satisfied reinforces." Therefore, it is important to educate family and peers to elicit socially desirable behaviors and to positively reinforce them. Depressed teens need to be encouraged to initiate appropriate social contacts in a variety of situations and to work on changing distorted thinking. Since distorted thinking has been found to be central to the development of depression in both children and adolescents, it is important to incorporate cognitive therapy techniques into treatment plans. One treatment that has been found to be very effective is using self-statement and self-management techniques in cognitive restructuring to modify internal stimulus conditions that trigger depression and negative self-concept (Clarizio, 1985; Meichenbaum, 1977).

Why Group?

Group therapy to treat adolescent depression has become an increasingly common modality; teens seem to benefit by sharing with others and by knowing that they are not alone. The literature identifies two programs that are quite helpful in decreasing adolescent depression. These programs serve adolescents who have elevated self-reported depressive symptoms and risks including marital conflict in the home, low family cohesion, and conduct problems.

The first program, the Coping with Stress (CWS) program, was developed by Clarke, Lewinsohn, and Hops (1990) for adolescents with elevated self-reported depressive symptomatology. CWS is a program using cartoons, group activities, and role-plays to teach adolescents techniques including cognitive-restructuring skills to identify and reorganize negative or irrational thoughts. CWS is focused on developing adaptive coping skills and consists of 15 group sessions of 45 minutes each, usually conducted after school. The group leaders are specially trained.

The second program, the Penn Prevention Program (PPP), was developed by Martin Seligman and his research team at Penn State University (Jaycox, Reivich, Gilham, & Seligman, 1994) with the purpose of altering cognitive distortions and improving coping skills for adolescents who are at risk for depression. Participants had elevated depressive symptomatology and high levels of perceived family conflict. PPP consists of twelve 90-minute group sessions in a program using instruction and homework techniques to teach interpretation and problem-solving/coping skills. Results showed a significant decrease in depressive symptoms at the end of the program and at the six-month follow-up posttreatment.

Proposed Group and Overall Objectives

This is a 12-week educational and CBT group for teens ages 13 to 17. The group is designed to provide peer support and education to teens about symptoms of depression and coping strategies. Objectives include identifying depression from a biopsychosocial perspective, understanding types of depression, and increasing self-esteem. Various coping skills are taught, including CBT, anger management, and communication skills. Suicide prevention is emphasized, as well as the importance of developing healthy support systems.

Group Profile: Outline of Sessions
Session 1

- Introduce the members to group rules and goals.
- Introduce members and the group leader.
- Have members share why they decided to be involved in group.

   Activity: Discuss personal definitions of *depression*.

   Depression is _____ .

Write different definitions on the board so members can see similarities and differences.

Session 2

- Discuss depression.
- Identify specific symptoms that are common.
- Discuss the impact of being depressed:
  - Biologically and physically
  - Psychologically and emotionally
  - Socially
- Explore the stigma of this diagnosis:
  - Weak
  - Mentally ill
  - Exaggerating ("drama queen" or "king")

Activity: Distribute each member a handout that lists three columns: Bio, Psycho, and Social. Ask members to note ways depression has impacted them in each of these three areas.

Session 3

- Discuss the types of depression.
- Identify different causes using the word *biopsychosocial*:
  - Biological: genetics, hormonal
  - Psychological: low self-esteem, cognitive (negative thinking)
  - Social: life stressors (e.g., loss, life changes, disappointment in self or others)

Activity: Have the group divide into pairs. Members are to identify to their partner the type(s) of depression they feel they have. Share as a group to see the variety that is likely to emerge.

Session 4

- Address the connection between self-esteem and depression.
- Explore ways of building self-esteem.

Activity: Do an exercise about strengths: Ask members how others would describe them. Ask them to think of one area they would like to feel good about, and explore ways to set goals to achieve this.

Session 5

- Introduce cognitive-behavioral therapy.
- Discuss concepts of the thoughts-feelings-action model.
- Explore negative thinking by reviewing negative thinking reminders:
  - Negative attitude
  - Disqualifying positive events
  - Exaggerating the negative
  - Absolute thinking
  - Name calling
  - Perfectionistic thinking
  - Blaming

Activity: Present various examples of the different negative thinking reminders and how they result in a depressed mood. Invite members to provide their own examples.

Session 6

- Introduce cognitive restructuring and its benefits.
- Teach cognitive restructuring skills.
- Practice challenging negative, irrational thoughts with more positive, rational ones.
- Suggest two steps: (1) thought stopping and (2) positive self-talk.
- Emphasize the power of perspective.

Activity: Model the two steps of cognitive restructuring. Give members scenario cards to use, and have them divide into pairs and practice these steps themselves.

Session 7

- Introduce letting go of anger.
- Discuss depression as anger turned inward.
- Explore ways to let go of anger in healthy ways.

Activity: Ask how many members experience angry feelings they keep inside. Explain ways to safely release pent-up anger.

Session 8

- Introduce the importance of communication skills.
- Identify communication problems in relationships with parents, teachers, peers, and others.
- Introduce different communication styles:
  ◦ Passive
  ◦ Assertive
  ◦ Aggressive
  ◦ Passive-aggressive

Activity: Ask members to give an honest appraisal of their primary communication style. The leader is to role-play each style with different members.

Session 9

- Continue to identify personal styles of communicating.
- Teach assertiveness skills to the group.
- Discuss positive and negative consequences of good communication.
- Encourage practicing these coping skills.

Activity: Have members identify real-life examples of problem areas in their life where assertion is necessary. Practice assertiveness in pairs using these examples. At the end of the session, have members share positives and negatives about being assertive.

Session 10

- Discuss the importance of healthy support systems.
- Explore ways of reaching out to others when depressed.
- Emphasize building strong relationships.

Activity: Via role-plays, have members practice reaching out to others when they need support.

Session 11

- Discuss depression and suicidal thoughts.
- Emphasize seeking help early on.

- Encourage members to use the coping skills they have been taught.

    Activity: Have members devise a personal suicide prevention plan.

Session 12

- Review their progress and evaluate the group.
- Anticipatory planning: "What can I do in the future if I feel depressed?"
- End: Deal with feelings of loss.

    Activity: Celebrate with a party. Provide self-esteem messages written on a personalized card to each member.

Agency Considerations

An outpatient depression support group for teens is typically found in counseling centers and departments of mental or behavioral health. Nonprofit counseling agencies, for-profit private counseling corporations, county or public mental health centers, and psychiatric or behavioral health departments in health maintenance organizations are examples. It is critical to have access to medical care, where a physician or psychiatrist is available to evaluate and prescribe antidepressant medication. It is also important to be prepared to enlist the help of professionals in conducting suicidal risk assessments if the need arises.

Additional Topics and Corresponding Group Profiles

As with children, there are many other issues relevant to working with adolescents. In the accompanying CD-ROM the following topics and corresponding "Group Profiles" are addressed in depth:

- Anger Management Teen Group
- Anxiety Support Group for Teens
- Nonviolent Teen Group
- Substance Abuse Teen Group
- Teen Pregnancy Support Group
- Teenage Fathers' Support Group

- Teen "Relationships" Support Group
- Teen Self-Esteem Support Group
- Trauma Survivors and Loss Teen Support Group (School Shootings, Accidents, Gang Violence)
- Latina Teens Empowerment Group
- Young Men's Support Group (Brother to Brother)

Group Work with Adults

Adults

Adulthood encompasses a vast age span from young adulthood, to middle age to later life. This section considers issues relevant to both young and middle-age adults. Older adulthood is examined later in this chapter.

Entering young adulthood can be both exciting and challenging. It is frequently a difficult phase, given the transition from focus on oneself to focus on others. Turning 18 years old marks formal entrance into adulthood from a legal perspective, yet many young adults are not yet ready to become independent, financially or emotionally, from their parents. For those who are expected to live independently and make life decisions on their own, this life stage can be very difficult. Additionally, young adults are generally dealing with intimacy issues and work and career decisions.

Physically, young adults are said to be at the peak of their development (Ashford, Lecroy, & Lortie, 1997). For some, emphasis is on becoming more health conscious than they were during their adolescent period. For young adult women, the reproductive system is at its prime, resulting in decisions to become pregnant and experience childbirth. Hormonal imbalances can be extreme at this time, especially during the menstrual cycle, and can lead to difficulties intra- and interpersonally.

Biologically, reproductive problems and cancer of the reproductive system for both men and women can develop during this period, as seen in the increased incidence of testicular and breast cancer. Moreover, the formal diagnosis of a mental illness, such as Schizophrenia, depression, and bipolar disorders, is often made during early adulthood.

Psychologically, there is the expectation that young adults are capable of engaging in formal operational thinking and are adept at problem solving. In reality, however, many entering adulthood have not yet mastered this cognitive level. Communication problems are common and contribute to many of the problems young adults have in their interpersonal relationships with family, friends, intimate relationships, professors, and employers. Erikson (1963) notes that individuals at this stage are struggling with issues of "intimacy versus isolation." As a result of this developmental task, young adults are often in search of intimate relationships and may pursue love interests. Isolation and loneliness can take a toll on the emotional state of those who have difficulty in relationships.

Making major life decisions and taking on major life responsibilities is integral to adults in this stage. As a result, many young adults experience some type of stress-related illness or condition. When faced with a medical or mental illness, financial or career-related struggles, or interpersonal problems, the stress can become unmanageable.

Socially, young adults face the task of individuation. Because of economic hardships common today, many remain at home. Some may find this to be overwhelming, while others may not yet be ready to venture out on their own. Those asked to move out by their family often feel great stress about surviving financially and emotionally.

Treatment Considerations for Working with Young Adults

- Be aware that young adults are as diverse as adolescents, with some very mature at age 18 and others still like adolescents in their behaviors at age 25.

- Recognize the pressures that many young adults face and the impact these pressures may have on them physically, psychologically, and socially.

- Be sensitive to the fact that many young adults have to juggle multiple responsibilities (e.g., work, school, family) that they may not be ready for.

- Consider the drug and alcohol problems that may be present at this stage, when freedom from parental control opens the door to increased experimentation.

- Assist young adults in understanding the risks of unprotected sexual activity.

- Be prepared to help young adults deal with intimacy issues and relationship struggles they have limited experience with; help them with concerns about marriage, career, and work.

- Be able to recognize the signs of mental illness (e.g., Bipolar Disorder, Schizophrenia, depression) that may first surface during this stage.

Young adults eventually enter middle age, which can be a time of great emotional growth or a time of physical, psychological, and social decline. The definition of middle age has changed in the last few decades, given the increase in life expectancy; not long ago, those who are middle age today would have considered themselves old. Today, middle age is a much more diverse period in life that is affected primarily by each person's experiences and life choices. Typically, middle-age adults are involved with launching their children, with career advancement, and with developing new perspectives about who they are. At this stage, some adults may begin to review their past and feel regret or sadness about their lack of accomplishment. Others may look to the future and feel anxious, depressed, and hopeless. In both of these cases, such contemplation may precipitate a crisis that may be tied to developmentally age-appropriate issues related to generativity versus stagnation.

Biologically, during middle age many adults must face the repercussions of their previous maladaptive behaviors including poor eating habits, excessive tanning, excessive substance use, and sexual acting out, to name a few. Stress may account for increasing medical and psychological problems faced by many middle-age individuals. Women may struggle with menopause, and both genders must deal with changes in their own sexual response. Of great significance is the fact that various life-threatening or chronic illnesses become even more of a concern for certain individuals during this stage. The incidence of breast cancer for women and prostate cancer for men is greater, as is heart disease for both genders.

Psychologically, middle age may be a time of crisis, better known as the midlife crisis. This can be a difficult phase of life, since the body is changing, children are leaving home, parents are growing older and perhaps more frail, and people are more realistic about their life goals and their own mortality. "Facing these issues often requires individuals to review their past to renew and reintegrate their identity. Even those who experience no major difficulties at this stage often have a period of reflection that can be emotionally stressful (Alle-Corliss & Alle-Corliss, 1999, p. 280). During this stage, it is not uncommon for individuals to be more serious about their social and moral responsibilities; some become more involved in socially responsible activities such as coaching, serving as representatives on community boards and task forces, participating in fundraisers and volunteer activities, or working for a particular cause or charity.

For some, alcohol or drug addiction has reached its peak, resulting in loss of health, of jobs, of relationships, and of freedom. It is during this time that many finally accept their addiction and seek treatment for chemical dependency. Codependency issues must also be confronted by significant others who previously placed blame on the alcohol user or drug user. The need to cope with psychological conditions, such as Major Depressive Disorder, Generalized Anxiety Disorder, and Bipolar Disorder, is also common during this stage.

Socially, many middle-age adults struggle with single parenting, divorce, remarriage, and the stress of a blended family. Stress resulting from spousal abuse, past sexual abuse or rape, and occupational and financial difficulties can be great during this stage. Also, there is a greater likelihood that conflicts will exist between midlife parents and their adolescent children, adult children, and aging parents. Some middle-age adults are struggling with teens and young adults; others, who started families later in life, are dealing with the many stressors of early parenthood. When aging parents are plagued by Alzheimer's or another serious medical or mental illness, the stress on these adults can be great. Grandparenting, usually a joy, can be stressful when middle-age adults are placed in a custodial role.

Treatment Considerations for Working with Middle-Age Adults

- Middle adulthood is a diverse period of life and must be recognized as such.

- Be aware and capable of helping with the crises that are common at this stage, given the presence of high-risk behaviors involving substance abuse, job loss, and marital conflicts that can lead to extramarital affairs, divorce, and remarriage.

- Recognize the need to be supportive of middle-age adults who are part of the "sandwich generation" and who may be called on to care for both their teen or adult children and their aging parents. The stressors are magnified for those who have started a second family.

Basic Guidelines for Group Work with Adults

- Orient members to the group purpose, goals, ground rules, and expectations.
- Discuss the importance of commitment, attendance, and promptness.
- Lay the foundation for the beginning development of trust and rapport among group members and with group leader(s).
- Be respectful, listen carefully, and refrain from being judgmental or critical.
- Arrive on time to the group and model appropriate group behavior.

Anxiety Adult Support Group

Issue

Anxiety disorders as a group are among some of the most common, frequently occurring disorders in the United States. According to the Anxiety Disorders Association of America (2008), anxiety disorders affect 40 million adults in the United States age 18 and older, or about 18.1% of the United States population. Anxiety disorders cost the United States more than $42 billion a year, or almost one-third of the $148 billion total mental health bill for the U.S. (Anxiety Community, 2008). Other reports find that individuals suffering from anxiety are three to five times more likely to seek medical care and six times more likely to be hospitalized for psychiatric disorders. Furthermore, approximately one in seven adults in the United States and Britain is affected by anxiety disorders each year (Brown, 2003; Roe-Sepowitz, Bedard, and Thyer, 2005).

Anxiety, also referred to as fear or nervousness, can be one of the most distressing emotions that a person can feel. Anxiety is a very common and at times powerful emotion from which no one is completely immune. Everyone experiences anxiety in varying degrees and under certain circumstances. The presence of life changes and stressors can result in anxious feelings that for the most part can be considered normal. For instance, individuals often feel anxious when reaching a new developmental stage, such as entering adolescence, starting college, and getting married, or when facing such stressors as divorce, job loss, death of a loved one, health crisis, or foreclosure. In fact, it has been found that "anxiety disorders can be the result of life stressors and events, learning, parenting, upbringing, illness-induced stress, genetic endowment and other biological conditions, and the inability to cope with and manage all of these factors at once" (Roe-Sepowitz et al., 2005, p. 13).

The effect of anxiety can be constructive or destructive; the outcome, of course, depends greatly on the intensity, duration, and cause. Anxiety can be constructive when there is enough emotion to generate energy and motivate a person to solve problems and move forward. Conversely, when anxiety exists beyond the optimal level, it can result in decreased effectiveness and can cause mild confusion, disorganization, or panic. In other words, "some anxiety is helpful, keeping persons alert and aware of their environment; too much anxiety, however, fatigues a person and can lead to diminished functioning" (Roe-Sepowitz et al., 2005, p. 13).

Dixon (1987) notes: "In panic anxiety, the disintegration of the personality or psychic system is so great that destructive behavior to self or others can occur. Anxiety is central to a crisis. When it becomes so intense, so overwhelming that it is unmanageable, personality disorganization occurs as a crisis develops" (p. 43). To be considered an anxiety disorder, anxiety must be severe enough to lead to pathological disturbances of affect, thinking, behavior, and physiological activity (U.S. Surgeon General, 1999).

Anxiety is typically manifested physiologically and mentally. Physical signs include: jitteriness, tension, light-headedness, difficulty breathing and flushed cheeks, heart palpitations, flushing, tightness in the chest, inappropriate perspiration, increased blood pressure, and rapid pulse. Some individuals experience tremors of various parts of the body when anxious; they may be restless or agitated, may pace the floor or may be unable to sit still. Sleep disturbances, insomnia, excessive sleeping, and disturbing dreams are common. A persistent cough, clogging of the throat, or a dry mouth is often experienced. Gastrointestinal problems such as nausea, heartburn, and diarrhea may occur, along with frequent urination, headaches, and backaches. Finally, disturbances in the menstrual cycle or changes in skin are not unusual.

Anxiety can greatly reduce a person's mental functioning; the anxiety can be manifested in the person's communication and speech patterns with slurring of words, rapid speech, or loud talking. Logical thinking capacity, judgment, decision making, reality testing, concentration, and attention span and memory may be impaired. An anxious person may feel confused and be unable to function socially. Dixon (1987) adds that "other indirect signs of anxiety include angry, hostile, or impulsive behavior. Various forms of acting out can be signs of anxiety;

for example, behavior that is unusual for the individual such as sexual promiscuity, stealing, running away, excessive drinking, or drug use" (p. 46).

Anxiety disorders can be categorized in these ways:

- *Phobias* involve the fear of specific things or situations, such as heights, elevators, insects, or flying in airplanes.
- *Panic attacks* are intense feelings of anxiety in which individuals often feel that they are about to die or go crazy.
- *Posttraumatic Stress Disorder* includes repeated memories of terrible traumas with high levels of distress.
- In *obsessive-compulsive disorders*, individuals are affected by repetitive thoughts (obsessions) that lead to repetitive behaviors (compulsions).
- *Generalized anxiety disorders* result in a mixture of worries and of anxiety symptoms experienced most of the time. As such, they are viewed as chronic.
- *Adjustment disorders with anxiety* relate to anxiety that is tied to the presence of life stressors with which the person is having difficulty coping.

Risk factors for anxiety disorders are various, ranging from genetics, brain chemistry, personality, and life events/life stressors. Treatment of anxiety is a very important area of clinical practice; anxiety disorders make up the most prevalent psychological conditions in the United States. According to ADAA (2008), "People with an anxiety disorder are three to five times more likely to go to the doctor and six times more likely to be hospitalized for psychiatric disorders than those who do not suffer from anxiety" (p. 30). According to Thyer and Birsinger (1994): "[Anxiety disorders are] more common than either alcohol abuse or depression, two conditions once thought to occur more frequently" (p. 272). It has been found that anxiety conditions can lead to virtually complete incapacitation, such as with Agoraphobia and obsessive-compulsive disorders, or can lead to suicidal thoughts, as with Panic Disorder (Corsini & Wedding, 2008).

Treatment

There are various treatment approaches to anxiety. Individual psychodynamic therapy, crisis intervention, and critical incident stress debriefing have been used to treat anxiety. Psychoeducational and cognitive-behavioral interventions have also become more common-place; individuals are educated about anxiety and its physical and psychological manifestations, taught breathing and relaxation techniques, and encouraged to learn how to challenge their negative and fearful thinking. Greenberger and Padesky (1995) believe that "anxiety is accompanied by the perception that we are in *Danger* or that we are *Threatened* or *Vulnerable* in some way [and that] cognitive methods . . . are highly effective in reducing and managing anxiety" (p. 179). Use of cognitive restructuring techniques is encouraged to help clients evaluate their anxious thoughts so that they may more quickly assess the danger and its consequences and may challenge their irrational, negative, and anxiety-producing thoughts with more positive and rational thinking. Along with cognitive restructuring, clients are encouraged to use relaxation training involving progressive muscle relaxation, controlled breathing, imagery, and distraction (Bourne, 2005). Overcoming avoidance is important; many individuals who suffer from anxiety are experts at evasion. Although anxiety is reduced when one avoids a difficult situation, the more the situation is avoided, the more anxious a person becomes about facing that situation in the future. Greenberger and Padesky (1995) emphasize that "to overcome anxiety, we need to learn to approach the situations or people we avoid. Learning to approach and cope with a situation in which we feel anxious is a lasting and powerful way of eliminating anxiety" (p. 187).

Medication may be used in conjunction with any of the just-mentioned treatments or when no treatment has been proven effective. Both antianxiety and antidepressants may be used. A medication evaluation with a psychiatrist is necessary for medication to be prescribed.

Why Group?
Group treatment has been proven very effective in the treatment of both depression and anxiety. Specifically, outpatient cognitive therapy has been recognized as a cost-effective and clinically sound treatment (Corsini and Wedding, 2008). "The same active, directive, and problem-focused approaches used in individual cognitive therapy are used with groups. . . . Group therapists strive to facilitate positive group cohesion and interactions, encouraging group members to be mutually collaborative and supportive of individual member's change efforts" (Greenberger & Padesky, 1995, pp. 180-181). Typically, members are introduced to both group and cognitive theory and then are taught a hierarchy of skills to combat anxiety. Systematic desensitization is

another highly versatile therapy that has been useful in treating anxiety disorders (Frew and Spriegler, 2008).

Proposed Group and Overall Objectives

This is a close-ended 16-week psychoeducational, cognitive-behavioral, and process group designed to help members develop coping skills for managing anxiety.

The overall purpose of this group is to reduce the rate of existing anxiety and to prevent the onset of additional anxiety problems. The group is geared toward adults suffering from Panic Disorder, Generalized Anxiety Disorder, and Posttraumatic Stress Disorder (PTSD) (if stable).

Specific objectives are to reduce the overall level, frequency, and intensity of the anxiety so that daily functioning is not impaired. The focus is on stabilizing anxiety while helping members increase their ability to function on a daily basis. Members learn to replace anxiety-producing cognitions with reality-based, self-affirming ones. Last, a goal is to increase members' self-esteem while reducing their feelings of inadequacy and insecurity regarding acceptance of others (Paleg & Jongsma, 2005, pp. 29–31)

Group Profile: Outline of Sessions
Session 1

- Introduce members to the group purpose.
- Review ground rules and expectations.
- Discuss anxiety symptoms.

Activity: Encourage members to share what symptoms led to their participation in the group. Discuss their history of anxious feelings.

Session 2

- Educate members about long-term predisposing causes of anxiety:
  - Genetic predisposition
  - Growing up in a family where parents fostered overcautiousness, perfectionism, emotional insecurity, and dependence, or where parents discouraged assertion.

Activity: Encourage members to share predisposing causes of anxiety that pertain to their own experiences.

Session 3

- Discuss how stress accumulates when not dealt with. Discuss how it can lead to psychophysiological illness.

Activity: Invite members to identify their own cumulative levels of stress and identify recent stressors that could be contributing to anxiety.

Session 4

- Discuss emotional, cognitive, and behavioral elements that maintain anxiety.
- Identify real-life situations.

Activity: Encourage members to identify the elements that maintain their own anxiety, such as anxious talk, mistaken beliefs, lack of assertiveness, muscle tension, and so on.

Session 5

- Teach deep (abdominal) breathing.
- Demonstrate the power of progressive relaxation techniques.

Activity: Lead the group through a detailed visualization and encourage the daily use of this imagery following progressive relaxation. Set up behavioral incentives for practicing.

Session 6

- Discuss the physiological and psychological impact of exercise:
  - Rapid metabolism or excess adrenaline and thyroxin in the bloodstream and brain, leading to improved concentration
  - Production of endorphins, reduced insomnia, and increased feelings of well-being
  - Reduced depression and anxiety

Activity: Formulate an exercise program building toward a goal of 20 to 30 minutes of exercise at least 4 days per week. Recommend reading *Exercising Your Way to Better Mental Health* by Larry M. Leith (1998). Review progress and actively confront resistance.

Session 7

- Clarify the distinction between thoughts and feelings.
- Teach major types of cognitive distortions:
  - Overestimating
  - Catastrophizing
  - Overgeneralizing
  - Filtering
  - Emotional reasoning
  - "Should" statements
- Identify these 7 negative thinking reminders:
  1. *Negative attitude.* You look at things in a dark way. Before something even happens, you decide it will be bad or turn out bad. Without really knowing, you think others do not like you or will think of you in a negative way.
  2. *Disqualifying positive events.* Even when good things happen, you do not let yourself believe them or feel good about them.
  3. *Exaggerating the negative.* You make small problems big. You think little things that go wrong are really bigger than they are.
  4. *Absolute thinking.* You see things in one way only, either as really great or very bad. Watch out for using words like "never," "always," "everyone," and "all."
  5. *Name calling.* You call yourself or others names because of a mistake that was made.
  6. *Perfectionistic thinking.* You believe that things have to be a certain way for you to feel okay about them. Be careful of words like "should," "ought," "need to," and "must."
  7. *Blaming.* You blame yourself or others for things that are not really correct.

Activity: Encourage members to note differences between thoughts and feelings. Ask members to complete this sentence:

When I feel anxious, I think _____ .

Help them to determine which of the negative thinking reminders their thoughts fit.

Session 8

- Teach cognitive-behavioral techniques through cognitive restructuring.
- Encourage the development and implementation of reality-based, self-affirming cognitions to counter cognitive distortions and anxiety-provoking self-talk.

Activity: Explore with the group their underlying mistaken beliefs, and practice using cognitive restructuring to counter these beliefs. Begin the process by identifying a personal negative thought and by countering it. Thereafter, encourage group members to practice in pairs. At the end of the session, review members' experiences with cognitive restructuring, reinforcing success and redirecting strategies that fail.

Session 9

- Continue to discuss the therapeutic use of positive affirmations to replace distorted, negative beliefs.
- Discuss the importance of identifying of symptoms and suppressed feelings that each person experiences, such as free-floating anxiety, depression, psychosomatic symptoms (e.g., headaches or ulcers, or muscle tension).

Activity: Distribute a handout on labeling feelings, and encourage members to review and apply the material to their own lives.

Session 10

- Explore the benefits of being able to tune in to their bodies to identify their feelings.
- Explore fears about expressing anger, including fears of losing control or of alienating significant people. Discuss how these fears are tied to anxiety.

Activity: Encourage and reinforce honest, assertive expression of feelings in the group and then with significant others. Help members to write out their angry feelings before communicating them to another person; reinforce controlled, respectful, assertive expression of feelings.

Session 11

- Discuss assertive communication, including the expression of emotional needs and personal desires and the ability to say no.
- Clarify the distinction among passive, aggressive, and assertive behavior.

Activity: In pairs, role-play situations where members make assertive requests of their partners.

Session 12

- Discuss problem-solving skills by teaching five steps to assertive problem-solving:
  1. Identify the problem.
  2. Brainstorm all possible options.
  3. Evaluate the pros and cons of each option.
  4. Implement a course of action.
  5. Evaluate the results.

Activity: In pairs, role-play the application of problem-solving skills to everyday life conflicts.

Session 13

- Discuss the importance of the implementation of daily self-nurturing behaviors.
- Identify examples of self-care and discuss how to implement them in one's life.

Activity: Help members develop a list of self-nurturing behaviors, such as soaking in a bath, reading a book, or listening to music. As a homework exercise, have members complete at least one item from the list daily.

Session 14

- Discuss the importance of daily social involvement.
- Explore the positives and negatives of developing social relationships.

Activity: Assign members to participate in one social activity per day and to report on their experiences to the group. Remind them to use CBT to enter the social arena with positive and realistic thinking.

Session 15

- Focus on sound nutritional habits to maintain a healthy, balanced lifestyle that will increase stress resistance.
- Educate members about problems associated with the consumption of caffeine and refined sugar.
- Discuss the reasons for the pros and cons of medication.

Activity: Explore with members how chemicals from the use of caffeine and sugar might influence their anxiety. Encourage members to evaluate their need for medication in handling their anxiety.

Session 16

- Review the group process.
- Encourage a commitment to a relapse-prevention program consisting of daily relaxation, physical exercise, good nutrition, and cognitive restructuring.
- Initiate anticipatory planning by encouraging members to predict possible anxiety situations and to consider how they plan to cope with these.
- Termination and ending: Members are encouraged to discuss feelings regarding the closure of group.

Activity: Celebrate the ending of the group with relaxing music and healthy desserts.

Agency Considerations

An anxiety adult support group can take place in a host of settings where counseling and mental health services are provided. For instance, this type of group can be offered in nonprofit counseling and family services agencies; in county or public mental health clinics and in private, for-profit psychology clinics; and in psychiatry and behavioral health departments of health maintenance organizations. In some cases, treatment groups can also be held in preventive medicine departments or within hospital or medical centers. Access to medical evaluation and care is important in case a group member presents with excessive anxiety that requires additional treatment.

Additional Topics and Corresponding Group Profiles

In working with adults, there are also many other issues that merit mention. The topics listed below and corresponding "Group Profiles" are addressed in depth in the accompanying CD-ROM:

- Assertiveness Training Adult Group
- Depression Adult Support Group
- Divorce Adjustment Support Group
- Domestic Violence Women's Support Group
- Mothers Victimized by Domestic Violence
- Eating Disorders Support Group (Anorexia Nervosa)
- Gay and Lesbian Support Group
- HIV and AIDS Adult Support Group
- Men's Support Group
- New Immigrant Support Group
- Parenting Group (for Children and Teens)
- Sexual Addictions Support Group
- Substance Abuse Support Group
- Support Group for Survivors of Suicide
- Women's Support Group for Incest Survivors
- Young Adult Group

Group Work with Older Adults and the Medically Ill

Working with Older Adults

The number of older adults rose dramatically in the 20th century and is now well over 13% of the entire U.S. adult population. In fact, it is estimated that by 2030, there will be 65 million adults age 65 and older (Burger, 2008). Furthermore, later life now spans a longer time frame, as adults are living much longer than ever before. Definitions of what an older adult is varies. The American Association of Retired Persons considers older adulthood to start at age 50; many discounts are available for those age 55 and older; and age 65 is the age when many are considered eligible for Social Security benefits. Besides specific age criteria, an individual's attitude and views about age have a great impact on overall functioning. For instance, someone age 55 can feel and look older, given a difficult life and/or negative attitude. Conversely, someone age 70 can still feel strong and vital and can view his or her stage of life in a positive way. Clearly, since the age range and attitudinal differences of this population are so broad, there is great diversity among people in their later years.

The fact that the number of older adults continues to rise will undoubtedly have a profound impact on human services. Burger (2008) has noted that "the chances of needing outside help increases sharply with age" (p. 7). With age comes an increased need for personal care and home management. Hospital stays are longer and medical visits are more frequent, given increased susceptibility to diseases such as cancer, heart disease, arthritis, and diabetes; rates of depression and suicide increase; and older adults are subject to multiple losses.

Physically, seniors are faced with bodily declines and more chronic health problems that can be costly to treat and serve to isolate and depress some people. Polypharmacology is an added hazard some seniors engage in to treat their many health problems. Psychologically, growing old can be a struggle. The stage of 'Ego Integrity versus Despair' reflects the importance of the life review process evident during this stage. Some older adults view aging as a gratifying period, as their demands are lighter and they have more time for leisure activities and to enjoy retirement and grandparenthood. Obviously, good health, strong support systems, and financial stability contribute to this positive outlook.

Other older adults find growing old very emotionally and physically difficult. Some suffer from mental decline, sensory deficits, and memory problems, and may also have to cope with medical problems. Loss is common in later life, whether it is physical, emotional, or social. Physically, older persons may see a decline in their vigor, vitality, and ability to function as before, and they may fear the ultimate loss of life through death. Emotionally, older adults experience loss of loved ones, cohorts, and sometimes children. Socially, some seniors experience loss of their identity in the workforce and may feel isolated, lonely, and regretful about retirement. Many times they feel useless and forgotten.

Because loss of any type is more prevalent for older adults, depression and anxiety are often greater. Suicide, although greatly underreported, has become more prevalent in this age group. Finally, with an increase in the lifespan, we have seen a rise in the diagnosis of Alzheimer's disease.

Certainly, the prospect of having to live with this condition or of having to be a caregiver of a loved one diagnosed with this condition can be extremely stressful— physically, emotionally, and socially.

There is great variation among older adults in terms of their social life. Some seniors remain active and involved socially, while others may feel isolated and view themselves as failures. Retirement can be a positive anticipated event or a negative event. Support from family and others is important in helping seniors cope with life changes.

For many seniors who live on a fixed income and struggle with healthcare costs, stress can be great. Many seniors live in poverty and are unable to obtain the benefits of medication interventions and nutritional supplements that are available to those with more financial resources (Alle-Corliss & Alle-Corliss, 1999; Burger, 2008; Hull & Kirst-Ashman, 2004; Neukrug, 2008).

Elder abuse and maltreatment have become more common in situations where the elderly are frail or too ill to care for themselves. Also, parent abuse often occurs in families where child abuse existed. Older adults are also victims of prejudice and discrimination because of their age and vulnerable status. Ageism is also prevalent and can affect older adults, either directly or subtly.

Psychosocial perspectives on aging are important to note. According to psychosocial theory, as individuals grow older, their behavior changes, their social interactions change, and the activities in which they engage change. *Aging* is defined here as "the transformation of the human organism after the age of physical maturity so that the probability of survival decreases, and it is accompanied by regular transformations in appearance, behavior, experience and social roles" (Parrot, 2004, p. 2). *Psychosocial aging* can be described as a result of the disuse of previously acquired skills, of random wear and tear, and of a change in the ability to adapt to environmental variables, to loss of internal and external resources, and to genetic influences over the lifespan. Social scientists believe that genetics (heredity) is a major factor in determining the length of human life, although environment plays an important role in modifying the expected lifespan.

Schneider, Corey, and Corey (2007) encourage helping professionals not to ignore the special needs and problems of the elderly. They go on to say:

> *The way you approach aging has a great deal to do with how you will treat older people. Rather than focusing on old age as being exclusively a time of loss, you can see it as a time of both positive and negative transformations.*

Be open to what older people can teach you, even if you are in the role of helping them. (p. 203)

Older adults have great wisdom and vast life experiences to draw from. Tapping into these can serve to enhance their self-worth as well as to teach future generations what is important about growing older.

General Treatment Considerations

- Demonstrate a deep sense of caring and genuine respect for older people and their cultural values. Understand how a person's cultural background continues to influence present attitudes and behaviors.
- Possess a healthy attitude regarding one's own aging and an ability and desire to learn from older adults. Promote "integrity" rather than "despair."
- When interviewing an older adult, it is important to follow five specific interviewing techniques:
  1. Invest proportionately more energy into the interview, since older adults often present with less energy.
  2. Pace the interview according to the client's fluctuating energy levels and physical constraints.
  3. Recognize sensory losses. Communication can be maximized if the practitioner sits close to older persons and face them directly. Be conscious of recruitment deafness, which is when a person cannot hear at a certain level, but shouting is too loud.
  4. Use touch as a meaningful communication bridge when working with the elderly. Be sensitive to individual and cultural concerns.
  5. Avoid information overload by speaking slowly, by using short sentences, by dealing with one thought at a time, and by asking for feedback to be certain meaningful communication has taken place. Elderly persons typically take 15% more time to respond than younger adults.
- Be knowledgeable of the special physiological, psychological, spiritual, and social needs of the aged. Be sensitive to the burdens and anxieties of older people.
- Consistently enhance older people's self-esteem by encouraging their maximum participation, and acknowledge their role as an authority on aging.

- Begin with focusing on problems the elderly can handle with success. This will help relieve feelings of helplessness that might otherwise lead them to withdraw from treatment. Don't overwhelm them.

- Set realistic goals and strive to restore any degree of functioning that is possible. It is important to be patient and flexible.

- Offer older adults choices, allow them to choose their priorities, and respect their decisions. Acknowledge your confidence in their abilities to make choices and to follow through.

- Be sensitive to need for sexual expression in late adulthood, and be cautious about being judgmental or critical.

- Be cognizant of issues tied to loss that the elderly commonly experience, and be skilled in the management of grief and depression that may result.

- Be willing to be an advocate for the elderly, who may not have the strength to cope with the confusions of bureaucracies. Be knowledgeable about AARP, Medicare, Social Security, and others.

- Be open to engaging in reminiscing and in the life review process with the elderly. These strategies may be helpful in linking relevant past events to the present as well as in helping to bring closure to an individual's life.

- Become skilled in crisis intervention strategies that are often necessary when working with older adults. Possess the ability to deal with extreme feelings of loss, depression, isolation, hopelessness, grief, hostility, and despair.

- Be prepared to work with significant others and families.

Guidelines for Group Work with the Elderly

- Develop a sound group proposal that minimizes resistance from the elderly. For instance, the name of the group is important; words such as *depression* or *mental health* often carry a stigma.

- Be clear about the purpose of the group.

- Be careful to properly screen and to make sure group members are similar in abilities and cognitive functioning.

- Be aware of such practical issues as group size, duration, setting, and techniques to be used, and make sure they are compatible with the older group members.

- Emphasize the importance of confidentiality.

- Be careful not to label quickly or diagnosis a group member without first getting to know him or her.
- Given the diversity among older adults, it is important to understand the social and cultural backgrounds of the group members and to make sure they are compatible with those of the other members.
- Use of touch is important in working with the elderly but must be done in an appropriate way, and only when the group leader feels comfortable doing so.

Some Dos and Don'ts in Group Practice with Elderly Clients

- Do not treat people as if they are frail when they are not.
- Avoid keeping members busy with meaningless activities.
- Affirm the dignity, intelligence, and pride of elderly group members.
- Do not assume that every elderly person likes being called by his or her first name, or by "honey" or "sweetie."
- Make use of humor appropriately. Avoid laughing at your members for failing to accomplish tasks, but laugh with them when, for instance, if they have created a funny poem.
- Avoid talking to them as if they were small children, no matter how severely impaired they may be.
- Allow your members to complain, even if there is nothing you can do about their complaints. Do not burden yourself with the feeling that you should do something about all of their grievances; sometimes venting can be sufficient.
- Avoid probing for the release of strong emotions that neither you nor they can handle effectively in the group sessions.
- Determine how much you can do without feeling depleted, and find avenues for staying vital and enthusiastic.

Loss Support Group

Issue

Facing some type of loss is an inevitable aspect of growing old. During the aging process, a person often experiences many losses without adequate time to recover. Moreover, when multiple and cumulative losses exist, the propensity for depression is heightened (Zarit, 1980). Intervening early in the grieving process is important in preventing complicated grief reactions for older adults. Recognizing the gamut of losses that are likely to affect the elderly is crucial in better understanding them. For instance, it is not uncommon for older persons to experience the loss of: physical health, social contacts, familiar roles, financial security, home, independence and power, mental stability, reaction time and intellectual acuity, and loved ones.

Grief and bereavement are common reactions to loss, especially to the loss of loved ones. *Grief* refers to the "cognitive and emotional reactions that follow the death of a loved one. Grief can vary in duration and intensity, and it can fade and reappear at unexpected moments" (Newman & Newman, 2003, p. 462). Much has been written about the grieving process. The Westberg Model (Zastrow & Kirst-Ashman, 2004) developed in 1962 to address sudden and tragic loss includes this progression:

- Shock and denial
- Eruption of emotions, including anger
- Possible development of stress-induced illnesses
- Panic
- Guilt
- Depression and loneliness
- Reentry difficulties
- Hope
- Affirming reality

Elisabeth Kübler-Ross is perhaps best-known for her model of grieving. Introduced in 1969, it is relevant to understanding the grief experienced from any loss. Her five-stage model consists of:

Stage 1. Denial

Stage 2. Rage and anger

Stage 3. Bargaining

Stage 4. Depression

Stage 5. Acceptance

Different types of loss can evoke a myriad of emotions. It has been found helpful to address these common emotional reactions to loss in treatment settings:

- Shock and denial

Shock. Many who have just been informed of a tragic loss are so "numb" and in such a state of "Shock" that they are almost devoid of feelings. It is believed that when emotional pain is unusually intense, a person's response system experiences "overload" and temporarily shuts down so that the individual hardly feels anything. Thus he or she may act as if nothing has happened. In other words, at the beginning, the loss may not seem real. Shock is the body's way of protecting itself until the person is able to adjust to the event.

Denial. This is a way of avoiding the impact of a loss when the individual is not ready to cope with reality. In this sense, denial is often considered "functional" as it helps cushion the impact of the loss. Further, it is often a first response to emotionally painful news and thus can be viewed as a defense mechanism in which anxiety-provoking thoughts are kept out of or isolated from conscious awareness. Denial can be a marvelous coping device, as it can help those through a time of crisis until they are ready to cope more constructively.

- Confusion and despair. Painful feelings are difficult to cope with and may lead to feelings of helplessness and hopelessness. Sometimes grieving individuals may search for reasons why the loss happened. At times this search can create further confusion and a sense of despair.

- Rage and anger. It is normal to feel angry when one has experienced a loss.

  1. At some point, often after the shock, denial, and despair stages, reality sets in, and it is normal to ask, "Why? This isn't fair." Often, anger is experienced at this time.
  2. The anger may be directed at God for causing the loss or at the deceased/departed one for "desertion." Many may question why this loss happened and may feel anger, even at themselves for not having done something to prevent this eventual loss.
  3. Anger can be a secondary emotion that underlies hurt and pain. Individuals often need permission to feel their anger.
  4. Likewise, it is important for individuals suffering from loss to be careful to not succumb to feeling guilty about their angry feelings, for they are natural and a normal process of grieving.
  5. The appropriate expression of anger is important and necessary to move on. Maladaptive coping, however, can hinder the process of grief resolution and actually cause more harm. Therefore, the importance of learning healthy coping skills is to be emphasized and addressed.

6. It is important to highlight the fact that some individuals may feel anger more readily at the onset of the grief process and/or throughout. It is important to emphasize that angry feelings in themselves are not bad; self-destructive or outwardly directed anger can be harmful however.

• Panic and guilt

Panic. People often feel panic when they realize that the loss is real. Not only has life changed, but the departed individual is no longer present to interact with. Often this panic is manifested in fears of going insane, in nightmares, in unwanted emotions that may seem uncontrollable, in physical reactions, and in concentration difficulties. These may further contribute to the sense of panic.

Guilt. Guilt is a very strong emotion that many feel, whether it is appropriate to the loss or not. People can feel guilt when they blame themselves for having contributed to the loss or for not having done enough. Often guilt may not fit the circumstances, yet it is a common among grieving people and needs to be acknowledged as such as well as respected.

• Depression and Isolation

Depression. When a person experiences a loss, there may be a deep and lasting feeling of sadness. Such sadness and a sense of hopelessness may become predominant emotional responses.

Isolation. Isolation and loneliness are common, as the grieving person may withdraw from others, especially when others are viewed as nonsupportive or incapable of understanding.

• Hope. Hope may be experienced as individuals people begin to put their lives back together and experience joy. Again, some may feel guilty for these feelings and may be tempted to punish themselves for allowing positive emotions to exist.

• Acceptance and/or adjustment. Acceptance begins when the individual learns to adjust to the loss. It signifies that the person has come to terms with the fact that the loss is real and universal. There may still be sadness, yet the intense emotions are either gone or are not so prominent and overwhelming. Sometimes acceptance is not possible, and an individual experiences only an adjustment to the loss.

According to Newman and Newman (2003), "Bereavement is the long term process of adjustment to the death of a loved one and is more all-encompassing than grief" (p. 462). Bereavement is often accompanied by physical symptoms, role loss, and a variety of intense emotions that include anger, sorrow, anxiety, and depression. Since bereavement can increase the likelihood of illness and even death among survivors, it is especially important to recognize and treat.

Five critical variables have been found to influence experiences of bereavement and grief:

1. The nature of the prior attachment or the perceived value that the lost person or thing has for the bereaved individual
2. The way in which the loss occurred and the concurrent circumstances of the bereaved person
3. The coping strategies that the bereaved individual has learned to use in dealing with previous losses
4. The developmental situation of the bereaved person—that is, how being a child, adolescent, adult, or elderly person influences one's grief and mourning
5. The nature of the support available to the bereaved person after the loss from the family members, friends, other individuals, and social institutions (Corr, Nabe, & Corr, 2006; Parkes, 1975; Sanders, 1989)

In helping individuals work through the grief process, it is important to assess into which of these stages they best fit.

Treatment

Treatment of grief reactions and bereaved individuals is especially common when working with the elderly, given their increased experience with loss. In helping individuals who have lost a loved one to grieve, it is important to encourage them to:

- Cry when needed: Crying releases tension and is part of the grieving process.
- Talk openly about their loss and their plans to friends, family, clergy, professional counselors, group members, and the like: Talking about one's grief eases loneliness and allows for appropriate ventilation of feelings.
- Be open to questioning their beliefs: If the loss is a death of a loved one, the bereaved may need to examine their faith and philosophy of life.

- Not dwell on their unhappiness: It is recommended that bereaved people become involved and active in life around them and not use their energy on self-pity.

- Recognize that holidays and anniversary dates of the birth and death of loved ones may be stressful: Explore positive ways of coping during this difficult time.

- Encourage survivors to move forward and recognize that a sense of purpose and meaning will eventually return, despite the severe impact of the loss.

- Be aware that grief can be very stressful and may lead to a variety of illnesses: Encourage that they seek medical help if needed.

- Be prepared to face sleeplessness, sexual difficulties, loss of appetite or overeating, intense dreams of the loved one, low energy, and poor concentration: Help normalize these reactions and encourage the bereaved to begin to take care of themselves.

- Understand that guilt, whether real or imagined, is part of the grieving process: Assist them to challenge their negative, irrational thoughts and to learn to resolve their guilt.

- Make an effort to talk to others about the loss or its impact: If possible, encourage members to inform significant others about how they can be most supportive.

- Refrain from making major life decisions, such as changing jobs or moving, until sufficient time has passed.

Why Group?

Loss is such a universal issue, and especially so for elderly persons. Participation in a group setting can be very therapeutic and serve to help the bereaved realize that they are not alone, and that others have sustained similar losses and understand them.

Proposed Group and Overall Objectives

This is a 12-week support, closed group for seniors who have recently sustained one or more losses that are creating grief-type reactions. Objectives are for members to: address the meaning of loss, no matter how different their loss is from that of others; understand the different types of loss; identify and express feeling attached to this loss; understand the danger of maladaptive coping; and learn more appropriate means to cope. The group also explores benefits of rituals and personal memorials, how to deal with special concerns such as anniversary dates of the loss, the importance of support systems, and positive ways of healing.

Group Profile: Outline of Sessions
Session 1

- Get started: Orient members to group purpose and process.

  Activity: Encourage members to share something about their loss and the reason for wanting to be in this group.

Session 2

- Begin to address the unique and ongoing nature of grief while emphasizing that there is no correct way to grieve, as it is an individual matter.
- Address the notion that loss can mean something different to everyone and that each person's feelings and experiences with loss must be respected, regardless of how minor (i.e., moving) the loss may seem in comparison to major losses (i.e., death).

  Activity: Ask members to identify their loss in more specific terms.

Session 3

- Identify and discuss in more detail different types of loss, including:
  - Death of a significant other by:
    - Suicide
    - Accident
    - Illness
    - Violence
- Separation
  - Separation/divorce
  - Departure of loved one
  - A move or the loss of a relationship

  Activity: Ask members to share their experience with different types of loss. Emphasize their past coping skills in dealing with loss of some sort.

Session 4

- Educate members about the common emotional reactions to loss:
  - Shock and denial
  - Confusion and despair
  - Rage and anger
  - Panic and guilt
  - Depression and isolation
  - Hope
  - Acceptance and adjustment

Activity: Ask members to identify which feelings they seem to be struggling with the most, and allow them to discuss these.

Session 5

- Encourage members to begin to consider emotions as part of the healing process.
- Encourage members to delineate which emotions they can relate to.
- Explore ways to express their feelings related to loss appropriately.
- Address the importance of ventilating these emotions.

Activity: Using a Feeling Chart, validate their feelings and note similarities among group members.

Session 6

- Discuss different coping styles.
- Identify maladaptive coping:
  - Using drugs and alcohol
  - Being sexually irresponsible
  - Isolating oneself from other people
  - Refusing to get help for a physical or psychological problem
  - Denying that anything is wrong, even if the person knows he or she has a problem
  - Lashing out at other people
  - Allowing emotions to control one's life
  - Being extremely passive or aggressive
  - Engaging in violent or criminal antisocial behaviors

- ◦ Refusing to learn more positive coping skills
- ◦ Allowing relationships with others to deteriorate

Activity: Explore group members' previous or current use of maladaptive coping. If the maladaptive coping methods are being used currently, guide and encourage the group to discuss ways to make positive changes.

Session 7

- Point out that it takes time to heal from the loss of someone you love but that choosing more positive ways of coping can help.
- Brainstorm some ways they could help heal themselves.
- Discuss why the more positive coping methods might be better in the long run, as self-destructive behavior can cause additional problems.

Activity: List positive coping methods that members have used successfully.

Session 8

- Discuss the value of rituals and personal memorials in assisting the grieved individual to progress through the grief process more easily.
- Share factual information regarding the purpose and process of funerals.
- Discuss the burial and its symbolism, and explain how burial rites may differ from culture to culture.
- With other losses such as divorce or a move, explain relevant factual information.

Activity: Encourage group members to be creative in planning a way to memorialize their loved one. Use a scrapbook or poem as an example.

Session 9

- Address the notion of special days such as holidays, anniversaries, birthdays, or the date when loss was first felt (through death or separation).

- Explore how to best cope with these painful moments yet still emphasize that each person will have to find what best fits his or her coping and personality style.

Activity: In pairs, have group members prepare for how to spend emotionally difficult days. Share their results with the group as a whole.

Session 10

- Examine the benefit of having a healthy support system to assist in the grief process.
- Explore what types of supports may more emotionally draining or induce further stress than actual supports. (Often, significant others may have the best of intentions, yet their "support" may not be truly helpful.)
- Discuss the fact that depending on the loss, support may be minimal.
- Discuss the unrealistic expectations others may have regarding the grief process. Reemphasize that grief is a unique and individual process.

Activity: Identify realistic supports and encourage reaching out to church and community.

Session 11

- Emphasize that going through grief is difficult, yet in time, things usually improve.
- Ideas that might be helpful include:
  - Do not be frightened to be angry at losing someone or something. They should find someone to talk to about the anger rather than taking it out on themselves or on those around them.
  - Grieving is a normal process, yet it does hurt. Members may benefit by finding a counselor who can help them further.
  - Advise members not to hold back and to share their feelings with family members or others who are supportive. Emphasize that they should not bottle up their feelings.
  - Members can write a letter to the departed, sharing all the things they might not have had a chance to say.
  - Hobbies encourage a sense of expertise and enjoyment.
  - Members can do things for others, but not at the expense of their own well-being.

○ It is important to take care of themselves, to get plenty of regular exercise, and to eat a balanced diet.
○ Sometimes getting a pet to talk to, to care for, and to love can be helpful, yet members should be aware that this cannot replace the loss.

Activity: Help members brainstorm ways to begin the healing process on a positive note. Encourage members to choose at least one of the ideas mentioned to follow through with.

Session 12

• Review and evaluate the group.
• Discuss gains made and growth experienced.
• Reinforce their strengths and ability to move forward.

Activity: Celebrate with a way to memorialize their loved ones collectively.

Agency Considerations

A loss support group can be conducted in a variety of settings including: hospitals; specialized senior centers; nursing and convalescent homes; nonprofit, public counseling, or mental health centers; and for-profit departments of preventive medicine and behavioral health in health maintenance organizations.

Additional Topics and Corresponding Group Profiles

Many additional topics relevant to working with older adults are important to consider. The following topics and corresponding "Group Profiles" are addressed in depth in the accompanying CD-ROM:

• Caregivers' (Alzheimer's) Support Group
• Depression Senior Support Group
• Grandparenting Support Group
• Healthy Living (Successful Aging) Support Group
• Long-term Care Support Group
• Widows' and Widowers' Support Group

- Preretirement Planning Support Group
- Reminiscing Therapy Group

Diabetes Support Group

Issue

In recent years, diabetes mellitus has become an increasing health problem in the United States and other industrialized nations. Considered a chronic disease, diabetes not only poses an obstacle to longevity but also impacts quality of life and results in rising healthcare costs. In fact, diabetes is considered one of the main threats to health in the 21st century (Zimmer, Alberti, & Shaw, 2001, p. 782). It is widely recognized as one of the leading causes of death and disability in the United States and was ranked as the sixth leading cause of death in 2002 (National Diabetes Information Clearinghouse [NDIC], 2008). Statistics that compare incidence from less than a decade ago to today illustrate why diabetes is viewed as an epidemic healthcare crisis. Specifically, in 1994, the prevalence of diabetes in the United States was estimated to be 2.98%, or 7.7 million people; in 2002, the number rose to 6.3%, or 18.2 million people. Additionally, the prevalence of diabetes diagnosed in those age 20 and older increased from 5.1% to 8.7% in a 10-year period. Centers for Disease Control (2003) data from 2002 reveals a yearly incidence among those 20 years and older to be 1.3 million. Also in 2002, there were 206,000 persons younger than age 20 formally diagnosed with diabetes. When unreported cases are taken into account, the number of actual cases may be much greater. More recent statistics reveal that the number of those afflicted with diabetes has risen to 23.6 million children and adults in the United States, or 7.8% of the population (American Diabetes Association, 2008).

Diabetes is a metabolic disorder in which the body does not produce or properly use insulin. Insulin is a hormone that is needed to convert sugar, starches, and other food into energy needed for daily life. According to the American Diabetes Association (2008), "the cause of diabetes continues to be a mystery, although both genetics and environmental factors such as obesity and lack of exercise appears to play roles" (p. 1).

There are various types of diabetes: type 1, type 2, and gestational. Type 1 diabetes mellitus (T1DM) was previously known as insulin-dependent or juvenile-onset diabetes; it usually develops before age 30 and is marked by insulinopenia. According to Lopez-Sandrin and Skyler (2005): "Type 1 diabetes is an autoimmune disease that causes the gradual inflammation and destruction of the insulin-secreting pancreatic beta cells and eventually leads to complete insulin deficiency. Patients are dependent on exogenous injections of insulin for survival" (p. 189). Bate and Jerums (2003) note that T1DM is the result of various factors, including genetic predisposition, certain environmental triggers, and immune activation targeted against the insulin-producing pancreatic islet beta cells.

Diabetes mellitus type 2 (T2DM) results from insulin resistance, which is a condition in which the body fails to properly use insulin, combined with relative insulin deficiency. Most of those who are diagnosed with diabetes have type 2 diabetes. In fact, as the percentage of obese persons has increased, so has the incidence of T2DM. Herold (2004) has noted that obesity seems to be the greatest environmental influence on the development of diabetes. Unlike type 1, type 2 is often preventable. It is associated with other health conditions, namely hypertension, dyslipidemia, and obesity (American Diabetes Association, 2003; American Heart Association, 2003).

Gestational diabetes leads to the immediate development of type 2 diabetes after birth in 5% to 10% of women. A last category important to mention are those who are prediabetic; their blood glucose levels are higher than normal but not high enough for the diagnosis of type 2 diabetes. Sadly, approximately 57 million Americans have prediabetes (American Diabetes Association, 2008). A major study has found that many who are prediabetic are able to lower their risk of developing diabetes by losing 5% to 7% of their body weight through diet and physical activity (NDIC, 2008).

According to NDIC (2008), the cost to the United States for diabetes is about $132 billion; $40 billion is estimated to be indirect costs, such as disability payments, time lost from work and premature death, and $92 billion from direct medical costs for diabetic care, including hospitalizations and medical supplies. These figures are not surprising if one considers the long-term complications of diabetes; diabetes often "leads to blindness, heart and blood vessel disease, stroke, kidney failure, amputations, and nerve damage. Uncontrolled diabetes can complicate pregnancy, and birth defects are more common in babies born to women with diabetes" (NDIC, 2008, p. 4).

Treatment

Psychological feelings on first being diagnosed with diabetes include shock, denial, fear, anxiety, anger, and depression. When the disease progresses, any or all of these symptoms are likely to be heightened. Psychological treatment that involves both support and education about the disease process and preventive measures is optimal. Individual, family, and group counseling can all be helpful when working with the newly diagnosed diabetic patient.

Why Group?

A group format is appropriate to provide education and support to individuals with similar concerns and issues. Since individuals with diabetes are often misunderstood by others, treating them in a group setting where they can feel understood and validated is helpful. Additionally, members are often more able to challenge one another since they are experiencing similar health struggles.

Proposed Group and Overall Objectives

This is a 9-week educational and support group for newly diagnosed diabetic patients. The group offers members much-needed information about diabetes. Different types of diabetes are discussed, as are treatments and ideas for making healthy lifestyle changes that can help minimize future medical problems. Group members receive support and encouragement necessary to look to the future with hope that they are taking charge of their health.

Group Profile: Outline of Sessions
Session 1

- Introduce members to the group and the group purpose.
- Review the group ground rules.
- Discuss feelings about being diagnosed with diabetes.

   Activity: Members introduce themselves and share their feelings about their new diagnosis.

Session 2

- Present statistics about diabetes mellitus.
- Educate members about diabetes.
   - Share basic facts about diabetic types and prevalence:

1. Type 1 (T1DM)
2. Type 2 (T2DM)
3. Gestational
4. Prediabetes

- Review various types of treatments.

Activity: Discuss myths and facts regarding diabetes.

Session 3

- Discuss the emotional aspects of being diagnosed:
  - Shock at the diagnosis, disbelief.
  - Denial: "No, it's a mistake." People continue to eat poorly.
  - Fear of many things (e.g., going places, eating certain foods), which can cause further problems.
  - Anxiety, which can exacerbate the disease process.
  - Depression: The person isolates and withdraws and continues poor self-care.

Activity: Explore the range of feelings among group members and the importance of accepting the diagnosis and beginning to deal with it.

Session 4

- Emphasize risk factors:
  - Genetics/family history
  - Obesity
  - Poor eating habits/diet
  - Substance use
- Additional factors to consider:
  - High-stress lifestyle
  - Lack of exercise
  - Limited rest or sound, restful sleep

Activity: Members assess their individual risk factors and prioritize them from one to three (with 1 being the higher risk factor). They are to make a commitment to begin working on the #1 priority, then #2, and finally #3.

Session 5

- Discuss treatment options: diet, medication, or both.
- Deal with fears and resistance regarding treatment.
- Emphasize complications:
  - Blindness
  - Heart disease
  - Stroke
  - Kidney failure
  - Wound infections and amputations
  - Nerve damage

Activity: Members share their individual struggles and gain feedback.

Session 6

- Explore dietary changes.
- Present facts about a healthful diet versus an unhealthful one.
- Discuss difficulties in eating healthful foods:
  - Motivation to change eating habits
  - Financial constraints
  - Family support

Activity: In pairs, have members work on describing specific dietary changes they need to make.

Session 7

- Consider the value of exercise.
- Discuss roadblocks to a regular exercise routine.
- Explore making small changes.

Activity: Devise a progressive exercise program for members.

Session 8

- Incorporate stress reduction measures.
- Discuss stressors and their impact on health/medical conditions.
- Explore new coping skills:
  - Deep breathing

- ○ Progressive relaxation
- ○ Problem solving

Activity: Demonstrate a progressive relaxation exercise. Apply problem solving to specific problems that group members identify.

Session 9

- Encourage active participation in healthcare.
- Discuss following medical advice (taking medication and adhering to a diet).
- Focus on taking control of one's own healthcare.

Activity: In pairs, come up with a list of questions to ask healthcare providers. Homework is to bring a healthful snack to share at the last group session.

Session 10

- Review and evaluate the group.
- Reinforce learning.
- Consolidate gains.
- Closure and ending.
- Discuss building new supports.

Activity: Celebrate with healthful foods from a menu group members have created.

Agency Considerations

A diabetes support group is best when conducted in a medical setting where medical care is also available. These medically based support groups are found in nonprofit and public heathcare agencies and in preventive medicine departments in for-profit health maintenance organizations.

Additional Topics and Corresponding Group Profiles

Besides diabetes, many other medical conditions lend themselves to group work. The following medical topics and corresponding

"Group Profiles" are addressed in depth in the accompanying CD-ROM:

- Breast Cancer Support Group
- Cardiac Rehabilitation Support Group
- Chronic Pain Support Group
- Disabilities Support Group
- Hospice Support Group (Terminally Ill)
- Spinal Cord Injury Rehabilitation Support Group
- Staff Support Group (Burnout Prevention)

REFERENCES

Abbey, S., & Farrow, S. (1998). Group therapy and organ transplantation. *International Journal of Group Psychotherapy, 48*(2), 1634–1685.

Abdudabeeh, N., & Aseel, H. A. (1999). Transcultural counseling and Arab Americans. In J. McFadden (Ed.), *Transcultural counseling* (2nd ed., pp. 283–296). Alexandria, VA: American Counseling Association.

Abramowitz, A. J., & O'Leary, S. G. (1991). Behavior interventions for the classroom: Implications for children with ADHD. *School Psychology Review, 20,* 221–235.

Abramson, J. (1983). *A non-client centered approach to program development in a medical setting.* Philadelphia: Temple University Press.

Adler, A. (1927). *Understanding human behavior.* New York: Greenberg.

Adler, A. (1964). *Social interest: A challenge to mankind.* New York: Capricorn.

Agars, W. S. (1987). *Eating disorders: Management of obesity, bulimia, and anorexia.* New York: Pergamon Press.

Agazarian, Y. M., & Janoff, S. (1993). Systems theory and small groups. In H. I. Kaplan and B. J. Sadock (Eds.), *Comprehensive group psychotherapy* (3rd ed., pp. 32–44). Baltimore: Williams & Wilkins.

Aguilera, D. C., & Messick, J. M. (1982). *Crisis intervention: Theory and methodology* (4th ed.). St. Louis, MO: C. V. Mosby.

Al-Abdul-Jabbar, J., & Al-Issa, I. (2000). Psychotherapy in Islamic society. In I. Al-Issa (Ed.), *Al-Junun: Mental illness in the Islamic world* (pp. 277–293). Madison, CT: International Universities Press.

Alberti, R., & Emmons, M. L. (1995). *Your perfect right: A guide to assertive living* (7th ed.). San Luis Obispo, CA: Impact.

Alberti, R., & Emmons, M. L. (2001). *Your perfect right: A guide to assertive living* (8th ed.). Atascadero, CA: Impact.

Al-Krenawai, A., & and Grahma, J. R. (2000). Culutrally sensitive social work practice with Arab clients in mental health settings. *Health & Social Work, 25*(1), 9–22.

Allan, R., & Scheidt, S. (1998). Group psychotherapy for patients with coronary heart disease. *International Journal of Group Psychotherapy, 48*(2), 187–214.

Alle-Corliss, L. & Alle-Corliss, R. (1998). *Human service agencies: An orientation to fieldwork.* Belmont, CA: Thomson-Brooks/Cole.

Alle-Corliss, L. & Alle-Corliss, R. (1999). *Advanced practice in human service agencies: Issues, trends, and treatment perspectives* (2nd ed.). Belmont, CA: Thomson-Brooks/Cole.

Alle-Corliss, L. & Alle-Corliss, R. (2006). *Human service agencies: An orientation to fieldwork.* (2nd ed.). Belmont, CA: Thomson- Brooks/Cole.

Alle-Corliss, R. (2006). Men's group (1994–2006). MMH. Montclair, CA.

Allen-Meares, P. (1995). *Social work with children and adolescents.* White Plains, NY: Longman.

Alzheimer's Association. (1998). *Caregiving and Alzheimer's?* Chicago: Author.

American Academy of Pediatrics. (2005). *Childhood obesity.* Retrieved July 2008, from http://aap.org/

American Cancer Society. (2003). *Breast cancer facts and figures: 2003–2004.* Atlanta, GA: Author.

American Counseling Association. (1995). *Code of ethics and standards of practice.* Alexandria, CA: Author.

American Diabetes Association. (2002/3). Economic costs of diabetes in the U.S. in 2002. *Diabetes Care, 26,* 917–932.

American Diabetes Association. (2008). *All about diabetes.* Retrieved July 2008, from http://www.diabetes.org/about-diabetes.jsp

American Foundation for Suicide Prevention (2005). Facts and Figures: National Statistics. New York: Author.

American Group Psychotherapy Association. (2001). *Principles of group psychotherapy: Faculty core course manual.* New York: Author.

American Heart Association. (2003). *Heart disease and stoke statistics: 2004 update.* Dallas, TX: Author.

American Medical Association. (2000). Washington, DC: Author.

American Psychiatric Association. (2000). *Diagnostic and statistical manual of mental disorders: DSM IV-TR* (4th ed., text revision). Washington, DC: Author.

American Psychiatric Association (Producer). (2004). *Film Tx: Myths and realities of growing old: Aging & long-term care in California* [Motion picture]. Monrovia, Ca.

American Psychological Association. (2000) Washington, DC: Author.

American Spinal Cord Injury Association. (2008). *Spinal cord injury.* Retrieved July 2008 from http://en.wikipedia.org/wiki/Spinal_cord_injury

Anderson, M. L., & Collins, P. H. (Eds.). (1995). *Race, class, and gender: An anthology* (2nd ed.). Belmont, CA: Wadsworth.

Anderson, R. N. (2001). Deaths: Leading causes for 1999. *National Vital Statistics Reports, 49* (11).

Ando, M. (2005). A case study of usefulness of cognitive therapy based on reminiscence method for cancer patient. *Japanese Journal of Health Psychology, 18*(2), 53–64.

Ansbacher, H. L. (1977). Individual psychology. In R. J. Corsini (Ed.), *Current personality theories* (pp. 45–85). Itasca, IL: F. E. Peacock.

Ansbacher, H. L., & Ansbacher, R. (Eds.). (1956). *The individual psychology of Alfred Adler.* New York: Basic Books.

Ansbacher, H. L., & Ansbacher, R. R. (Eds.). (1964). *The individual psychology of Alfred Adler.* New York: Harper & Row/Torchbooks. (Original work published 1956)

Anthony, J. (1972). The history of group psychotherapy. In H. I. Kaplan & B. J. Sadock (Eds.), *The evolution of group therapy* (pp. 1–26). New York: Dutton.

Anxiety Community. (2008). Retrieved Decemember 2008, from www.healthyplace.com/Communities/Anxiety/

Anxiety Disorders Association of America. (2008). Retrieved December 2008, from www.adaa.org

Arendell, T. (1995). *Fathers and divorce.* Thousand Oaks, CA: Sage.

Arkowitz, H. (1997). Integrative theories of therapy. In P. L. Wachtel & S. B. Messer (Eds.), *Theories of psychotherapy: Origins and evolution* (pp. 227–288). Washington, DC: American Psychiatric Association.

Armistead, L., Kotchich, B. A., & Forehand, R. (2004). Teenage pregnancy, sexually transmitted diseases, and HIV/AIDS. In L. A. Rapp-Paglicci, C. N. Dulmus, & S. Wodarski (Eds.), *Handbook of preventive interventions for children and adolescents* (pp. 227–274.) Hoboken, NJ: John Wiley & Sons.

Arredondo, P. (2002). Counseling individuals from marginalized and underserved groups. In P. E. Pedersen, J. G. Draguns, W. J. Lonner, & J. E. Trimble (Eds.), *Counseling across cultures* (pp. 233–250). Thousand Oaks, CA: Sage.

Arredondo, P., Toperek, T., Brown, S. P., Jones, J., Locke, D. C., Sanchez, J., & Stadler, H. (1996). Operationalization of the multicultural counseling competencies. *Journal of Multicultural Counseling and Development, 24*(1), 42–78.

Arzin, N. H., Donahue, B., & Besalel, V. A. (1994). Youth drug abuse treatment: a controlled outcome study. *Journal of Child and Adolescent Substance Abuse, 3,* 1–16, 1995.

Ashford, J. B., Lecroy, C. W., & Lortie, K. L. (1996/1997). *Human behavior in the social environment: A multidimensional perspective.* Pacific Grove, CA: Brooks/Cole.

Association for Specialists in Group Work. (1992). Professional standards for the training of group workers. *Journal for Specialists in Group Work, 17,* 12–19.

Association for Specialists in Group Work. (1998). Best practice guidelines. *Journal for the Specialists in Group Work, 23*(3), 237–244.

Association for Specialists in Group Work. (1998/1999). Principles for diversity-competent group workers. *Journal for Specialists in Group Work, 24*(1), 7–14.

Association for Specialists in Group Work. (2000). Professional standards for the training of group workers. *The Group Worker, 29*(3), 1–10.

Atkisson M. (2008). Cognitive-Behavioral Depression and Anxiety Adult Group. OMH. Ontario, CA.

Attig, T. (1991). The importance of conceiving of grief as an active process. *Death Studies, 15,* 385–393.

Baars, B. J. (1986). *The cognitive revolution in psychology.* New York: Guilford Press.

Backhaus, K. (1984). Life books: Tools for working with children in placement. *Social Work, 29,* 551–554.

Bagley, C. (1992). Development of an adolescent stress scale for use by school counselors. *School Psychology International, 13,* 31–49.

Baird, B. N. (2002). The internship practicum and field placement handbook: A guide for the helping professions (3rd ed.). Upper Saddle River, NJ: Prentice Hall.

Bandura, A. (1977). *Social learning theory.* Englewood Cliffs, NJ: Prentice Hall.

Barker, R. (1996). *The social work dictionary.* Washington, DC: NASW Press.

Barkley, R. A. (1990). *Attention deficit hyperactivity disorder: A handbook for diagnosis and treatment.* New York: Guilford Press.

Barkley, R. A. (1997). *ADHD and the nature of self-control.* New York: Guilford Press.

Barrett, T. W., & Scott, T. B. (1990). Suicide bereavement and recovery patterns compared with nonsuicide bereavement patterns. *Suicide and Life-Threatening Behavior, 29,* 1–15.

Bass, D. D., & Yep, R. (Eds.). (2002). *Terrorism, trauma, and tragedies: A counselor's guide to preparing and responding.* Alexandria, VA: American Counseling Association.

Bass, D. M., & Bowman, K. (1990). The transition from caregiving to bereavement. The relationship of care-related strain and adjustment to death. *Gerontologist, 30,* 35–42.

Bate, K. L., & Jerums, G. (2003). Preventing complications of diabetes. *Medical Journal of Australia, 179*(9), 498–503.

Beck, A. T. (1963). Thinking and depression. *Archives of General Psychiatry, 9,* 324–333.

Beck, A. T. (1976). *Cognitive therapy and the emotional disorders.* New York: International Universities Press.

Beck, A. T., Rush, A. J., Shaw, B. P., & Emergy, G. (1979). *Cognitive therapy of depression.* New York: Guilford Press.

Beck, A. T., & Weishaar, M. (1989). Cognitive therapy. In A. Freeman, K. M. Simon, L. E. Beutler, & H. Arkowitz (Eds.), *Comprehensive handbook of cognitive therapy* (pp. 21–36). New York: Plenum.

Beisser, A. (1970). The paradoxical theory of change. In J. Fagan & I. L. Shepherd (Eds.), *Gestalt therapy now* (pp. 77–80). New York: Harper & Row.

Belkin, G. S. (1984). *Introduction to counseling* (2nd ed.). Dubuque, IA: William C. Brown.

Bell, N. J., & Bell, R. W. (Eds). (1993). *Adolescent risk taking.* Newbury Park, CA: Sage.

Bengston, V. L. (2001). Beyond the nuclear family. The increasing importance of multigenerational bonds. *Journal of Marriage and Family, 63,* 1–16.

Berliner, L. (1995). Child sexual abuse: Direct practice. *In Encyclopedia of social work* (19th ed, Vol. *1,* pp. 408–417). Washington, DC: NASW Press.

Berliner, L., & Elliott, D. M. (1996). Sexual abuse of children. In J. Briere, L. Berliner, J. Bulkley, C. Jenny, & T. Reid (Eds.), *The APSAC handbook on child maltreatment* (pp. 51–71). Thousand Oaks, CA: Sage.

Berliner, L., & Elliott, D. M. (2002). Sexual abuse of children. In J. E. B. Myers, L. Berliner, J. Briere, C. T. Hendrix, C. Jenny, & T. A. Reid (Eds.), *The APSAC handbook on child maltreatment* (pp. 55–78). Thousand Oaks, CA: Sage.

Bernard, M. E., & DiGiuseppe, R. A. (1989). Rational-emotive therapy today. In M. E. Bernard & R. A. DiGiuseppe (Eds.), *Inside rational-emotive therapy: A critical appraisal of the theory and therapy of Albert Ellis* (pp. 1–7). San Diego: Academic Press.

Berne, E. (1964). *Games people play*. New York: Grove Press.

Berrier, S. (2001). The effects of grief and loss on children in foster care. *Fostering Perspectives*, 6(1).

Berry, B. (1965). *Race and ethnic relations* (3rd ed.). Boston: Houghton Mifflin.

Betcher, H., & Maple, F. (1985). Elements and issues in group composition. In M. Sundel, P. Glasser, R. Sarri, & R. Vinter (Eds.), *Individual change through small groups* (2nd ed., pp. 180–203). New York: Free Press.

Beutler, & H. Arkowitz (Eds.). *Comprehensive handbook of cognitive therapy* (pp. 21–36). New York: Plenum.

Birkenemaier, J., & Berk-Weger, M. (2007). *The practical companion for social work. Integrating class and fieldwork* (2nd ed.). Boston: Allyn & Bacon.

Birmaher, B., Brent, D. A., & Benson, R. S. (1998). Summary of the practice parameters for the assessment and treatment of children and adolescents with depressive disorders. *Journal of the American Academy of Child and Adolescent Psychiatry*, 37(11), 1234–1238.

Blanter, A. (2000). *Foundations of psychodrama: History, theory and practice* (4th ed.). New York: Springer.

Blanter, A. (2003). Not mere players: Psychodrama applications in everyday life. In J. Gershoni (Ed.), *Psychodrama in the 21st century: Clinical and educational applications* (pp. 103–115). New York: Springer.

Bludworth, J. (2006). A Successful Aging Group. In M. S. Corey & G. Corey (Eds.), *Groups: Process and practice* (7th ed., pp. 417–423). Belmont, CA: Thomson Brooks/Cole.

Blumenfeld, W, J. (1992). *How we all pay the price*. Boston: Beacon Press.

Bograda, M. (2005). Strengthening domestic violence theories: Intersections of race, class, sexual orientation, and gender. In N. Sololoff & C. Pratt (Eds), *Domestic violence at the margins: Readings on race, class, gender, and culture* (pp. 25–38). New Brunswick, NJ: Rutgers University Press.

Bolman, L. G., & Deal, T. E. (2003). *Reframing organizations: Artistry, choice and leadership* (3rd ed.). San Francisco: Jossey-Bass.

Botvin, C. J., Schinke, S., & Orlandi, (1995). *Drug abuse prevention with multiethnic youth*. Thousand Oaks, CA: Sage.

Bound, J., Duncan, G. J., Laren, D. S., & Oleinick, L. (1991). Poverty dynamics in widowhood. *Journal on Gerontology*, 46, 5115–5124.

Bourne, E. J. (2005). *The anxiety and phobia workbook* (4th ed.). Oakland, CA: New Harbinger Publications.

Bowman, R., & Bowman, V. (1998). Life on the electronic frontier: The application of technology to group work. *Journal for Specialists in Group Work*, 23(4), 438– 445.

Boy, A. V., & Pine, G. J. (1999). *A person-centered foundation for counseling and psychotherapy* (2nd ed.). Springfield, IL: Charles C. Thomas.

Boyd, N. (1935). Group work experiments in state institutions in Illinois. In *Proceedings of the National Conference of Social Work* (p. 344). Chicago: University of Chicago Press.

Bozarth, J. D., & Brodley, B. T. (1986). Client-centered psychotherapy: A statement. *Person-Centered Review*, 1(3), 262–271.

Brabender, V. (2002). Introduction to group therapy. Hoboken, NJ: John Wiley & Sons.

Brabender, V. A., Fallon, A. E., & Smolar, A. I. (2004). *Essentials of group therapy*. Hoboken, NJ: John Wiley & Sons.

Brackett, J. (1895). The charity organization movement: Its tendency and its duty. In *Proceedings of the 22nd national conference of charities and corrections*. Boston: G. H. Ellis.

Bragg, H. L. (2003). *Child protection in families experiencing domestic violence*. Washington, DC: U.S. Department of Health and Human Services.

Bragger, G., & and Halloway, S. (1978). *Changing human service organizations*. New York: Free Press.

Brammer, L. M. (1985). *The helping relationship: Process and skills* (3rd ed.). Englewood Cliffs, NJ: Prentice Hall.

Brammer, L. M. (1998). *The helping relationship: Process and skills* (4th ed.). Englewood Cliffs, NJ: Prentice Hall.

Brannigan, G. G., & Young, R. C. (1978). Social skills training with the MBD adolescent: A case study. *Academic Therapy, 13,* 214–222.

Bremmer, J. D., Krystal, J. H., Southwick, S. M., & Charney, D. S. (1995). Functional neuro-anatomical correlates of the effects of stress on memory. *Journal of Traumatic Stress, 8,* 527–550.

Brieland, D., Costin, L. M., & Atherton, C. R. (1980). *Contemporary social work* (2nd ed.). New York: McGraw-Hill.

Brill, N. (1990). *Working with people* (4th ed.). White Plains, NY: Longman.

Brill, N., & Levine, J. (2000). *Working with people: The helping process* (6th ed.). Boston: Allyn & Bacon.

Brill, N., & Levine, J. (2002). *Working with people: The helping process* (7th ed.). Boston: Allyn & Bacon.

Britton, P. J. (2001). Guidelines for counseling clients with HIV spectrum disorders. In E. R. Welfel & R. E. Ingersoll (Eds.), *The mental health desk reference* (pp. 60–66). New York: John Wiley & Sons.

Brooks-Harris, J. E. (2008). *Integrative multitheoretical psychotherapy.* Boston: Lahaska Press.

Brown, D. T., & Prout, H. T. (1999). Behavioral approaches. In H. T. Prout & D. T. Brown (Eds.), *Counseling and psychotherapy with children and adolescents: Theory and practice for school and clinical settings* (pp. 203–346). New York: John Wiley & Sons.

Brown, L. K., & Brown, M. (1988). Dinosaurs divorce: A guide for changing families. New York: Little Brown Books for Young Readers.

Brown, P. (2003, September 6). In the shadow of fear. *New Scientist, 30.*

Brown, S. S., & Einsenberg, L. (Eds.) (1995). *The best intentions: Unfinished pregnancy and the well-being of children and families.* Washington, DC: National Academy Press.

Brownlee, S. (1991, August 12). Alzheimer's: Is there hope? *U.S. News & World Report,* 40–49.

Brueggermann, W. G. (1996). *The practice of macro social work.* Chicago: Nelson-Hall.

Brueggermann, W. G. (2006). *The practice of macro social work* (3rd ed.). Belmont, CA: Thomson Brooks/Cole.

Buckingham, S. L., & Van Gorp, W. G. (1988). Essential knowledge about AIDS dementia. *Social Work, 33*(2), 112–115.

Burchum, J. L. R. (2002). Cultural competence: An evolutionary perspective. *Nursing Forum, 37*(4), 5–15.

Burgdorf, R. L. Jr. (Ed). (1980). *The legal rights of handicapped persons.* Baltimore, MD: Paul Brookes.

Burger, W. R. (2008). *Human services in contemporary American* (7th ed.). Belmont, CA: Thomson Brooks/Cole.

Burgess, A., & Roberts, A. R. (2002). Crisis intervention for persons diagnosed with clinical disorders based on the stress-crisis continuum. In A. R. Roberts (Ed.), *Crisis intervention handbook: Assessment, treatment and research* (2nd ed., pp. 56–77). New York: Oxford University Press.

Burns, D. D. (1999). *Feeling good: The new mood therapy* (Rev. ed.). New York: Wholecare.

Burns, D. D., & Nolen-Hoeksema, S. (1992). Therapeutic empathy and recovery from depression in cognitive-behavioral therapy: A structural equation model. *Journal of Consulting and Clinical Psychology, 60,* 441–449.

Butler, R. (1963). The life review: An interpretation of reminiscence in the aged. *Psychiatry, 26*(1).

Butler, S. (1996). *Conspiracy of silence.* San Francisco: Volcano Press.

Cancer Network. (2008). In *Psychological and social aspects of breast cancer.* Retrieved July 2008 from http://www.cancernetwork.com/breast cancer/article/10165/1160706page_Number =2

Canning, M. (2006, February). Exploring sexual compulsivity and its healing path. In *Pioneers in Recovery.* Symposium conducted at the annual meeting of the Medows, La Jolla, CA.

Canto, J. G., & Iskandrian, A. E. (2003). Major risk factors for cardiovascular disease. Debunking the "only 50%" myth. *Journal of the American Medical Association, 290,* 947–949.

Caplan, G. (1961). *An approach to community mental health*. New York: Grune & Stratton.

Caplan, G. (1964). *Principles of preventive psychiatry*. New York: Basic Books.

Capuzzi, D., & Gross, D. R. (2003). *Counseling and psychotherapy: Theory and interventions* (3rd ed). Upper Saddle River, NJ: Merrill Prentice Hall.

Capuzzi, D., & Gross, D. R. (2007). *Counseling and psychotherapy: Theory and interventions* (4th ed). Upper Saddle River, NJ: Merrill Prentice Hall.

Cardemil, E. V., & Battle, C. L. (2003). Guess who's coming to therapy? Getting comfortable with conversations about race and ethnicity in psychotherapy. *Professional Psychology: Research and Practice, 34*(3), 278–286.

Carkhuff, R. R., & Berenson, B. G. (1977). *Beyond counseling and therapy* (2nd ed.). New York: Holt, Rinehart & Winston.

Carnes, P. (1991). *Don't call it love: Recovery from sexual addiction*. New York: Bantam Books.

Carnes, P. (2006). *Facing the shadow: Starting sexual and relationship recovery: A gentle path to beginning recovery from sex addiction*. Carefree, AZ: Gentle Path Press.

Carnes, Delmonico, and Griffin. (2001). *Sexual addiction*. Retrieved July 31, 2008, from http://en.wikipedia.org/wiki/Sexual-addiction

Caroll, J. L., & Wolpe, P. R. (1996). *Sexuality and gender in society*. New York: HarperCollins.

Carr, D., House, J. S., Wortman, C., Neese, R., & Kessler, R. C. (2002). Psychological adjustment to sudden and anticipated spousal loss among older widowed persons. *Journal of Gerontology, 56B*, 5237–5248.

Carter, E. A., & McGoldrick, M. (Eds.). (1988/1989). *The changing life cycle. A framework from for family therapy* (2nd ed.). New York: Gardner Press.

Cartwright, D. (1968). The nature of group cohesiveness. In D. Cartwright & A. Zonder (Eds.), *Group dynamics: Research and theory* (3rd ed.). New York: Harper & Row.

Castex, G. M. (1994). Providing services to Hispanic/Latino populations: Profiles on diversity. *Social Work, 39*(3), 288–296.

Center for Cognitive Therapy. (2000). *About us*. Retrieved in 2000, from http://www.padesky.com/about_us.htm

Center for Mental Health. (1998). *Children's and adolescents' mental health*. Retrieved 2007 from http://www.mentalhealth.org/publications/allpub/CA-0004/default.asp

Centers for Disease Control and Prevention. (1999). *Suicide deaths and rates per 1,000,000*. Retrieved 2007 from http://www.cdc.gov/ncipc/data/us9794/;suic.htm

Centers for Disease Control and Prevention. (2003). *National diabetes fact sheet*. Rockville, MD: U. S. Department of Health and Human Services.

Chang, T., & Yeh, C. J. (2003). Using online groups to provide support to Asian American men: Racial, cultural, gender, and treatment issues. *Professional Psychology: Research and Practice, 34*(6), 634–643.

Chermack, S. T., Fuller, B. E., & Blow, F. C. (2000). Predictors of expressed partner and nonpartner violence among patients in substance abuse treatment. *Drug and Alcohol Dependency, 58*, 43–54.

Cheston, S. E. (2000). A new paradigm for teaching counseling theory and practice. *Counselor Education and Supervision, 39*, 254–269.

Chiaferi, R., & Griffin, M. (1997). Developing fieldwork skills: A guide for human services, counseling, and social work students. Pacific Grove, CA: Brooks/Cole.

Child Trauma Academy (2002). *Trauma and children: An introduction for foster parents*. Vol 10, Issue 1. Retrieved November 2005, from http://www.fosteringperspectives.org/fp_v10n1/v10n1 .htm

Chiles, J., Miller, M., & Cox, G. (1980). Depression in adolescent delinquent population. *Archives of General Psychiatry 37*, 1179–1184.

Christensen, T. (2006). A group for children who have been abused. In M. S. Corey & G. Corey (Eds.), *Groups: Process and practice* (7th ed.). Belmont, CA: Thomson Brooks/Cole.

Clarizio, H. (1985). Cognitive-behavioral treatment of childhood depression. *Psychology in the Schools, 22*(3), 308–322.

Clarke, G. N., Lewinsohn, P. M., & Hops, H. (1990). *Instructor's manual for the adolescent coping with depression course.* Portland, OR: Kaiser Permanente Center for Health Research.

Cobb, H. C., & Warner, P. J. (1999). Counseling and psychotherapy with children and adolescents with disabilities. In H. T. Prout & D. T. Brown (Eds.), *Counseling and psychotherapy with children and adolescents: Theory and practice for school and clinical settings* (pp. 401–425). New York: John Wiley & Sons.

Collier, H. V. (1982). *Counseling women: A guide for therapists.* New York: Free Press.

Comer, R. J. (1995). *Abnormal psychology* (2nd ed.). New York: Freeman.

Conte, J. (Ed.). (2002). *Critical issues in child abuse.* Thousand Oaks, CA: Sage.

Copeland, M. E. (2001). The depression workbook: A guide for living with depression and manic depression. Oakland, CA: New Harbinger Publications.

Copeland, N. J. (2000). Brain mechanisms and neurotransmitters. In D. Nutt, J. Davidson, & J. Zohar (Eds.), *Post-traumatic stress disorder* (pp. 69–100). London: Martin Dunitz.

Corey, G. (1995). *Theory and practice of counseling and psychotherapy* (5th ed.). Pacific Grove, CA: Brooks/Cole.

Corey, G. (2001). *Theory and practice of group counseling* (5th ed.). Pacific Grove, CA: Brooks/Cole.

Corey, G. (2004). *Theory and practice of group psychotherapy* (6th ed.). Belmont, CA: Thomson Brooks/Cole.

Corey, G. (2005). *Theory and practice of counseling and psychotherapy* (7th ed.). Belmont, CA: Thomson Brooks/Cole.

Corey, G. (2008). *Theory and practice of counseling and psychotherapy* (8th ed.). Belmont, CA: Thomson Brooks/Cole.

Corey, G. (2009). *The art of integrative counseling.* Belmont, CA: Thomson Brooks/Cole.

Corey, G., & Corey, M. (2002). *I never knew I had a choice: Explorations in personal growth* (7th ed.). Pacific Grove, CA: Brooks/Cole.

Corey, G., & Herlihy, B. (1997). *Dual/multiple relationships: Toward a consensus of thinking.* New York, NY: Hatherleigh Press.

Corey, G., Schneider-Corey, M., & Callanan, P. (2007). *Issues and ethics in the helping professions* (7th ed.). Belmont, CA: Thomson Brooks-Cole.

Corey, G., Schneider-Corey, M., Callanan, P., & Russell, M. (2004) *Group techniques* (3rd ed.). Pacific Grove, CA: Brooks/Cole.

Corey, M. S., & Corey, G. (2003). *Becoming a helper* (4th ed.). Pacific Grove, CA: Brooks/Cole.

Corey, M. S., & Corey, G. (2004). Reframing resistance. The Group Worker: Association for Specialists in Group Work, *32*(2), 5–8.

Corey, M. S., & Corey, G. (2006). *Groups: Process and practice* (7th ed.). Belmont, CA: Thomson Brooks/Cole.

Corey, M. S., & Corey, G. (2007). *Becoming a helper.* (5th ed.). Belmont, CA: Thomson Brooks/Cole.

Cormier, S. & Cormier, B. (1998). *Interviewing strategies for helpers: Fundamental skills and cognitive behavioral interventions* (4th ed.). Pacific Grove, CA: Brooks/Cole.

Cormier, S., & Hackney, H. (2005). *Counseling strategies and interventions* (6th ed.). Boston, MA: Allyn & Bacon.

Cormier, S., & Nurius, P. (2003). Interviewing and change strategies for helpers: Fundamental skills and cognitive-behavioral interventions. Pacific Grove, CA: Brooks/Cole.

Corr, C. A., Nabe, C. M., & Corr, D. M. (2006). *Death and dying, life and living* (6th ed.) Belmont, CA: Wadsworth/Cengage Learning.

Corsini, R. J., & Wedding, D. (2008). *Current psychotherapies* (8th ed.). Belmont, CA: Thomson Brroks/Cole.

Coryell, W., Noyes, R., & House, J. D. (1986). Mortality among outpatients with anxiety disorders. *American Journal of Psychiatry, 143,* 508–510.

Cosby and Sabin (1995). *Use of therapy groups.* Paper presented at meeting of Kaiser Permanente, Portland, OR.

Costello, E. G., Angold, A., Burns, B. J., Stangel, D. K., Tweed, D. L., & Erkanli, A. (1996). The Great Smoky Mountains study of youth: Goals, design, methods, and the prevalence of DSM III-R disorders. *Archives of General Psychiatry, 53,* 1129–1136.

Covin, A. B. (1977). Using Gestalt psychodrama experiments in rehabilitation counseling. *Personnel and Guidance Journal, 56*, 143–147.

Coyle, G. L. (1930). *Social process in organized groups.* New York: Richard R. Smith.

Crary, E, (1992). *I'm frustrated: Dealing with feelings series.* Seattle, WA: Parenting Press, Inc.

Craske, M. G., Barlow, D. H., & O'Leary, Y. (1992). *Mastery of your anxiety and worry.* Albany, NY: Graywind.

Crooks, R., & Baur, K. (1993). *Our sexuality* (5th ed.). Redwood City, CA: Benjamin/Cummings.

Crosson-Tower, C. (2008). *Understanding child abuse and neglect* (7th ed.). Boston: Pearson Allyn & Bacon.

Culbertson, S., & Mansergh, G. (Producer). (2004). Long term care choices. In American Psychiatric Association (Producer), *Film Tx: Myths and realities of growing old: Aging and long-term care in California* [Motion picture]. CA: The Toy Box Press and Gil Mansergh.

Cummings, E., & Henry, W. E. (1961). *Growing old: The process of disengagement.* New York: Basic Books.

Curb, J. D., Belleau, G. C., Wilcox, B. J., & Abbot, R. D. (2005). Heart disease. In C. N. Dulmus & L. A. Rapp-Paglicci (Eds.), *Handbook of preventive interventions for adults.* Hoboken, NJ: John Wiley & Sons.

Damschen, S. (2007, Fall). *Developing an Alzheimer's support group for caregivers.* Paper presented at Fullerton, CA.

D'Andrea, M., Daniels, J., & Heck, R. (2004). *The Multicultural awareness, knowledge, and skills survey* (MAKSS). Department of Counselor Education, University of Hawaii, HI.

Daniels, R., & Kitano, H. H. L. (1970). *American racism: Exploitation of the nature of prejudice.* Englewood Cliffs, NJ: Prentice Hall.

Danish, J., D'Aguielli, A., & Hauer, A. (1980). *Helping skills: A basic training program.* New York: Human Services Press.

Dattilio, F. M., & Norcross, J. C. (2006). Psychotherapy integration and the emergence of instinctual territoriality. *Archives of Psychiatry and Psychotherapy, 8*(1), 5–6.

Davis, C. (2005). Breast cancer. In C. Dulmus & L. A. Rapp-Paglicci (Eds.), *Handbook of preventive interventions for adults* (pp. 214–225). Hoboken, NJ: John Wiley & Sons.

Day, S. X. (2004). *Theory and design in counseling and psychotherapy.* Boston: Lahaska Press.

Day, S. X. (2009). *Theory and design in counseling and psychotherapy* (2nd ed.). Boston: Lahaska Press.

DeLeon, P. H., Uyeda, M. K., & Welch, B. L. (1985). Psychology and HMDS: New partnership or new adversary? *American Psychologist, 40*(10), 1122–1124.

DeLucia-Waack, J. L. (1996). Multicultural group counseling: Addressing diversity to facilitate universality and self-understanding. In J. L. DeLucia-Waack (Ed.), *Multicultural counseling competencies: Implications for training and practice* (pp. 157–195). Alexandria, VA: Association for Counselor Education and Supervision.

DeLucia-Waack, J. L. (1999). What makes an effective group leader. *Journal for Specialists in Group Work, 24*, 131–142.

DeLucia-Waack, J. L., & Donigan, J. (2004). The practice of multicultural group work: Visions and perspectives from the field. Belmont, CA: Thomson Brooks/Cole.

DePanfilis, D., & Zuravin, S. (1999). Predicting child maltreatment recurrences during treatment. Child Abuse and Neglect, *23*(8), 729–743.

deShazer, S. (1991). *Putting difference to work.* New York: Norton.

Devore, W., & Schlesinger, E. G. (1995). *Ethnic social work practice.* St. Louis, MO: C. V. Mosby.

Dinkemeyer, D. C., & Muro, J. (1979). *Group counseling: Theory and practice.* Itasca, IL: F. E. Peacock.

Dinkemeyer, D. Jr., & Sperry, L. (2000). Counseling and psychotherapy. *Psychiatric Quarterly, 24*, 788–799.

Dixon, S. L. (1987). *Working with people in crisis* (2nd ed.) Columbus, OH: Merrill.

Dobson, K. S. (1989). A meta-analysis of the efficacy of cognitive therapy for depression. *Journal of Consulting and Clinical Psychology, 57*, 414–419.

Domestic Violence Intervention Project. (2007). *Wheel of child abuse.* Retrieved 2007, from

http://www.theduluthmodel.org/pdf/
AbuseChl.pdf

Donigan, J., & Malnati, R. (1997). *Systemic group therapy: A triadic model.* Belmont, CA: Thomson Brooks/Cole.

Donigan, J., & Malnati, R. (2006). *Systemic group therapy: A triadic model.* Belmont, CA: Thomson Brooks/Cole.

Dover, R. B. (1990). Defining mental retardation from an educational perspective. *Mental Retardation, 28,* 147–154.

Dower, J. W. (1986). War without mercy: Race and power in the pacific war. New York: Pantheon.

Driekurs, R. (1950). Techniques and dynamics of multiple psychotherapy. *Psychiatric Quarterly, 24,* 788–799.

Dreikurs, R. (1967a). Psychodynamics, psychotherapy, and counseling: Collected papers of Rudolf Dreikurs, M.D. Chicago: Alfred Adler Institute.

Dreikurs, R. (1967b). The function of emotions. In R. Dreikurs, Psychodynamics, psychoatherapy, and counseling: Collected papers of Rudolf Dreikurs, M.D. (pp. 205–217). Chicago: Alfred Adler Institute.

Dufort, M., & Reed, L. (Eds.). (1995). *Learning the way: A guide for the home visitor working with families on the Navajo reservation.* Watertown, MA: Hilton/Perkins Project of Perkins School for the Blind and Arizona Schools for the Deaf and Blind.

Duke University Health System (2004–2008). *Assertiveness training.* Retrieved December 2008, from www.dukehealth.org

DuPaul, G. J., Guevremont, D., & Barkley, R. (1992). Behavior treatment of attention-deficit hyperactivity disorder in the classroom: The use of the Attention Training System. *Behavior Modification, 16,* 204–225.

DuPaul, G. J., & Stoner, G. (1994). *ADHD in the school.* New York: Guilford Press.

Dykfman, B. (2007). Cognitive behavior treatment of expressed anger in adolescents with conduct disorders. *Education, 121*(2), 298–300.

D'Zurilla, T. J. (1988). *Problem-solving therapies.* In K. S. Dobson (Ed.), *Handbook of cognitive behavioral therapies.* New York: Guilford Press.

Ebersole, P. P. (1976). Reminiscing and group psychotherapy with the aged. In I. M. Mortenson Burnside (Ed.), *Nursing and the aged.* New York: Blakeston Publications.

Echterling, L. G., Cowan, E., Evans, W. F., Staton, A. R., McKee, J. E., Presbury, J., & Stewart A. L. (2008). *Thriving: A manual for students in the helping professions* (2nd ed.). Boston: Lahaska Press.

Edelwish, J., & Broadsky, A. (1982). Training guidelines: Linking the workshop experiences to needs on and off the job. In W. S. Pain (Ed.), *Job stress and burnout* (pp. 133–154). Beverly Hills, CA: Sage.

Egan, H. (2002). *The skilled helper* (7th ed.). Pacific Grove, CA: Brooks/Cole.

Ellis, A. (1996). Overcoming resistance: Rational-emotive therapy with difficult clients. New York: Springer.

Ellis, A., & Bernard, M. E. (1985). What is rational-emotive therapy (RET)? In A. Ellis & R. M. Grieger (Eds.), *Handbook of rational-emotive therapy* (pp. 1–30). New York: Springer.

Ellis, A., & Dryden, W. (1997). *The practice of rational-emotive therapy* (2nd ed.). New York: Springer.

Ely, G., & McGuffey, K. (2005). Partner violence. In C. N. Dulmus & L. A. Rapp-Paglicci (Eds.), *Handbook of preventive interventions for adults* (pp. 360–374). Hoboken, NJ: John Wiley & Sons.

Emmelkamp, P. M. (1994). Behavior therapy with adults. In S. L. Garfield & A. F. Bergin (Eds.), *Handbook of psychotherapy and behavior change* (4th ed., pp. 379–427). New York: John Wiley & Sons.

Engel, G. L. (1977). The need for a new medical model: A challenge for biomedicine. *Science, 196,* 129–136.

Equal Employment Opportunity Commission and the U.S. Department of Justice. (1991). *Americans with Disabilities Act handbook.* Washington, DC: U.S. Government Printing Office.

Erikson, E. H. (1963). *Childhood and society.* New York: Norton.

Erikson, E. H. (1968). *Identity: Youth and crisis.* New York: Norton.

Erikson, E. H. (1998). *The life cycle completed.* New York: Norton.

Ethers, W., Austin, W., & Prothero, J. (1976). *Administration for the human services: An introductory programmed text.* New York: Longman.

Fairburn, C. G. (1984). Bulimia: Its epidemiology and management. In A. J. Stunkard & E. P. Stellar (Eds.), *Eating and its disorders.* New York: Raven Press.

Fairburn, C. G., & Wilson, G. T. (Eds.) (1993). *Binge eating: Nature, assessment, and treatment.* New York: Guilford Press.

Faiver, C., Eisengart, S., & Colonna, R. (2004). *The counselor intern's handbook* (3rd ed.). Belmont, CA: Brooks/Cole.

Fanning, P., & McKay, M. (1993). *Being a man: A guide to the new masculinity.* Oakland, CA: New Harbinger Publications.

Fantuzzo, J., Boruch, R., Beriama, A., Atkins, M., & Marcus, S. (1977). Domestic violence and children: Prevalence and risk in five major U.S. cities. *Journal of the American Academy of Child and Adolescent Psychiatry, 36,* 116–122.

Farber, B. A. (Ed.). (1983). *Stress and burnout in human service professions.* New York: Pergamon Press.

Federal Interagency Forum on Child and Family Statistics. (2002). *America's children: Key national indicators of well-being, 2002.* Washington, DC: U.S. Government Printing Office.

Fender, B. (1994). Safety and danger in the Gestalt group. In B. Feder & R. Ronall (Eds.), *Beyond the hot seat: Gestalt approaches to group* (pp. 41–52). Highland, NY: Gestalt Journal Press.

Fennel, D. L., & Weinhold, B. K. (1989). *Counseling families: An introduction to marriage and family therapy.* Denver, CO: LOVE.

Fentiman, I. S. (2001). Fixed and modifiable risk factors for breast cancer. *International Journal of Clinical Practice, 55*(8), 527–530.

Ferguson, E. D. (1984). *Adlerian theory: An introduction.* Chicago: Adler School of Professional Psychology.

Ferree, M. C. (2001). *Females and sex addiction: Myths and diagnostic implications.* Nashville, TN: Brunner-Routledge.

Film Tx (2005). *Spousal/Partner abuse: Assessment, detection & intervention* [Motion picture]. Website available at: www.filmtx.com

Fiore, T. A., Becker, E. A., & Nero, R. C. (1993). Educational interventions for students with attention deficit disorders. *Exceptional Children, 60*(2), 163–173.

Fisher, R., Ury, W., &, Patton, B. (1997). *Getting to yes: Negotiating agreement without giving in* (2nd ed.). London: Arrow Business Books.

Flegal, K. M., Carroll, M. D., Kuczmarski, R. J., & Johnson, C. L. (1998). Overweight and obesity in the United States: Prevalence and trends, 1960–1994. *International Journal of Obesity, 22,* 39–47.

Flores, P. J. (1998). *Group psychotherapy with addicted populations.* New York: Haworth Press.

Fortune, A., Pearlingi, B., &, Rochelee, C. (1992). Reactions to termination of individual treatment. *Social Work, 37*(2), 171–178.

Fostering Perspectives. (2005) *Trauma and children: An introduction for foster parents.* Vol 10, Issue 1. Retrieved November 2005, from http://www.fosteringperspectives.org/fp_v10n1/v10n1.htm

Fowler, M. (1992). CH.A.D.D. educators manual: An in-depth look at attention deficit disorders from an educational perspective. Plantation, FL: CH.A.D.D.

Franz, M., MacCartie, B., & BCATA Ethics Committee members: C. Gold & B. Skyward. (1999). *Technology guidelines: BCATA recommendations for ethical practice* Vancouver, BC: BCATA Technology Guidelines.

Fraser, M. W., & Williams, S. A. (2004). Aggressive behavior. In L. A. Rapp-Paglicci, C. N. Dulmus, & S. Wodarski (Eds.), *Handbook of preventive interventions for children and adolescents* (pp. 100–129). Hoboken, NJ: John Wiley & Sons

Freidman, A. S., Schwartz, T., & Utada, A. (1989). Outcome of a unique drug abuse program: A follow-up study of clients of Straight, Inc. *Journal of Substance Abuse Treatment, 6,* 259–268.

Frew, J., & Speigler, M. D. (2008). *Contemporary psychotherapies for a diverse world.* Boston: Lahaska Press.

Frick, P., & Lahey, E. (1991). Nature and characteristics of attention deficit hyperactivity disorder. Austin, TX: Pro-Ed.

Fuhriman, A., & Burlingame, G. (1994). Group psychotherapy: Research and practice. In A. Fuhriman & G. M. Burlingame (Eds.), *Handbook of group psychotherapy* (pp. 191–222). New York: John Wiley & Sons.

Fuller-Thomson, E., Minkler, M., & Driver, D. (1977). A profile of grandparents raising grandchildren in the United States. *Gerontologist, 37*, 406–411.

Gambone, J. (2000). *Retirement: A boomer's guide to life after 50.* Minneapolis, MN: House Publishing.

Garner, J. (1995). Long-term care. In R. Edwards & H. J. Hopps (Eds.), *Encyclopedia of social work* (pp. 1625–1634). Washington, DC: NASW Press.

Gary, R. E. (1988). The role of the school counselor with bereaved teenagers: With and without peer support groups. *The School Counselor, 35*, 185–192.

Gattai, F. B., & Musatti, T. (1999). Grandmothers' involvement in grandchildren's care: Attitudes, feelings, and emotions. *Family Relations: Interdisciplinary Journal of Applied Family Studies, 48*, 35–42.

Gazda, G. M., Ginter, E. J., & Horne, A. M. (2001). *Group counseling and group psychotherapy: Theory and application.* Boston: Allyn & Bacon.

Gladdi. D. (2006). Life review: Implementation, theory, research, and therapy. *International Journal of Aging & Human Development, 63*(2), 153–171.

Gladding, S. T. (2003). *Group work: A counseling specialty* (4th ed.). New York: Merrill.

Gladding, S. T. (2004). *Counseling: A comprehensive approach.* Columbus, OH: Pearson Merrill Prentice Hall.

Gladding, S. T. (2005). *Counseling theories: Essential concepts and applications.* Upper Saddle River, NJ: Pearson Merrill Prentice Hall.

Gilbert, L. A., & Schere, M. (1999). *Gender and sex in counseling and psychotherapy.* Boston: Allyn & Bacon.

Gilham, J. E., Reivich, K. J., Jaycox, L. H., & Seligman, M. E. (1995). Prevention of depressive symptoms in schoolchildren: Two-year follow-up. *Psychological Science, 6*, 343–351.

Gilliland, B., & James, R. K. (1993). *Crisis intervention strategies* (2nd ed.). Pacific Grove, CA: Brooks/Cole.

Gilliland, B., & James, R. K. (2003). *Crisis intervention strategies* (5th ed.). Pacific Grove, CA: Brooks/Cole.

Glasser, W. (1965). *Reality therapy: A new approach to psychiatry.* New York: Harper & Row.

Glueckauf, R. L., Pickett, T. C., Ketterson, T. U., Loomis, J. S., & Rozensky, R. H. (2003). Preparation for the delivery of telehealth services: A self-study framework for expansion of practice. *Professional Psychology: Research and Practice, 34*, 159–163.

Goldstein, E. G. (1995). Psychosocial approach. In R. L. Edwards (Ed.), *Encyclopedia of social work* (19th ed., pp. 1948–1954). Washington, DC: NASW Press.

Goldstein, S. (1999). Attention deficit hyperactivity disorder. In S. Goldstein & R. Reynolds (Eds.), *Handbook of neurodevelopmental and genetic disorders in children* (pp. 154–188). New York: Guilford Press.

Goodwill, S. (1987). Dance movement therapy with abused children. *Arts in Psychotherapy, 14*, 59–68.

Goodman, M., Brown, J., & Dietz, F. (1992). *Managing managed care: A mental health practitioner's survival guide.* Washington, DC: American Psychiatric Press.

Gooren, B., Fliers, E., & Courtney, K. (1990). Biological determinants of sexual orientation. *Annual Review of Sex Research, 1*, 175–196.

Gornet, B. (2004). *Myths and facts about hospice care.* Hospice of Marin: www.hospicebythebay.org

Gravold, D. K. (Ed.). (1996). *Cognitive and behavioral treatment modalities and applications.* Pacific Grove, Ca: Brooks/Cole.

Gray, R. E. (1988). The role of the school counselor with bereaved teenagers: With or without peer support groups. *School Counselor, 35*, 185–192.

Greenblat (2003). Obesity epidemic [Electronic version]. *CQ Researcher, 13*(4). Retrieved June 2007, from http://www.cqpress.com/product/Researcher-Obesity-Epidemic-v13-4.html

Greenberg, D., & Padesky, C. A. (1995). *Mind over mood: A cognitive therapy treatment manual for clients.* New York: Guilford Press.

Greenberg, L. I. (1975, July). Therapeutic grief work in children. *Social Casework,* 396–403.

Greenberg, P. E., Sistisky, T., & Kessler, R. C. (1999). The economic burden of anxiety disorders in the 1990s. *Journal of Clinical Psychiatry, 60,* 427–435.

Greenfield, L., Rand, M., & Craven, D. (1998). *Violence by intimates: Analysis of data on crime by current and former spouses, boyfriends, and girlfriends.* Washington, DC: U.S. Department of Justice.

Guerrero, M. (2007). *Obesity prevention group proposal.* Unpublished paper, California State University, Fullerton.

Guilliland, B., & James, R. K. (1993). *Crisis intervention strategies* (2nd ed.). Pacific Grove, CA: Brooks/Cole.

Haake, C. A. (1991), Behavioral markers and intervention strategies for regular and special education teachers. In P. Accardo, T. Blondis, & B. Whitman (Eds.), *Attention deficit disorders and hyperactivity in children* (pp. 251–285). New York: Marcel Dekker.

Haber, D. (2006). Life review: Implementation, theory, research, and therapy. *International Journal of Aging & Human Development, 63*(2), 153–171.

Hackney, H., & Cormier, S. (2005). *The professional counselor: A process guide to helping* (5th ed.). Boston: Pearson.

Haines, A. A. (1992). Comparison of cognitive-behavioral stress management techniques with adolescent boys. *Journal of Counseling and Development, 70,* 600–605.

Hallahan, D. P., & Kauman, J. M. (2000). *Exceptional learners: Introduction to special education* (8th ed.). Boston: Allyn & Bacon.

Halley, A., Kopp, J., & Austin, M. (1998). *Delivering human services: A learning approach to practice.* New York: Longman.

Halmi, K. A. (2003, October). *Effective treatment strategies for anorexia and bulimia nervosa.* Paper presented at the Behavioral Healthcare Symposium: Mind and Body: An Integrated Approach to Care, Kaiser Permanente, Indian Wells, CA.

Hansfeneld, Y. (1983). *Human service organizations.* Englewood Cliffs, NJ: Prentice Hall.

Hare, A. (1976). *Handbook of small group research* (2nd ed.). New York: Free Press.

Harrigan, M. P., & Farmer, R. L. (2000). The myths and facts of aging. In R. L. Schneider, N. P. Kroft, & A. J. Kisor (Eds.), *Gerontological social work: Knowledge, service settings, and special populations* (2nd ed., pp. 26–65). Pacific Grove, CA: Thomson Brooks/Cole.

Harrow, J., Nelson-Brambir, M., Harrow, G. (1996). *Counseling basics for wiccan clergy.* Retrieved 1996 from, http://www.proteusco ven.org/proteus/counselbook.html

Hatcher, R. A., Trussel, J., Steward, F., Cates, W., Jr., Steward, G. K., Guest, F., & Kowal, D. *Contraceptive technology* (17 ed.). New York: Ardent Media.

Haveman, R., & Wolfe, B. (1994). *Succeeding generations.* New York: Russell Sage.

Hawkins, J. D., Catalano, R. F., & Miller, J. Y. (1992). Risk and protective factors for alcohol and other drug problems in adolescence and early adulthood: Implications for substance abuse problems. *Psychological Bulletin, 112,* 64–105.

Hayes, S. C., Follette, V. M., & Linehan, M. M. (2004). *Mindfulness and acceptance.* New York: Guilford Press.

Hayes, S. C., Luoma, J. B., Bond, F. W., Masuda, A., & Lillis, J. (2006). Acceptance and commitment therapy: Model, processes and outcomes. *Behaviour Research and Therapy, 44,* 1–25.

Hays, P. A. (2001). *Addressing cultural complexities in practice: A framework for clinicians and counselors.* Washington, DC: American Psychological Association.

Henderson, D. A., & Gladding, S. T. (2004). Group counseling with older adults. In J. L. DeLucia-Waack, D. Gerrity, C. R. Kalodner, & M. T. Riva (Eds.), *Handbook of group counseling and psychaotherapy* (pp. 469–478). Thousand Oaks, CA: Sage.

Henry, S. (1992). *Group skills in social work. A. four-dimensional approach* (2nd ed.). Pacific Grove, CA: Brooks/Cole.

Hepworth, D. H., Rooney, R. H., & Larsen, J. A. (2002). *Direct social work practice: Theory and skills* (5th ed.). Pacific Grove, CA: Brooks/Cole.

Herbert, M. & Wookey, J. (2004). *Managing children's disruptive behavior: A guide for practitioners working with parents and foster parents.* Hoboken, NJ: John Wiley & Sons.

Herek, G. M., & Berril, K. (1990). Violence against lesbians and gay men: Issues for research, practice, and policy. *Journal of Interpersonal Violence, 5*(3), 359–364.

Herman, J. L. (1992). *Trauma and recovery.* New York: Basic Books.

Herold, K. C. (2004) Achieving antigen specific immune regulation. *Journal of Clinical Investigation, 113,* 346–349.

Herrmann, D. S., McWhirter, J. J., & Sipsas-Herrmann, A. (1997). The relationship between dimensional self-concept and juvenile gang involvement: Implications for prevention, intervention, and court referred diversion programs. *Behavioral Sciences and the Law, 15,* 181–194.

Hetherington, E. M., Stanley-Hagan, M., & Anderson, E. R. (1989). Marital transitions: A child's perspective. *American Psychologist, 44,* 303–312.

Hetherington, E. M., Cox, M., & Cox, R. (1985). Long-term effects of divorce and remarriage on the adjustment of children. *Journal of the American Academy of Psychiatry, 24,* 518–530.

Higgins, S. T. (1999). Principles of learning in the study and treatment of substance abuse. In M. Galanter & H. D. Kleber (Eds.), *Textbook of Substance Abuse Treatment* (2nd ed.). Washington, DC: American Psychiatric Press, Inc.

Hoff, L. A. (1989). *People in crisis: Understanding and helping* (3rd ed.) Redwood City, CA: Addison-Wesley.

Hollon, S. D., DeRubeis, R. J., Evans, M.D., Wiemer, J. J., Garvey, J. G., Grove, W. M., & Tuason, V. B. (1992). Cognitive-therapy and pharmacotherapy for depression: Singly and in combination. *Archives of General Psychiatry, 49,* 774–781.

Hollon, S. D., & Najaitis, L. (1988). Review of empirical studies of cognitive therapy. In A. J. Frances & R. E. Hales (Eds.), *American Psychiatric Press review of psychiatry* (Vol. 7, pp. 643–666). Washington, DC: American Psychiatric Press.

Hollon, S. D., Shelton, R. C., & Loosen, P. T. (1991). Cognitive therapy and pharmacotherapy for depression. *Journal of Consulting and Clinical Psychology, 59,* 88–99.

Homan, M. S. (2004). Promoting community change: Making it happen in the real world. Pacific Grove, CA: Brooks/Cole.

Hooyman, N. R., & Kiyak, H. A. (1991). *Social gerontology: A multidisciplinary perspective* (2nd ed.). Boston: Allyn & Bacon.

Howard, M., Delva, J., Jenson, J. M., Edmond, T., & Vaughn, M. G. (2005). Substance abuse. In C. N. Dulmus & L. A. Rapp-Pagilicci (Eds.), *Handbook of Preventive Interventions for Adults,* pp. 92–124. Hoboken, NJ: John Wiley & Sons.

Howard, M., & Jenson, J. (2003) Clinical guidelines and evidence-based practice in medicine, psychology and allied professions. In A. Rosen & K. Proctor (Eds.), *Developing practice guidelines for social work intervention: Issues, methods, and research agenda* (pp. 83–107). New York: Columbia University Press.

Hsieh, H., & Wang, J. (2003). Effect of reminiscence therapy on depression in older adults: A systematic review. *International Journal of Nursing Studies, 40*(4), 335–345.

Hsu, J., Tseng, W., Ashton, G., McDermott, J., & Char, W. (1985). Family interaction patterns among Japanese Americans and Caucasian families in Hawaii. *American Journal of Psychiatry, 142,* 577–581.

Hulewat, P. (1996). Resettlement: A cultural and psychological crisis. *Social Work, 41*(2), 129–135.

Hulka, B. S., & Moorman, Z. G. (2001). Breast cancer: Hormones and other risk factors. *Maturitas, 38*(1), 102–113.

Hull, G. H., & Kirst-Ashman, K. K. (2004). *The generalist model of human services practice.* Belmont, CA: Thomson Brooks/Cole.

Hulse-Killacky, D., Killacky, J., & Donigan, J. (2001). *Making task groups work in your world.* Upper Saddle River, NJ: Merrill/Prentice Hall.

Humphreys, K., Winzelberg, A., & Klaw, E. (2000). Psychologists' ethical responsibilities in Internet-based groups: Issues, strategies, and a call for dialogue. *Professional Psychology: Research and Practice, 31*(5), 493–496.

Institute of Medicine. (1994). *Reducing risks for mental disorders: Frontiers for preventative intervention research.* Washington, DC: National Academy Press.

Ivey, A. E. (1991). *Developmental therapy: Theory into practice.* San Francisco: Jossey-Bass.

Ivey, A. E., Pedersen, P. B., & Ivey, M. B. (2001). *Intentional group counseling: A microskills approach.* Pacific Grove, CA: Brooks/Cole.

Jacobs, E. E., Masson, R. L., & Harvill, R. I. (2002). *Group counseling: Strategies and skills* (4th ed.). Belmont, CA: Thomson Brooks/Cole.

Jacobs, E. E., Masson, R. L., & Harvill, R. I. (2006). *Group counseling: Strategies and skills* (5th ed.). Belmont, CA: Thomson Brooks/Cole.

James, R. K. (2008). *Crisis intervention strategies.* Belmont, CA: Thomson Brooks/Cole.

James, R. K., & Gilliland, B. E. (2001). *Crisis intervention strategies* (3rd ed.) Belmont, CA: Thomson Brooks/Cole.

Janosik, E. H. (1984). *Crisis counseling: A contemporary approach.* Belmont, CA: Wadsworth.

Jaycox, L. H., Reivich, K. J., Gilham, J., & Seligman, M. E. P. (1994). Prevention of depression symptoms in school children. *Behaviour Research and Therapy, 32*, 801–816.

Jehn, K. C., & Chartman, J. (2000). The influence of proportional and perceptual conflict composition on team performance. *International Journal of Conflict Management, 11*(1), 56–73.

Jesor, R., & Jesor, S. L. (1977). *Problem behavior and psychosocial development: A longitudinal study of youth.* New York: Academic Press.

Johnson, A. B. (1990). Out of Bedlam: The truth about deinstitutionalization. New York: Basic Books.

Johnson, D. R., Feldman, S. C., & Southwick, S. M. (1994). The concept of the second-generation program in the treatment of PTSD among Vietnam veterans. *Journal of Traumatic Stress, 7*, 217–235.

Johnson, G. (2008). *Sex addiction has devastating effects.* Retrieved December 2008, from http://www.straight.com/article-170662/too-much-sex-brain

Johnston, L. D., O'Malley, P. M., & Bachman, J. G. (2002). *The monitoring the future national survey results on adolescent drug use: Overview of key findings, 2001.* (NIH Publication No. 02–5105). Bethesda, MD: National Institute on Drug Use.

Jones, K., & Robinson, E. H. (2000). Psychoeducational groups: A model for choosing topics and exercises appropriate to group stages. *Journal for Specialists in Group Work, 25*, 356–365.

Kabat-Zinn, J. (1990). Full catastrophe living: The program of the stress reduction clinic at the University of Massachusetts Medical Center. New York: Delta.

Kadden, R, N., Cooley, N. L., & Getter, H. (1989). Matching alcoholics to coping skills or interactional therapies: Posttreatment results. *Journal of Consulting Clinical Psychology, 57*, 698–704.

Kaiser Permanente. (2004). *Diversity Newsletter.* Fontana, CA: Author.

Kalodner, C. R. (1998). Systematic desensitization. In S. Cormier & B. Cormier (Eds.), *Interviewing strategies for helpers* (4th ed., pp. 497–529). Pacific Grove, CA: Brooks/Cole.

Kamerman, S. B., & Khan, A. J. (1976). *Social services in the United States: Policies and programs.* Philadelphia: Temple University Press.

Kaminer, Y. (1994). Adolescent Substance Abuse: A comprehensive guide to theory and practice. New York: Plenum, 1994.

Kanel, K. (1999). *A guide to crisis intervention.* Cleveland, OH: Custom Publishing.

Kanel, K. (2003). *A guide to crisis intervention.* (2nd ed.). Pacific Grove, CA: Brooks/Cole.

Kanel, K. (2005/2007). *A guide to crisis intervention* (3rd ed). Pacific Grove, CA: Brooks/Cole.

Kanel, K. (2008). *An overview of the human services.* Boston, MA: Lahaska Press.

Kann, L., Kinchen, S., A., Williams, B. I., Ross, J. G., Lowry, R., Grunbaum, J. A., & Kolbe, L. J. (2000). Youth at risk behavior surveillance: United States, 1'999, Morbidity and Mortality Weekly Reports, *49*, 1–96.

Kannel, W. B. (1990). Contribution of the Framingham Study to preventive cardiology (Bishop lecture). *Journal of the American College of Cardiology, 15*, 206–211.

Kannel, W. B., & Sytkowski, P. A. (1987). Artherosclerosis risk factors. *Pharmacology and Therapeutics, 32*, 207–235.

Kanuha, V. K. (2005). Compounding the triple jeopardy: Battering in lesbian of color relationships. In N. Sololoff & C. Pratt (Eds.), *Domestic violence at the margins: Readings on race, class, gender, and culture* (pp. 25–38). New Brunswick, NJ: Rutgers University Press.

Kaplan, B. (1984). Anxiety states. In F. J. Turner (Ed.), *Adult psychopathology: A social work perspective*, pp. 260–279. New York: Free Press.

Kaufman, J., Cullinan, D., & Epstein, M. (1987). Characteristics of students placed in special programs for the seriously emotionally disturbed. *Behavioral Disorders, 12*, 175–184.

Kazdin, A. E. (1993). Adolescent mental health: Prevention and treatment programs. *American Psychologist, 48*, 121–141.

Keen, S. (1991). *Fire in the belly: On being a man.* New York: Bantam Books.

Kepner, E. (1994). Gestalt group process. In B. Feder & R. Ronall (Eds.), *Beyond the hot seat: Gestalt approaches to group* (pp. 5–24). Highland, NY: Gestalt Journal Press.

Kerson, T. (1994). Field instruction in social work settings: A framework for teaching. New York: Haworth Press.

Khantzian, E. J., Golden, S. J., & McAuliffe, W. E. (1999). Group therapy. In M. Galanter & H. D. Kleber (Eds.), *Textbook of substance abuse treatment* (2nd Ed.). Washington, DC: American Psychiatric Press, Inc.

Kim, B. S. K., Atkinson, D. R., & Umemoto, D. (2001). Asian cultural values and counseling process: Current knowledge and directions for future research. *Counseling Psychologist, 29*, 570–603.

Kirst-Ashman, K. K., & Hull, G. H. Jr. (1993). *Understanding generalist practice.* Chicago: Nelson-Hall.

Kiser, P. M. (2008). *The human services internship* (2nd ed.). Belmont, CA: Thomson Brooks/Cole.

Kish, M. (1991). Counseling adolescents with L.D. *Intervention in School of Mental Retardation Reviews, 5*(5), 22–26.

Kitano, H. H. L. (1981). Asian Americans, the Chinese, Japanese, Koreans, Filipinos, and Southeast Asians. *The Annuals 454*, 125–138.

Kitchener, K. S. (1984). Intuition, critical evaluation and ethical principles: The foundation for ethical decisions in counseling psychology. *Counseling Psychologist, 12*(3), 43–55.

Klerman, G. L. (1978). Affective disorder. In A. M. Nicholi (Ed.), *The Harvard guide to modern psychiatry* (pp. 253–282). Cambridge, MA: Belknap.

Knaus, W. (2006). *The cognitive behavior workbook for depression.* Oakland, CA: New Harbinger Books.

Kock, M. O., Dotson, V., & Troast, T. P. (2001). Interventions with eating disorders. In C. Zastrow (Ed.), *Social work with groups* (5th ed., pp. 433–453). Pacific Grove, CA: Brooks/Cole.

Korb, M. P., Gorrel, J., & Van de Reit, V. (1989). *Gestalt therapy: Practice and theory* (2nd ed.). Boston: Allen and Bacon.

Kornblum, W., & Julian, J. (2001). *Social problems* (10th ed.). NJ: Prentice-Hall

Kornhaber, A. (1996). *Contemporary grandparenting.* Thousand Oaks, CA: Sage.

Koss-Chioino, J. D. (1999). Depression among Puerto Rican women: Culture, etiology and diagnosis. *Hispanic Journal of Behavioral Sciences, 21*(3), 330–350.

Kottler, J. A. (1994). *Advanced group leadership.* Pacific Grove, CA: Brooks/Cole.

Kottler, R. M. (1986). *On being a therapist.* San Francisco: Jossey-Bass.

Kramer, R. M. (1981). *Voluntary agencies in the welfare state.* Berkeley: University of California Press.

Krames (2002). Managing your chronic pain. *Health and Safety Education,* Stamford, CT: StayWell.

Kraus, K., & Hulse-Killacky, D. (1996). Balancing process and content in groups: A metaphor. *Journal for Specialists in Group Work, 21*, 90–93.

Kübler-Ross, E. (1969). *On death and dying.* New York: Collier Books.

Kuybers, J., & Benston, V. (1973). Competence and social breakdown: A social-psychological view on aging. *Human Development, 16*(2), pp. 37–49.

LaFountain, R. M., Garner, N. E., & Eliason, G. T. (1996). Solution-focused counseling groups: A key for school counselors. *School Counselor, 43,* 256–267.

Lambert, M. J. (1992). Implications of outcome research for psychotherapy integration. In J. C. Norcross & M. R. Goldstein (Eds.), *Handbook of psychotherapy integration* (pp. 94–129). New York: Basic Books.

Landeros, L. (2008). *Hermanos a Hermanos* : Presentation on group/fieldwork. Fullerton, CA: Author.

Landlaw, S., & Moore, L. (1991). Social skills deficits in children with attention deficit hyperactivity disorder. *School Psychology Review, 20*(2), 235–251.

Lange, A. J., & Jubkowski, P. (1976). *Responsible assertive behavior. Cognitive behavioral procedures for trainers.* Champaign, IL: Research Press.

Larsen, S. (2008, August). *Serving individuals with severe and or multiple disabilities.* Benson Clinical Review, Vol. *53.*

Larsen, S. (2008). Trends in foster care: A review of the statistics. *Hannah's Harold.*

Larsen, S. (2008). The sexual exploitation of children on the Internet. *Hannah's Harold.*

Larsen, S. (2008). A practical understanding of the social work profession in the United States. *Hannah's Harold.*

Larsen, S., Dashtipour, K., & Brown, S. (2008). Depression. *The Benson House Clinical Review,* Vol. *53.*

Laudenslager, K. K. (2006). A group for elementary school children of divorce and changing families. In M. S. Corey, & G. Corey (Eds.), *Groups: Process and practice* (7th ed.). Belmont, CA: Thomson Brooks/Cole

Lauffer, A. (1984). *Understanding your social agency.* Beverly Hills, CA: Sage.

Lawson, G. W., Ellis, D. C., & Rivers, P.C. (1984). *Essentials of chemical dependency counseling.* Rockville, MD: Aspen Systems.

Lazarus, A. A. (1986). Multimodal therapy. In J. C. Norcross (Ed.), *Handbook of eclectic psychotherapy* (pp. 65–93). New York: Brunner/Mazel.

Lazarus, A. A. (2006). Multimodal therapy: A seven-point integration. In G. Stricker & J. Gold (Eds.), *A casework of psychotherapy integration* (pp. 17–28). Washington, DC: American Psychiatric Association.

Lazarus, A. A., & Beutler, L. E. (1993). On technical eclecticism. *Journal of Counseling and Development, 71,* 381–385.

Lecroy, C. W., & Mann, J. E. (2004). Substance abuse. In L. A. Rapp-Paglicci, C. N. Dulmus, & S. Wodarski (Eds.), *Handbook of Preventive Interventions for children and adolescents* (pp. 1098–1224). NJ: John Wiley & Sons.

Lee, C. C., & Ramsey, C. J. (2006). Multicultural counseling: A new paradigm for a new century. In C. C., Lee (Ed.), *Multicultural issues in counseling: New approaches to diversity* (3rd ed.) Alexandria, VA: American Counseling Association.

Lefrancois, G. R. (1999). *The lifespan* (5th ed.) Belmont, CA: Wadsworth.

Lehmann, P., & Rabenstein, S. (2002). Children exposed to domestic violence: The role of impact, assessment, and treatment. In A. R. Roberts (Ed.), *Handbook of domestic violence: Intervention strategies* (pp. 343–364). New York: Oxford University Press.

Leith, L. M. (1998). *Exercising your way to better mental health.* Morgantown, WV: Fit Information Technology.

Lerner, J. W., Lowenthal, B., & Lerner, S. (1995). *Attention deficit disorders: Assessment and teaching.* Pacific Grove, CA: Brooks/Cole.

Leslie, R. S. (1993, July/August). Confidentiality. *Californian Therapist,* p. 5.

Lessa, N. R., & Scanlon, W. F. (2006). *Wiley concise guides to mental health substance disorders.* Hoboken, NJ: John Wiley & Sons.

Levant, R. F. (1992). Toward the reconstruction of masculinity. *Journal of Family Psychology, 5* (3/4), 379–402.

Levant, R. H., Hirsch, L., Celentano, E., Cozza, T., Hill, S., MacEachern, M., Marty, M., & Schnedeker, J. (1992). The male role: An investigation of norms and stereotypes. *Journal of Mental Health Counseling, 14,* 325–377.

Levitt, M. J., Weber, R.A., & Guacci, N. (1993). Convoys of social support: An intergenerational analysis. *Psychology and Aging, 8,* 323–3216.

Lewinsohn, P. F., Rohde, P., & Crozier, L.C. (1991). Age and depression: Unique and shared effects. *Psychology and Aging, 6,* 247–260.

Lewis, J. A., Lewis, M. D., Packard, T., & Souflee, F. (2006). *Management of human service service programs* (3rd ed.) Pacific Grove, CA: Brooks/Cole.

Liebowitz, M. R., Salman, E., Jusino, C. M., Garfunkel, R., Street, L., Cardenas, D. L., Siverstre, J., Fyer, A. J., Carrasco, J. L, Davies, S., Guarnaccia, J. P., & Klein, D. (1994). Ataque de nervios and panic disorder. *American Journal of Psychiatry 151*(6), 871–875.

Lindemann, E. (1944). Symptomatology and management of acute grief. *American Journal of Psychiatry, 101,* 141–148.

Linehan, M. M. (1993). Skills training manual for treating borderline personality disorder. New York: Guilford Press.

Litt, M. D., Babor, T. F., & DelBoca, F. K. (1992). Types of alcoholics. II: Application of an emperically derived typology to treatment matching. *Archives of General Psychiatry 49,* 609–614.

Lloyd, G. A. (1995). HIV/AIDS overview. In *Encyclopedia of social work* (19th ed., pp. 1257–1290). Washington, DC: NASW Press.

Long Beach Area Child Trauma Council (1992). *About Us*. Retrieved 1992, from http://www.endabuselb.org/

Long, V. O. (1996). *Facilitating personal growth in self and others*. Pacific Grove, CA: Brooks/Cole.

Lopez-Sandrin, M., & Skyler, J. S. (2005). Diabetes mellitus. In C. M. Dulmus & L. A. Rapp-Paglicci (Eds.), *Handbook of preventive interventions for adults* (pp. 187–213). Hoboken, NJ: John Wiley & Sons.

Los Angeles Times. (2008). *Barack Obama wins presidency, making history* [Article by Mark Z. Barabak]. Retrieved November 5, 2008, from http://www.latimes.com/news/ nationworld/washingtondc/la-na-ledeall5-2008nov05,0,2092786.story

Loza, N. (2001, May). *Insanity on the Nile: The history of psychiatry in pharaonic Egypt*. Paper presented at the Second Biennial National Conference on Health Issues, in the Arab American community, Dearborn, MI.

Lubrosky, L. (1984). Principles of psychoanalytic psychotherapy: A manual for supportive-expressive treatment. New York: Basic Books.

Luepker, E. T. (2003). *Record keeping in psychotherapy and counseling. Protecting confidentiality and the professional relationship*. New York: Brunner-Routedge.

Lum, D. (2004). *Social work practice and people of color* (5th ed.). Belmont, CA: Thomson Brooks/Cole.

Lyness, J. M. (2008). *Patient information: Depression in adults*. Retrieved August 2008, from http://www.update.com

Mackelprang, R., & Salsgiver, R. (1999). *Disability*. Pacific Grove, CA: Brooks/Cole.

MacKenzie, K. R. (1990). *Introduction to time-limited group psychotherapy*. Washington, DC: American Psychiatric Press.

MacKenzie, K. R. (1994). Where is here and when is now? The adaptational challenge of mental health reform for group psychotherapy. *International Journal of Group Psychotherapy, 44,* 407–428.

MacKenzie, K. R. (1995). *Effective use of group therapy in managed care*. Washington, DC: American Psychiatric Press.

Mader, S. H. (Producer). (2004). Benefits of grandparenting. In American Psychiatric Association (Producer), Film Tx: *Myths and Realities of Growing Old: Aging and long term care* [Motion Picture]. CA: The Toy Box Press and Gil Mansergh.

Maheu, M., Whitten, P., & Allen, A. (2001). *E-Health, telehealth, and telemedicine: A guide to start-up and success*. San Francisco: Jossey-Bass.

Malley-Morrison, K., & Hines, D. A. (2004). Family violence in a cultural perspective: Defining, understanding, and combating abuse. Thousand Oaks, CA: Sage.

Manson, J. E., Tosteson, H., Ridker, P. M., Satterfield, S., Hebert, P., & O'Conner, G. T. (1992). The primary prevention of myocardial infarction. *New England Journal of Medicine, 326,* 1406–1416.

Marin (Producer). (2004). Myths and facts about hospice care. In American Psychiatric Association (Producer), Film Tx: *Myths and Realities of Growing Old: Aging and long term care* [Motion Picture]. CA: The Toy Box Press and Gil Mansergh.

Markus, H. E., & King, D. A. (2003). A survey of group psychotherapy training during predoctoral psychology internship. *Professional Psychology: Research and Practice, 34*(2), 203–209.

Martikaninen, P., & Valkonen, T. (1996). Mortality after death of a spouse: Rates and causes of death in a large Finnish cohort. *American Journal of Public Health, 86,* 1087–1093.

Martin, B. C. (2008). *Sexual addiction 101.* Retrieved July 2008, from http://www.sandiegotherapists.com/sexaddiction.html

Maslack, C. (1982). Understanding burnout: Definitional issues in analyzing a complex phenomenon. In W. S. Paing (Ed.), *Job stress and burnout* (pp. 29–40). Beverly Hills, CA: Sage.

Maslow, A. (1962). *Toward a psychology of being.* New York: Van Nostrand Reinhold.

Mayo Foundation for Medical Education and Research. (2007). *Compulsive sexual behavior.* Retrieved August 2008, from http://www.mayoclinic.com/health/compulsive-sexual-behavior/DS00144

McAdam, T. W. (1986). *Careers in the nonprofit sector: Doing well by doing good.* Farmington Hill, MI: Taft Group

McAnulty, B. D., & Burnetter, M. M. (2001). *Exploring human sexuality: Making healthy decisions.* Boston: Allyn & Bacon.

McClure, B. A. (1994). The shadow side of regressive groups. *Counseling and Values, 38,* 77–89.

McDonald, R., Jouriles, E., Ramisetty-Miker, S., Caetano, R., & Green, C. E. (2006). Estimating the number American children living in partner-violent families. *Journal of Family Psychology 20*(1), 137–142.

McDonald-Wikler, L. (1987). Disabilities: Developmental. In *Encyclopedia of social work* (Vol. 1) Silver Spring, MD: NASW.

McGregor (1960). *Careers in the nonprofit sector: Doing well by doing good.* Farmington Hill, MI: Taft Group.

McKay, M., & Rogers, P. (2003). *The anger control workbook.* Oakland, CA: New Harbinger Publications.

McKenna, K. Y. A., Green, A. S., & Gleason, M. E. J. (2002). Relationship formation on the Internet: What's the big attraction? *Journal of Social Issues, 58*(1), 9–13.

McKinney, J., Montague, M., & Hocutt, A. (1993). Educational assessment of students with attention deficit disorders. *Exceptional Children, 60,* 125–131.

McKnight, D. L., Nelson-Gray, R. O., & Barnhill, J. (1992). Amethasone suppression test and response to cognitive therapy and antidepressant medication. *Behavior Therapy, 1,* 99–111.

McLemore, S. D. (1994). *Racial and ethnic relations in America* (4th ed.). Boston: Allyn & Bacon.

McMahon, A., & Rhuddick, P. (1964). Reminiscing: Adaptation significance in the aged. *Archives of General Psychiatry,* 292–298.

McMahon, M., Neville-Sorvilles, J., & Schbert, L. (1999). Undoing harm to children: The Duluth Family Visitation Center. In M. L. Shepard & E. L. Pence (Eds.), *Coordinating community responses to domestic violence: Lessons from Duluth and beyond* (pp. 151–167). Thousand Oaks, CA: Sage.

McManus, M. C. (1991). Serving lesbian and gay youth. *Focal Point, 5,* 1–4.

McMinn, M. R., Buchanan, T., Ellens, B. M., & Ryan, M. K. (1999). Technology, professional practice, and ethics: Survey findings and implications. *Professional Psychology: Research and Practice, 20*(2), 165–172.

McWhirter, J., McWhirter, B. T., McWhirter, A. M., & McWhirter, E. H. (1998). *At-risk youth: A comprehensive response.* Pacific Grove, CA: Brooks/Cole.

Meachaum, J. A. (1995). Reminiscing as a process of social construction. In B. K. Haight & J. D. Webster (Eds.), The art and science of reminiscing: Theory, research, methods, and applications (pp. 37–48). Washington, DC: Taylor & Francis.

Meara, N. M., Schmidt, D., & Day, J. (1996). Principles and virtues. A. foundation for ethical decisions, policies, and characters. *Counseling Psychologist, 24*(1), 4–77.

Mears, D. P. (2003). Research and interventions to reduce domestic violence revictimization. *Trauma, Violence, and Abuse, 4,* 127–147.

Meenaghan, T. M., & Gibbons, W. G. (2000). Generalist practice in larger settings: Knowledge and skill concepts. Chicago: Lyceum Books.

Meenaghan, T. M., & Kilty, K. M. (1993). Policy analysis and research technology: Political and ethical considerations. Chicago: Lyceum Books.

Meichenbaum, D. H. (1975). Theoretical and treatment implications of development research on verbal control of behavior. *Canadian Psychological Review, 16,* 22–27.

Meichenbaum, D. H. (1977). *Cognitive-behavior modification: An integrative approach.* New York: Plenum.

Meichenbaum, D. H. (1985). *Stress inoculation training.* Elmsford, NY: Pergamon.

Meier, S. T., & Davis, S. R. (1993). *The elements of counseling* (2nd ed.). Pacific Grove, CA: Brooks/Cole.

Melchert, T., & Burnett, K. F. (1990). Attitudes, knowledge and sexual behavior of high-risk adolescents: Implications for counseling and sexual education. *Journal of Counseling and Development, 68*(3), 293–298.

Mellonie, B. (1983). Lifetimes: *A beautiful way to explain death to children.* Toronto, Canada: Bantam Books.

Meris, D. (2001). Responding to the mental health and grief concerns of homeless HIV infected gay men. *Journal of Gay & Lesbian Social Services: Issues in Practice, Policy, & Research, 13*(4), 103–112.

Merta, R. J. (1995). Group work: Multicultural perspectives. In J. G. Ponterotto, J. M. Casas, L. A. Suzuki, and C. M. Alexander (Eds.). *Handbook of multicultural counseling* (pp. 567–585), Newbury Park, CA: Sage.

Miedel, W. T., & Reynolds, A. J. (2004). Parent involvement in early intervention for disadvantaged children: Does it matter? *Children and Youth Services Review, 26*(1), 39–62.

Miller, J. B., & Stiver, I. P. (1997). The healing connection: How women form relationships in therapy and in life. Boston: Beacon Press.

Miller, M. (1986). *Counseling geriatric clients* (Cassette recording No. 14). Memphis, TN: Memphis State University, Department of Counseling and Personal Services.

Miller, M. J. (1996). Some comparisons between Taoism and person-centered therapy. *Person-Centered Journal, 3,* 12–14.

Miller, S. C. (1969). *The American image of the Chinese, 1785–1882.* Berkeley: University of California Press.

Miller, W., & Rollnick, S. (Eds.). (2002). *Motivational interviewing: Preparing people for change.* New York: Guilford Press.

Milliren, A. P., & Clemmer, F. (2006). Introduction to Adlerian psychology: Basic principles and methodology. In S. Slavik & J. Carlson (Eds.), *Readings in the theory and practice of individual psychology* (pp. 17–43). New York: Routledge (Taylor and Francis).

Milliren, A. P., Evans, T. D., & Newbauer, J. F. (2003). Adlerian theory. In D. Capuzzi, & D. R. Gross (Eds.), *Counseling and psychotherapy: theories and interventions* (3rd ed.) Upper Saddle River, NJ: Merrill Prentice-Hall.

Minuchin, S., & Fishman, C. (1981). *Family therapy techniques.* Cambridge, MA: Harvard University Press.

Morales, A. T., & Sheafor, B. W. (1995). *Social work: A profession of many faces.* (7th ed.). Boston: Allyn and Bacon.

Moreno, J. L. (1972). *Psychodrama* (4th ed.). Beacon, NY: Beacon House. (Original work published 1946).

Mosak, H. (2000). Adlerian psychotherapy. In R. J. Corsini & D. Wedding (Eds.), *Current psychotherapies* (6th ed., pp. 54–98). Itasca, IL: F. E. Peacock.

Mosak, H. H. (2005). Adlerian psychotherapy. In R. J. Corsini & D. Wedding (Eds.), *Current psychotherapies* (7th ed., pp. 52–95). Belmont, CA: Brooks/Cole.

Mosak, H. H., & Maniacci, N. (1999). *A primer on Adlerian psychology.* Philadelphia: Brunner/ Mazel.

Moses, A. E., & Hawkins, R. O. (1982). *Counseling lesbian women and gay men: A lifetime approach.* St. Louis, MO: Mosby.

Murase, K. (1977). *Minorities and Asian Americans.* In J. B. Turner (Ed.), *Encyclopedia of social work* (Vol. 2, p. 953) Washington, DC: National Association of Social Workers.

Myers, J. E., Sweeney, T. J., & Witmer, J. M. (2000). The Wheel of Wellness counseling for wellness: A holistic model for treatment planning. *Journal of Counseling and Development, 78,* 251–266.

Nasser-McMillan, S. C. (1999). *Mental health considerations in the Arab community.* Paper presented at the Second Biennial National Conference on Health Issues in the Arab American Community, Dearborn, MI.

Nasser-McMillan, S. C., & Hakim-Larson, J. (2003). Counseling considerations among Arab Americans. *Journal of Counseling & Development, 81*(2), 150–159.

National Association of Social Workers. (1999). *Code of ethics.* Washington, DC: Author.

National Association of Social Workers. (2004). *Code of ethics.* Washington, DC: Author.

National Breast Cancer Coalition. (2004). *Facts about breast cancer in the United States: Year 2003.* Washington, DC: Author.

National Center on Domestic Violence and Sexual Violence (2008). *Abuse of children violence wheel.* Retrieved July 2008, from http:// www.ncdv.org/images/Childrenviolence wheel

National Center for Health Services. (2001). *Prevalence of overweight among children and adolescents: United States 1999.* Washington, DC: National Center for Health Statistics.

National Commission on Children (1991). *Speaking of kids: A national survey of children and parents* (ASI Publication No. 15528–2). Washington, DC: U.S. Government Printing Office

National Diabetes Information Clearinghouse. (2008). *Diabetes overview.* Retrieved July 2008, from http://diabetes.niddk.nih.gov/ dm/pubs/overview/index.htm

National Institute of Health (2003). *Older adults: Depression and suicide facts.* (NIH Publication No. 03–4593).

National Institute of Mental Health. (2000). *Adolescent depression.* Retrieved 2002 from http:// www.nimh.nih.gov/

National Institute of Mental Health. (2001). *Trauma.* Washington, DC: U.S. Government Printing Office.

National Institute of Mental Health. (2008). The numbers count: Mental illness in America. In *Science on our minds* [Fact sheet]. Bethesda, MD: Author.

National Institute of Mental Health (Producer). (2004). Depression in the elderly. In American Psychiatric Association (Producer), Film Tx: *Myths and realities of growing old: Aging and long term care* [Motion picture]. CA: The Toy Box Press and Gil Mansergh.

National Organization for Human Services (NOHS) (2000).

National Spinal Cord Injury Statistical Center. (2008). *Facts and Figures at a glance 2008.* Birmingham: University of Alabama at Birmingham.

Native American Research and Training Center. (1995). *Some alarming facts.* Tucson: University of Arizona.

Neimeyer, Y., & Feixas, G. (1990). The role of homework and skill acquisition in the outcome of group cognitive therapy for depression. *Behavior Therapy, 21,* 282–292.

Nelligan, A. (1994). Balancing process and content: A collaborative experience. *Together, 23,* 8–9.

Neugarten, B., & Weinstein, R. (1964). The changing American grandparent. *Journal of Marriage and the Family, 26,* 199–204.

Neukrug. E. (1994). *Theory, practice, and trends in human services: An Introduction.* Pacific Grove, CA: Brooks/Cole.

Neukrug, E. (2002). *Skills and techniques for human service professionals: Counseling environment, helping skills, treatment issues.* Pacific Grove, CA: Brooks/Cole.

Neukrug, E. (2004). *Theory, practice, and trends in human services: An introduction* (3rd ed.) Pacific Grove, CA: Brooks/Cole.

Neukrug, E. (2008). *Theory, practice, and trends in human services: An introduction* (4th ed.). Belmont, CA: Thomson Brooks/Cole.

Neumark-Sztainer, D., Butler, T., & Palti, H. (1995). Eating disturbances among adolescent girls: Evaluation of a school-based primary prevention program. *Journal of Nutrition Education, 27,* 24–31.

Newman, B. M., & Newman, P. R. (1999). *Development through life: A psychosocial approach* (7th ed.). Belmont, CA: Thomson Wadsworth.

Newman, B. M., & Newman, P. R. (2003). *Development through life: A psychosocial approach* (8th ed.). Belmont, CA: Thomson Wadsworth.

Ney, P. (1987). The treatment of abused children: The natural sequence of events. *American Journal of Psychotherapy, 41,* 391–401.

Nickelson, D. (2000). Telehealth, health care services, and health care policy: A plan for action in the new millennium. *New Jersey Psychologist, 50*(1), 24–27.

Nixon, R. (2002). Treatment of behavior problems in preschoolers: A review of parent training programs. *Clinical Psychology Review, 22,* 525–546.

Norcross, J. C., & Beutler, L. E. (2008). Integrative psychotherapies. In R. J. Corsini & D. Wedding (Eds.), *Current psychotherapies* (8th ed., pp. 481–511). Belmont, CA: Brooks/Cole.

Norcross, J. C., Beutler, L. E., & Levant, R. F. (2006). *Evidence-based practice in mental health: Debate and dialogue on the fundamental questions.* Washington, DC: American Psychological Association.

Norcross, J. C., Karpiak, C. P., & Lister, K. M. (2005). What's an integrationist? A study of self-identified integrative and (occasionally) eclectic psychologists. *Journal of Clinical Psychology, 61,* 1587–1594.

Norcross, J. C., & Newman, C. F. (1992). Psychotherapy integration: Setting the context. In J. C. Norcross, & M. R. Goldfried (Eds.), *Handbook of psychotherapy integration* (pp. 3–45). New York: Basic Books.

Nowinski, (2000). Twelve-step facilitation. In K. M. Carroll (Ed.), *Approaches to drug abuse counseling* (NIH Publ. no. 00-4151). Bethesda, MA: National Institute on Drug Abuse.

Nugent (1990). *An introduction to the profession of counseling.* Columbus, OH: Merrill.

Nydell, M. (1987). *Understanding Arabs: A guide for westerners.* Yarmouth, ME: Intercultural Press.

O'Brien, E. M. (1992). American Indians in higher education. *Research Briefs, 5*(5). Washington, DC: American Council on Education, Policy Analysis and Research.

Ochberg, F. M. (Ed.). (1988). *Post-traumatic therapy and victims of violence.* New York: Brunner/Mazel.

O'Dea, J. A. (1995). *Everybody's different: A self-esteem program for young adolescents.* Sydney, Australia: University of Sydney Press.

Office for Equal Opportunity and Diversity Management (2003).

Office of Juvenile Justice and Delinquency Prevention (2002). Juvenile arrests. Retrieved 2007 from http://www.ojjdp.ncjrs.org/ojstatbb/asp/html/qa251.html

Office of Juvenile Justice and Delinquency Prevention (2002a). Juvenile arrests. Retrieved 2007 from http://ojjdp.ncjrs.org/ojstatbb/asp/html/qa251.html.

Offord, D. (2000). Selection of levels of prevention. Addictive Behaviors, *25,* 833–842.

Okun, B. K. (1990). *Seeking connections in psychotherapy.* San Francisco: Jossey-Bass.

Olafson, M. (2002). When paradigms collide. In *Critical Issues in Child Abuse.* New Haven, CT: Yale University Press.

Olds, D. L. (2002). Prenatal and infancy home visiting by nurses: From randomized trials to community replication. *Prevention Science, 3*(3), 153–172.

O'Leary, E., & Nieuwstraten, I. M. (2001). The exploration of memories in Gestalt reminiscence therapy. *Counseling Psychology Quarterly, 14*(2), 165–180.

O'Leary, K. D. (2000). Developmental and affective issues in assessing and treating partner aggression. *Clinical Psychology: Science and Practice, 6,* 400–414.

Olmstead, M. (1959). *The small group.* New York: Random House.

Olsen, L. D. (1971). Ethical standards for group leaders. *Personnel and Guidance Journal, 50,* 288.

O'Neil, M. K. (1984). Affective disorders. In F. J. Turner (Ed.), *Adult psychopathology: A social work perspective* (pp. 148–180). New York: Free Press.

Oregon State. (2008). *Suicide Bereavement Support.* Retrieved August 2008, from http://www.oreegon.gov/DHS/ph/ipe/ysp.sbs.shtml

Ormont, L. R. (1988). The leader's role in resolving resistances to intimacy in the group setting. *Interpersonal Journal of Group Psychotherapy, 38*(1), 29–46.

Ortiz, L. (1995). Sectarian agencies. In R. Edwards & J. Hopps (Eds.), *Encyclopedia of social work* (pp. 2109–2116). Washington, DC: NASW Press.

Osborne, W. L. (1982). Group counseling: Direction and intention. *Journal for Specialists in Group Work, 7,* 275–280.

Osgood, N. J. (1985). *Suicide and the elderly: A practitioner's guide to diagnosis and mental health intervention.* Rockville, MD: Aspen.

Osofsky, J. D., & Thompson, M. D. (2000). Adaptive and maladaptive parenting: Perspectives on risk and protective factors. In J. P. Shonkoff & S. J. Meisels (Eds.), *Handbook of early childhood intervention* (2nd ed., pp. 54–76). New York: Cambridge University Press.

Oxford, D. (2000). Selection of levels of prevention. *Addictive Behaviors, 25,* 833–842.

Oxford, J. (1985). *Excessive appetites: A psychological view of addictions.* New York: John Wiley & Sons.

Pack-Brown, S. P., Whittington-Clark, L .E., & Parker, W. M. (1998). *Images of me: A guide to group work with African American women.* Boston: Allyn & Bacon.

Page, B. J. (2004). Online group counseling. In J. L. DeLucia-Waack, D. Gerrity, C. R. Kalodner, & M. T. Riva (Eds.), *Handbook of group counseling and psychotherapy* (pp. 609–620). Thousand Oaks, CA: Sage.

Page, B. J., & Jencius, M. J. (2009). *Groups: Planning and leadership skills.* Boston: Lahaska Press.

Paleg, K., & Jongsma, A. E., Jr. (2005). *The group treatment planner.* Hoboken, NJ: John Wiley & Sons.

Papalia, D. E., Olds, S. W., & Feldman, R. D. (1998). *Human development* (7th ed.). Boston: McGraw-Hill.

Papalia, D. E., Olds, S. W., & Feldman, R. D. (2001). *Human development* (8th ed.). Boston: McGraw-Hill.

Parkes, C. M. (1975). Determinants of outcome following bereavement. *Omega Journal of Death and Dying, 6,* 303–323.

Parrto, V. M. (2004). Theories on aging. *Theories of Aging* [Collected notes]. Retrieved from www.angelfire.com/ns/southeasternnurse

Parsons, R. D. (2007). *Counseling strategies that work! Evidence-based interventions for school counselors.* Boston: Pearson.

Passons, W. R. (1975). *Gestalt approaches in counseling.* New York: Holt, Rinehart, and Winston.

Patterson, G. R., Dishion, T. J., & Yoerger, K. (2000). Adolescent growth in new forms of problem behavior: Macro- and micro-peer dynamics. *Prevention Science, 1*(1), 3–13.

Peck, R. C. (1968). Psychological developments in the second half of life. In B. L. Neugarten (Ed.), *Middle age and aging* (p. 88). Chicago: University of Chicago Press.

Pedersen, P. (2000). *A handbook for developing multicultural awareness* (3rd ed.) Alexandria: VA: American Counseling and Development.

Perls, F. (1969). *Gestalt therapy verbatim.* Lafayette, CA: Real People Press.

Perls, F., Hefferline, R. F., & Goodman, P. (1951). *Gestalt therapy: Excitement and growth in the human personality.* New York: Julian Press.

Piper, W. E., & Ogrodniczuk, J. S. (2004). Brief group therapy. In J. L. DeLucia-Waack, D. Gerrity, C. R. Kalodner, & M. T. Riva (Eds.), *Handbook of group counseling and psychotherapy* (pp. 641–650). Thousand Oaks, CA: Sage.

Polster, E., & Polster, M. (1973). *Gestalt therapy integrated: Contours of theory and practice.* New York: Brunner/Mazel.

Poser, E. G. (1970). Toward a theory of behavior prophylaxis. *Journal of Behavior Therapy and Experimental Psychiatry, 1,* 39–43.

Poser, E., & King, M. (1975). Strategies for the prevention of maladaptive fear responses. *Canadian Journal of Behavioral Science, 7,* 279–294.

Postmes, T., Spears, R., & Lea, M. (1999). Social identity, group norms, and "deindividuation": Lessons from computer-mediated communication for social influence in the group. In N. Ellemers, R. Spears, & B. Doosje (Eds.), *Social identity: Context, commitment, content* (pp. 164–183). Oxford, UK: Blackwell.

Postmes, T., Spears, R., Sakhel, K., & deGroot, D. (2001). Social influence in computer-mediated communication: The effects of anonymity on group behavior. *Personality and Social Psychology Bulletin, 27,* 1245–1254.

Posthuma, B. W. (2002). *Small groups in therapy settings: Process and leadership* (4th ed.). Boston: Allyn & Bacon.

Price, C. A.(Producer). (2004). Crisis of old age: Facts about retirement. In American Psychiatric Association (Priducer), *Film Tx: Myths and Realities of Growing Old: Aging and Long Term Care* [Motion Picture]. CA: The Toy Box Press and Gil Mansergh.

Pritchard, C. (1996). *Suicide: The ultimate rejection? A psycho-social study.* Bristol, PA: Open University Press.

Prochaska, J., DiClimente, C., & Norcross, C. (1992). In search of how people change. *American Psychologist, 41*(4), 1102–1114.

Puig-Antich, J. (1982). Major depression and conduct disorders in prepuberty. *Journal of the American Clinical Psychiatry, 21,* 118–128.

Raja, S. N., McGee, T., & Stanton, W. R. (1992). Perceived attachment to parents and peers and psychological well-being in adolescence. *Journal of Youth and Adolescence, 21,* 471–486.

Rapport, L. (1996). Crisis intervention goals and steps. Retrieved October 2008, from http://childlaw.law.sc.edu/usermanual/crisissea tonz.htm

Rapp-Paglicci, L. A. (2002). Children and adolescents from violent homes. In L. A. Rapp-Paglicci, A. R. Roberts, & J. S. Wodarski (Eds.), *Handbook of violence* (pp. 54–66). Hoboken, NJ: John Wiley & Sons.

Rapp-Paglicci, L. A., Dulmus, C. N., & Wodarski, J. S. (Eds.). (2004). *Handbook of preventive interventions for children and adolescents.* Hoboken, NJ: John Wiley & Sons.

Ray, M. (2008). Be strong: A suicide survivor's group. Presentation on Group/Fieldwork, presented in, Fullerton, CA.

Reamer, F. G. (1998). Ethical standards in social work: A review of NASW code of ethics. Washington, DC: NASW Press.

Regier, D. A., Narrow, D. E., Rae, D. S., Manderscheid, R., W., Locke, B. Z., & Goodwin, F. K. (1993). The defective U.S. mental and addictive service system: Epidemiologic catchment areas prospective 1-year prevalence rates of disorders and services. *Archives of General Psychiatry, 50,* 80–94.

Reid, K. (1981). *From character building to social treatment: The history of the use of groups in social work.* Westport, CT: Greenwood Press.

Reid, K. (1997). Social work practice with groups: A clinical perspective (2nd ed.). Pacific Grove, CA: Brooks/Cole.

Remley, T. P., & Herlihy, B. (2001). *Ethical, legal, and professional issues in counseling.* Upper Saddle River, NJ: Merrill/Prentice Hall.

Reinecke, M. A., Ryan, N. E., & DuBois, D. L. (1998). Cognitive behavioral therapy of depression and depressive symptoms during adolescence: A review and meta-analysis. *Journal of the American Academy of Child and Adolescent Psychiatry, 37*(1), 26–34.

Reiss, A. J., Jr., & Roth, J. A. (Eds.). (1993). *Understanding and preventing violence: Social influences* (Vol 3). Washington, DC: National Academy Press.

Reiter, M. D. (2008). *Therapeutic interviewing: Essential skills and contexts of counseling.* Boston: Allyn and Bacon

Riordan, R. J., & Beggs, M. S. (1987). Counselors and self-help groups. *Journal of Counseling and Development, 65,* 427–429.

Roberts, A. (2000). *Crisis intervention handbook: Assessment, treatment, and research.* New York: Oxford Press.

Roberts, A. R., & Yeager, K. R. (Eds.). (2004). *Evidence-based practice manual: Research and* outcome measures in health and human services. New York: Oxford University Press.

Robins, L. N., & Reiger, D.A. (Eds.). (1991). Psychiatric disorders in America: The epidemiologic catchment areas study. New York: Free Press.

Robinson, M., & Wilson, G. (2006). Everyone's wired for sexual addiction. Reuniting: Healing with sexual relationships. Retrieved December, 2008, from http://www.reuniting.info/science/porn_addiction_wired_for_sexual_addiction

Robinson, P., Wischman, C., & Del Vento, A. (1996). A manual for primary care and mental health providers. Reno, NV: Context Press.

Roe-Sepowitz, D. E., Bedard, L. E., & Thyer, B. A. (2005). Anxiety. In C. N. Dulmus & L. A. Rapp-Paglicci (Eds.), Handbook of preventive interventions for adults. Hoboken, NJ: John Wiley & Sons.

Roe-Sepowitz, D. E., & Thyer, B. (2004). Adolescent mental health. In L. A. Rapp-Paglicci, C. N. Dulmus, & J. S. Wodarski (Eds.), Handbook of preventive interventions for children and adolescents (pp. 67–99). Hoboken, NJ: John Wiley & Sons.

Rogers, C. R. (1970). Carl Rogers on encounter groups. New York: Harper & Row.

Rogers, C. R. (1986). Carl Rogers on the development of the person-centered approach. Person-Centered Review, 1, 257–259.

Roller, B., & Nelson, V. (1991). The art of cotherapy. New York: Guilford Press.

Rooney, R. H., & Chovanec M. (2004). Involuntary group. In C. D. Garvin, L. M. Gutierrez, & M. J. Galinsky (Eds.), Handbook of social work with groups (pp. 212–226). New York: Guilford Press.

Rose, S. D. (1989). Working with adults in groups. San Francisco: Jossey-Bass.

Rose, S. D., & Edleson, J. (1987). Working with children and adolescents: A multimodal approach. San Francisco: Jossey-Bass.

Rosen, A., & Proctor, E. (Eds.). (2003). Practice guidelines for social work interventions: issues, methods, and research agenda. New York: Columbia University Press.

Rosenberg, M., Giberson, R., Rossman, B., & Acker, M. (2000). The child witness of family violence. In R. Ammerman & M. Hersen (Eds.), Case studies in family violence (pp. 259–291). New York: Plenum Press.

Rosenberg, S., & Zimet, C. (1995). Brief group treatment and managed mental health care. International Journal of Group Psychotherapy, 45, 367–379.

Ross, M. (1989). Relation of implicit theories to the construction of personal histories. Psychological Review, 96, 341–357.

Rothschild, B. (2000). The body remembers: The psychophysiology of trauma treatment. New York: Norton.

Rowe, J. W., & Khan, R. L. (1998). Juvenile sexual offending: Causes, consequences, and correction. San Francisco: Jossey-Bass.

Rowe, J. W., & Kahn, R. L. (1998). Successful aging. New York: Pantheon Books.

Royse, D., Dhopper, S. S., & Rompf, E. (1999). Field instruction: A guide for social work students (3rd ed.). New York: Longman.

Rutan, J. S. (2003). Sandor Ferenczi's contributions to psychodynamics group therapy. International Journal of Group Psychotherapy, 53, 375–384.

Rutan, J. S., & Stone, W. N. (2001). Psychodynamic group therapy (3rd ed.). New York: Guilford Press.

Sanders, C. M. (1989). Grief: The mourning after. New York: John Wiley & Sons.

Santhiveeran, J. (1998). Virtual group meetings on the Net: Implications for social work practice. Paper presented at the meeting of the Association for the Advancement of Social Work with Groups, Miami, FL.

Santoyo, R. (2008). Chica power. Presentation on Group/Fieldwork, presented in Fullerton, CA.

Saxton, A. (1971). The indispensable enemy: Labor and the American-Chinese movement. Berkeley: University of California Press.

Schaefer, C. E., Johnson, L., & Wherry, J. N. (1982). Group therapies for children and youth. San Francisco: Jossey-Bass.

Schaefer, R. T. (1988). Racial and ethnic groups. Glenview, IL: Scott Foresman.

Schein, E. H. (1985). Organizational culture and leadership. San Francisco: Jossey-Bass.

Schopler, J., Galinsky, M., & Abell, M. (1977). Creating community through telephone and computer groups: Theoretical and practice perspectives. *Social Work with Groups, 20*(4), 19–34.

Scott, J. & Lynton, R. (1952). The community factor in modern technology. Paris: United Nations Educational, Scientific, and Cultural Organization.

Scurfield, R. M. (1985). Post-trauma stress assessment and treatment: Overview and formulations. In C. R. Figley (Ed.), *Trauma and its wake: The study of post-trauma stress disorder* (pp. 219–256). New York: Brunner/Mazel.

Seekins, T. (1997). Native Americans and the ADA. *The Rural Exchange, 10,* 1–17.

Seligman, M. E. P. (1975). *Helplessness.* San Francisco: W. H. Freeman.

Seligman, M. (1995). *The optimistic child: A revolutionary program that safeguards children against depression and builds lifelong resilience.* New York: Houghton Mills.

SeniorNet (Producer). (2004). Depression in the elderly. In American Psychiatric Association (Producer), *Film Tx: Myths and realities of growing old: Aging and long-term care in California* [Motion Picture]. Monrovia, CA: The Toy Box Press and Gil Mansergh.

Shapiro, J. L., Peltz, L. S., & Bernadett-Shapiro, S. (1998). *Brief group treatment: Practical training for therapists and counselors.* Pacific Grove, CA: Brooks/Cole.

Sharf, R. S. (2008). *Theories of psychotherapy and counseling: Concepts and cases.* Belmont, CA: Brooks/Cole.

Sharma, S. (1997). Domestic violence against minority women: Interventions, preventions and health implications. Equal Opportunity International, *16,* 1–14.

Shulman, L. (1984). *The skills of helping: Individuals and groups* (2nd ed.). Itasca, IL: F. E. Peacock.

Shulman, L. (1999). *The skills of helping individuals, families, groups* (4th ed.). Itasca, IL: F. E. Peacock.

Sigelman, C. K., & Shaffer, D. R. (1995). *Life-span human development* (2nd ed.). Pacific Grove, CA: Brooks/Cole.

Skinner, B. F. (1953). *Science and Human Behavior.* New York: Macmillan.

Slaikeu, K. (1990). *Crisis intervention: A handbook for practice and research.* Boston: Allyn & Bacon.

Slater, J. R., & Spetalnick, D. (2001). Compassion fatigue: A personal perspective. In T. McClam & M. Woodside (Eds.), *Human service challenges in the 21st century* (pp. 215–224). Birmingham, AL: Ebsco Media.

Smith, D. C. (1997). *Caregiving: Hospice proven techniques for healing body and soul.* New York: Macmillan.

Smolowe, J. (1995). The downward spiral. Time [On-line Serial]. Available: America Online, Education.

Sonstegard, M. A. (1998). The theory and practice of group counseling. *Journal of Individual Psychology, 54*(2), 217–250.

Sonstegard, M. A., & Bitter, J. R. (2001). *Adlerian group therapy: Step-by-step.* Unpublished manuscript.

Sowa, C. J., May, K., & Niles, S. G. (1994). Occupational stress within the counseling profession: Implications for counselor training. *Counselor Education and Supervision, 34,* 19–29.

Spar, J., & LaRue, A. (2006). *Clinical manual of geriatric psychiatry.* Washington, DC: American Psychiatric Publishing.

Speigler, M. D. (1980, November). Behavioral primary prevention: Introduction and overview. In M. D. Speigler (Chair), *Behavioral primary prevention: A challenge for the 1980s.* Symposium conducted at the annual meeting of the Association for the Advancement of Behavior Therapy, New York.

Speigler, M. D., & Guevremont, D. C. (2003). *Contemporary behavior therapy* (4th ed.). Pacific Grove, CA: Brooks/Cole.

Spence, S. H. (2003). Social skills training with children and young people: Theory, evidence and practice. *Child and Adolescent Mental Health, 8*(2), 84–96.

Spence, S. H., & Dadds, M. R. (1996). Preventing childhood anxiety disorders. *Journals of Behavior Change, 13,* 241–249.

Sperry, L., Carlson, J., & Kjos, D. (2003). *Becoming an effective therapist.* Boston: Allyn & Bacon.

Spira, H. I. (1997). Understanding and developing psychotherapy groups for medically ill patients. In J. L. Spira (Ed.), *Group therapy for medically ill patients* (pp. 3–51). New York: Guilford Press.

Spitz, H. I., & Spitz, S. T. (1999). *A pragmatic approach to group psychotherapy*. Philadelphia: Brunner/Mazel.

Stivers, C. (1990). Promotion of self-esteem in the prevention of suicide. *Death Studies, 14*, 301–327.

Stockton, R., Morran, D. K., & Kreiger, K. M. (2004). Review and perspectives of critical dimensions in therapeutic small group research. In G. M. Gazda (Ed.), *Basic approaches to group psychotherapy and group counseling* (3rd ed., pp. 37–85). Springfield, IL: Charles C. Thomas.

Stoddard, S., Jans, L, Ripple, J., & Kraus, M. (1998). *Chartbook on work and disability in the United States*. Berkeley, CA: InfoUse.

Stolberg, A. L., & Mahler, J. (1994). Enhancing treatment gains in a school-based intervention for children of divorce through skill training, parental involvement and transfer procedures. *Journal of Consulting and Clinical Psychology, 62*(1), 147–156.

Storms, M. D. (1981). A theory of erotic orientation development. *Psychological Review, 88*, 340–353.

Straus, M. A., & Gelles, R. J. (Eds.). (1990). *Physical violence in American families: Risk factors and adaptation to violence in 8,415 families*. New Brunswick, NJ: Transaction.

Stricker, G., & Gold, J. (Eds.). (2006). A casebook of psychotherapy integration. Washington, DC: American Psychological Association.

Strong, B., & DeVault, C. (1983). *The marriage and family experience* (2nd ed.). New York: West.

Strumpfel, U., & Goldman, R. (2002). Contacting: Gestalt therapy. In D. J. Cain & J. Seeman (Eds.), *Humanistic psychotherapies: Handbook of research and practice* (pp. 189–219). Washington, DC: American Psychological Association.

Strupp, H. H., & Binder, J. L. (1994). *Psychotherapy in a new key: A guide to time-limited dynamic psychotherapy*. New York: Basic Books.

Substance Abuse and Mental Health Service Administration, Office of Applied Studies. (2005). *Results from the 2004 national survey on drug use and health: National findings*. Retrieved November 2005, from http://www.oas.samhsa.gov/2k4/NSDUH/nsduh.pdf

Sue, D. W. (2001). Multidimensional facets of cultural competence. *Counseling Psychologist, 29*, 790–821.

Sue, D. W., Arredondo, P., & MacDavis, R. J. (1992). Multicultural counseling competencies and standards: A call to the profession. *Journal of Counseling and Development, 70*(4), 477–486.

Sue, D. W., & Sue, D. (2003). *Counseling the culturally diverse: Theory and practice* (4th ed.). Hoboken, NJ: John Wiley & Sons.

Sue, D. W., & Sue, D. (2008). *Counseling the culturally diverse: Theory and practice* (5th ed.). Hoboken, NJ: John Wiley & Sons.

Summit, R. (1983). The child abuse accommodation syndrome. *Child Abuse and Neglect, 7*, 177–193.

Sweitzer, H. F., & King, M. A. (2004). *The successful internship* (2nd ed.). Belmont, CA: Brooks/Cole.

Sweitzer, H. F., & King, M. A. (2009). *The successful internship* (3rd ed.). Belmont, CA: Brooks/Cole.

Szapocznik, J., and Hernandez, R. (1988). The Cuban American family. In C. H. Mindel, R. Witabenstein, & R. Wright Jr. (Eds.), *Ethnic families in America* (3rd ed., pp. 160–172). New York: Elsevier.

Taylor, R. L. (Ed.). (1994). *Minority families in the United States: A multicultural perspective*. Englewood Cliffs, NJ: Prentice Hall.

Texas Council on Family Violence (Producer). (2005). Film Tx: *Spousal/partner abuse: assessment, detection and intervention* [Motion Picture]. Monrovia, CA: The Toy Box Press and Gil Mansergh.

Teyber, E. (2000). *Interpersonal process in psychotherapy: A relational approach* (4th ed.). Belmont, CA: Wadsworth.

Thomas, A. R., & Cobb, H. C. (1999). Culturally responsive counseling and psychotherapy with children and adolescents. In H.T. Prout & D. T. Brown (Eds.), *Counseling and psychotherapy with children and adolescents: Theory* and practice for children and clinical settings (3rd ed., pp. 49–73). New York: John Wiley & Sons.

Thomlison, B. (2004). Child maltreatment: A risk and protective factor perspective. In M. W. Fraser (Ed.), *Risk and resilience in childhood: An ecological perspective* (2nd ed., pp. 89–131). Washington DC: NASW Press.

Thomlison, B., & Craig, S. (2005). Ineffective parenting. In C. Dulmas & L. Rapp-Paglicci (Eds.), *Handbook of preventive interventions for adults.* Hoboken, NJ: John Wiley & Sons.

Thompson, M. P., Kaslow, N. M. J., & Kingree, J. B. (2002). Risk factors for suicide attempts among African American women experiencing recent intimate partner violence. *Violence and Victims, 17*, 283–295.

Thyer, B. A., & Birsinger, P. (1994). Treatment of clients with anxiety disorders. In D. K. Granvold (Ed.), *Cognitive and behavioral treatment: Methods and Applications.* Pacific Grove, CA: Brooks/Cole.

Tice, C. J., & Perkins, K. (1996). *Mental health issues and aging: Building on the strengths of older persons.* Pacific Grove, CA: Brooks/Cole.

Tolan, P. H. (2001). Emerging themes and challenges in understanding youth violence involvement. *Journal of Clinical Child Psychology, 30*, 233–239.

Tomlin, A. M., & Passman, R. H. (1989). Grandmothers' responsibility in raising 2 year-olds facilitates their grandchildren's adaptive behavior: A preliminary intrafamilial investigation of mothers' and maternal grandmothers' effects. *Psychology and Aging, 3*, 119–121.

Toseland, R. W., & Spielberg, G. (1982). The development of helping skills in undergraduate social work education: Model and evaluation. *Journal of Education for Social Work, 18*(1), 66–73.

Toseland, R. W., & Rivas, R. S. (1984). *An introduction to group work practice.* Boston: Allyn & Bacon.

Toseland, R. W., & Rivas, R. S. (2001). *An introduction to group work practice* (3rd ed.). Boston: Allyn & Bacon.

Toseland, R. W., & Rivas, R. S. (2009). *An introduction to group work practice* (6th ed.). Boston: Allyn & Bacon.

Tower, C. C. (1989). *Understanding child abuse and neglect.* Needham Heights, MA: Allyn & Bacon.

Triffon, B. J. (1977). Grandparents: Parenting again. *Columbus Parent, 9*, 17.

Trotzer, J. (1999). *The counselor and the group* (3rd ed.). Philadelphia: Taylor & Francis.

Truax, P., & Jacobson, N. S. (1992). Marital distress. In P. H. Wilson (Ed.), *Principles and practice of relapse prevention* (pp. 290–321). New York: Guilford Press.

Tsang, H. W. H., & Cheung, L.C.C. (2005). Social skills and training for people with schizophrenia: Theory, practice and evidence. In J. E. Pletson (Ed.), *Progress in schiozophrenia research* (pp. 181–207). Hauppauge, NY: Nova Science Publishers.

Tuckman, B. (1965). Developmental sequence in small groups. *Psychological Bulletin, 63*, 384–399.

Tyson, E. H., Dulmus, C. N., & Wodarski, J. S. (2002). Assessing violent behavior. In L. A. Rapp-Paglicci, A. R. Roberts, & J. S. Wodarski (Eds.), *Handbook of violence* (pp. 148–168). Hoboken, NJ: John Wiley & Sons.

Uba, L. (1994). *Asian Americans: Personality patterns, identity, and mental health.* New York: Guilford Press.

United Kingdom Alcohol Treatment Trial (UKATT) Research Team. (2005). Effectiveness of treatment for alcohol problems: Findings of the randomized UK alcohol treatment trial. *British Medical Journal, 331*, 331–339.

U.S. Census Bureau. (2000). U.S. census of population and housing profiles of general demographic characteristics. Washington DC: Author.

U.S. Census Bureau. (2002). Statistical abstract of the United States. Retrieved July 15, 2002, from http://www.census.gov/prod/www/statistical-abstract-02.html

U.S. Census Bureau. (2003). Disability status 2000: Census 2000 Brief. Retrieved October 30, 2005, from http://www.census.gov/prod/2003 pubs/c2kbr-17.pdf

U.S. Census Bureau. (2004). U.S. Interim projections by age, sex, race, and Hispanic origin. Retrieved September 1, 2004, from http://www.census.gov/ipc/www/usinterimproj/natprojtab01a.xls

U.S. Department of Health and Human Services. (2006). The AFCARS report: Preliminary FY 2005 estimates as of September 2006 (13). Retrieved November 21, 2006, from http://www.acf.hhs.gov/programs/cb/stats research/afcars/tar/report13.htm

U.S. Department of Labor. (2001) The Americans with Disabilities act: Public law 101–366. Retrieved October 30, 2005, from http://www.dol.gov/odep/pubs/fact/ada92fs.htm

U.S. Surgeon General's Report on Mental Health. (1999). *Mental health: A report of the Surgeon General: Executive summary.* Rockville, MD: U. S. Department of Health and Human Services.

Van Puyenbroeck, J., & Maes, B. (2006). Program development of reminiscence group work for ageing people with intellectual disabilities. *Journal of Intellectual & Developmental Disability, 31*(3), 139–147.

Vasterling, J. J., & Brewin, C. R. (2005). *Neuropsychology of PTSD: Biological, cognitive, and clinical perspectives.* New York: Guilford Press.

Vergeer, G. E. (1995). Therapeutic applications of humor. Directions in Mental Health Counseling, *5*(3), 4–11.

Volpe (2008) (Site internet doc on Effects of DV on Children and Adolescent: An Overview: Joseph S. Volpe, Director, Prof Development.)

Wagner, W. G. (1996). Optimal development in adolescence: What is it and how can it be encountered? *Counseling Psychlologist, 24,* 360–399.

Walker, C. E., Hedberg, A. G., Clement, P. W., & Wright, L. (1981). *Clinical procedures for behavior therapy.* Englewood Cliffs, NJ: Prentice Hall.

Walker, L. (1979). *The battered woman.* New York: Harper & Row.

Wall, V. D., & Nolan, L. L. (1987). Small group conflict: A look at equity, satisfaction and styles of conflict management. *Small Group Behavior, 18,* 188–211.

Wallerstein, J. S. (1998). Children of divorce: Stress and developmental tasks. In N. G. Garmezy & M. Rutter (Eds.), *Stress, coping, and development in children.* Baltimore: John Hopkins University Press.

Wallerstein, J. S., & Blakeless, S. (1989). *Second chances.* New York: Ticknor & Fields.

Watson, D. L., & Tharp, R. G. (1997). Self-directed behavior: Self-modification for personal adjustment (7th ed.). Pacific Grove, CA: Brooks/Cole.

Weber, M. (1946). In H. Gerth & C. W. Mills (Eds.), *From Max Weber: Essays in sociology.* New York: Oxford University Press.

Webster-Stratton, C. (Ed.). (2003). Aggression in young children: Services proven to be effective in reducing aggression. In R. Tremblay, R. Barr, & T. L. Peters (Eds.), *Encyclopedia of early childhood development.* Retrieved August 12, 2004, from http://www.child-encyclopedia.com/documents/Webster-StratonANGxp_rev.pdf

Wegscheider-Cruse, S. (1989). *Another chance: Hope and health for the alcoholic family.* Palo Alto, CA: Science and Behavior.

Weinberg, H. (2001). Group process and group phenomena on the Internet. *International Journal of Group Psychotherapy, 41,* 361–378.

Weiner, M. (1990). *Human service management: Analysis and applications.* Belmont, CA: Wadsworth.

Weinstein, B. (1994). *I'll work for free: A short-term strategy with a long-term payoff* [Cassette Recording]. New York: Henry Holt.

Weiss, R. S. (Ed.). (1973). *Loneliness: The experience of emotional and social isolation.* Cambridge, MA: MIT Press.

Weissman, M. M., Markowitz, J. C., & Klerman, G. L. (2000). *Comprehensive guide to interpersonal psychotherapy.* New York: Basic Books.

Welfel, E. R. (2002). *Ethics in counseling and psychotherapy: Standards, research, and emerging issues* (2nd ed.). Pacific Grove: CA: Brooks/Cole.

Weyandt, L. L. (2001). *Attention deficit hyperactivity disorders: An AD/HD primer.* Boston: Allyn & Bacon.

Whalen, C. K., & Henker, B. (1986). Cognitive behavior therapy for hyperactive children: What do we know? *Journal of Children in Contemporary Society, 19,* 123–141.

Williams, C. (2007). *Teen anger management group program.* Ontario, CA: Ontario Mental Health.

Williams, E. E., & Ellison, F. (1996). Culturally informed social work practice with American Indian clients: Guidelines for non-Indian workers. *Social Work, 41*(2), 147–151.

Wilson, G. T. (2004). Acceptance and change in the treatment of eating disorders: The evolution of manual-based cognitive behavioral therapy. In S. C. Hayes, V. M. Follette, & M. Linehan (Eds.), *Acceptance, mindfulness, and behavior change.* New York: Guilford Press.

Wilson, G., & Ryland, G. (1980). The social group work method. In A. Alissi (Ed.), *Perspectives on social group work practice* (pp. 169–182). New York: Free Press.

Wilson, J. (2007). Foster parent training [Handout]. San Bernardino, CA: Foster Family Network

Wilson, J. Q. (1995). Crime and public policy. In J. Q. Wilson & J. Petersilla (Eds.), *Crime* (pp. 489–507). San Francisco: ICS.

Wodarski, L. A., & Wodarski, J. S. (2004). Obesity. In L. A. Rapp-Paglicci, C. N. Dulmus, & J. S. Wodarski (Eds.), *Handbook of preventive interventions for children and adolescents* (pp. 301–323). Hoboken, NJ: John Wiley & Sons.

Wolak, J., & Finkelhor, D. (1998). Children exposed to partner violence. In J. L. Jasinski & L. M. Willimans (Eds.), *Partner violence: A comprehensive review of twenty years of research* (pp. 73–112). Newbury Park, CA: Sage.

Wolf, A. (1975). Psychoanalysis of groups. In G. M. Gazda (Ed.), *Basic approaches to group psychotherapy and group counseling* (2nd ed.). Springfield, IL: Charles C. Thomas.

Wolf, A., & Kutash, I. L. (1986). Psychoanalysis in groups. In I. L. Kutash & A. Wolf (Eds.), *Psychotherapist's casebook* (pp. 332–352). San Francisco: Jossey-Bass.

Wolpe, J. (1958). *Psychotherapy and reciprocal inhibition.* Palo Alto, CA.: Stanford University Press.

Wolpe, J. (1990). *The practice of behavior therapy.* New York: Pergamon Press.

Wong, P. H., & Watt, L. M. (1991). What types of reminiscence are associated with successful aging? *Psychology and Aging, 6,* 272–279.

Woodside, M. R, & McClam, T. (1994). *An introduction to human services* (2nd ed.). Pacific Grove, CA: Brooks/Cole.

Woodside, M. R., & McClam, T. (2009). *An introduction to human services* (6th ed.). Belmont, CA: Thomson Brooks/Cole.

Worden, J. W. (2002). *Grief counseling and grief therapy: A handbook for the mental health practitioner* (3rd ed.). New York; Springer.

World Health Organization. (1990). *Cancer pain relief and palliative care.* (WHO Technical Report Series-804). Geneva, Switzerland: Author.

Wright State University. (2008). *Breast cancer: How your mind can help your body.* Retrieved July 2008, from http://www.wright-counseling .com/Brochures/BreastC.htm

Wulf, R. (1998). The historical roots of gestalt therapy. *The Gestalt Journal, 21*(1), 81–92.

Yalom, I. (1975). *The theory and practice of group psychotherapy.* New York: Basic Books.

Yalom, I. (1995). *The theory and practice of group psychotherapy* (4th ed.). New York: Basic Books.

Yalom, I. (2005). *The theory and practice of group psychotherapy* (5th ed.). New York: Basic Books.

Yontef, G. (1993). *Awareness, dialogue and process: Essays on Gestalt therapy.* Highland, NY: Gestalt Journal Press.

Yontef, G. (1999). Awareness, dialogue and process: Preface to the 1998 Gestalt edition. *Gestalt Journal, 22*(1), 9–20.

Young, M. E. (2001). *Learning the art of helping. Building blocks and techniques* (2nd ed.). Upper Saddle River, NJ: Pearson, Merrill Prentice Hall.

Zarit, S. (1980). *Aging and mental disorders.* New York: Macmillan.

Zastrow, C. H. (1985). *Social work with groups.* Chicago: Nelson-Hall.

Zastrow, C. H. (2009). *Social work with groups: A comprehensive workbook* (7th ed.). Belmont, CA: Brooks/Cole Cengage Learning.

Zastrow, C. H., & Kirst-Ashman, K. (2004). *Understanding human behavior and the social environment* (6th ed.). Belmont, CA: Thomson-Brooks/Cole.

Zick, C. D., & Smith, K. R. (1991). Patterns of economic change surrounding the death of a spouse. *Journal of Gerontology, 46*, 5310–5320.

Zigmound, N., & Brownlee, J. (1980). Social skills training for adolescents with learning disabilities. *Exceptional Education Quarterly, 2*, 77–83.

Zimmer, P., Alberti, K. G. M., & Shaw, J. (2001). Global and societal implications of the diabetes epidemic. *Nature, 414*, 782–787.

Zinker, J. (1978). *Creative process in Gestalt therapy.* New York: Random House Vintage.

Zogby, J. (2001). *What ethnic Americans really think: The Zogby culture polls.* Washington, DC: Zogby International.

Zusman, J. (1966). Some explanations of the changing appearance of psychotic patients: Antecedents of the social breakdown syndrome concept. *Millbank Memorial Fund Quarterly, 64*(1), 20.

Zylestra, S. (2006). United [Letter to the editor]. *Therapist, 18*(1), 6.

Author Index

Triffon, B. J., 383
Troast, T. P., 371
Trotzer, J., 23, 383
Truax, P., 383
Trussel, J., 368
Tsang, H. W. H., 138, 383
Tseng, W., 189, 369
Tuason, V. B., 369
Tuckman, B., 64, 65, 383
Tweed, D. L., 363
Tyson, E. H., 383

Uba, L., 189, 383
UKATT Research Team, 156, 383
Umemoto , D., 189, 371
Ury, W., 81, 366
U.S. Bureau of Census, 384
U.S. Census Bureau, 183, 383, 384
U.S. Department of Health and Human Services, 384
U.S. Department of Labor, 384
U.S. Surgeon General, 325
U.S. Surgeon General's Report on Mental Health, 312, 384
Utada, A., 366
Uyeda, M. K., 177, 364

Valkonen, T., 374
Van de Reit, V., 123, 371
Van Gorp, W. G., 361
VanPuyenbroeck, J., 384
Vasterling, J. J., 384
Vaughn, M. G., 369
Vergeer, G. E., 48, 384
Volpe, 384

Wagner, W. G., 384
Walker, C. E., 384
Walker, L., 384
Wall, V. D., 80, 384
Wallerstein, J. S., 384
Wang, J., 369

Warner, P. J., 363
Watson, D. L., 136, 384
Watt, L. M., 385
Weber, M., 168, 384
Weber, R. A., 373
Webstrer-Stratton, C., 384
Wedding, D., 129–133, 135, 146, 208, 326–327, 363
Wegscheider-Cruse, S., 384
Weinberg, H., 248, 384
Weiner, M., 167, 384
Weinhold, B. K., 366
Weinstein, B., 174, 384
Weinstein, R., 376
Weishaar, M., 143, 359
Weiss, R. S., 384
Weissman, M. M., 105, 106, 384
Welch, B. L., 177, 364
Welfel, E. R., 237, 239, 384
Weyandt, L. L., 302, 384
Whalen, C. K., 304, 385
Wherry, J. N., 36, 380
Whitten, P., 247, 373
Whittington-Clark, L. E., 55, 378
Wiemer, J. J., 369
Wilcox, B. J., 364
Williams, 132
Williams, B. I., 370
Williams, C., 385
Williams, E. E., 194, 385
Williams, S. A., 366
Wilson, G., 268, 380, 385
Wilson, G. T., 131, 366, 385
Wilson, J., 385
Wilson, J. Q., 385
Winzelberg, A., 248, 370
Wischman, C., 380
Witmer, J. M., 376
Wodarski, J. S., 311, 379, 380, 383, 385
Wodarski, L. A., 385
Wolak, J., 385

Wolf, A., 106, 107, 385
Wolfe, B., 368
Wolpe, J., 129, 137, 385
Wolpe, P. R., 362
Wong, P. H., 385
Woodside, M. R., 165, 166, 168, 169, 173, 175–176, 178–180, 197, 198, 228, 385
Wookey, J., 369
Worden, J. W., 385
World Health Organization (WHO), 385
Wortman, C., 362
Wright, L., 384
Wright State University, 385
Wulf, R., 385

Yalom, I., 3, 15, 18, 20, 23, 24, 35–41, 49, 63, 65, 66, 71, 79, 83, 87, 240, 270, 278, 284, 385
Yeager, K. R., 285, 379
Yeh, C. J., 248, 362
Yep, R., 153, 359
Yoerger, K., 378
Yontef, G., 123, 126, 385
Young, M. E., 138, 385
Young, R. C., 361

Zarit, S., 339, 385
Zastrow, C., 371
Zastrow, C. H., 40, 71, 72, 233, 264, 265, 311, 340, 385, 386
Zick, C. D., 386
Zigmound, N., 386
Zimet, C., 14, 380
Zimmer, P., 350, 386
Zinker, J., 126, 386
Zogby, J., 187, 386
Zuravin, S., 364
Zusman, J., 386
Zylestra, S., 386
Zylstra, 213

Subject Index

Token economy and behavior
therapy, 136, 304
Training for group leaders, 6,
13, 21, 61, 234–237, 249,
250
Training (T)-group movement,
18, 19
Transference
group psychotherapy, 13
middle stage of group, 84
and psychodynamic
therapeutic approach,
107
Transition phase, middle stage
of group, 76–86
Trauma, 14. *See also* Post
traumatic stress disorder
(PTSD)
Treatment groups, 5
Treatment plans, 14, 20, 101,
134, 140, 305, 314
Trends in group work,
27–29
integrative approach, 20, 29,
30, 157–159

Trust
and acceptance, 41, 54, 76
beginning stage of group,
72–74
behavior therapy, 140
building, 15
group members, 41, 43, 54,
282
importance of, 72
and informed consent, 222
level of trust, 43, 73, 74, 282
middle stage of group, 76
person-centered therapy,
118
teen and adolescent groups,
311
as therapeutic factor, 41
12-step programs, 16, 211, 212
Types of groups, 6–16, 127,
263, 264

Universality, 36, 37, 42

Values
agencies, 167, 178

ethics and core values, 215–
217
group leader, 45, 46, 54, 56,
57, 61, 218, 219
group work, 217
Vicarious learning, 24, 42
Videoconferences, 242
Virtual groups, 245, 246
Voluntary group membership,
43, 270, 271

Watson, John, 129
Wender, Louis, 18
Wolpe, Joseph, 129
Women
and gender differences, 198,
199
poverty, 196, 200
as practitioners, 201, 203
sexism, 199
Working phase, middle stage
of group, 76, 77,
86–90

Yalom, Irvin, 20

About the CD-ROM

This appendix provides you with information on the contents of the CD that accompanies this book. For the latest and greatest information, please refer to the ReadMe file located at the root of the CD. Here is what you will find:

- System Requirements
- Using the CD with Windows, Linux, and Macintosh
- What's on the CD
- Troubleshooting

System Requirements

Make sure that your computer meets the minimum system requirements listed in this section. If your computer doesn't match up to most of these requirements, you may have a problem using the contents of the CD.

- PC running Windows 98 or later or a Macintosh running Mac OS X
- An Internet connection
- A CD-ROM drive

Using the CD

1. Insert the CD into your computer's CD-ROM drive. The license agreement appears.

Note to Windows users: The interface won't launch if you have autorun disabled. In that case, click Start→Run (For Windows Vista, Start→All Programs→Accessories→Run). In the dialog box that appears, type D:\Start.exe. (Replace D with the proper letter if your CD drive uses a different letter. If you don't know the letter, see how your CD drive is listed under My Computer.) Click OK.

Note for Mac Users: The CD icon will appear on your desktop, double-click the icon to open the CD and double-click the "Start" icon.

2. Read through the license agreement, and then click the Accept button if you want to use the CD.

The CD interface appears. The interface allows you to install the programs and run the demos with just a click of a button (or two).

What's on the CD

This CD-ROM contains Group Profiles in addition to those found in the book. The many topics covered in the Group Profiles are presented in a clear, concise, and relevant manner facilitating the translation of concepts, ideas, and skills into actual practice. The Group Profiles are Word documents to allow practitioners to customize them to readily meet their specific needs. Each individual Group Profile includes information on evidence-based practice, detailed group treatment plans, group objectives, week-to-week group content, and suggested group activities. The comprehensive overview represents mental health concerns commonly treated in today's diverse agency settings.

Addressing a wide variety of psychological issues frequently encountered in therapy work with groups, the Group Profiles cover an range of clients across the lifespan—children, adolescents, adults, older adults, and the medically ill. Topics covered in these Group Profiles include anxiety, depression, divorce adjustment, substance abuse, foster care, trauma, chronic pain, anger management, hospice, weight management/obesity prevention, teen pregnancy, HIV/AIDS, and many more.

The CD-ROM also includes several documents from the Association for Specialists in Group Work (AGSW): Best Practices Guidelines, Professional Standards for the Training of Group Workers, and Principles for Diversity-Competent Group Workers.

Applications

The following applications are on the CD: Word for Windows and Mac.

OpenOffice – freeware
For your convenience, we have included OpenOffice, which is a program that allows you to view Microsoft Word documents.

> *Shareware programs* are fully functional, trial versions of copyrighted programs. If you like particular programs, register with their authors for a nominal fee and receive licenses, enhanced versions, and technical support.
>
> *Freeware programs* are copyrighted games, applications, and utilities that are free for personal use. Unlike shareware, these programs do not require a fee or provide technical support.
>
> *GNU software* is governed by its own license, which is included inside the folder of the GNU product. See the GNU license for more details.
>
> *Trial, demo, or evaluation versions* are usually limited either by time or functionality (such as being unable to save projects). Some trial versions are very sensitive to system date changes. If you alter your computer's date, the programs will "time out" and will no longer be functional.

Troubleshooting

If you have difficulty installing or using any of the materials on the companion CD, try the following solutions:

- **Turn off any anti-virus software that you may have running.** Installers sometimes mimic virus activity and can make your computer incorrectly believe that it is being infected by a virus. (Be sure to turn the anti-virus software back on later.)
- **Close all running programs.** The more programs you're running, the less memory is available to other programs. Installers also typically update files and programs; if you keep other programs running, installation may not work properly.
- **Reference the ReadMe.** Please refer to the ReadMe file located at the root of the CD-ROM for the latest product information at the time of publication.

Customer Care
If you have trouble with the CD-ROM, please call the Wiley Product Technical Support phone number at (800) 762-2974. Outside the United

States, call 1(317) 572-3994. You can also contact Wiley Product Technical Support at **http://support.wiley.com.** John Wiley & Sons will provide technical support only for installation and other general quality control items. For technical support on the applications themselves, consult the program's vendor or author.

To place additional orders or to request information about other Wiley products, please call (877) 762-2974.